# HEROES, HONCHOS & HUMDINGERS

*To Julie*

*Toby McDaniel*

• *Toby McDaniel* •

Published by The State Journal-Register
One Copley Plaza, Springfield, Illinois 62701

Printed in the United States of America
by Phillips Brothers Printers
Springfield, Illinois

First printing 1999

Library of Congress Catalog Number 99-96117

ISBN: 0-9675600-0-4

Special thanks to The State Journal-Register, Publisher and Editor Patrick Coburn, Managing Editor Barry Locher, Promotion Manager Nancy Evans, SJ-R prepress, advertising, photography, news and library departments, HIP Advertising, contributors to this column and my faithful readers. ~ Toby McDaniel.

Toby McDaniel has no peer when it comes to puncturing pomposity and this philosophy shines through every page. This definitely is not a collection of columns that follows the adage, "It's the kind of book that once you put it down, you can't pick it up."

When he wrote his first column in 1969, Toby was making $120-a-week while Paul Powell, the infamous Illinois secretary of state, was well on his way to stuffing a shoe box with cash — to the tune of $800,000.

Since that time, Toby's columns have gone through six more secretaries of state, five governors and five mayors of Springfield. None went unnoticed, and at the same time, the lesser known were featured and never ignored.

If you want to laugh along with Toby and not get bogged down in right- or left-wing minutiae, this book is for you. There is chuckle after chuckle and no doubt lingers why Toby McDaniel is an institution.

Chicago has Irv Kupcinet. St. Louis has Jerry Berger. The Quad Cities has Bill Wundram and Springfield has Toby McDaniel, a journalistic treasure.

Readers have been rewarded with more than 3,500 of Toby's columns over a 30-year period and here is how I would sum up "Heroes, Honchos & Humdingers," his first book writing venture:  Give us more by 2004!

*Gene Callahan*

After reporting and writing a daily column for the Illinois State Register for 10 years, Gene Callahan was assistant press secretary to Illinois Gov. Samuel Shapiro, then press secretary to Lt. Gov. Paul Simon and was assistant Illinois secretary of state for several years before moving to Washington, D.C., where he was chief of staff for U.S. Sen. Alan Dixon from 1981-93. For the next five years, he was director of governmental relations for Major League Baseball.

(A.) At fire scene in 1968. (B.) Telephone interview in 1976. (C.) Aboard submarine tender USS Sperry during storm at sea in 1960. [As U.S. Navy journalist]. (D.) Interviewing heavyweight boxing champion Floyd Patterson in 1958. (E.) Noting light-heavyweight boxing champ Archie Moore's piano prowess, 1958.

(F.) Co-judging 1979 Jaycees Miss Witch Pageant with Mayor Mike Houston (center) and mystery judge in gorilla suit. (G.) Hurling one at Chatham Cow Chip Throw in 1977. (H.) Chatting with Archie Moore in 1958. (I.) Press conference in Mayor Nelson Howarth's office, 1970. (J.) Accompanying city officials on inspection tour of crumbling Old Town branch sewer in 1970. (K.) Boarding Mid-America Airline's first flight out of Capital Airport in 1970.

To my wife Sharon
and daughter Mindy

# 1969

## CALL IT CAPITOL PUNISHMENT ~

A telephone transmitting device was discovered fastened to the bottom of a chair in a state legislature committee hearing room. 'Twas not what it seemed to be.

A practical joker apparently was trying to throw a scare into someone. Since this particular chair is usually occupied by a state legislator, guess who?

Telephone company engineers were consulted and confirmed the simulated bugging device was harmless. Totally harmless; in fact, the same piece of equipment is in the mouthpiece of every telephone in use today.

## CASE OF THE MISSING SPOON ~

Taxpayers will have every reason in the world to cry "uncle" when they have to pick up the tab — conservatively estimated at $2,500 to date — for medical treatment for Sangamon County Jail inmate William McGuff, required after he swallowed a spoon. He did it voluntarily, of course.

It was no ordinary spoon, so there was no ordinary remedy. After several uncomfortable days with a 7-inch-long tablespoon in this stomach, McGuff underwent surgery at a Springfield hospital.

He's still there, in a $40-a-day private room and under 24-hour guard (which costs more than $40 a day). In addition to that expense, taxpayers are paying for a public defender to represent McGuff on the burglary charge against him.

Sheriff Eddie Ryan, who doesn't look forward to paying the bill, says the spoon swallower won't be given silverware from now on and will have to eat with his hands.

The surgeon turned the spoon over to Ryan and he presented it to Police Chief Silver Suarez because McGuff did his old spoon-swallowing trick when he was locked up in the city jail.

## SO MUCH FOR PLAYING FAIR ~

Health-Safety Department inspector Frank Mohan thinks he has some food for thought for political candidates. Then again, maybe not.

When a building at Ninth and Cass was being remodeled, he found a political campaign poster boosting M.J. Daughton as a Democratic candidate for sheriff in 1914. His motto was: "A Knocker Never Wins — A Winner Never Knocks."

Daughton lost the election.

## TO NOT TELL THE TRUTH ~

Jury selection was under way before Circuit Judge Creel Douglass. A robbery defendant was about to go on trial.

When an obviously age-shy middle-aged woman became the focus of routine questioning, the Q & A went like this:
Question: "Are you a native resident of this county?"
Answer: "Yes."
Question: "How long have you resided in this county?"
Answer: "All my life."

## WHAT A BUCK BOUGHT THEN ~

High school and college students working city/county government summer jobs this year were paid $1.54 to $1.79 an hour.

The new Lincoln Tower apartment hi-rise, heralded by promoters as "red carpet living," is calling for tenants. Rent varies according to floor, higher up meaning higher on the rent scale, with one-bedroom units starting at $150 monthly and two-bedrooms at $270.

And the city of Springfield "splurged" on a new fire engine: $32,000. (Today's cost: six to eight times as much.)

## SIGN LANGUAGE ~

A fried chicken restaurant claimed: "WE'RE PROUD OF OUR FOWL COOKING."

## GOVERNMENT 'COVER-UP' ~

Mini-skirted employees (just the women, fortunately) in Secretary of State Paul Powell's vast domain proved too much of too little for him. He ordered a cover-up.

Though that was comical in itself, his method of enforcing the rule was downright laughable.

Powell deployed matronly types to every division of his agency. Armed with yardsticks, they patrolled day to day, measuring hemlines.

*Paul Powell*

Powell's little snit provided plenty of comic relief not only for local media; it became a joke coast-to-coast. That included a bit on NBC's "Today Show." And for that exposure, a film clip showed the "mini-measurers" on routine patrol — wielding their yardsticks — and Powell himself in a dead-serious interview.

Powell later told the local media: "I didn't want any publicity on this."

## COURTROOM CLOWN ~

Prospective jurors were being screened by Chief Circuit Judge William Chamberlain lickety-split until he ran up against a decided unwilling-ness-to-serve on the part of one fellow.

Barely beyond identifying himself, he volunteered to the judge that he had a preconceived notion about the case — he already had decided whether the criminal defendant was innocent or guilty.

But after Chamberlain had bounced a few pointed questions off the guy, it was obvious he knew nothing about either the defendant or the case at hand. He was then asked where the preconceived notion came from.

"A little bird told me," the man cracked.

No question about it; no one would want this goof on a jury. Chamberlain excused him from jury duty but ordered him to sit tight.

Not only did the guy have to sit through the rest of jury selection, he was made to sit through the trial and until the jury returned its verdict — two days later.

## THE GENDER TRAP ~

A "lady" isn't always a lady; just ask Sangamon County Sheriff Eddie Ryan.

In all innocence, Logan County Sheriff Glen Nichols prevailed on Ryan to temporarily house "a lady prisoner" because there was no vacancy in the women's cellblock in his county lockup in Lincoln. Transfer of the inmate was accomplished, a female sheriff's deputy processed "Shirley" — mug shot, body frisk, et al. — and put her in the southeast (women's) cellblock.

All was calm for a while. Then one of Shirley's cellmates slipped a note to the turnkey. It said she "sensed something wrong."

Deputies hauled Shirley back for reprocessing; body search included, only more thorough. Indeed, something was wrong. Shirley turned out to be LeRoy.

Minutes later, Nichols' phone was ringing. Come and get LeRoy, he was told. Faster than you can say "I was duped by a female impersonator," a red-faced Logan County sheriff showed up to haul LeRoy back to Lincoln and put him where HE belonged: in the men's cellblock.

## A FAIR GONE BY ~

The King Family, Eddie Arnold and Liberace lead advance ticket sales for the Illinois State Fair's grandstand lineup this year. But all other acts are selling well: the Baja Marimba Band, comic George Kirby, Judy "Laugh-In" Carne, comedian Stu Gillman, John Davidson and the Doodletown Pipers, Marty Robbins and Faron Young.

## BEHIND THE MARCHING SCENE ~

The protest march that the Southern Christian Leadership Conference will stage in Springfield later this month will, for the second time in a six-week period, hit the police department right in the breadbasket (pun intended). The group's daylong visit and march on the Statehouse May 14 all but taxed the 114-man department (not to mention taxpayers) to the limit. That policing job required a force of 77 men throughout most of one eight-hour shift, which normally is staffed by 22 officers. Days off were canceled and off-duty officers were called in in order to make up the 77-man force.

Result: Taxpayers lost 330 man hours of routine police services.

The tab likely will be exceeded when the SCLC comes back to stage another "Operation Breadbasket" demonstration because it's being heralded as bigger than the last.

## LUCKILY THE ROPE BROKE ~

Five city firefighters probably owe their lives to a strand of rope that broke at the scene of the extra-alarm blaze that destroyed the G&E furniture warehouse last week.

Engine and truck companies arrived on the scene, just a few blocks from fire department headquarters, quickly that night. Six firefighters went into the alley at the rear of the big building, laying a hose line and attempting to chop the lock off a steel door. That failed.

Firefighter Jimmy Cauthen then returned to his rig to get a steel-cutting power saw so he could cut into the door and gain access to the conflagration inside. But the pullcord broke as he tried to start the power saw. He went back to the firetruck, grabbed another saw and returned to the back door.

Cauthen barely had time to start the saw, much less cut into the door, when the two-story brick building's rear wall collapsed without warning, burying him and almost covering Capt. Frank Embree, who was a few feet away. No one had detected the usual warning signs — bowing or cracking — that the wall had weakened.

Cauthen was killed, Embree critically hurt. Firefighters Sydney Letz Jr. and Bob Stoker also were injured. Driver Engineer John Hinds and Capt. Thomas Bestudik narrowly escaped injury.

Fire officials all agreed; had the pullcord not snapped and had the first saw functioned, the rear door undoubtedly would have been open, all six men would have been much closer to the falling wall and probably killed.

## SECURE AND SAFE ~

Probably no other Illinois chief executive has been afforded such security as blanketed Gov. Richard Ogilvie during his GOP Day appearance at the state fair Wednesday.

Extra-duty city and auxiliary police officers, escorting the auto caravan and controlling traffic at most intersections along the route, whisked Ogilvie from his downtown mansion to the fairgrounds nonstop. His enclosed limousine (past governors usually rode in convertibles) was surrounded by state troopers for the parade across the fairgrounds to the grandstand. And the grandstand was crawling with uniformed and plainclothes police.

Little more security would have protected President Richard Nixon had he been there, it was said.

*Gov. Richard Ogilvie samples apples at state fair.*

The grandstand security detail reportedly consisted of more than 300 officers. That would mean the Cairo United Front demonstrators, who had warned they would make it *their* day at the fair, were outnumbered by at least 20 to one. But the handful of demonstrators merely waved signs expressing their dislike of Ogilvie, behaving far better than grandstand show audiences that booed him earlier.

## MISSPELLING LESSON ~
Attorney J. Waldo Ackerman gets the last laugh.

Our mention last week that he, in filing Gov. Ogilvie's appeal of a city zoning action that would permit expansion of the Mansion View Motel (across the street from the governor's mansion), twice misspelled Ogilvie's name brought a courier-dispatched letter to this column.

From Ackerman, it was addressed to "Mr. Tuby McDaniel." He wrote that the column "was delightful and we at the Pfeifer, Fixmer, Gasaway and Ackerman law firm all enjoyed it greatly."

However, we have a hunch he's really poking fun. Numerous sources, and our own eyes, had already told me that, in my haste to point out his spelling errors, I misspelled Ackerman's name.

# 1970

## NECK AND NECK ~

Conversation between two grade-schoolers aboard a mass transit bus, the subject being their respective teachers:

"You ought to see his neck, he looks like an ostrich," one boy said,
"Yeh, I know who he is," replied the other. "His wife was my teacher last year."
"Well, I don't know who'd marry him!"
"Another ostrich."
"You mean . . ."
"Yeh, she looks like one too."

## SIGN LANGUAGE ~

In front of a commercial establishment at South Grand and MacArthur:

"Stick your nose in our business anytime."

~

## DIGGING FOR DIRT ~

A discussion among city council members Monday concerned fill dirt for a planned police training facility. It was noted that dirt will be available from a Peoria Road construction project.

Mayor Nelson Howarth, urging prompt action to obtain that dirt before someone beats the city to it, capped the discussion with:

"I know more than 10 people who are looking for dirt — not including some newspaper people I know."

## SIGN LANGUAGE ~

Out on Stevenson Drive:

"Optimist: Husband who checks to see if his marriage license has expired."

## YOU HAVE TO BE 16 TO DRIVE ~

The Easter egg hunt at a south-side shopping center last weekend was interrupted by a loudspeaker announcement:

"Will the woman driving the gold Chevrolet please go to your car; your 6-month-old baby is crying."

That prompted a conversation something like this between two women bystanders:

"Isn't that awful to leave a 6-month-old baby alone in a car?" one asked the other.

"I don't see anything wrong; the kid can't go anywhere," was the reply.

## QUOTABLE ~

Two small boys were riding bikes along a west-side street when one yelled to the other: "I can't ride worth a damn; let's go back."

## 'PRIVATE EYES' ~

None of that "I-don't-want-to-get-involved" attitude in Farmersville, one of those small towns where citizens look out for each other.

~

Last week when a strange car pulled up to a Farmersville bank, a woman nearby quickly jotted down the car's license number.  A man painting his garage also noted the car and scratched the license number on the building. Minutes later when the bank robbers emerged, bent the license plate down and sped away, the man and woman ran to the bank to investigate.

No doubt their action played a big part in the quick apprehension of suspects.

(Among items of evidence gathered by FBI agents, who canvassed every house in the town during the investigation, was the section of the garage bearing the license number.  The man was promised the FBI would pay for repairs.)

## WHO ME? ~

The alibi defense of convicted murderers Michael and Robert Dukett counted heavily on a tavern owner who appeared in court here last Saturday to identify one or both Duketts as being in his St. Louis establishment the night that gas station attendant David Burch was robbed and slain.

But the tavern owner, looking for Michael Dukett, pointed to the man sitting directly in front of the witness stand, court reporter Jerry Wedeking.

Then the witness, also attempting to identify the younger Dukett, sized up the packed courtroom and pointed into the spectator gallery, putting the finger on this writer.

(After some coaching, however, the witness finally identified the defendant, Dukett.)  We'd judge that the problem arose because both Wedeking and yours truly were wearing green shirts, the same color that Michael Dukett wore. Of course, the alibi witness had been told to point out the guy in the green shirt.

## SCHOOL KIDS LOSE A GOOD BUDDY ~

First day of school is a long way off but no doubt it will be sad for many Butler and Blessed Sacrament grade-schoolers.  Those who cross the busy Laurel Street-MacArthur Boulevard intersection probably won't realize until then the passing of their pal, crossing guard Joe Overby.

Joe died last week after a brief illness.

The slightly stooped Negro, despite his 88 years, never missed a day on the job. Joe, always neatly dressed (white shirt and tie every day), was a familiar figure in white police cap and orange vest for the past seven years. He was alert to the movement of every kid and every car. He'd whistle traffic to a halt, then trot out into the street to usher his charges across safely.

He always had a smile for the kids and it wasn't unusual for one of them to reward Joe with a fresh flower, piece of candy or Crayola sketch. The love the kids had was never more obvious than on every Nov. 17 when Butler students tossed a big birthday party for him. Joe also had a host of friends among the motoring public; many of those who passed by daily always had a wave or beep on the horn for him.

Friends were important to Joe, for he had almost no family. No one was more appreciative of Joe's dedication and perfect safety record than the police, and they reciprocated with a floral tribute and dual motorcycle escort for his short funeral procession.

## CASE OF THE MISSING 'N' ~

At a south-side motel where police chiefs convened last month, the marquee originally read,

"WELCOME INTNL. ASSN. OF CHIEFS OF POLICE."
All except one night because someone swiped one of the N's.

(Guess which one.)

## NOW CUT THAT OUT ~

Springfield Finance Com. James Dunham was sauntering down an empty hallway toward his office shortly after a city council meeting the other day. Purchasing agent Andy O'Neill happened to enter the hall through a doorway Dunham had just passed.

O'Neill, with a gleam in his eye, broke the sound barrier. "Commissioner!" bellowed O'Neill.

Dunham stopped dead in his tracks and spun around. "Don't do that!" blurted Dunham when he spied O'Neill.

"What's the matter commissioner, did I scare you?" O'Neill asked.

"Yes, I thought it was the mayor, " confessed Dunham in relief.

## BUILDING A 'FAIR' REPUTATION ~
Springfield's oldest practicing architect, Murray Hanes, has been to all but two Illinois State Fairs since 1888.

Count 'em. That's 80 state fairs.

## HE'S NO 'PERRY' MASON ~
Decatur attorney Louis Mason, who's entertaining a full house in Sangamon County circuit court where he's defending an armed robber, has complained to Judge Paul Verticchio about some of the newspaper reviews he's getting.  He didn't like being described in news stories as "flamboyant" but, after looking up the word in the dictionary, said that he wouldn't object because the word can be considered either critical or complimentary.

## LADY IN THE STATION HOUSE ~
The Springfield Police Department has its first female officer, Pat Sutton, and a fashion problem.

What will her uniform skirt length be?
Midi, mini or maxi?
Chief Silver Suarez skirts the issue by saying the hemline will be "around" the knee.

## MASON'S COLORFUL IMAGE EXTENDS BEYOND THE COURTROOM ~
In a resume in which he describes himself as a "lawyer's lawyer," Louis Mason notes he is a licensed schoolteacher, funeral director, real estate and insurance broker, once operated his own detective agency, holds the rank of colonel in the Air Force reserves, has free-lanced as an actor in local theater and has been a Boy Scout troop master.

He also is a former restaurant and motel operator, a referee for high school and Big Ten sports, and has an application pending to referee professional basketball and football.

He also speaks seven languages.

## CANINE CATERER ~

A guy out by Washington Park is getting his fill of sandwiches and apples. Every day his dog brings home a brown bag lunch that always consists of two sandwiches and an apple.

Seems a student at nearby Butler School isn't fond of sandwiches and apples, and ditches his lunch in the bushes every day.

## DEAD DRYER ~

A telephone call to Coroner William Telford's office went something like this:

"My dryer just died," blurted the caller.
"Just a minute," replied secretary Nancy Clark as she buzzed Telford.
"Who died?" Telford asked.
"My dryer, my dryer," the caller repeated. "Who is this?"
"This is the coroner."
"Oh, oh! I've got the wrong number," the caller apologized. "I was calling the appliance repair man."

## CHAIN LINK ~

Illinois State Journal reporter Marcia Bullard (she's now president, CEO and editor of USA Weekend Magazine) has found there's a trick to riding a bicycle without getting bell-bottom jeans caught in the chain.

She hasn't learned how to prevent it but she knows how to get out of such a predicament.

After becoming entangled the other day, and all other measures of escape failed, she just slipped herself out of the jeans — in the privacy of her garage, naturally.

〜

## THE GOOD, THE BAD AND THE TRUTH ～

An old gent rushed across Washington Street to assist two young mini-skirted gals who were struggling with giant packages . . . A 10-year-old boy in a doughnut shop, enjoying a cup of hot chocolate and a cigarette, and cussing a blue streak . . . A guy nabbed by sheriff's deputies in a raid that netted thousands of dollars worth of loot and narcotics was asked by the judge what he did for a living. "Nothing," he said. "I am just a bum."

## 'HIGHER' EDUCATION ～

Among the more unusual accredited courses offered by Sangamon State University:

"Rock Poetry as Literary Expression," described as "poetry of rock music viewed as a response to a world of beauty and ugliness, of sex and drugs, of politics and withdrawal."

"Women's Liberation: The Contemporary Struggle and Its Background," described as "historical and literary perspective of the current agitation for sexual equality," focusing on such areas as "women's educational and intellectual opportunity, woman's status with regard to legal, social, religious and political institutions, woman's unique psychological tensions and woman's image in various media."

## BELIEVE IT OR NOT ～

A guy appearing in magistrate court on a speeding charge here the other day admitted to doing 47 mph in a 30 mph zone just as the arresting officer testified, and the judge pronounced him not guilty.

## LET IT SNOW, LET IT SNOW! ～

An elderly lady, discussing Wednesday's weather forecast, shocked her cab driver with this:

"If it snows, I hope it's brassiere-high to a tall woman."

# 1971

## GRINCH STOLE CHRISTMAS FROM NEEDY ~

The spirit of giving didn't infect quite everyone at Christmas time. At least one crumb demonstrated the spirit of taking.

Under the guise of a "sleigh driver" for the Salvation Army, someone swiped food baskets that were to have provided Christmas Day dinner for poor families. At least 25 baskets were stolen.

It was one of the lowest con games yet devised.

Volunteering to deliver some of the 500 baskets the Salvation Army had promised to the needy, the culprit went so far as to pretend to have made his assigned rounds, forging signatures of the intended recipients to receipt cards, then returned the cards to Salvation Army officials. After numerous callers inquired about their baskets, the thefts were realized.

A crash program of grocery purchasing, packing and special deliveries ensured a merrier and a more filling Christmas for the 25 families that could be traced. But it was feared other families didn't report being "missed" and lost out.

It was theorized that the Christmas thief was only heartless, not hungry.

## ILLINOIS IN THE (S)LIMELIGHT ~

The scandalous Paul Powell story got big play not only in Illinois and neighboring states, but coast to coast as did the Orville Hodge scandal that smeared the state political scene in 1956.

In fact, Powell's pile of cash appears to be getting more media attention than did the Hodge episode.

*Paul Powell*

As soon as Powell's $800,000 hoard (much of it crammed into a shoe-box) was revealed last week, a Los Angeles television station called for a big hunk of newsreel on the late secretary of state. Gene Tyhurst, vice president of the St. Nicholas Hotel, where the cash had been stashed, was photographed showing Powell's old room to the press. He's still getting calls from friends saying they saw his picture in papers in various parts of the country.

Tyhurst has been besieged by newsmen since the story broke nine days ago. An NBC television news team just pulled out after occupying Powell's old room for five days. Interviews with Attorney General William Scott, Tyhurst and Powell's chauffeur, among others, were filmed in the room — or, as they say in the business, on location.

By the way, it's room No. 546 and it's for rent. Surprisingly, there's no waiting list.

There's a historic note, too. Hodge, like Powell, also was a regular tenant at the St. Nicholas when he was state auditor. And Hodge had a room one floor up, directly above Powell's, when his scandal broke 14 years ago.

## COMEDY CRASH SCENE ~

A gent driving along South MacArthur Boulevard last Saturday afternoon smacked into the rear of a car that was slowing for traffic. His inability to stop in time was due to ice-coated pavement in front of a drive-through car wash.

Seeing two women dangling over the front seat in the car he hit, he bailed out fast and — fearing the worst — ran to the rescue.

He found the driver, city hall secretary Paula Heien, in hysterical laughter and the other gal, a Lincoln bank teller — her shortly cropped hair literally standing on end — desperately pawing the floorboard.

"I'm not getting out of this car until I find that damned wig," she kept muttering.

The impact had sent her wig flying.

Finally, she retrieved it from beneath the seat and plopped it back on her head. But it landed sideways. A glance in the mirror sent her into hysterics. It was determined no one was hurt and everybody left laughing.

## YA DON'T SAY! ~

One of the candidates for city council dropped this profound statement the other day:

"The future is coming."

## CHICKEN SNOOP ~

The following advertisement will appear Sunday in The State Journal-Register's want-ad section.

"CHICKEN SEXER WANTED — Salary $1.00 per hundred chicks. Minimum one year's experience plus willingness to travel. Apply Illinois State Employment Service office.

A placement manager for the ISES says men and women with the skill to judge a chick's sex usually are of Japanese descent since that nationality has delicate hands and superior eyesight. A chick sexer's pay most often runs in excess of $8 per hour and, since they're kept busy the year 'round (their schedule of hatcheries is arranged through the American Chick Sexing Association of Philadelphia, Pa.), annual salary hits the $20,000 to $30,000 bracket.

## HIT ME AGAIN, DEALER ~
One of several boys nailed for playing cards in school yesterday was getting the third-degree from his mother:

"Why would you do such a thing?" mom asked.
"But I wasn't playing cards," her teenager replied.
"You know you were, the principal caught you," she argued.
"I wasn't playing cards, mom, I was dealing."

## BALLGAME FOR THE BIRDS ~
Fans at the Griffin Cyclones' regional game in the armory saw the "ol' pigeon drop." Pranksters snared several pigeons, attached gold streamers to their legs, stuffed them under their jackets and smuggled the birds into the armory.

Griffin's first basket was hailed with release of most of the pigeons.

A couple of kids were left with birds-in-hand. Two pigeons suffocated under the boys' jackets.

More than one spectator was spattered before the flying pigeons calmed and roosted.

School officials didn't think the prank too funny. Two Griffin students drew suspensions.

## NEVER FEAR; SHE'S MY GIRLFRIEND ~
A city council candidate, stumping in a local tavern the other night, caught hail Columbia from a gal who didn't like the answer to her question on a campaign issue.

She pledged to vote for the candidate's opponent, then stomped back to her seat.

The man with her later apologized to the candidate for his "girlfriend's" actions, telling the politico that "she" may not vote for him but his "wife" sure would.

## MAIL BAG ~

"I enjoyed your article relating to Griffin students releasing pigeons at the regional basketball tournament and their subsequent suspension.

"However, I should point out that such antics aren't without precedent. An earlier group of Griffin students (then Cathedral High School) accomplished the same stunt during the 1954 regional, the pigeons being smuggled in by Griffin cheerleaders and equipped with streamers upon their release.

"Certain members of this earlier ring are still Springfield residents. One is a prominent Democrat attorney and politico, another a federal agent and another a C.P.A.

"One other difference: The earlier culprits weren't apprehended. Please excuse my not signing this (letter) but I don't know the statute of limitations on such an offense. Griffin authorities may still be looking for us."

## TIME LINES ~

The haircut business is hurting. Long hair, of course, is what's hurting it. It's been hurting since the fad started several years ago with the younger generation. Now it's the older generation of longhairs that's hurting it worse than ever; paying the lonesome barber a visit only about once a month instead of every 10 days to two weeks. Besides the downhill business trend, there's the constantly rising cost of living index. So look for the price of a haircut to go up 25 cents (to $2.75) in about two weeks . . . Girls are invading the previously all-male McDonald's fast-food crews . . . The off-and-on gas price war is off again: A north-side gas station shot its price from 31 to 39 cents-a-gallon yesterday.

## GOVERNMENT CURSE ~

This "Important Notice" is posted in several city hall offices:

"Due to increased competition and a keen desire to remain in business, we find it necessary to institute a new policy.

"Effective immediately, we are asking that somewhere between starting time and quitting time and without infringing too much on the time usually devoted to lunch periods, coffee breaks, rest periods, story telling, ticket selling, vacation planning and rehashing of yesterday's television programs, that each employee endeavor to find some time that can be set aside and be known as 'work break.'

"To some this may seem a radical innovation, but we honestly believe that the idea has great possibilities. It can conceivably be an aid to steady employment and it might also be a means of assuring regular pay checks."

## THE 'EARL' OF CASH ~

An estate auction on South Walnut last weekend attracted a big crowd but an even bigger crowd probably would have shown up had the big money find there a couple of years ago been disclosed in advance.

An inventory of the home back then by attorney Earl Bice, shortly after the woman moved out, produced $108,000 in cash. She didn't believe in banks and had stashed $86,000 in the oven of an electric range, the other thousands in coffee cans.

The range, which should prove to be some sort of a collector's item, was sold at the auction.

Bice apparently has a knack for running into money. In the 1940s, he was executor of a barber's estate on the north side and among items for auction there was a box of shotgun shells. A guy bought them, dropped them and $5,750 fell out of the box.

But, as Bice notes, he's only been the finder and not the keeper.

## LEGACY OF AN AD MAN ~

Jay Slaven, retiring today after 40 years as a classified ad man for the Journal-Register, has written at least one ad on about every subject imaginable and there's a story behind many of them.

He got the most personal satisfaction from this ad, which he paid for himself, in 1943:

"We've no place to go. Must have large home. Splendid Christian family just received notice from landlord to vacate eight-room home as he desires to sell rather than rent. Man, wife and seven children, ages 3 to 16, must find similar size house. Father is bedridden due to recent accident and only means of support is 16-year-old daughter's salary. House must be moderately priced. Any house in any location considered."

*Jay Slaven*

Father Meara, then pastor of St. Joseph's Church, notified Slaven to cancel the ad three days later. Only one reply to the ad was received but it was a good one.

The man who owned the house the family lived in had read the ad, had a change of heart and decided not to sell the property. Not only that. He repaired the roof, sent the family two tons of coal and told his tenants they had a home as long as they desired.

## TIGHTWAD-OF-THE-YEAR ~
A wealthy Springfield man who lost his wallet, bulging with $2,000, at the state fair.

A 16-year-old girl found the wallet and returned it to him. He managed to cough up only a 50-cent reward.

But she's still smiling, and convinced that honesty really does pay.

## WARNING: ILLINOIS LEGISLATURE IN SESSION ~
Talk about a waste of time, state Rep. John Wall introduced a House bill to amend the Beauty Culture Act. This bill would change the terminology of "shampoo girl" to "shampoo assistant."

## WRITER'S CRAMP FOR NOTHING ~
A rookie policeman wrote more than 100 parking meter tickets his first day out last week, then went back to the station for more tickets.

It wasn't until then that he realized he'd left all three copies of each ticket on the cars he had ticketed.

That left the city with no record of the tickets, meaning that no one had to pay.

## NO SMOKING/HACKING SECTION ~

From a deep conversation between three older ladies dining out:

"She quit smoking like the doctor told her but now she's choking to death."

## NIXON AND KIDS ~

Shortly after President Richard Nixon emerged from the Old Capitol and plunged into the crowd of thousands on the plaza for handshaking he heard sobbing from down under. Spying a small hand jutting from the mass of humanity, he stooped and discovered 7-year-old Mike McDaniel. Mike was on the verge of being trampled by the pushing crowd.

*President Richard Nixon at Old Capitol Plaza.*

Nixon asked if he was hurt, then reached into his coat pocket and handed Mike a presidential pen, telling Mike he could have it for being a good boy.

Nixon, who showed a lot of interest in the younger generation throughout his travels here, cast somewhat of a spell over two boys outside the Junior Livestock Building at the state fair. A 6-year-old, upon hearing the president's voice over a loudspeaker, broke into a run toward the building while yelling back to his parents: "It's Nixon, it's Nixon."

A short distance away, a 10-year-old boy sidled up to a ring of state troopers guarding the presidential limousine. Admiring the empty car, he asked a trooper to "touch it for me."

## FROM WHERE SANTA SITS ~

There's never a dull minute when you're Santa Claus. Dick Little, the man behind the whiskers on the north side of the square, testifies to that.

Only slightly frayed after three weeks of wear and tear, the 6-foot, 220-pound Little has listened to more than 2,500 kids rattle off their Christmas lists. From that he draws these parallels: the girls still want dolls while walkie-talkies and tape recorders are big with boys this year; kids who visit Santa without their moms and dads ask for more than do those who show up with their parents; and poor kids want shoes and clothes more than toys.

It's the same old line of questioning, but the answers vary.

"And what do you want for Christmas?" Little asked one 5-year-old cutie.

"A dolly that leaks," she blurted, as a shock wave bounced from Little to the blushing mother and grandmother nearby.

Then there was a 2-year-old girl who Little recalls as the "best" kid. She climbed onto his knee, clearly stated her Christmas requests, then rewarded Santa with a big hug and kiss.

Seldom does anyone confess to Santa Claus that they've been bad. Little classifies those who do (always boys, incidentally) as "smarties." Falling into the same category are the beard-pullers. Little's beard has had it. He's had to order a new one.

Little occasionally is confronted by the longhair set. A 15-year-old boy, playing the "tell-Santa-what-you-want-for-Christmas" game for the candy cane reward, asked for a pound of marijuana. On another occasion, Little was "cussed out in either Spanish or Italian" by an 18-year-old hippie type.

"But those kind are few and far between," Little boasts, "because practically everybody loves Santa Claus."

As long as Little wears the red and white suit, the feeling is mutual.

"I love kids and right now I'm in seventh heaven," admits the grandfather of six who recently retired after traveling 49 of the 50 states for Remington Rand and Bell & Howell.

～

Little takes his role seriously. He makes no promise of what Santa will deliver. At most, if he catches an affirmative nod from a parent on the sidelines, he explains to the youngster on his knee that Santa will consult with mom and dad to try to work out the request.

If Santa doesn't make promises, then Santa doesn't break promises, says Little. Above all else, he's concerned that Santa Claus hold onto his reputation as a good guy.

Little also sits as counselor when the need arises.

One such occasion was when a 10-year-old boy asked for a real .22-caliber rifle. Little told him that Santa simply couldn't fill that request, explaining the responsibilities, danger and some of the laws involved. A compromise resulted, the boy changing his request to a toy gun.

# 1972

## CAT YARN HAS UMPTEEN LIVES ~

That darned cat, the dead one mentioned by this column several months ago, keeps cropping up. Not only around here, but in other corners of the nation.

Variations of the story are many. But there's no doubt it's the same old tale.

And, apparently it's only a tale. Its source can be narrowed only to someone who claims — in all sobriety — that it actually happened to a friend of a dear friend. Our version went something like this:

A frenzied mother with a carload of kids and the family cat pulled into a shopping center parking lot. The kids bailed out, so did the cat and it was squashed by another car swinging into the next parking slot.

Hysteria struck the kids. Mom, in an attempt to restore calm, promised a proper burial for the cat, scooped the remains into a paper sack and placed it on the fender of the car before setting off on the shopping tour.

Minutes later, a woman spotted the sack, grabbed it and ran. Ducking into a nearby coffee shop, the woman opened the sack to assess her treasure, spied the dead cat and keeled over in a dead faint. Somebody called an ambulance. The woman was loaded onto a stretcher. So was her purse and the sack with the dead cat before she was hauled away. End of yarn.

A few weeks after the story swept the countryside here, it popped up in a Memphis, Tenn., newspaper column written by Lydel Sims. He labeled it: "That Dead Cat Is The Liveliest Beast."

Sims, noting that he had carried the strange story often over the years, warned readers it "rages periodically over the land, sweeping all skeptics before it, (and is) accepted as absolute truth by citizens who normally wouldn't believe their own mothers without independent evidence."

He found a moral to it all: "If you see a paper sack somewhere unattended, don't grab it and run because if you do, the crazy story might turn out to be true."

## SEA STORY ~

The sinking of the oceanliner Queen Elizabeth in early January jogged a few memories for WMAY newsman Dick Shaughnessy. He crossed the Atlantic aboard the giant ship 28 years ago, only it was no pleasure cruise.

It was 1943, the "Queen" was a troopship and Shaughnessy was a PFC in the Army Air Corps. Shaughnessy's outfit, the 81st Air Drone Squadron, accounted for part of the 14,000 troops (three times the ship's normal passenger load) on board for the trip from New York to Scotland.

Staterooms had been stripped of their luxurious fittings — even the mattresses were gone — and four men were jammed into two-bunk quarters. Dining was no picnic, either. Two meals a day. That's all anyone had time for. Chow lines were a mile long. As soon as you got through one line, you got into another one for the next meal, Shaughnessy recalls.

Although the Atlantic was crawling with deadly German submarines, the Queen traveled without escort. She was fast, capable of outrunning anything at sea. And she did.

～

Shaughnessy's voyage, even on a zig-zag course, took only five days compared to the average troopship convoy that took twice as long.

## HINDSIGHT ～

Anyone applying for jobs as Springfield police officers or firefighters from now on will find one part of the physical exam — the eye test — quite a bit tougher.

Recent discovery that a rookie patrolman is colorblind prompted police officials to ask him how he passed the eye test. He told them. Seems the good doctor held up two fingers.

"How many fingers to you see?" he asked the prospective officer.
"Two," he answered.
"That's right," the doctor announced, "you pass."
Another doctor will be conducting the tests from now on.

## SMORGASBORD ～

• That new Motel 6 about to go up on 31st Street will mean tough competition. Rooms rent for $6-a-night.

• Abbie Hoffman's book, "Steal This Book," was stolen from Lincoln Library even before it could be processed and put on the shelf.

• A mother asked her 10-year-old daughter what she liked most about the Girl Scout meeting she'd just attended: "We have a new janitor and he let us see inside the boys' restroom," was her enthusiastic reply.

• A motorist, blocked by a car in the driveway of a department store parking lot, slapped this note on the guy's windshield: "If you'd park your car where you're supposed to, it wouldn't get hit." He figured the guy would go crazy trying to find where his car had been hit — which, of course, it hadn't been.

• A call to the Lincoln Police Department at 3 o'clock in the morning sent a squad car in search of a nude woman running around a motel. After a thorough investigation, officers on the scene radioed to headquarters that they "couldn't find hide nor hair of her."

## POSTMAN 'NEXT OF KIN' ~

There are those who have no one to turn to. Such was the case of an elderly southwest side woman. She had no living relatives. But she had a big-hearted mailman, Charles Dodd. He befriended her, as he has others, many times while delivering mail in her neighborhood.

A few months ago, she felt her life drawing to a close and asked Dodd to take her to a funeral home, assist her in selecting a casket and help make funeral arrangements. He obliged. She died a few weeks later.

Dodd then performed his last deed for the woman. He arranged for a minister to preach the funeral and secured pallbearers: three other post office employees, an Illinois Bell employee, a neighbor and himself.

## PENNIES FOR HER THOUGHTS ~

A downtown insurance company secretary, with a little spite in her eye, paid off a fistful of parking meter tickets with pennies. She dropped off a 5½ pound package of coins at the city treasurer's office but didn't stick around for the count. But she should have.

Only 698 pennies, secured to cardboard by layers of Scotch tape, accompanied the seven tickets. She was two cents shy.

Another error was detected by the treasurer's staff. Date of issuance on one of the tickets had been adjusted to take it out of the regular delinquent category. That ticket price had doubled to $2. So, that made her $1.02 short, and she's being billed for it.

## POSTAGE ADO ~

A mailman lost his cool and dropped a four-letter word when confronted by a big  snarling dog.

His remark was monitored by a lady who promptly contacted postal authorities.

He was surprised to learn that the post office has what is called a "courtesy council" and he was summoned to appear before it — and was exposed to a lecture on courtesy.

## SHOT DOWN ~

The host of a Springfield radio talk show, expounding his philosophy for gun control, stated flatly that guns have no place in the home. He certainly didn't have a gun in his house, he said, and confessed further that he probably couldn't hit anything — like a burglar — even if he had a gun.

He had a caller at that point, a man who said he might pay a visit to the radio man's home some night, now that he knew he didn't have a gun around the house.

"You must be a burglar," the talk show host told the caller.
"I didn't say that," the caller retorted.
"But you talk like a burglar," insisted the radio man.

Their conversation continued something like that until a commercial break.

Immediately afterward, he changed his mind about guns. He told his listening audience he was convinced the man who called was a burglar and he warned that he in fact DOES have a gun (although he contended it doesn't belong to him) in his home.

We don't know if he sat up all night — gun in hand — waiting for the burglar to show up.

## SMALL (FRY) BUSINESS ~

A cute little gal was tending a lemonade stand on Fifth near Laurel. A cold glass of lemonade was advertised at three cents.

A guy driving by with his family stopped and bought six glasses. He tipped the industrious little girl seven cents.

Finishing off the lemonade, he asked where he could throw the paper cups. She quickly retrieved the empties, wiped each one dry with paper towel and set them back on the counter for her next customers.

## SHORTCUT IN THE KITCHEN ~

The bake-off at the Sangamon County Fair drew brownie entries from Mary Beth Powell and her sister Debbie Powell Bailey of Auburn.

To simplify the chore, the girls combined talents and baked one batch.

Each then placed a sample on separate plates and entered them in the competition. They fooled the judges. Debbie won first place and Mary was awarded fourth place.

## MAIL BAG ~
From state Rep. Eugene Schlickman of Arlington Heights:

"In your July 21 column, you reported that I owe $6 to the city of Springfield for parking meter violations. As you may know, while in Springfield, I reside at the State House Inn, and occasionally, due to the press of legislative matters, have ignored the presence of my automobile. You're absolutely right that legislators are no more immune from local parking regulations than the average taxpaying motorist they represent. Enclosed is a copy of a letter I have sent to the city of Springfield regarding my indebtedness." (Schlickman's letter to the city was accompanied by a check and an apology for this negligence.)

## NOW, THAT'S NOT NICE ~
There's a rule at Lincoln State School, where Larry Buzzard is superintendent, that anyone parking on school grounds must lock their car.

Buzzard, while guiding a couple of visitors around the facility the other day, neglected to follow that rule. But when he returned to his car, he wished he'd locked it. A mean little kid had taken advantage of the situation and literally "done his business" on both the front and back seats.

## BEHOLDIN' TO NOBODY ~
A Chatham woman phoned the secretary of state's office about a job and was encouraged to apply. But when she went in for an interview, talk was limited to patronage positions. She was interested only in the "equal opportunity" system.

It is possible to "apply" for certified positions, the interviewer admitted, but a political endorsement by the right party guarantees immediate placement, he emphasized. That's the way it is in this branch of state government — patronage or else, she was told. She wasn't impressed.

"You're not too hungry are you?" the interviewer quipped.

"Not that damned hungry," the woman replied.

## HERE'S LOOKIN' ATCHA ~

The scene was an alley behind the Emerson Building at the state fairgrounds. It was 5 o'clock, quitting time for Illinois Department of Agriculture employees there.

One woman driving a pickup truck started through the alley. Another woman, driving a car, pulled in from the opposite direction about the same time to pick up a passenger.

Both drivers, determined to drive through, motioned to each other. Neither would give.

So, for the next 2½ hours (until 7:30 p.m.), the two women stared at each other.

What the woman in the car apparently didn't know was that the truck was stalled.

## SHORT SUBJECTS ~

The city has collected $434 worth of delinquent parking tickets from state legislators since we listed 58 lawmakers who had ignored citations the past couple of years . . . Illinois State Journal writer Bob Estill isn't bragging about it, but his disabled 14-foot outboard "yatch" (with Estill and his family aboard) was towed to shore by a canoe at Lake Springfield.

## LBJ: GET A HAIRCUT! ~

Springfield barber Ed Murphy, who sent $2.75 and a note to Lyndon Johnson urging the former president to hurry to the nearest barber shop and have his shoulder-length white hair sheared, received a letter from Texas this week.

It was from LBJ's secretary, who had a full explanation for her boss's long locks. She said Johnson's activities, such as going to the barber shop, have been curtailed since his hospitalization in July. Murphy was assured Johnson is "feeling much better" these days, that he is expected to resume regular office hours soon and at that time will consult a hair-stylist.

Murphy also was assured that his comments "will be called to Johnson's attention" later, at a time when he is feeling more like his old self. And Murphy's $2.75 was refunded.

## SCHOOL DAZE ~
A first-grader at Jane Addams School, returning home with the first day of school under his belt, was asked by his father how he liked it:

"Great," he replied excitedly. "One kid threw up twice in my room."

## BUMPER SNICKER ~
"MAJORITY NOT SILENT — GOVERNMENT'S DEAF."

## DEAD LETTER FILE ~
Campaign fund-raisers for Democrat presidential candidate George McGovern sent a letter to "The Hon. Paul Powell, Secretary of State's Office", appealing for a contribution last month. And this week, a similar letter addressed to "Paul Powell, St. Nicholas Hotel, Springfield, Ill.," arrived from President Nixon's fund-raising committee.

"As you know," the letters to the late secretary of state said, "we are now in the final stages of an historic presidential election campaign which will surely determine how you and your family live for many years to come. Your whole way of life is at stake."

Although both political parties had bum mailing lists, the GOP had the best address considering that the hotel was where Powell's money was hidden.

## BUMPER SNICKER ~
"WANNA FIGHT POLLUTION? GAG A POLITICIAN."

## SOBERING REMINDER ~
Tacked to Assistant Sangamon County Schools Superintendent Harold Funk's office bulletin board is a small worn-out shoe.

Funk spotted it on a third-grade boy, whose foot protruded through a gaping hole in the sole, in the dead of winter several years ago.

He bought the boy a new pair of shoes and hung up the old one as a reminder that life could be a whole lot worse.

## MECHANICAL DUNSTER ~

A computerized statement from Passavant Hospital at Jacksonville went to a Bluffs man who, the computer considered, is delinquent in paying his hospital bill. On the bill was this "personal" message:

"Hello there, I am the hospital's computer. As yet, no one but me knows that you have not been making regular payments on this account. However, if I have not processed a payment from you within ten days, I will tell a human who will resort to other means of collection."

Now, for what the tattletale computer doesn't know.

An insurance policy will pay the bill if and when another computer — the one the man's employer fed it to — ever gets the message.

A human element on one side suggests a showdown between the two computers, squaring off at 20 paces with magnets.

## COLLECTOR'S ITEM ~

A mother found this note, scribed by her 7-year-old daughter to a neighbor boy, in the milk box:

*Dear Mike*
*We can't go on like this.*
*Love, Cindy*

## LANGUAGE BARRIER ~

Circuit court received a letter from a prison inmate requesting a free transcript of his trial record.

He explained he can't afford to pay for the transcript because he is a "poorpus."

He meant he is a pauper, of course, but for a minute there was a temptation to forward the letter to Marineland.

## JUDGE DRESSES DOWN ~

Judge J. Waldo Ackerman and his son went fishing Saturday morning. Then they headed for home in plenty of time for Ackerman to tidy up for a wedding ceremony in the afternoon.

But no one was at home when they returned and they found themselves locked out.

Ackerman looked at himself: unshaven, clad in grubby fishing togs and sneakers. He awaited rescue. But there was no rescue.

So, with time growing short, he made a dash to the courthouse, grabbed his black robe and proceeded to a home where the wedding party was anxiously awaiting his arrival. With the robe hiding everything but his whiskers, the lower legs of his faded pants and the green sneakers, he faced the music. His apologies flowed like wine following the ceremony. Ackerman confesses he now knows firsthand what it's like to plead for mercy.

## KEEP THY HORN UNTO THYSELF ~

A fellow was waiting for a traffic light to change when he spied a bumper sticker on the car in front of him.

"HONK IF YOU LOVE JESUS," the sticker read.

Showing his strong affection, the guy laid on his horn. Out of the car in front jumped a very large gentleman who stomped back to confront the honking motorist. Half scared out of his wits, the guy, pointing to the bumper sticker, meekly explained that he was only honking because he loved Jesus.

"Well don't honk your. . . . . horn at me," the big guy shouted, "my son put that . . . . . thing on there!"

# 1973

## ALL IN THE FAMILY ~

The estate of an area woman was being processed in court and the judge was asking the routine questions to determine her survivors.

A brother who had preceded her in death was found to have had somewhat of an unusual marriage history. He had married three sisters — one at a time, of course. As one died, he married another until he had married all three.

At the close of the proceedings, curiosity overpowered the judge and he asked the obvious question:

"Were there any more sisters in that family?"

"No," quipped one relative, "but if there had been, he would've married 'em."

⌣

## SCHOOL DAZE ~

Springfield Police Officer Tom Marvel's school lectures on traffic safety sometimes have a reverse effect on small fry. Here's one that backfired:

"And what have you been learning in school?" a father asked his young son one evening.

"Well, dad, they took my class way out on the other side of town to a graveyard and took us into this big monument (Lincoln's Tomb)," the wide-eyed boy replied. "A man in there had been shot and they told us all about him.

"Then a policeman came to our school to talk to us. He told us all about his badge and whistle and gun and . . . say, I think he's the one who shot that guy at the graveyard."

## MAIL BAG ~

From Mrs. Lloyd Wall of Springfield: "Thank you for your story concerning the gentleman who married three sisters. That was my father-in-law, David E. Wall.

"Your story came about due to the death of his sister, Belle Squires of Divernon. We got a big kick out of your story, which is true, except there was one other unmarried sister who we used to kid (before her death) that if she stayed around she still might marry Dave. He died while still married to his third wife.

"There is another part of this story which makes it so lovable. Dave used to tell anyone who commented on his marrying three sisters that 'I've got the greatest and most wonderful mother-in-law and I want to keep her.' I wonder how many of us present-day mothers-in-law could have such a wonderful tribute paid to us?"

## SLIP OF THE TONGUE ~

A local radio DJ, reading a report on the Chicago school teacher strike, said the teachers wanted "radioactive" pay.

## 'COURTHOUSE BETTY' ~

The manner and dress of the woman led most people to believe she was a kook.

Her portly frame usually was draped with an old choir robe. She wore sneakers or desert boots, a pound of dime store jewelry and layers of lipstick and rouge. An artificial flower sometimes jutted from the top of her head.

She was a daily sight in the county courthouse for years and became an avid spectator at criminal trials. That earned her the nickname of "Courthouse Betty."

She also was a familiar figure in the Statehouse, where she kept an eagle-eye on the legislature and attended all of the committee hearings she could find. Betty also found an interest in some meetings of the city council, Historical Sites Commission and Springfield Art Association. As one acquaintance put it, she seldom missed anything that was free.

Not only was she a spectator at such events, she often participated in the discussion of business at hand. She usually asked bold questions, which made her offensive to some.

That got her into trouble at the courthouse a few years ago. She repeatedly interrupted courtroom proceedings by shouting questions at the lawyers and judges. And on one occasion, as all spectators at a murder trial were being searched, Betty was found to be carrying a knife in her purse.

"She was continually disturbing the court and we finally had to do something," recalls Sheriff Eddie Ryan. "I talked to her and suggested she go to the library instead. She didn't do those things intentionally. I felt sorry for her, the poor soul had nothing else to do. That knife we found was just a small one. She carried it strictly for her own protection, I'm sure."

That was the end of her courthouse residency.

Betty made the news three times in her life.

Eight years ago, she marked Memorial Day by having state Rep. J. David Jones and Air National Guard Col. Ralph Bush preside at the dedication of a flagpole in front of her home. A plaque honored the memory of the first member of the Army Air Corps to fly the Atlantic Ocean. He was Col. Frank Kennedy, her father. Kennedy also was one of 12 volunteers for the Army's first aviation school back in 1911.

Then, in 1967, Betty formed the short-lived NDCPA, the designation for "Naked Dogs, Clothe People Association." Idea of the movement (prompted by publication of a pattern for a dog sweater in the newspaper) was to "take clothes off dogs and put them back on people," Betty told snickering newsmen.

"Dogs should be prohibited from wearing clothes unless it is recommended by a licensed veterinarian for the health and welfare of the animal," she contended.

She aimed the second phase of the movement — putting clothes back on people — primarily at topless dancers. No one signed the petition she circulated.

Betty next made headlines in 1971 when she pressed the city council to rename Capital Airport as Circling Eagle Airport in recognition of her father's efforts to protect rights of the American Indian and his role as a pioneer aviator. Her father was adopted by the Comanche tribe and named "Circling Eagle." Betty, who claimed to be "Princess Peaceful Bear," failed to move the council.

Jones, a neighbor of Betty's, has long been convinced of her "vital interest" in government. She telephoned him late one night and urged him to sponsor her for the position of state director of aeronautics.

Jones, as well as many local political figures, knew her as a member of the League of Women Voters. It was at one of the league's meet-the-candidates meetings last fall that Betty asked some of her bold questions:

"Are you going to try the first woman who has a legal abortion in Sangamon County as a murderess?" she asked State's Attorney Joseph Cavanagh.

"What funeral home are you in cahoots with and where do you send all your bodies?" she asked Coroner Norman Richter.

Betty also was a daily caller on radio station talk shows.

That was "Courthouse Betty." Her real name was Betty Kennedy and that's the way it appeared in the obituary column this week.

It took only a couple of paragraphs to say she was found dead in her modest home on Walnut Street, that she was 52 years old, that she served her country as a WAC during World War II and that she had no survivors.

## THE LITTLEST THINGS COUNT ~

Among a long list of items awarded to a woman in Sangamon County divorce court the other day was "grandfather's shovel," "remains of Aunt Dorothy's hi-chair" and the plaintiff's mother's rolling pin.

## GOVERNOR BE SEATED! ~

Illinois Gov. Dan Walker said it:

"They've done a great job remodeling (millions of dollars worth) the Executive Mansion but there's not a comfortable chair in the whole damned place."

## KID STUFF ~

The scene was the men's restroom at the Holiday Inn East. A gent entered last night and was confronted by a serious-minded 5-year-old boy, arms folded across his chest, standing at attention.

Upon inquiry, the boy proudly identified himself as Roy Ziegler Jr. and explained that he was merely waiting for a man to emerge from the middle booth so he could retrieve his toys.

"No toys in here," bellowed the voice inside.

So the gent took young Roy in tow to look for the toys, described only as "swords."

Minutes later, the guy in the booth caught up with the search party, which at this point included innkeeper Lacey Brooks. Roy got his swords back.

No wonder the guy in the booth didn't recognize them at first — they were miniature swords, the kind that come in cocktail glasses, otherwise known as swizzle sticks.

Brooks promptly contributed about 100 more to Roy's arsenal.

## STRAIGHT TALK ~

Ex-state's attorney assistant Walter Kasten, who's about to resume his role as public defender, is well known for his less-than-subtle way of saying things both in and out of the courtroom.

He once lectured a parole violator (considerably bigger than he) in a corner of the courthouse like this:

"Well, Harry, you've been a bad boy. And you know what we do with bad boys, don't you? Sure you do. We send bad boys to the big house. That's where I'm gonna send you."

## PRAISE THE LORD . . . AND PASS THE RESOLUTION! ~

So it went at Monday's meeting of the Sangamon County Board.

As usual, the monthly session opened with bowed heads for the invocation and recitation of the Pledge of Allegiance to the flag. The Rev. Andrew Templeman, pastor of the First Presbyterian Church, was clergyman of the month. He sidestepped tradition and prefaced his prayer by quoting a minister who once spoke before the Pennsylvania state legislature:

"Oh Lord, if in this day we aren't deeply concerned for the need for justice, then make our steaks tough and our martinis sweet."

Templeman, having gained the undivided attention of his "congregation," then launched the invocation.

A few minutes later, after disposing of routine matters, the board tackled what turned out to be the most controversial matter of the day; the question of whether clergymen should be paid $15 for performing the monthly invocation.

"Why, all of a sudden, should we start paying preachers?" one board member asked.

One of the board's finance committee members who introduced the "religious resolution" explained that the lack of pay for preachers was an oversight in the first place, that it had been assumed they were being paid for their services.

"Do the ministers need the money?" another board member asked.

"If we can spend $10,000 on a drug rehabilitation program, we can afford to spend $180 (a year) for a little religion," spouted a supporter of the resolution.

"Amen," chimed another.

Before the burning question could be brought to a vote, there was a hassle over when the pay — if granted — should be effective. One board member suggested the proposed June 1 date be changed to make the preacher pay retroactive to Jan. 1.

"Why not make it retroactive to December, the start of the fiscal year?" someone asked.

"Why not go all the way back to 1910?" countered another.

Finally, the Jan. 1 date was adopted and the roll was called up yonder. A voice vote was far from unanimous but the resolution passed.

That prompted board member Huck Huckaby to rise and, tongue-in-cheek, offer a motion that the county pay fellow board man Buck Jones to lead the Pledge of Allegiance. Chairman Dean Collins quickly gaveled down the motion, ruling it dead for lack of a second.

But the issue may not be dead yet. Another board member, who wants to remain anonymous for the time being, says he'll nominate both Huckaby and Jones to serve as assistant chaplains at the next board meeting and compensate them with proceeds from a freewill offering.

~

## SOME OPERATION! ~
Dr. Lyle Wacaser drives a pickup truck that carries this sign:

"Lyle Wacaser — Neurology and Light Hauling."

## GUN CONTROL ~
Nine-year-old Phil Ackerman spotted a city policeman standing in line at a carry-out restaurant and, pursuing a youngster's fascination for guns, asked if he could look at the officer's revolver.

"You certainly can," said the officer.

"Will you take it out of the holster and show it to me?" Phil asked.

"Sorry, but I can't," replied the officer. "If I did that, all the water might run out of it."

## FORGET THE ALPO ~
There's a guy on the south side who must be chomping at the bit.

He has two dogs that share his household at night. One is a big dog with a strange appetite. He's eaten two or three of his master's expensive shoes.

A few nights ago, the dog found the guy's false teeth and ate 'em.

## OUCH! ~
City health inspector Al Brittin hauled a gang of kindergartners to an inoculation clinic at fire department headquarters. One little boy in the group clung tight to Brittin all the way.

"Is this gonna hurt?" he asked on the way inside.

"No, it'll just tickle a little," Brittin assured him.

The wide-eyed boy grimaced and his eyes watered when the needle was inserted but he uttered not one word.

Brittin returned his charges to the school and the little boy was still hang-

44

〜

ing onto his hand as they crossed the playground. It was at that point that the silence was broken.

"You big son-of-a-bitch, it did too hurt!" the boy blurted as he broke away and ran for his life.

## FINALLY CONVINCED ~

State Rep. Roscoe Cunningham of Lawrenceville tried to cut across two other traffic lanes in an attempt to make a right turn at Fifth and North Grand. But his car collided with another car driven by a Springfield woman.

Cunningham told investigating patrolman Bob Williamson he was immune from arrest and continued on his way to the legislature. Williamson figured otherwise, wrote a ticket citing Cunningham for an improper turn and went to the Statehouse to hand it to the lawmaker.

Cunningham put off the patrolman again, claiming he didn't have his driver's license with him or $25 for bail. Williamson didn't give up. He later mailed the summons to Cunningham.

Cunningham, a former Lawrence County state's attorney and now a member of the legislative judiciary committee, finally threw in the towel and mailed his "fine" with the following letter (on official House stationery) to Associate Judge Jerry Rhodes:

"Dear Judge Rhodes:

"My lawyer's advised that plausible defense is available since intersection lacked appropriate signs to warn that right lane only permitted me to turn right on arrow. However, other handlers were apprehensive that relentless resistance might provoke a Watergate situation disproportionate to the joy of vindication.

"Accordingly, per telephone conversation, I enclose my check for $15. Consent that matter be heard in my absence. If the prosecution fails to appear, I move for dismissal and request that the check be endorsed to the delightful street art fair that I've attended on Old Capitol square in other years.

"I appreciate your kindness. If you're in County Lawrence, stop and see us. Guarantee your safe conduct through this county. If I can assist you in the General Assembly, do not hesitate.

"Best Wishes, Roscoe E. Cunningham"

## TAXPAYER TRANSPORTATION CO. ~

State-owned cars turn up in the darndest places and under such extenuating circumstances. Here are some recent sightings:

U9480 — At a drive-in movie theater during the wee morning hours on a weekend.

U5723 — Parked in front of a bakery thrift shop on Clear Lake Avenue while the woman driver, attired in a bright green silky pantsuit, shopped for day-old goodies.

U1860 — At McDonald's, where the driver treated his wife and kids to hamburgers on the weekend. Later at Sears, where the family went shopping.

U7681 — Carrying a man, woman and two children, buzzing along U.S. 67 north of St. Louis on a weekend.

U8390 — Cruising through eastern Colorado.

Caught in the act, you say? But wait. Consider these "logical" explanations.

The car with U9480 plates is an unmarked Ford assigned to the director of the state Environmental Protection Agency. Rule of thumb is that department heads enjoy unlimited use of a state-owned car. So that means any high-ranking state official can drive a state car to the movies, supermarket, church, etc.

The car at the thrift shop was driven by a home economist from the University of Illinois. She was picking up supplies for a U of I exhibit at the state fair, according to a university official.

The man who took his family to McDonald's and Sears had recently moved in from Chicago to go to work for the secretary of state and had been authorized by a superior to temporarily make personal use of the state car until he could buy his own car. But he was directed not to drive it to McDonald's or Sears any more.

The head baseball coach at Western Illinois University (Macomb) was driving the state car spotted in Missouri. He had taken his wife and kids along on a "recruiting" trip to Baldwin, Mo., a university spokesman said. He dropped them off at a relative's home in Missouri, which was "on the way" to Baldwin, and picked them up on his return trip two days later. He had obtained permission to take his family on the trip. Such practice is permitted but not encouraged, says the university.

The driver of the car with U8390 plates was a professor and former dean of students at Southern Illinois University (Carbondale). He was crossing Colorado on a return trip from Oregon State University, where he attended a two-week seminar and received an excellence award for teaching. He had driven to Oregon alone, then brought back his mother-in-law and two brothers-in-law for a visit.

Now, Mr. Taxpayer, you be the judge. Were those cars used for official business or monkey business?

## LONG WAY AROUND ~

A funny thing happened to a woman on her way to surgery at Memorial Hospital the other night. Two new nurses loaded her onto a cart and wheeled her out of a sixth-floor room, and headed for the operating room on the seventh floor.

Ten minutes later, relatives left her room for the solarium, on the eighth floor, to wait out the operation. Rounding the corner to catch an elevator, they were surprised to find the two nurses — patient in tow — still waiting for the elevator doors to open.

That elevator was out of order. So the surgical detail moved on to another elevator, climbed aboard, pushed the button for the seventh floor and went straight to the basement. Another punch of the button took the nurses and their patient to the eighth floor, at which point they disembarked in search of the operating room. After wheeling the woman through the solarium, across an enclosed rooftop ramp and around the eighth floor in another building, the nurses were directed back to the solarium and onto the elevator.

Down they went in an attempt to hit the seventh floor but they missed it again. Up again they went. Down. Up.

Finally, the elevator doors opened to a safe landing on the seventh floor. Doctors were waiting and wondering what had happened to their patient. It had been about 30 minutes since the woman was wheeled out of her room just one floor below.

She had really been taken for a ride but, sporting a good sense of humor, admitted she enjoyed every minute of it. She's still laughing because everything came out okay in the operating room.

## LITE FACTOR ~

A guy near First and Elliott called City Water Light & Power to report one of the new high-wattage street lights in his neighborhood had burned out. A crew got it going, then it went out again — on purpose. CWLP turned it off at the request of a greenhouse operator who complained that the bright light made his poinsettias grow too fast.

## TAKEN FOR A RIDE ~

A woman dropped off her car at a department store service center to have a flat tire repaired and skipped off to do some shopping.

About 30 minutes later she returned, found the repair job yet to be done and, after a few words with the mechanic, stomped back into the store. She returned a little later to find the tire fixed but the trunk lid open.

Still miffed, she slammed the lid shut, hopped in and drove off. But she was startled by a pounding noise and a man's voice a few blocks away. It was coming from the trunk.

Seems the mechanic had crawled into the trunk to bolt down the spare tire and unintentionally was taken captive by the woman.

He was mad, mad, mad. He demanded she drive him back to the store.

She did but he refused to sit up front with her. He rode in the trunk.

## SPRINGFIELD NOTORIETY ~

The January issue of Esquire magazine lists Springfield for a dubious achievement award, citing a man wearing a jockstrap over his head who robbed a White Hen Pantry store here.

Such a masked man (staged) appears on the magazine cover.

A number of armed robberies at White Hen stores were reported during the year but lawmen say they don't recall one in which a man hid behind a jockstrap.

# 1974

## PENNY'S GREAT ADVENTURE ~

It was the long way home from kindergarten for 5-year-old Penny Talkington last Thursday. A total of about 6 miles, in fact.

Patrolman David Haynes, working a school zone assignment with representatives of the Traffic Safety Council, intercepted Penny on Monroe Street near Fairhills Shopping Center. She was in tears, obviously lost.

Penny blurted only enough to tell Haynes she was trying to find her way home from school. He figured she meant Dubois School, a few blocks away, and suggested she climb into his patrol van so he could drive her home.

"No, no, please," she insisted. "I can't ride with strangers."

Haynes talked until his complexion matched his blue uniform. No way would the little girl accept his offer of a ride.

Nancy Dodson, a safety council member, offered to go along.

"You're a stranger too," Penny responded.

She finally agreed to let Haynes "escort" her. So off she went, back toward Dubois School, with Haynes driving alongside in his patrol van.

"Is that the school you go to?" Haynes inquired a few blocks later.

"No, it doesn't look like that," Penny said.

She kept walking. Haynes, driving at a snail's pace with red lights flashing, kept following. The tears were still flowing as the patrolman halted her just west of busy Walnut Street for another conference.

With the help from two women and a couple of youngsters in the neighborhood, Penny remembered her last name. Haynes was in the process of radioing headquarters when Penny's parents called to report she was missing.

By that time, she decided that Haynes was no longer a stranger and she climbed into the van to ride the rest of the way home — another 25 blocks.

Penny goes to kindergarten at Lincoln School, located at 11th and Monroe. When she began the seven-block trek home about three hours earlier that afternoon, she headed west instead of east. That took her straight through the downtown business district, across nine major street intersections and two railroads.

Penny summed it up this way: "I made a wrong turn."

## DAZE GONE BY ~

There've been some changes at Memorial Hospital since this fee schedule and set of house rules were in effect 100 years ago. A bed in a ward cost $4 per week and had to be paid for in advance. An additional $5 to $10 was charged if surgery was performed. Private rooms were $7 to $10 per week, payable two weeks in advance. But that rate didn't cover such things as special nurses, physician fees, use of operating rooms, wine or liquors and patients back then were also required to have at least a two-week supply of clothing because the hospital offered no personal laundry services.

## KID STUFF ~

A number of lawmen looking for a murder suspect had surrounded an old building when a small boy happened on the scene.

"What's going on?" he asked.

"We're looking at this building, we're thinking about buying it," one officer replied.

"Then why does that cop have his gun out?" the kid persisted.

"Well, there's rats inside and we may have to shoot 'em," quipped the officer.

## UNCONVENTIONAL LIVING ~

A guy in Springfield is preparing to put his wife and five kids in a convent. He'll go with them, of course. It's a surplus convent at Rochelle that he bought to "convert" into a home.

Don't laugh, it's a nice brick building with plenty of possibilities. Upstairs are eight bedrooms in a row, a huge bathroom with four lavatories, tub, shower stalls and four johns.

The chapel will be converted into a "rec" room and a telephone will be installed in the confession booth. Amen.

## NAKED CITY ~

It was pretty dull Saturday night until Illinois State Journal police reporter Lee Aschoff got a phone call from a nude woman.

She told him she was nude, anyway. And she told him why. She was steamed.

Seems she'd been to a west-side supermarket and bought a bar of soap for 34 cents. She went home, stripped and hopped into the shower. It was then, as she removed the wrapper from the soap, that she noticed she'd just bought a "free sample."

Her first reaction was to call the Journal, so that's why she called in the nude, she told Aschoff. Good thing her first thought wasn't to dash back to the supermarket for a refund.

## SAFETY FIRST ~
An eighth-grader was letting his dad in on his plans for the science fair at school.

"I'm going to build an atomic bomb," the boy calmly announced.

"You can't do that," his father sputtered.

"Just a little one."

"You'd better talk it over with your teacher."

"I did."

"What did she say?"

"To be careful."

## COURT JESTER ~
Judge Simon Friedman was in the process of selecting a jury for a murder trial Monday. Clerk Kenneth Richards announced the number and name of the next prospective juror.

"Wheeee, that's me," a woman chirped as she headed for the jury box.

"It's just like playing bingo, isn't it, lady?" the judge cracked.

## HYSTERICAL SITE ~
When Sam Sgro reopened the St. Nicholas Hotel a few weeks ago, he revealed he would promote Paul Powell's old room where the late secretary of state stashed nearly a million bucks in cash (much of it in a shoebox) as a tourist attraction of sorts.

But he's reconsidering. Sgro has gotten a lot of flak from Powell admirers who don't like the idea. Sgro says he doesn't want to do anything to jeopardize the hotel, so he's inclined at this point to let Powell rest in peace.

Too bad. Powell and his shoebox fortune would be a natural draw for the historic old hotel. That story went around the world and, more than three years later, hasn't been forgotten. Letters with news clippings about the St. Nick, addressed to the "Shoebox Hotel," are still coming from the four corners.

*St. Nicholas Hotel in Paul Powell days.*

## BEHIND BARS ~

Chief Judge Howard Lee White was touring the county jail and listening to gripes from inmates. One complained about the food.

"What's wrong with it?" the judge asked.

"You should have seen what they gave me for breakfast — two doughnuts and a cup of coffee," the prisoner blurted.

"That's more than I had for breakfast," White countered.

## WISH I HADN'T SAID THAT? ~

There's an old song titled "Please Don't Talk About Me When I'm Gone."

Seems that would have been good advice for some people in high places who were at no loss for words when Secretary of State Paul Powell died.

Admittedly, it's just been accusations and investigations the past three years concerning Powell's racetrack stock, his hotel room cash horde and countless other suspicious dealings he was involved in.

But last week, a federal grand jury here named Powell an unindicted conspirator in connection with the indictment of two contractors accused of bribing him to get lucrative Statehouse remodeling contracts.

Point being, if Powell wasn't dead, he also would have been indicted.

With that in mind, we resurrect some of the "haunting" eulogies that poured forth upon his passing in 1970, prior to the expose of any illegal activities. And, in parenthesis, are our 1974 interpretations:

Then-Gov. Richard Ogilvie said:

"Paul Powell quickly grasped the infinite complexities of man and government."

(Not to mention cash-laden shoeboxes.)

Chicago Mayor Richard Daley said:

"Powell never lost the common touch."

(That was common?)

Then-Lt. Gov. Paul Simon said:

"Education in Illinois has had no better friend than Paul Powell."

(True, Illinoisans have learned a lot about him.)

Southern Illinois University President Delyte Morris said:

"He was a legend."

(So was Benedict Arnold.)

Former Springfield Mayor Nelson Howarth said:

"Paul Powell's word was his bond."

(Yes, Powell would have been able to post his own bond.)

State Rep. Clyde Choate said:

"Paul Powell's virtues and human touch made him the most unforgettable man to ever walk the halls of this building (the Statehouse)."

(And pad his pockets at the same time.)

## MAN, THAT'S WEAK! ~

Public defender Walter Kasten summed up his closing argument in an armed robbery trial like this the other day:

"The state's case is as weak as broth made from the shadow of a chicken that starved to death," he told the jury with a straight face.

Kasten was rewarded with a verdict of not guilty.

## COLD STREAK ~

Four kids streaked police headquarters the other night but only three were captured. What happened to the other streaker? He ran faster and took refuge under a parked car.

It was 1 o'clock in the morning, cold and he was nude. Some time later, he scooted (very carefully) out from under the car, found a jacket and, with that wrapped around him, made his way to the railroad tracks. Then he hopped a slow freight that took him to within walking distance of his south-side home.

All that in his birthday suit. Guess what: It just happened to be his birthday.

## THERE GOES LUNCH! ~

Patrolman Bob Squires was one of the first officers on a murder scene at Fourth and Washington five months ago. This week, while testifying in the James Young trial, he revealed a new method of protecting evidence at a crime scene.

Squires, explaining that his diet lunch was in his squad car, said he used radishes and celery sticks from his brown bag to mark items of evidence he found near the body in the street.

The vegetables served the purpose well. Radishes and celery were about the first things that caught the eye of investigators as they arrived on the scene.

For the record, Squires skipped lunch that night.

## MR. CLEAN? ~

A county resident called the sheriff's office to complain of an intruder. Seems a man knocked on the door and asked to use the bathroom. Permission granted.

Some 20 minutes later, the man was still in the bathroom. At that point, the man of the house decided to investigate.

He was shocked to find the mystery man really was using the bathroom — he was taking a bath.

## SHAGGY DOG STORY ~

A woman telephoned the Laketown Animal Clinic to report that her dog had swallowed a knee-length sock.

"What'll I do?" she gasped.

A secretary advised that the doctor was in surgery at the time but would return her call in a few minutes.

The woman, before hanging up, stressed the emergency nature of the situation — she needed the sock by Monday.

## MOM DIDN'T HAVE A CLUE ~

A mother was startled when she discovered her son and a pal, both grade-schoolers, playing "shop."

One was the shopkeeper and the other was the shoplifter.

## THANKS, BOSS ~

Judge George Coutrakon presided at the wedding of his court reporter, Jerry Wedeking, the other day. He capped the ceremony with the same phrase that closes every criminal proceeding:

"You have 30 days in which to appeal," Coutrakon advised the groom.

## 'SHORT' STORY ~

Insurance agent John Cavanaugh, a fairly big fellow, was on his knees looking for something behind the sales counter when a woman walked up to make a payment.

Able to reach the counter top from that position, he remained on his knees while accepting the payment and writing the receipt.

The woman departed and Cavanaugh continued his search under the counter.

Next day the same woman returned and asked another agent if she could talk to the "midget."

## SHOEBOX 'SANDALS' ~

We know what ex-Secretary of State Paul Powell did with shoeboxes. But Bud Sutton was even more inventive.

Sutton, an employee of Baker Plumbing & Heating, was on a job at Myers Brothers department store that required him to step out of an upper story window onto a freshly tarred roof.

His crepe shoe soles soaked up the sticky stuff.

The only way out was through the store, so he slapped a shoebox lid on each sole to protect the carpeting and tromped through the crowd of shoppers.

"Do you have anything in a size 12 box?" Sutton quipped as he stalked through the shoe department.

## LOOK OUT BELOW! ~

Painters were putting the finishing touch on the Lincoln City Hall but couldn't quite reach the top of the tower. So the fire department, housed in the same building, contributed its hook-and-ladder truck to the cause.

The owner of the painting firm personally took brush and paint bucket in hand, climbed the aerial ladder and started applying the coat of silver. Then it happened. Somehow the bucket of paint broke loose and bounced rung-by-rung down the long ladder, splattering both the shiny red fire truck and the city hall wall before plopping onto the street.

Painters, firemen and volunteers formed a rag brigade and rubbed, and rubbed, and rubbed, and . . .

## ERA ENDING ~

Coal was once big business in Springfield. Seven coal yards, plus several mines, were operating here when Achille Designe opened his coal yard at 2729 South Grand Ave. E. about 30 years ago.

Designe is the only coal man left and this probably will be his last year in business. Besides the dwindling market for coal, skyrocketing prices in the industry are driving him out.

What is known as egg-size Kentucky coal was selling for $32.80 a ton at Designe's yard about a year ago. It's twice that much now and the price will be "something else" by winter, Designe predicts.

That's considering he can get coal to sell. Mining companies aren't interested in supplying independent dealers any more, he says. Designe has coal left over from last winter that he expects will keep him in business this season.

Now 73, Designe eyes retirement in 1975.

"Guess I'll just be a G-man the rest of my life," he reckons.

"G" stands for "government," Designe explains, which is where his pension will come from.

## TINKLE TIME ~

Motorists traveling U.S. 66 thought they were seeing an invasion as a long convoy of Army trucks pulled to the side of the highway and a platoon of soldiers made a mad dash into a cornfield at the edge of Mount Olive.

But it was a different kind of mission, obvious by the strategic positions the men took up in the field.

Passing motorists stared, grinned and honked. Within minutes, the men climbed back into their trucks and the convoy moved out.

Needless to say, everyone was relieved.

## CAMPAIGN DAZE ~

The toughest part of the campaign for county board candidate Norm Schultz was sidestepping dogs — not issues. He often found himself face to face with a snapping canine and was even bitten by one.

Near the end of the campaign trail, though, he knocked on a door and a little dachshund ran out.

"Get Schultzy! Get Schultzy!" someone yelled from inside.

Schultz thought he'd really had it. Then he realized Schultzy was the name of the dog.

## WITCH'S BREW? ~

Here's what one guy served to Halloween party guests.

Ingredients included acetone, methul acetate, furan, diacetyl, butanol, methyl furan, methyl butanol, isoprene, various oils, propional aldehyde, methanol, acetaldehyde, methul formate, ethanol and dimethyl sulfide and caffeine.

Deadly witch's brew?

Nope. That's a plain old cup of coffee.

## GET THE PICTURE? ~

A young county jail inmate was rushed to a hospital for X-ray after telling deputies he swallowed a razor blade. Doctors were inspecting the third set of X-rays when the prisoner abruptly coughed up a confession. He admitted his story was a hoax after being told that his mother — not the taxpayers — would be getting the hospital bill.

Seems he dreamed up the story after learning another inmate was granted trustee status after a razor blade gulping stunt some time ago. He aspired to be a trustee, too.

# 1975

## JONESY'S FLAG ~

It was a small world for Reese Harold Jones. His life revolved around the Piccadilly Tavern on North Fifth Street.

"Jonesy" had a "job" there — putting up the American flag each morning. Tavern patrons grew concerned for him when they noticed the flag was missing the other day. Jonesy was in the hospital, tavern owner Duke Thompson informed them. A few days later, Jonesy died.

He was a loner many of his 54 years. He had a son somewhere. Also an elder sister some distance away. But the gang at the Piccadilly was his real family.

A proud ex-Marine, Jonesy lived day to day. He didn't always remember the day before. Something to do with the silver plate in his head, they said. That was the patch-job for a wound he suffered in a battle for an island in the Pacific during World War II.

"He'd been around here for 12 years that I know of," Thompson recalled. "I inherited him when I took over the place."

Jonesy lived in a room above the tavern. He existed on his veteran's pension and a little help from friends. He did little favors for the other roomies there, all pensioners. And he ran errands for Thompson.

"Jonesy was always doing something nice for somebody, but his job was putting up the flag," said Thompson. "Everybody around here liked him, that's for sure."

There were times when he annoyed people, though. Like just about every day at 4:30 in the morning. He got up at that hour to take a shower. His "neighbors" often suggested that he refrain from getting up so early.

That was just part of the Marine Corps that rubbed off on him.

Little things meant a lot to Jonesy. Like the half-dozen name tags he'd saved from Christmas packages over the years and taped to the otherwise bare walls in his room.

But a discharge certificate from the Marine Corps, neatly folded and tucked into his billfold, probably was his most cherished possession.

Thompson made the funeral arrangements. Regulars at the tavern filled a cigar box with contributions for flowers. They started gathering in the tavern at 7 a.m. Monday, more than 90 minutes prior to the funeral.

"It was really something," Thompson mused. "People you'd think wouldn't give a damn about anything showed up to go to the funeral."

After a short prayer service at a funeral home, a nine-car procession wound its way into Camp Butler National Cemetery. Four men and two women, patrons of the Piccadilly, carried Jonesy's casket to the gravesite. A detail from World War I Veterans Barracks 185 conducted the service.

"It was strictly military," said Thompson. "That's the way Jonesy would have liked it."

## SIGN NOT A WELCOME MAT ~

The sign outside the governor's mansion hints visitors are welcome. It ain't necessarily so. Just ask the woman who drove onto the grounds Wednesday night.

*Illinois' Executive Mansion in early 1970s.*

She was taking her sister and two small kids on a sightseeing tour around town. While viewing the mansion from Fifth Street, they noticed the big gate at the driveway was open. Her sister suggested they drive through for a closer look.

As the woman steered her little old Chevy up to the front of the mansion, she saw that the gate ahead, through which she had planned to exit, was closed. At that point, she shifted into reverse and started backing up. That's when she heard a shrill whistle and looked up to see a well-dressed man bounding toward the car.

"What in the hell do you think you're doing?" he yelled.

"I'm sorry," the woman gasped. "We just wanted to get a better look at the mansion."

"Don't you know this is private property?" the man shouted. "How in the hell would you like someone to drive a car through your front yard in the middle of the night?" (It was about 8:30 p.m.)

"We're sick and tired of people coming through here and causing trouble," the man continued. "What kind of a troublemaker are you, anyway? I have half a notion to call the police and have you thrown in jail."

"Look, mister, I'm really sorry," the woman interjected. "We're just taking a little tour of Springfield."

"I don't want to see your car on these grounds again, or even driving by, or I'll have you thrown in jail," the verbal assault continued. "And you better damned well not hit anything backing out of here."

Needless to say, the woman exercised extreme caution in her retreat. Who was the man? She doesn't know. He didn't offer any identification. But she does know that it wasn't the governor.

## BOWS OUT LIKE A GENTLEMAN ~
Monday night's sign-off was Wayne Cody's last on WMAY. But he gave no hint of it, bowing out with his familiar "Goodnight, ladies and gentlemen."

He was a casualty of the Rock Age.

Cody, who billed himself as the "Old Campaigner and Last of the Redhot Lovers," was one of the few piano playing disc jockeys in the nation when he joined WMAY in 1955. He already had 20 years of radio under his belt plus a long musical career in vaudeville. His "Cody Quartet" toured every state in the union.

"It was simple," Cody says of his exit. "They told me I could stay if I'd play rock 'n' roll.

"I couldn't do that. Neither my sponsors nor my listeners would stand for it. And I wouldn't either."

## COLLECTOR'S ITEM ~
Here's how one guy fights inflation at the post office. He mails everything "Half-Class." (I think that's what he said.)

## HAND-CANCELED ~
Even barbers get hate mail. Here's a letter a disgruntled 10-year-old boy sent to his barber who trimmed a little too much off his locks:

"Dear Scalphunter:

"Some day I'll repay you for taking all my hair. You dirty facest thief. I'll get you for it.

⌣

"Your X Customer

"P.S.-You Stink!!!"

## GETTING EVEN ~
A 70-year-old woman left her favorite wool head scarf in a shopping cart while meandering through a drug store. Somebody swiped it.

To torment the thief, she put out the word that she'd been shopping for something to treat head lice.

## REVEILLE IN THE COURT ~
The trial of bank robber George Alewelt in federal court apparently reached the boring point for the defendant. He fell asleep.

U.S. Attorney Donald Mackay noticed the dozing defendant and nudged defense attorney Michael Costello, who nudged his client.

Then, when the prosecution closed its case, Costello handed Judge Harlington Wood Jr. a written motion for mistrial on grounds that Alewelt had fallen asleep and missed part of the testimony. Motion denied.

The trial continued and Alewelt was convicted — of bank robbery, not sleeping.

## LOOKED LIKE GRASS ~
It was an early harvest for one farmer south of town, thanks to a city slicker.

A young man was hired by Roosevelt National Development Corp. to mow the grass in its Hyde Park complex. He mowed the grass and everything he thought was grass. That included 10 acres of wheat on a neighboring farm.

The farmer figured his loss at somewhere around $2,000 and was promptly reimbursed by the development company.

## MONKEYSHINE AIRLINES ~
There's a new resident at the Henson Robinson Zoo — a monkey named

"Pearl" who arrived this week on a flight from Brownsville, Texas.

Like many air travelers, Pearl has a story to tell.

She departed on a Braniff Airlines flight with plans to transfer to TWA in Kansas City. But upon landing there, she learned that someone had neglected to tell TWA she was coming. And since the temperature was 90-plus degrees, TWA declined to accept responsibility for her, fearing that the heat might get the best of the old girl. That left the monkey on Braniff's back.

So, the airline put Pearl on its next flight to Minneapolis. That was the only way Pearl could get to St. Louis on a Braniff plane.

During another layover in Minneapolis, Pearl was pampered with a banana and orange lunch, not to mention a lot of attention from Braniff employees.

She arrived at St. Louis after a 22-hour trip and, from there, was chauffeured to Springfield by zookeeper Linda Pride.

Fortunately, Pearl didn't have any luggage.

## ADLAI IS CATS' MEOW ~

The great ongoing debate in Springfield over a leash law for cats is nothing new. Back in 1949, the state legislature passed the "Act To Provide Protection To Insectivorous Birds by Restraining Cats."

But then-Govenor Adlai Stevenson saw fit to veto the controversial measure. This sympathetic note, which he wrote to explain his veto, ranks among his most quoted compositions:

"I cannot believe there is a widespread public demand for this law or that it could,

Gov. Adlai Stevenson , left, welcomes President Harry Truman to Springfield in 1952.

as a practical matter, be enforced.

"I cannot agree that it should be the declared public policy of Illinois that a cat visiting a neighbor's yard or crossing the highway is a public nuisance. It is in the nature of cats to do a certain amount of unescorted roaming.

"Consider the owner's dilemma: To escort a cat abroad on a leash is against the nature of the cat, and to permit it to venture forth for exercise unattended into a night of new dangers is against the nature of the owner. In my opinion, the state of Illinois and its local governing bodies already have enough to do without trying to control feline delinquency."

## GAWK AT YOUR OWN RISK ~

The professional artists have struck again. Take a gander at some of their work in the Exposition Building at the Illinois State Fair.

Try not to laugh.

"And they call that art" is the comment heard from most fairgoers who meander through what one observer calls a "Monument to Malpractice."

This year's exhibit even tops the 1974 show in which one of the most memorable displays appeared to be a pair of pantyhose that would fit an elephant. For 1975, the winning sculpture is "Logarhythms." It resembles a sheet of crinkled aluminum foil.

Second place for sculpture is a pile of white sand in a corner of the exhibit room. At first glance — and second glance — one would assume workmen neglected to tidy up after a construction project. It's described by the artist as a "floor piece" but is "untitled."

"Looks exactly like what we have in the back yard for the kids to play in," one man equipped.

Another bit of sculpture also is found on the floor. It's dark brown in color, obviously something one should avoid stepping on — or in.

"What the hell is that?" one guy asked his wife.

〜

"I think I know, but I'm not going to say in front of the kids," she quipped.

Then, there's the "Bird," a bigger-than-life wooden woman that appears to have the capability of flight. She has no eyeballs, is topless and is in position for takeoff.

It isn't all that funny. She carries a $5,000 price tag.

Fiber sculpture is another category. Here you'll find "Blue Tongue" on exhibit.

It resembles a tongue, all right, one you might expect to find in the mouth of a rhinoceros. And it's all broken out with orange welts.

Fortunately, it doesn't cost anything to look.

## MOONLIGHT SERENUDE 〜

A man fishing on Lake Springfield late last Saturday night made it to shore on a trolling motor after his boat battery fizzled out. But while he went after his car and trailer, the boat worked loose from its mooring and drifted away.

He stripped to his undershorts, dived in and swam out to retrieve the boat. During the swim, his shorts drifted down to his ankles. In an attempt to hoist them, he lost them. So he finished his swim, climbed into the boat and steered it back to shore in the nude.

Otherwise, the outing was uneventful. He didn't catch a thing, not even a cold.

## JAILHOUSE BLUES 〜

The jailing of state Sen. John Knuppel for contempt of court was a landmark in more ways than one for the judicial system. Throwing a lawyer in jail for anything — let alone for wearing "objectionable" attire (a turtleneck T-shirt) in the courtroom — is almost unheard of around here. And the 30-day term Knuppel got — burglars, dope pushers and other low life often get off much easier.

And even though Knuppel is in the process of appealing his fine, he goes to the slammer. Convicted felons often go free while their convictions are appealed.

By the way, all the talk about transferring Knuppel to the Sangamon County Jail because of no air-conditioning in the Cass County Jail was so much hot air.

The jail here isn't air-conditioned. Better medical facilities, with which to treat the senator's heart condition, may be available here but the jail doesn't have a cardiac cell, either.

*John Knuppel and his troublesome turtleneck.*

As it turned out, Knuppel was placed in a cell next to the detention cell, commonly referred to by inmates as the "hole." The hole happened to be occupied by an inmate who'd been refusing to take a shower. All in all, it was a breathtaking experience for the senator.

Back to the senator's first day in the Sangamon County Jail. After the official reception, he was issued a mattress, half a blanket, a piece of a towel and coveralls that were too small. He rolled up the coveralls, used them for a pillow and slept in his B.V.D.s.

And, Knuppel says: "You should have seen the look on the jailer's face when I told him I'd have to take my nitroglycerin into the cell, in case I have a heart attack."

## KNOCK KNOCK ~

Two guys in a southwest-side apartment complex knocked on a neighbor's door late Saturday night. When he opened it, they doused him with a bucket of water.

A few minutes later they heard a knock on their door, followed by the terse announcement that "this is the police."

Had to be the guy down the hall out for revenge, they figured. So they grabbed their bucket, jerked open the door and let fly with the water. Next thing they knew, they were looking at two dripping-wet policemen.

One of the men in blue sputtered something about everyone being under arrest but the officers were laughing so hard, the practical jokers figured they didn't mean it. And they didn't.

## QUOTABLE ~

A sheriff's deputy from Perry County was testifying at one of those rare probation revocation hearings in circuit court here. Responding to a question from the defense attorney, the deputy said he thought the defendant should be sent to prison:

"What good would that do him?" the defense lawyer asked.

"I don't know what it would do for him but it would do society a lot of good," the deputy replied.

## A HELOISE HINT? ~

It's that time of year and a Pawnee, Ill., woman decided to take precautions with her female doggie, now known as "Crazy Leggs."

To protect her during the canine social season, the woman slips a pair of pantyhose over the dog's hindquarters. Good thing.

Crazy Leggs escaped from the confines of the house the other day and ran loose for more than an hour. She finally returned home.

The pantyhose were full of runners but intact.

## PUNK KID ~

An 8-year-old boy ran into a neighborhood tavern and gasped out an order for six hamburgers, six cheeseburgers and "a whole lotta them" potato chips. He was obviously bent on treating his pals.

The bartender inquired about how he planned to pay for the order. The kid plopped a $20 bill on the bar.

"Where did you get that kind of money?" the barkeep asked.

"My old lady went to sleep on the couch and I ripped her off," the boy shot back.

(NO SALE!)

# 1976

## CHARLIE ~

The obituary column carried Charles S. Hanson's name the other day. It didn't command a lot of attention. Most people didn't know "Charlie." That was their loss.

"Some kind of guy — one in a million" is the way he was described by the staff at a Springfield nursing home where his zest for life inspired so many.

Charlie, stricken with cerebral palsy since birth, lived his 52 years without taking a single step. He was never even able to lift a drink of water for himself. And his affliction was complicated by tuberculosis.

His mother took care of him for as long as she was able. About four years ago, Charlie entered a sanitarium, then went to the nursing home where he lived the last two years of his life.

His body was frail and drawn. But he remained alert.

"Who is that?" someone once asked while staring at Charlie's seemingly lifeless form. "Why would God let anyone like that live?"

"Oh, no, no, no," Charlie countered. "I like to live."

Nursing home staffers say Charlie often expressed a strong desire for life.

"His faith put anyone else's to shame," a nurse said. "He really made you count your blessings. He was an inspiration to everyone who knew him."

Charlie was known for two expressions. "Thank you" and "that's okay." Never an unkind word for anyone, not even for the guy who he heard question his right to live.

"Charlie had real faith all right," says a priest who got to know him well. "He was an inspiration to me."

Most of the things Charlie considered special were simple.

One of the nurses once loaded him into her van and took him on a tour of the city on her day off. Another took him for cookouts. He got to meet a lot of kids in the neighborhood that way. He liked that because the kids he met were always stopping at the nursing home to visit him.

Other staff members catered to Charlie on their off hours, taking him his favorite things to eat: a hamburger, a piece of lemon pie or a milkshake.

There was more to it than just taking. He had to be fed, and that was a time-consuming task. It wasn't unusual for someone to spend 90 minutes feeding Charlie a meal.

Then, there was Charlie's lighter side. He was a St. Louis Cardinals fan. He listened to broadcasts of the games with all the enthusiasm of a fan in the stands. He sported a Cardinal emblem on his nightgown.

And so it went when Gov. Dan Walker walked in the nursing home unannounced last spring. Charlie got his picture taken with the governor, despite the difficulty the nurses had with the camera. Walker waited until a good picture was taken.

At Christmas time, Charlie insisted on using his meager allowance to buy everyone a gift. His gifts were things like mini-packages of Kleenex but they went over like fifty-dollar bills.

Charlie showed signs of failing last fall. In November he heard there would be a mass anointing of the sick at the Cathedral and insisted on going. He made the trip in a wheelchair cushioned with pillows.

That was the last time he left his bed.

"Just about everybody around here cried for Charlie," a nurse said. "He was special. We really miss him."

## WHO'S IN CHARGE HERE? ~

A guy walked into Lepardo's liquor store the other night to pull an armed robbery but apparently didn't see owner Lawrence Crifasi sitting behind the counter. He stood there gawking around and fiddling with the ski mask he was wearing.

Meanwhile, Crifasi decided somebody was playing a practical joke. He decided to be practical, too. So he reached up, stuck his finger in the guy's back and gave a "don't move" order. Up went the masked man's hands.

Then he turned around and noticed Crifasi's finger wasn't loaded. He whipped out a revolver and gave the "stick 'em up" order.

He made off with $104.

## HEY ABBOTT, WHERE'S COSTELLO? ~

Remember, folks, you can find it all in the minutes of Springfield City Council meetings. Every word of every session since verbatim transcripts were ordered a few weeks ago.

But, so far, the voluminous documents are just gathering dust. No one is rushing to city hall to review them.

Therefore, we offer a sample of what city fathers are sparing no expense to record for prosperity.

Out of the 70-page transcript of the Dec. 23, 1975, session, the day Vietnamese refugees were welcomed to town, comes this patter between Mayor William Telford and Hung Manh Vu:

Hung: "May I have a request on my own?"

Mayor: "Yes, sir."

Hung: "My name is not on the list of refugees. I came here as a student but my name is not on the list. I would like to ask my name be in there."

Mayor: "All right, and . . . uh . . . what is your name?"

Hung: "My name is Hung . . . Hung . . . Hung."

Mayor: "Hung."

Hung: "Manh."

Mayor: "Manh."

Hung: "Vu is my family name."

Mayor: "Vu."

Hung: "Yes."

Mayor: "Hung Manh Vu, is that right?"

Hung: "Yes."

Mayor: "Hung Manh Vu."

Hung: "Thank you very much."

Mayor: "Thank you!."

*Mayor William Telford*

Then, there was this exchange between Telford, Finance Com. Jim Dunham, Utilities Com. Jim Henneberry and Streets Com. Frank Madonia at the Dec. 30 meeting:

Henneberry: "Did we ever get the hourly rates that a . . . ?"

Dunham: "Yes . . . "

Telford: "I got them. Yes, I'm sure that you got them in your mail. Maybe you haven't got around to it yet but it's there."

Henneberry: "Probably . . . "

Madonia: "They were detailed . . . "

Dunham: "I'd uh . . . you know . . . "

Henneberry: "There is, I'm sorry . . . "

Dunham: "Ah . . . we have the other rate, there it is, standard rate. I'll read them."

Moving along to page 49 of the minutes, the mayor and Health and Safety Com. Pat Ward teamed up for this inspirational adjournment:

Ward: " . . . I wish a very, very pleasant and prosperous, safe New Year to everyone in Springfield."

Mayor: " . . . Mr. Ward, I was just going to adjourn the meeting by wishing . . . uh . . . all the people, not only of the city of Springfield, but of the world . . . uh . . . a happy and hopeful, prosperous and peaceful year in 1976."

(Frick and Frack, eat your hearts out!)

## DOGGONE! ~

The fuss over the county animal shelter prompted collector King Hostick to scan his historical file. He has one letter, written by a Colorado state senator to United Mine Workers boss and former Springfield resident John L. Lewis, which reminds him of another letter he once owned.

It was written by President Harry Truman to the senator in 1949, responding to the senator's tongue-in-cheek suggestion that Lewis be appointed ambassador to Russia.

〜

Truman wrote that he "appreciated the humor but wouldn't appoint Lewis dogcatcher," much less ambassador.

Hostick bought that letter as a historical document for $1,000 about 15 years ago and doubled his money by selling it to a Chicago doctor.

And, for the record, Hostick thinks Lewis would have made a great dogcatcher.

## SILLY HALL ~

A man who recently purchased an electrified fence was at last week's city council meeting when the ordinance outlawing electrified fencing was passed.

He didn't mince words. "I was SHOCKED," the man exclaimed.

## SIGN LANGUAGE ~

On the back of a local garbage truck:
"YOUR GARBAGE IS OUR BREAD AND BUTTER."

## READY, AIM . . . ~

They say it was a shot heard 'round town, and will go down in history, as Divernon's "Bicentennial Blast." After the dust settled, village police reconstructed the event this way:

George Becker was experimenting with his homemade cannon at the edge of town. He loaded it with a ball bearing almost as big as a baseball, aimed it at a railroad embankment about 200 feet away and opened fire.

It was a good shot. But it missed the target.

The ball went screaming over the embankment, through four walls of an abandoned lumberyard building and on to Joe Bolosh's house. It ripped through the kitchen wall and sailed through a narrow space between the refrigerator and a cabinet.

Bolosh was sitting at the kitchen table, right in the line of fire. The ball bopped him in the shoulder, knocking him off his chair.

～

Bolosh, a war veteran who experienced the real thing, was only bruised and took the "shelling" in stride. No charges filed.

Police say the case — and the cannon — is closed.

## WHO'S ON FIRST? ~

Those verbatim transcripts of Springfield City Council meetings are piling up — and gathering dust — at city hall.

Since the order for typewritten blow-by-blow accounts of every meeting was issued eight months ago, 30 volumes containing more than 1,300,000 words have been produced.

So far, the transcripts (Five copies of each go to council members) have cost taxpayers nearly $10,000.

There has been one change since the verbatim record began with the council meeting of Dec. 23. Shortly after our publication several months ago of excerpts from some of the first transcripts, typists were directed to delete all "uhs," "ahs," grunts and groans.

Since no one has stopped in at city hall to read any of the transcripts, we present the following patter from the 185-page report of the council's marathon meet April 13. There was this exchange between Mayor William Telford and Utilities Com. Jim Henneberry, the subject at hand being a wage hike for utility employees:

Henneberry: "If the city council wants to negotiate these agreements, then that's all well and good. Let the city council do it."

Telford: "We're not gonna do it!"

Henneberry: "You can't have your cake and eat it too. You can't partici-pate half of the way."

Telford: "Neither can . . ."

Henneberry: "You can't be half pregnant, mayor."

Telford: "Well, I've seen girls half pregnant."

Henneberry: "Is that right?"

Telford: "Yeh! Haven't completed a term."

Henneberry: "Well, I think you'd better consult an obstetrician or a gyne-cologist."

Telford: "Well, they haven't completed the term. They're fully pregnant when they're ready to deliver, Mr. Henneberry."

Henneberry: "They're fully pregnant from the time of conception!"

Telford: "Well, if you want to get into that..."

Henneberry: "You want to argue that point, (you) will have to call some doctor in."

Telford: "Well anyway, your analogies are very poor."

Henneberry: "I still say you can't if the city council is gonna negotiate these agreements. Then they ought to do so. But you can't be as I said."

Telford: "I'm saying..."

Henneberry: "You can't be half in and half out."

(Skipping on, the debate between Telford and Henneberry continues.)

Telford: "Oh, that has nothing to do with it!"

Henneberry: "Yes, it does."

Telford: "That doesn't have a thing to do with it."

Henneberry: "You can't be happy, for crying out loud!"

Telford: "You're trying to crawl out of a hole you got yourself into."

Henneberry: "No, I'm not!"

Telford: "Well, you are, too..."

And so ends page 87. For those who've worked up an appetite, the other 181 pages are on a shelf in the city clerk's office.

## FOR GULPING GOURMETS ~
From the "My Favorite Recipe Cookbook" supplement Bob Gonko is preparing for publication.

> Elephant Stew
> 1 Elephant
> 2 Rabbits
> Salt and Pepper

Cut elephant into bite-size pieces. Should take about two months. Add enough brown gravy to cover, about half a tank car full. Cook over kerosene for four months at 465 degrees. Serves 3,800 people.

If more are expected, two extra rabbits may be added. But do this only when necessary because most people don't like HARE in their stew.

## TRICK OR TREAT? ~
The abstract statue of Abraham Lincoln at Lincoln Library took on a new look this week.

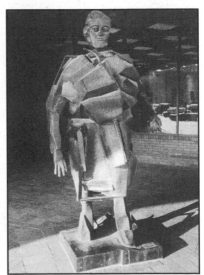

Scraps from the library construction job were fashioned by volunteers into a variety of accessories and added to the bronze form. An orange traffic safety cone was placed on the head, wire-rimmed glasses were added, an earring was attached to one ear, a cigarette stuck in the mouth, a peace symbol dangled from the neck, an empty paint bucket put in one hand and a caulking gun in the other.

*Controversial Abe Lincoln sculpture.*

A sign, "REFUSED BY SID'S JUNK YARD," was posted. And to that, someone inscribed: "Artists — Sanford & Son."

1977

## TAKING A TIP FROM ABE ~

Old defense tactics never die. A burglary trial at Virginia, Ill., last week so proved.

A man charged with burglary was acquitted by a Cass County jury after attorney John Knuppel rested his case on the same defense used in the historic Duff Armstrong murder trial.

It was none other than Abraham Lincoln who successfully defended Armstrong 119 years ago a few miles away in Beardstown.

Thrust of Lincoln's defense was an almanac that convinced the court the prosecution's star witness couldn't have seen the slaying by "the light of the moon," as he testified. According to the almanac, the moon was setting at the time of the slaying. Hence, darkness.

Last week Knuppel used National Weather Service charts to counter testimony by Illinois Bureau of Investigation agents and Cass County sheriff's deputies.

Lawmen said they were on stakeout and observed the defendant attempt to pry open a barn door from their vantage point some 400 feet away. That, they said, enabled them to identify the man when he was later apprehended at a farm house in the area.

However, it was too dark for the officers to pursue their suspect when he ran from the scene.

Knuppel, using the weather charts, pointed out the incident occurred one hour after sunset and two hours before the moon appeared. He argued it would have been too dark for police to have determined whether the defendant or a second man (an informant who was never charged in the case) was prying on the barn door. Knuppel also contended entrapment, arguing the information was encouraging his client to commit a crime.

A jury deliberated 45 minutes before returning the innocent verdict. Thus, it was the second time a lawyer-politician from Menard County went to Cass County and won a criminal case with an "almanac" defense.

Knuppel hastens to point out that any similarity between himself and the Great Emancipator ends there. He has no plans to push his political career beyond the state legislature.

# McKINNEY THE McCRIMINAL ~

The scene was Franklin Middle School. It was Feb. 19, 1975. Subject at hand for a Springfield School District teachers' workshop was "Use-Abuse of Controlled Substances."

Among the guest speakers was one George Patrick McKinney. His topic was "Crime and Drugs."

A convicted bank robber who had been paroled in 1972 after serving nearly 20 years in a federal penitentiary, McKinney was billed as "a Springfield resident having personal experience with criminals involved in drug trafficking."

The workshop was one of five "intercultural affairs" training sessions for teachers that year. It was an Illinois Office of Education approved program.

McKinney gave an award-winning performance. His audience grew steadily until he played to a standing-room-only crowd at his third lecture that day.

Teachers called him "extremely interesting" and "very stimulating." He was so popular, in fact, that teachers voted to invite him back for an encore at the next workshop at Washington Middle School. He accepted and drew capacity crowds at each lecture.

Where is McKinney today? In jail at Santa Monica, Calif., awaiting word from a jury that's weighing the evidence presented at his four-month-long murder trial.

McKinney is the key figure in what is called one of California's most bizarre and complex homicides. He is charged with murder, kidnapping and extortion in connection with the execution-type killings of a reputed Mafia bagman, the man's wife and a cocktail waitress.

The murders occurred seven months after McKinney's last workshop lecture in Springfield. He was arrested in Springfield, as one of the FBI's most wanted fugitives, about two weeks after the slayings.

Besides participating in the school workshops, McKinney was known to have been active in several community youth programs.

"He was very convincing," said one teacher who heard him lecture.

# AD LIBS ~
There've been some changes at the White House since the Carter family moved in:

• The fleet of limousines has been replaced by a pickup truck, two campers and a Model A Ford.
• The swimming pool has been stocked with catfish.
• Lawnmowers have been replaced by 100 head of sheep.
• Rose bushes have given way to peanut plants.

• The putting green has been converted to a potato patch.
• White House guards now wear overalls and clodhoppers, and tote double-barrel shotguns.

## MORE ON McKINNEY ~
George Patrick McKinney, the 49-year old Springfieldian who will be sentenced next week for the execution-style murder of a man and woman in California, has already escaped the gas chamber.

Midway through his sensational four-month trial, the California Supreme Court declared that state's death penalty unconstitutional. That left McKinney facing, at most, a life-without-parole prison term.

Little is known about McKinney's activities since he located in Springfield shortly after being released from federal prison at Marion in 1972. That's where he served nine years on his second bank robbery conviction.

According to murder trial testimony, McKinney worked as a senior cost accountant in St. Louis briefly, then came to Springfield where — in his words — he "was forced to hustle for a living." He sold cars and carpeting and worked in an ice cream store and as a musician. He also was employed for awhile as an accountant for the state of Illinois.

McKinney made his mark with the FBI back in 1953 when he kidnapped the manager of a Long Island bank and single-handedly robbed the bank of $190,000.

It was one of the biggest hauls ever made by a lone bandit, and the crime ranked as one of the FBI's most difficult cases of the time. But one year later, shortly after his automobile dealership in Florida went bankrupt, McKinney was captured.

## BITE-SIZE ADVICE ~
A bumper sticker circulated by the Illinois Dental Association:

"IGNORE YOUR TEETH AND THEY'LL GO AWAY."

## THE HIJACKER WHO BAILED OUT ~
It was about five years ago that FBI agent Victor Schaefer worked the

〜

most notorious case of his 26-year career. He recalled the story, an airline hijacking that made worldwide headlines, as he worked his last day as special agent in charge of the bureau's Springfield office.

The hijacking unfolded April 7, 1972. Schaefer was assistant agent in charge of the FBI office at Salt Lake City at the time and had charge of the investigation.

A United Air Lines jet with 91 passengers aboard was commandeered in western skies by a man who demanded $500,000. Following release of the passengers at a West Coast airport, the hijacker — who turned out to be Richard Floyd McCoy of Provo, Utah — forced the pilot to fly him back over Utah where he parachuted from the jetliner with the half-million dollar ransom. McCoy had made off with the biggest ransom ever paid in a skyjacking.

McCoy, a former helicopter pilot with the Green Berets in Vietnam, had first dropped two parachutes over Texas and New Mexico. But the FBI soon determined they were decoys and Schaefer concentrated his investigation in the Provo area. That led to McCoy as a suspect.

Agents came up with two good pieces of evidence. A fingerprint lifted from a magazine found in the seat the hijacker occupied on the plane matched McCoy's. Then the handwriting on a note he had passed to a stewardess was compared to handwriting in McCoy's military service record. It also matched.

"I took 10 agents out to McCoy's home in Provo real early in the morning," Schaefer recalled. "One agent went with me to the front door. I knocked. No answer. I knocked again, announcing it was the FBI and to let us in."

Agents detected movement inside the house. Schaefer began to wonder, realizing that McCoy was a recognized sharpshooter.

"But I kept knocking and ordering him to open up," Schaefer continued. "Finally the door opened and there was McCoy, dressed in his flight suit."

He offered no resistance.

A search warrant was obtained and agents started going through the house with a fine-tooth comb shortly after daybreak. They also dug around in the yard. Several hours later they found the gun and a dummy hand grenade McCoy had displayed on the plane. Then they found the ransom money, or $499,970 of it, on the back porch, ending a three-day investigation.

"We never did find the other $30 and still don't know what he did with it," Schaefer said.

McCoy was sentenced to 40 years in a federal prison in Pennsylvania. But in 1974, he and four other prisoners escaped. Three were caught just outside the prison gate, but McCoy and the other inmate remained at large until FBI agents got onto their trail after a $90,000 bank robbery on the East Coast.

Tracing them to Virginia Beach, Va., agents staked out a cottage. It wasn't long until McCoy, a gun in one hand and a key in the other, unlocked the front door. He reached around the door and flipped the light switch.

"That switch set off the squelch on the agents' portable radio inside," Schaefer said. "McCoy reacted by firing a shot into the room. Agents inside returned the fire with shotguns and blew him clear off the porch."

That was the end of Richard Floyd McCoy.

## BEEP, BEEP!!! ~

Hundreds of people in Springfield have found the buy of a lifetime, they think — a brand new Jeep, still in the crate and minus only tires and battery, for the unbelievable price of $125.

The Army was stuck with thousands of Jeeps at the end of the Vietnam War and is willing to practically give them away, or so the story goes.

Stipulations are that the Jeeps be ordered in lots of 1,000 (a train load), picked up at a central shipping point in Peoria and that the buyers keep their Jeeps a minimum of five years. Word of the sale has spread by word of mouth only, but more than 1,000 anxious buyers have already signed up, according to one source. It's strictly C.O.D.

Can this be true?

Sure can, some say. They remember a big motorcycle clearance by the Army at the old munitions plant near Illiopolis at the end of World War II. That's when the Army supposedly disposed of its unneeded motorcycles for $50 each.

But back to Jeeps. Is the government offering new Jeeps for $125 each?

"It never has and never will," says a spokesman for the U.S. government's surplus sales division at Battle Creek, Mich. "This is a wild rumor that's cropped up several times during the past 14 years or so."

Not long ago, the story circulated in the Florida and Georgia area and now has spread north, according to the surplus depot. Another wild rumor that makes the rounds claims the government has just discovered thousands of motorcycles, WWII leftovers, somewhere in Europe and is selling them at a ridiculously low price.

It's pointed out by the surplus spokesman that any military vehicles unloaded by the federal government usually are in poor to fair condition and certainly not new. Besides, such sales are by competitive bid only at military installations.

## MAIL BAG ~

Leno Petrilli of Springfield writes: "Read your column concerning the Edwards Jewelry Store robbery. To you it seemed so damned funny. I was the mailman involved, and it was no damned funny incident. I didn't just wander into the store, as was stated. I was on my tour of duty and I was delivering mail.

"As I opened the door, I saw two ladies on the floor and they waved me back, saying, 'There is a robbery going on.' I stepped back out, but the man with the gun was already charging toward me, yelling, 'Come back in here.' He came out the door and, with his gun, grappled with me to force me back inside. He knocked the mail from my hand. He forced me back inside.

"Once inside, I noticed the man with the gun was looking at the scattered mail and people started to gather outside. I locked the door, not trying to be brave, just trying to get the big glass door between me and the gun.

"The man yelled for me to unlock the door, and then I realized he had a partner in the store who came charging at me with his hand in his coat pocket, demanding I open the door. I did, and the other man came back in a rage and forced me to the back of the store.

"The two robbers decided to leave. They pushed me at gunpoint to the door, and I was sure that they would take me hostage. At the door they split. I aged 10 years in those few minutes, and I see no humor for a comedy movie as you stated. The gun barrel looked like a cannon.

"I could give these few minutes to you and put you in my shoes. Then hand you pencil and paper to write your column. You'd use the paper, but not to write your column."

NOTE: You read me wrong. The joke was the bandits — not the victims — for the way they bungled the holdup. But you're right about the paper. — T.M.

## DEMOLITION DERBY ~
Ryan VanPickerill flunked his first driver's test this week. He wrecked the car. But that's not all of the story.

Ryan is only 2 years old.

Seems his mother left him in the family car for a few seconds while she dashed into their house for something. He somehow started the car and put it in gear.

As the car lurched forward, Ryan was thrown to the floorboard and against the accelerator, as best his mother can figure. That propelled the car through the garage door, through the back of the garage and into a big tree in the back yard.

Everything is a wreck, except Ryan. He escaped unscathed — so far.

## 'COWBOY'S SWEETHEART' ~
The National Barn Dance, once the pride of Chicago radio station WLS, is long gone. But a few of its star performers are still going strong. One is Patsy Montana, whose singing and yodeling propelled her to fame on the

⌇

Barn Dance more than four decades ago.

Since then, only her age has changed. Still billed as the "Cowboy's Sweetheart," Patsy appears in flashy cowgirl outfits complete with boots and hat, sings the same songs, yodels as good as ever and chats between songs about Barn Dance days.

*Patsy Montana*

Her act is pure nostalgia. And it may be more popular than ever.

Patsy, a Californian since the Barn Dance faded away in the early '50s, currently is on her annual Midwest tour. She'll be at the Sangamon Valley Opry in Edinburg, Ill., Saturday night and at the Prairie Land Opry in Modesto the following Saturday night.

Although somewhat of a stranger in most parts of the country since the Barn Dance era, Patsy has never quit the business. Mostly she plays the nightclub circuit on the West Coast "because there aren't enough auditoriums around any more."

"You have to play them (clubs) if you want to work," she said in an interview this week. "That's why I'm looking forward to the opry dates."

A few areas in the United States — like central Illinois — still are showcases for country entertainers.

Last month Patsy played some of the old country dance halls in southeast Texas where her friend, the late Bob Wills, once reigned. A few weeks earlier, she starred at California's biggest folk festival with old timers like Johnny Bond, Hank Penny and Smokey Rogers. She was on other bills recently with the fabled Sons of the Pioneers and her former Barn Dance co-stars, the Hoosier Hotshots.

"Despite a published report that I'd quit show business to sell real estate, I haven't retired," Patsy says firmly. "I've been busier than I've been in a long time."

One reason for that is Patsy's European tours with her daughter, singer Judy Rose, the past four years.

"They love our country music over there," she boasts. "Audiences are simply great and I love 'em. I went the first time on the popularity of 'Cowboy's Sweetheart.' They had never heard of me but they knew the song."

Her reference was to "I Want To Be A Cowboy's Sweetheart," most popular of more than 200 songs she has written and published. That song gave Patsy the distinction of being the first female singer to have a million-seller record. It happened in 1936.

"I've been at it 42 years now," she admits. "I tell everybody I started when I was 2."

Patsy got her start by winning an amateur show in 1934. She took her road show act to the Barn Dance the next year. A number of years later, she helped launch the Louisiana Hayride at Shreveport, La., where she encountered then-unknowns Hank Williams, Kitty Wells and the Wilburn Brothers.

"It just happened that I was on as a guest the last night of the WLS Barn Dance in the old 8th Street Theater," Patsy recalls. "It was just like the last page of a book. Just think how big country music used to be in Chicago. There's nothing like that (Barn Dance) now."

The 8th Street Theater was razed years ago.

"I was appearing in Chicago and I knew they were tearing it down. I was riding a cab down Michigan Avenue. I thought I'd look the other way when I passed the theater. I just didn't want to see it going down. But I had to look, and when I did, I saw the big steel ball on the wrecking crane go crashing into what used to be my dressing room.

〜

"Well, times change," Patsy said. "And I think we're seeing progress. Of course, sometimes you wonder. There's quite a controversy in Nashville about what's happening to country music. It's very commercial now. That's what hurts it. That takes the heart out of it."

Patsy has one big complaint.

"I don't think we need dirty lyrics in our music. They say that's life. Sure, it's life. We have murder and kidnapping but who wants to sing about it?

"I believe there's a change coming, though. I really do. I feel it."

Patsy and Judy recorded an album ("Mum 'n Me" on the Look label) while touring England last year. And Patsy expects to have another album, recorded in Chicago by Birch Records, out soon.

"I'm really enjoying things now," Patsy says. "Maybe it's that I'm at the point in my career where I'm not trying to push anything. I'm really not out to sell anything. I've already been there. I enjoy meeting people and my singing makes that possible.

"I always look forward to coming to the Midwest. As long as I can keep my voice, I'll keep working. And I'll always come back here at least once a year. After all, this is my old corral."

## SIGN LANGUAGE ~
On the side of a local plumber's truck:
"Chief Commode Consultant."

And on the rear:
"A Flush Beats A Full House."

## A BRUSH WITH DEATH ~
The Springfield coed and two sorority sisters who were abducted at gunpoint near Indianapolis last week are convinced their lives were saved by a "very brave and dedicated" sheriff's deputy who survived a shootout with the gunman.

Amy Lindsay of Springfield was scratched on one arm by flying glass as she huddled with the other women in the back of the gunman's car.

"Amy realizes she is lucky to be alive," her mother said.

Miss Lindsay, Priscilla Hart and Lisa Shull had started back to Indiana University at Bloomington after celebrating Amy's 21st birthday. As they approached Interstate 465 about 2:30 a.m., their car was forced off the road by another car.

They locked the doors of their small foreign car as the other driver, identified by police as William Turner of Indianapolis, approached. He was armed with a .22-caliber revolver.

Turner smashed a window in the car, then fired a shot into the side of the vehicle, threatening to kill the women if they didn't follow orders. Two of the women obeyed his command to get out. When the other moved too slow, he fired another shot into the car. Turner then forced the coeds into the back of his car and sped away.

Meanwhile, the shots were heard by Indiana State Trooper David Kemper, who was a short distance away. He alerted other law enforcement agencies. Within minutes, Kemper found the coeds' abandoned car. In addition to the bullet holes, he found two purses and a shoe they had left behind.

Marion County Sheriff's Deputy Joseph Hecko, who was familiar with side roads in the area, played a hunch and soon found Turner's car parked on a lover's lane. About that time, Turner discovered the women had only a few dollars and was telling them he would assault them instead of rob them.

Pulling his squad car alongside, Hecko shined his spotlight into the vehicle and ordered Turner to get out with his hands up. Turner replied he was "just with my lady."

That was when the three women — who Turner had ordered to duck down and stay out of sight — raised their heads enough for the deputy to see them. Seconds later, Turner fired two shots into the deputy's car from point-blank range. The deputy returned six shots from his .357 magnum revolver, firing straight through the door on the driver's side.

⌐

Then there was silence.

The women, still on the back floorboard of the gunman's car, feared the deputy had been killed. Slowly, the kidnapper's car started pulling away. Still, there was no reaction from the deputy.

A short distance down the road, the car rolled to a stop and the women heard gurgling sounds. They knew then their abductor had been wounded.

"I'm going to die . . . I'm going to die," Miss Shull quoted Turner as saying.

The door on the driver's side opened. The domelight went on, and the women saw Turner covered with blood.

He got out, then reached back and picked up his gun. Then Turner put the gun to his head, pulled the trigger and fell to the ground.

Not knowing if he was dead, the women crawled into a ditch and hid to await police. Then they saw Deputy Hecko had reloaded his gun and radioed for help in the few minutes that had elapsed since the burst of gunfire.

Turner was dead.

The women crawled out of the ditch as a dozen squad cars converged on the scene.

They'd had a close call, all right. And so had the deputy. So close, in fact, he said he felt a breeze as the bullets fired by Turner whizzed past his head.

## JAIL JIVE ~
A number of changes are taking place to tighten security at the Sangamon County Jail in the wake of that big escape:

• Effective immediately, the doors will be locked at night.

• Visitors carrying violin cases will no longer be admitted unless the cases have violins in them.

• Use of courtesy cars by inmates will be limited to weekends only.

• Inmates must return all tools, including chisels, hacksaws and blow-torches, to the jail hobby shop until further notice.

• Inmates no longer will be allowed to use explosive devices within the jail except to celebrate the 4th of July.

• Certain educational classes, such as "Gunsmithing for Beginners" and "Rope Ladder Weaving," will be discontinued at the end of the current semester.

## NOT CLEAR FOR TAKEOFF ~

Now the Sangamon County Sheriff's Department realizes it set its sights too low when trying to acquire a surplus military airplane. Something a lot slicker than a helicopter — a B-2 bomber — is ready and waiting to be adopted by a friendly law enforcement agency.

Actually, Sheriff Martin Gutschenritter has already put the wheels in motion to add it to his "fleet." He's appointed a blue ribbon logistics committee known as "Laymen to Organize my Air Force" (LOAF) to arrange for inner-governmental transfer of the plane. A sheriff's top aide, Deputy I. Doolittle, says the World War II plane, although old, is low mileage. Army Air Corps records show it flew only six hours on a training flight before the pilot, being fired at by civilians on the ground, had to make a forced landing on a peanut farm outside Plains, Ga., in 1944. There it remained until snipe hunters stumbled onto it three months ago. A military surplus spokesman describes the plane, having been shielded by a grove of peanut trees, as being in relatively good condition. Repair costs are estimated at less than $2 million.

"But that's nothing for the county board to get flustered about," says a LOAF spokesman. "There'll be fringe benefits from flying this plane. In the long run, the county will make money."

The plane primarily will be used for law enforcement purposes: search-rescue missions, traffic surveillance and transportation of prisoners, according to Doolittle. It also will have strafing capabilities for high-speed chases and recapturing escapees.

When it's not in use, the plane will be made available to the public for cut-rate charter flights and junkets for county officials. Authorization for weekend flights to Newark, N.J., Slippery Rock, Ark., and Tijuana, Mexico, already has been granted, according to one source. Overseas flights to countries normally visited only by U.S. congressman are to be added later.

By eliminating such frills as in-flight movies, meals, beverages, stewardesses, seats, co-pilots, radar and baggage, charter air fares will be only one-third that charged by reputable airlines.

All flights, emergency and charter, will originate from the Lincoln Home area. The 8th Street Mall will be used for takeoffs and landings.

"It's perfect," said a LOAF member. "All we have to do is cut down a few trees, get rid of that silly bridge and pour a little extra concrete. The plane will be able to clear other obstructions (city hall and the courthouse) by several inches."

Since the plane will be parked in front of the Lincoln Home, it will be open to tourists. That will qualify the county for federal funds to build the runway.

Other grants totaling more than $2 million will be sought from the FAA, DOT, HUD, MUD and DUD, according to Doolittle. That should result in a profit of about $5,000-a-day for the sheriff's department, and that money will be used to buy more airplanes.

In an effort to win county board approval of the plane project, Doolittle says each board member will be offered a free flight to the country of their choice. However, they will not be informed that the flights are one-way.

As an expression of gratitude to the county for taking the bomber off its hands, the Army is throwing in two tanks, four Jeeps, three flame-throwers, a bazooka and 25 pup tents.

"We'll be able to handle anything," Doolittle beams, "even a war."

## A TWISTER'S TAIL ~

The tornado that ravaged Glenwood Park subdivision east of Chatham, Ill., was literally a rude awakening for 15-year-old Audrey James. She had returned to her home on Stoney Creek Drive after attending a cheerleading contest at White Oaks Mall. She went to her bedroom to take a nap.

Before long it happened. She was awakened by debris raining down on her.

Leaping from bed, she ran to open the door to an adjoining bedroom where she expected to find her mother napping. Her mother wasn't there. Neither was the bedroom. Neither was the rest of the ranch-style house.

*Chatham tornado damage.*

Only the walls of Audrey's bedroom were left.

The twister had made a direct hit on the house. As Audrey tried to run to a neighbor's home, the wind picked her up and threw her about 100 feet across the street and into a lagoon. She had to swim across the lagoon before making it to safety.

Later, she learned her mother had left for work before the tornado hit.

Among many other escapes:

Steve Miller spotted the funnel from in front of his home on Carefree Drive. Miller and his wife grabbed their kids and ran to the basement.

"We could hear boards creaking and cracking, and all sorts of horrible sounds," Miller recalled. "We knew the house was being torn apart. I thought it would never end. We just huddled together and cried."

When it did end, the Millers were surprised to find their house had sustained major damage but is repairable.

But next door the Louie Dean's weren't as lucky. Dean had been dozing in an easy chair. His wife was on the couch.

"The noise woke me," Dean said. "But I only had time to take a few steps across the room before it hit."

He was knocked down by a flying refrigerator that pinned him to the floor. His wife ended up beneath the overturned couch. She was trapped, too.

"Then it (the twister) struck again," Dean says without doubt. "I know it hit again because the second time it knocked the refrigerator off of me and I was able to get up."

Much of the house was blown away. Dean says he still hasn't found the roof. The rest caved in on the couch and on the chair Dean had been sitting in.

"He would have been killed if he hadn't gotten out of that chair," Dean's son says.

"I don't know how we got out alive," Dean added. "But we did, so we don't have anything to complain about."

## DARTS FOR THE ARTS ~

Brace yourself for another run through the Illinois State Fair's professional art gallery. Among the more notable rejects:

"Natural Rhythm" — Yards upon yards of recording tape tacked to the wall. (Looks like a grass skirt for Wilt Chamberlain.)

"He and She" — A small oil portrait of a man and woman with the tops of their heads cut off. (Any amateur with an Instamatic can do that.)

"Firehose" — Sections of worn-out firehose striped with bright colored oils and draped between two ladders. (Looks like spring cleaning at a gay fire-house.)

## DOWN SOUTH ~

Donna Bandor and sister-in-law Debra Clark, both of Hillsboro, made a last-minute decision to attend Elvis Presley's funeral in Memphis. Their decision was made Thursday morning. The funeral was Thursday afternoon.

They made a made dash to the airport and hopped a plane. Everyone they talked to told them they were wasting their time and money.

They arrived in Memphis 15 minutes before the funeral was scheduled to start. A policeman told them they wouldn't be able to get within four blocks of either Graceland mansion or the cemetery.

Telling their problem to a taxi driver, they got some sympathy. He promised to get them there "no matter what." He drove a back route and deposited the women at the cemetery gate where thousands had been waiting hours for a glimpse of the funeral procession. They ended up on the front row where they became acquainted with a nurse who had been on duty when Presley was rushed to the hospital a couple of days earlier. After the procession entered the cemetery, the nurse escorted the women back to Graceland where they watched celebrities return from the cemetery.

They arrived back home Thursday night in time to see a television news report on the funeral. There they were, on television, standing at the cemetery gate.

## HANKY PANKY ~

There was a going-away party Thursday night for Fiat-Allis engineer Steve Green who's moving to Arkansas. When things got into full swing, some of Green's friends slipped away with his pickup truck.

He was pleasantly surprised to see it later with a bed in the back and a nifty young woman in a sexy nightgown  perched on the bed. A sign on the truck identified it as the "Arkansas Welcome Wagon." Green was "forced" to sit next to the woman on the bed while the truck was driven around the northeast part of town.

## SHAGGY DOG STORY ~
A dog named Scarlett had a batch of puppies. Since the dog's owner didn't want the pups, she placed a newspaper ad offering to give them to good homes.

The ad was tagged: "Mother, Scarlett. Father, Gone With the Wind."

Two of the pups were given away. Then there was this phone call from a man who had read the ad:

"Are you the woman whose dog Scarlett had pups?" he asked.
"Yes, I am," she said.
"Well," the man blurted, "frankly, I don't give a damn!"

## ENGLANDERS REMEMBER ~
It's Veterans Day in this country today. But every day is Veterans Day in another part of the world.

It's observed daily at Mendelsham, England, a village about 75 miles northeast of London, where American forces established and operated Mendelsham Air Base during World War II.

Although the "aero dome" was closed down at war's end, villagers have not forgotten who defended them.

Wally Jackson, a salesman at Springfield Dodge Inc. who flew with the Mendelsham-based 34th Heavy Bombardment Group in 1944-45, just found that out on his first post-war visit to England.

The countryside was unchanged but Jackson, who flew 26 bombing missions from the base as a tailgunner on a B-17, found little of the once-giant facility remains; just a couple of huts and one hangar that is now used as a grocery warehouse. The rest is a sugar beet field. However, Jackson found something that wasn't on the a base when he left it 33 years ago.

At the tip of what was the runway where the giant bombers roared for takeoff stands a simple brick wall erected by the villagers in 1949. A plaque reads:

*"To the American airmen of the 34th who in valor gave their lives to the victory that made real the challenge for world peace and unity. April 1944 to June 1945."*

Three vases at the memorial were filled with fresh-cut flowers. Villagers, he learned, replace the flowers every day.

The visit rekindled countless memories — good and bad — for Jackson. Among the good was this gem:

Jackson was preparing to fly another mission. His wristwatch was on the blink and it was important for him, as a tailgunner, to know the time. He went to the PX and found only one watch in stock.

It was a genuine Mickey Mouse watch. But it was a watch, so he bought it. He paid $4.03 for it.

The routine was to fly from Mendelsham, bomb Germany and fly on to Russia. Planes reloaded there with bombs and fuel. Targets in Germany were hit again on the return flight.

Landing in Russia after the first leg of the mission, Jackson stood by while the bombers were fueled. Suddenly, a Russian colonel in charge of the operation ran up and grabbed Jackson by the arm. He kept jabbering in Russian to another officer.

"What's the matter with him?" Jackson asked an interpreter.

"The colonel wants your wristwatch," the officer said. "He'll pay you for it."

"It's not for sale," Jackson snapped.

The colonel refused to give in. Finally he offered to pay ANY price for the watch. He struck a nerve.

Jackson was thinking about the refueling arrangement. Each bomber held nearly 3,000 gallons of fuel and the Russians charged a dollar per gallon, cash on the line. And only American greenbacks were accepted.

That kinda burned Jackson.

"Okay, I'll sell the watch," Jackson said. "The colonel can have it for one-thousand American dollars."

To his surprise, the colonel peeled off $1,000. And that, Jackson chuckles, had to be the most expensive Mickey Mouse watch ever made.

## QUOTABLE ~
A woman driver ran a red light at Ninth and Capitol, smacked another car broadside and knocked it over the curb.

"I know I ran the light," she told the investigating officer. "But wasn't it his responsibility to swerve and get out of my way?"

## CLUES FOR CLAUS ~
This was among letters to Santa's substation at Springfield Recreation Department offices:

Dear Santa

How are you? This year I'd like an Odyssey with hockey, handball and tennis. Also a record, my stocking filled and any other crazy things you and your elves can stir up with your magical brains. I know I've been a little bad. But so has everyone else.

Love, David

# 1978

## STRESS REHEARSAL ~

There was a special practice session in the Rochester High School gym last Friday, shortly before the Rockets upset the Riverton Hawks for the Sangamon County basketball championship. But it wasn't basketball practice. The session went like this:

Jim Jost, coach of the Rockets, placed a ladder beneath a goal on the home court. Senior star Andy Lunt then climbed to the hoop and, under Jost's tutoring, cut down the net.

"We'd practiced everything else," says Jost. "So I thought we might as well work on cutting down the net, too. I figured it would have a good psychological effect on the guys."

As it turned out, Lunt wielded the knife like a veteran at the traditional net-snipping ceremony that followed the championship game. Just as though he'd rehearsed it.

## INSINCERELY YOURS ~

A woman sent a letter to Gov. Jim Thompson. She noted how the Executive Mansion had always appeared "cold, homeless and ugly" to her but, she told the governor, "you have added just what it needs — dogs."

She went on to tell of watching "Guv," Thompson's Irish setter, "prancing around, looking proud" on mansion grounds. Guv gives the mansion "warmth — it looks like someone lives there," she wrote.

*Gov. James Thompson*

Thompson replied with the following "form" letter:

"Thank you for the recent letter. You can be assured I will take your views and comments under consideration. I certainly appreciate receiving recommendations from concerned citizens such as yourself."

## WIND CHILL FACTOR ~

Mother Nature can be cruel to joggers. Just ask a local handball star.

He was preparing for his daily run around the neighborhood one frigid day when he discovered his wife had laundered his athletic apparel. It was still on the wet side but he suited up anyway. He jogged through the sub-zero cold without difficulty. But when he ended his run, he found himself in deep trouble.

The cold temperature had put the bite on his damp duds. And when he peeled down so far, he discovered he was literally frozen to a strategic piece of jogging paraphernalia.

It took some time — and the help of a doctor — to defrost him.

## SILLY HALL ~

The absence of Finance Com. Jim Dunham prompted this patter at Monday's executive city council session:

"How's the finance department getting along?" Mayor William Telford

~

asked Comptroller Bill Smith, who represented Dunham.

"Okay, I guess," Smith replied.

"Did we make any money last week?" Telford pressed.

"No," Smith quipped, "the printing press broke down."

"You're funnier than the commissioner," cracked Health-Safety Com. Pat Ward.

## AD LIBS ~
• Let's hear it for Peruvian Air Lines for flying those 160 breeder hogs from Springfield to Peru. Now there's an airline that's rootin' for business.
• The stewardess will ask the passengers on that flight: "Coffee grounds, tea leaves or sour milk?"
• The airline had a heckuva time qualifying a crew for the upcoming flight. Couldn't find a pilot that speaks pig Latin.

## FIREFIGHTERS TURN MEDICINE MEN ~
It was medicine time but the elderly woman, at home alone, couldn't get the newfangled safety cap off the prescription bottle.

Her medication was vital, so she decided to seek help from a neighbor. But she found no one at home. As a last resort, she called the fire department. An engine company from Firehouse No. 9 rolled up in front of her house minutes later.

One by one, three burly firefighters tried to open the bottle. After 20 minutes, they gave up. One firefighter finally cut off the cap with a knife.

The safety caps, of course, are meant for the protection of children. There are no children in the woman's home.

She phoned her friendly pharmacist, explained her predicament and asked for advice. He told her to write her congressman.

## COLLECTOR'S ITEM ~
Kids in the front row had concentrated on their gum chewing during

church service. Elders prepared to pass the collection plates. Suddenly, a 5-year-old girl leaped from her seat and rushed to her mother several rows back.

"Here, hold my gum," she blurted. "They're going to pass out treats."

## FINGER OF FATE ~

It was a typical day at the Marine Motor Bank until a computer department employee, Brenda Barker, entered a teller's cage on the drive. The teller she needed to consult with was busy with a customer, so she waited.

"I don't have all —— day!" a motoring customer shouted through the intercom to the teller. "First you're on the phone. Now you're talking to this smiley girl!"

The teller replied he was working as fast as he could, then he turned off the intercom. As Miss Barker stood by, she became aware that the customer was "staring a hole" through her.

"Please don't stare at me," Miss Barker mouthed through the window to the man. "I don't have to take this."

The man replied by sticking out his tongue and making faces at her. Miss Barker says she lost her cool. She responded by rendering the single digital designation of duress.

"I flipped him the bird," she admits. "It was a reflex reaction."

That sent the man into a rage. He jumped out of his car and tried to open the teller cage door. Realizing he couldn't gain access to the cage, he went to the bank's main lobby, calling Miss Barker a despicable name on the way. He was soon accompanied by a female bank supervisor back to the teller's cage. She asked Miss Barker to apologize.

"I'm terribly sorry," Miss Barker recalls saying to the man.

"Is this your IQ?" he blurted while giving her the same finger salute.

"Yes, sir," she said.

The man proceeded to tell her she "should be working in a red light district instead of a bank" and called her some more choice names. He at first refused to accept her apology.

"No, wait," Miss Barker quotes him as saying to the supervisor. "I will accept but I have to have her job, too."

At that point, Miss Barker was fired.

The man is said to have also berated Miss Barker's supervisor by calling her ugly names and saying he also wanted her fired.

Senior bank officials upheld Miss Barker's dismissal. A bank spokesman would say only that "it was an unfortunate incident" but he said Miss Barker's firing is final.

## WRONG ANSWER ~
A man was arraigned on a rape charge in circuit court the other day. The judge was asking the routine questions, like if he could afford a lawyer and if any other charges were pending against him. The quiz continued something like this:

"Are you employed?" the judge asked.

"No, I'm on disability," the defendant replied.

"How long have you been on disability?" the judge pressed.

"Since I accidentally killed that man in Louisiana," the man said coolly.

Bond was set at $100,000 and the defendant was hustled back to jail.

## PRAYER OF ALLEGIANCE ~
A 5-year-old girl was hosting a 5-year-old neighbor boy for supper. "I'll say the prayer," the little hostess chirped as they sat down at the table. And she did.

"Now wait while I say mine," her guest blurted, adding a warning that "it's a long one."

Hands clasped and heads bowed once again, he began his prayer. "I pledge allegiance, to the flag, of the United States of America," he prayed. "And to the Republic . . . etc., etc."

He missed nary a word.

"Amen!"

## HOSPITAL ZONE ~

A call for help was sounded by a patient at St. John's Hospital. He announced he needed assistance with the bedpan.

"I get your drift all the way out here," chirped a young nurse's aide from the hallway.

"Well," the patient countered, "I never promised you a rose garden!"

## OJARS OR LUTAK? ~

Jimmy Carter proposes to curb crime with OJARS (an agency called the Office of Justice Assistance, Research and Statistics).

Another program known as LUTAK sounds better. That stands for Lock 'em Up and Throw Away the Key.

## SILLY QUESTION ~

A referendum asking voters whether a ceiling should be put on taxes is circulating. That's like asking school kids if they like recess.

## BEHIND PRISON WALLS ~

Lack of maintenance in the mid-1970s paved the way for the "deplorable" condition of riot-torn Pontiac State Prison, says the Department of Corrections. Putting it back into shape would cost an estimated $17 million.

*Illinois State Police close in on riot-torn Pontiac Prison.*

While conditions for the 2,000 prisoners are poor, guards don't have it much better. Guard towers, for instance, are heated by pot-belly stoves in the winter, not air-conditioned in the summer and buckets are the only restroom facilities.

## 'LIB' QUIP ~

There's a guy in town who blames his sore knee on women's lib. He tells it this way.

There was a knock on the back door. He went to answer it, slipped on the slick floor and fell. He pulled himself up and finally got to the door. It was a woman from CWLP wanting in to read the meter.

Women's lib gave us "meterwomen," he reasons tongue-in-cheekly, so why not blame that movement for his fall? He was laid up with the bum knee for several weeks.

To stretch the lib point further, he says the pain he endured during emergency hospital treatment made him think he "was having a baby."

## CABBAGE CAPER ~

The batch of slaw prepared in the Sangamon County Jail kitchen for Sheriff Martin Gutschenritter's fund-raiser got the cook in hot water. Gutschenritter sent a memo to the cook, informing him he was guilty of "bad judgment" in that he used jail equipment (a meat slicer) for unofficial business (preparing food for the campaign party).

"This practice shall be discontinued immediately," the memo said.

Gutschenritter sent another memo to the chairman of the county board's building and grounds committee. Attached was a check for $5 "to cover electricity and wear and tear" on the slicer.

That settled the matter, although there was no mention of the cook's transportation to and from the jail to make the slaw during the wee hours. Deputies say a squad car was dispatched to pick up the cook at his home, then again to take him home.

## JUMPING TO A CONCLUSION ~

The first day of classes at a north-side grade school Monday was routine until one 8-year-old boy confronted a volunteer parent whose job was to complete a questionnaire for third-grade students.

"Gee, what pretty brown eyes you have," the woman said to the boy in an attempt to relax any tension.

"Thank you, ma'am," the boy beamed.

Then she asked his name and wrote it down. "Grade?"

"Third," he replied.

The next two blanks were to designate race and sex. So, without further questioning, the woman wrote in "B" and "M."

"What's that 'B' and that 'M' for?" the boy asked.

"Well," the woman started to explain, "this word is race, so I put 'B' to indicate black. And this word is sex and . . ."

"Oh," the boy interrupted, "I haven't had any of that yet!"

## SOUNDS FAIR ~

The Illinois State Fair's survey of 12,000 fairgoers turned up some real zingers. Besides the legitimate list of most-wanted or wanted-more-of attractions, there were these:

Belly dancing, cleaner bleacher seats, beer tents closer to the Main Gate, more shade, strip shows, better management, no church food. And baby-sitter service, a big air-conditioned tent, more good-looking men, more good-looking women, a symphony, escalator sidewalks, peaches, parking ramps, sand instead of asphalt in Happy Hollow.

And still others said they want go-go girls, a muscle man contest, less politics, a prostitution tent, more queens.

And a wet T-shirt contest, doors on restrooms, more orange juice, free beer, a tobacco spitting contest, decaffeinated coffee. A place to change baby diapers, a crop dusting contest, golf carts for everyone, nude wrestling and — last but not least, as they say — more surveys.

In the immortal words of fair manager Nick Stone, most of the fine folks who made those suggestions need not hold their breath.

## VEGETABLE TORTURE ~
A sign in a Farmer City theater:

"NO SMOKING. Anyone caught will be hung by their toenails and pummeled into unconsciousness with an organic carrot."

## LAW & ORDER ~
A couple of young ministers from out of town were driving through Lincoln Park after an outing on the tennis courts. Suddenly, as they were rejoining families and friends for a cookout, they were confronted by a park police car, red lights flashing and siren screaming. One of the preachers started to get out of the car.

"Get back in the car!" one of two advancing patrolmen ordered.

"But, I . . ." the young man countered.

"Get back in the car!" the officer growled.

He got back into the car. A few questions and answers later, the ministers learned they had been going the wrong way on a one-way street. Less than a Class X offense, of course, but there was more.

One of them — the one who happened to be driving — discovered he'd left his driver's license at home. But, eventually, all was forgiven and the park patrolmen — after giving the wrong-way ministers a 10-minute "crime does not pay" lecture — left them off with a warning.

## 'CRAZY' JAY ~
The new "Crazy Guggenheim's Auto Sales" on North Ninth, across from St. John's Hospital, is getting plenty of attention.

It's the name. A takeoff on the Jackie Gleason television show character, of course, but Jay Guggenheim actually owns the place.

## TEXAS STRANGER ~

A big talker from Texas, who latches on to lonely women through want ads in national publications, made a profitable swing through Springfield this summer and appears to have left several broken hearts in his wake. At least three women here, all divorcees, apparently fell for the reputed gigolo — one of them so hard she married him before he blew town.

The man, who appears to be known to law enforcement authorities far and wide, passed himself off here as a Texas oil tycoon. He wined, dined and romanced women while at the same time relieving them of things like credit cards, cash and cars.

However, he was known to work more than one area at the same time. During his involvement with one Springfield woman, the smooth-talking Texan is said to have had a woman from another state stashed in a local motel. After marrying the Springfield woman, acquiring her luxury car and credit cards, he departed on a business trip a few weeks ago and never returned.

The man is remembered well from when he appeared with the Springfield woman at the Sangamon County Courthouse in mid-July to apply for a marriage license. Conspicuous in his western-style hat and cowboy boots, he talked about the yacht he owns, and flashed diamond rings and a roll of money padded generously with $100 bills. Listing himself as being 49 years old and a widower, the cigar-smoking, paunchy Texan strongly resembles the sheriff character in Dodge truck television commercials. He topped his act by making a dollar sign out of the "S" in his name when he signed the license application.

"He was weird," says one county employee, "but he sure seemed like a millionaire."

Although he listed his marriage here as his second, investigators have estimated he's made 25 to 50 trips to the altar. He had openly boasted that his personal friend, Norman Vincent Peale, would come to Springfield to perform the marriage ceremony. He didn't, of course.

Since the Texan vanished, his Springfield wife has filed to have the marriage annulled. Her suit alleges he forced her to consume "stupefying" drugs and liquor prior to the ceremony that rendered her irresponsible for her actions.

Meanwhile, a warrant from Sangamon County just led to his arrest for felony theft (her car).

## OPEN WIDE ~
There's a complex of new dental offices in Clock Tower Village. One dentist asked another what the development should be named. He suggested "Tooth Acres."

## RIDING IN STYLE ~
Springfield police put a new paddy wagon on the streets recently. It's used to patrol the downtown area and, when the occasion arises, to haul people to jail. Unlike the black Maria of the past, this one is pure white and it is making a good impression with the gentlemen-of-the-street. They think it's an ambulance.

## CANDY MAN ~
The young employee who lost $30 of her own money in the holdup at the Fannie Mae Candy Shop a couple of weeks ago was soon confronted by a gent who insisted on reimbursing her for the loss.

*Brenton Coffey*

Brenton Coffey, the blind man who's been a fixture on Old Capitol plaza for many a year and a daily visitor to the candy shop, had left the shop minutes before the holdup. He told the gal he had a premonition something was going to happen and he neglected to return to warn her. He blamed himself for the robbery and insisted on reimbursing her for what she lost to the robbers. She declined.

## THE THANKS YA GET ~
A guy in a country town not far from here traditionally hands out apples to kids on Halloween. This year was no exception. He washed and pol-

ished a big pile of apples, and awaited the trick-or-treat crowd.

One little girl who showed up announced her mission and held out her trick-or-treat sack. The man took aim and dropped an apple inside.

The little girl stared down into the sack, then looked the guy straight in the eye and growled, "You (bleep), you busted my cookie!"

## ODE TO BIG BROTHER/BIG BUCKS ~

The great big (40 percent) pay raise for state officials inspired our poet laureate Vernon Harris of Rochester to pen "The Money Lovers."

Way back in the dim beginning, when they doubted they were winning, there were promises to serve the voters well.
But with victory came temptation — sticky fingers, exploitation — and a story that's ridiculous to tell.
All our fat and happy "servants" — in a ghastly, sad observance — got together and decided on a raise.
Twenty thousand lousy dollars, for their white and shiny collars, wasn't adequate for all those working days.

So they pooled their greed and cunning — little men, who once were running — and agreed that 40 was a just percent.
Having won their noisy battle, riding tall now in the saddle, we can wonder where their dedication went.
In our rightful indignation, with a worsening inflation, we have less money than ever we can keep.
With a wealthy legislature — monuments to human nature — we can pay these vultures while they sit and sleep.

All these whining politicians, making masterful decisions, have betrayed the trusting public once again.
But the day is surely coming, when — despite their tearful bumming — we shall have the chance to vote for honest men.
All the lying, all the dreaming, all the petty little scheming, on Election Day will be concealed from view.
But with will power and precision, we can make a wise decision — we can vote for those content with thirty-two.

(Harris took another poke at the legislative pay raise with this verse,

⌒

"Money Lovers, Part II.")

Down the highway, fairly flying — driving fast is satisfying — race those little men adept in riding free.
These, our noble legislators — these our callous perpetrators — are above the laws that govern you and me.
How they whimpered for election! How they boasted of perfection, when we "common folk" were due to cast our votes.
How they begged us, every hour, 'til we put them into power — then they rammed their legislation down our throats.

What is honor to the greedy? What's compassion for the needy? Where's the switch to turn their lust for money off?
While we're poorer still, and grieving, they have no intent of leaving — we must feed them, and they're waiting at the trough.
Those pay raises, raw and recent, brand them now as gross, indecent little pagans worshipping the dollar bill.
We, the "common folk," are learning — as our pocketbooks are burning — and one day we'll rise above their selfish will.

May we have the sense, and vision, to effect a mass decision — to elect some men who recognize our rights.
May we strip these preening beauties of their glory, of their "duties" and divest ourselves of all these parasites.
In this special Christmas season, decent people search for reason — there are many things to ponder, as we pause.
But, from those we once elected, very little is expected — each of them is now his own sweet Santa Claus.

## PAWS FOR THE CAUSE ~

A woman took her car into Capital Chrysler-Plymouth for service. She was accompanied by the biggest dog the guys there had ever seen. After awhile, the woman asked a salesman for directions to the ladies restroom. He didn't give it a second thought as he guided her to the office area, but the dog lumbered along at her side. Finally, the woman reached her destination, then paused.

"My *dog* has to go the bathroom," she told the salesman.

She then opened the door and escorted the dog into the john. No one knows for sure, but it's assumed the dog is potty-trained and performed as would be expected.

That gave employees plenty to talk about the rest of the day. One guy, for example, quipped to a secretary: "What would you have done if you had walked in and found that dog sitting on the pot reading the newspaper?"

Get in line, no doubt. There was this thought-provoking question, too: "Did the dog write on the wall?"

## ON GUARD FOR 1979 ~

The New Year will be full of surprises. As usual, we feel obligated to let a few of them out of the bag. So, tongue-in-check, here's a sample of what's in store for 1979:

• The battle over ERA will resume. A final vote will be called in November after ERA proponents swarm onto the Senate floor and stage a tug-of-war with a pair of extra-large pantyhose — with an ERA opponent in them.

• The Sangamon County Animal Shelter will announce the birth of the first test tube stray dog.

• The successful auction of worn-out, state-owned cars will inspire expansion of that program. Immediately following inauguration ceremonies next month, the state will auction off worn-out state officials.

• The city will crack down on dance parlors, inspiring operators of the social establishments to rename them checker parlors. Then the routine will be for a guy to enter and see how many moves he can make before he gets crowned by an undercover cop.

• During the city's next snow, when downtown streets receive the usual 6-inch layer of salt, a man standing on the curb waiting on a bus will find that his shoes have rusted out.

• The "Smokey Jokey," advertised as the ultimate radar detection device for motorists who want to avoid speed traps, will hit the market. It not only alerts the motorist to the radar cop ahead, but with the press of a button, it also lets the air out of all four tires on the police car.

# 1979

## DEAR JOHN ~

The Pontiac running around town with an ash tray, roll of toilet paper and urinal mounted on the rear belongs to William Hennessey. It's his answer to self-serve gas stations that offer no fringe benefits.

## TODDLIN' TOWN ~

Chicago officials called in outside help for snow removal. A Springfield man took his snowplow-equipped truck to the Windy City and was assigned to clear alleys.

He found the alleys full of rats — thousands of rats, he says. They literally attacked, climbing all over his truck and trying to get into the cab.

Scared him.

## ROYAL FLUSH ~

The men's room at city police headquarters just got a paint job. As one wag put it: "The slate has been wiped clean for a new generation of poets."

## LIFE IN AN ELEVATOR ~

At the time there didn't seem to be anything funny about being trapped for three hours in that elevator at the Washington Street parking ramp Tuesday night, says Linda Dickson. But now she can see some humor — just a little bit.

Finding herself imprisoned between the fourth and fifth floors, all she could think of at first was how worried her husband would be when he realized she was missing. Finally gaining some composure, she started rummaging through her purse. Anything to concentrate on, she told herself.

First, she found some chewing gum. She chewed one stick. Then two. Then three and four — all at the same time. Then she decided to balance her checkbook. That seemed reasonable. She's employed at a downtown bank. But she never did get around to that task. Instead, she listened for any sign of life outside and periodically pushed the elevator alarm button that triggered a loud bell in the stairwell. There is no telephone in the elevator.

About an hour and one-half later, Linda heard someone. She screamed and beat on the elevator door.

That did the trick. Vickie Stadtman heard the racket. She first thought it might be kids at play, but she called police to be on the safe side. Police responded and called the fire department.

Guess who was on the fire engine that pulled up? Firefighter Steve Stadtman, Vickie's husband. Linda was soon freed.

A little something else calmed Linda's nerves: an apology from the ramp manager and free parking for the next month.

## SURPRISE PARTY ~

A couple of play-for-pay girls hailed a motorist near Ninth and Jackson one night. They said that the man driving the car was wearing clerical garb but they hopped in anyway.

"Are you the police?" one gal asked.

"Do I look like the police?" the man countered.

"No," she said.

From that point on, it was strictly business. Without further ado, the girls stated their proposition.

Seconds later, uniformed police officers moved in and arrested them. Yes, girls, your prey was a policeman in priest's clothing.

## JUSTICE SPINNING ITS WHEELS ~

There was a knock at the door of a southeast-side home. It was about 8:30 p.m. German Roncancio answered and was surprised to see two sheriff's deputies. Roncancio was more surprised to learn they had a warrant for his arrest.

"What's the charge?" he asked.

He was told he had neglected to pay a $1 parking ticket in Macomb and, therefore, he was under arrest.

"You must be kidding," Roncancio said.

"No," said one deputy, "you have to come with us — right now."

Roncancio finally realized he was about to be hauled off to jail.

"I was scared," he recalls. "I'd never been in a jail in my life."

He asked the deputies to give him time to phone a lawyer. They did, and then agreed to the lawyer's request that Roncancio be allowed to surrender voluntarily at the county jail the next morning.

The alleged fugitive from a no-parking zone turned himself in and was formally booked. However, he was spared the usual mug shot and fingerprinting process.

"This is insanity," Roncancio commented to a sheriff's aide in the jail. "I can't believe this is happening. All for a parking ticket."

General reaction from jail personnel, he said, was that the whole episode was "kinda silly."

"Does this mean I now have a police record?" he asked a deputy.

"Yes."

Roncancio spent more than an hour at the jail but only for booking. He was immediately released on $35 cash bond without being locked up.

What disturbed Roncancio most, though, is that a law-abiding citizen is subject to being jailed for such a petty offense.

"I can't believe someone can be dragged out of their home any time and put in jail for something like that."

## WRONG NUMBER ~

A man phoned the secretary of state's office and requested license plate registration information. He was referred to a man on the supervisory level. He explained such information is available by phone only to law enforcement authorities. However, he noted, citizens may request license information in writing for a $2 fee.

"By the way," the state employee asked, "how did you get this phone number?"

"I'm not at liberty to give you that information on the phone," the citizen replied. "But if you put your request in writing and send $2, I'll be glad to send that information to you."

## HOLD THE RELISH ~

Two elderly couples walked into a fast food restaurant and carefully studied the menu before placing an order.

When served, one of the women complained to the cashier about being charged a dime extra for cheese on her hamburger. Although it was pointed out the menu lists the extra charge, the woman continued to complain, contending that she had been deceived and was the victim of a rip-off.

Then, with her companions in tow, she stalked out of the restaurant, climbed into a new Cadillac and drove away.

## LAZY DAISY ~
A woman who was a patient at Memorial Medical Center hated being awakened so early in the morning. She let hospital staffers know it.

Then, last Sunday, doctors and nurses found this sign on the door to her fourth floor room:

"Do Not Disturb! It's my birthday and I intend to sleep late. My blood pressure is fine — that is, unless you wake me!!"

## BYE-BYE BIRDIE ~
A bird flew into the Centennial Building the other day. Employees rallied to keep it supplied with food and water. Then the Department of Conservation was notified. A team of birdmen arrived to investigate.

The bird was a whippoorwill, a rarity for Sangamon County. It was captured and was being removed when an employee asked its destination.

It's very rare, so it will be stuffed and placed on exhibit in the museum, one state employee quotes one of the birdcatchers as saying. That prompted an impassioned plea for a stay of execution. No need for that. Just a little joke by the birdcatcher.

The bird had already been sentenced to life in Carpenter Park.

## ABE WAS FIRE-SAFETY CONSCIOUS ~
A trio of 7-year-olds were touring the Lincoln Home this week. The guide was telling how rough Mr. Lincoln had it in those days — no electric lights, no air-conditioning, no inside plumbing, etc.

"But," one safety-conscious youngster said, pointing to the modern electronic fixture on the wall, "at least he had a smoke alarm."

〜

## NAKED CITY ~

A young man strolled into Kent's IGA store on Monroe Street about 8 o'clock Thursday morning. He went straight to the bakery counter. Employees and customers stared.

No wonder. The young man was nude.

He mumbled something about a "dee-dee for breakfast." The woman behind the counter decided he was referring to a doughnut. So she handed him one.

About that time a male employee took him by the hand and escorted him to the door. Then across the parking lot and into a nearby apartment complex where he found the door of one apartment standing wide open, just as the young man had left it.

Turned out the young man had awakened before the rest of the family, lifted the apartment key from his father's pants pocket and gone out for breakfast.

Incidentally, the young man is 3 years old.

## QUOTABLE ~

An elderly woman touring the Executive Mansion asked this burning question:

"What kind of shorts does Gov. Thompson wear?"

"I really don't know," the woman guide responded. "I haven't been briefed on that yet."

## KID STUFF ~

A group of kids toured the Executive Mansion the other day.

"Did you see Governor Thompson?" one of the kids was asked by his father when he returned home.

"No," the boy said in all seriousness, "they had him put away in a room somewhere."

The father assumes his son was referring to the Thompsons' dog, "Guv," but he has yet to convince the boy that they don't lock up the governor on visitors' day.

## BENEFITS OF STARDOM ~

Stars of the state fair's grandstand shows aren't quite as demanding as they used to be when it comes to fringe benefits. This year, for example, the disco group Chic attached a rider to its $35,000 contract specifying the dressing rooms be stocked with two cases of soft drinks, one gallon of orange juice, two dozen doughnuts, coffee and assorted breakfast cereals. Lasagna with the usual trimmings was ordered for the group's evening meal.

In addition, Chic ordered four cases of ginger ale and Pepsi, two cases of Heineken beer, one case of Lowenbrau Light beer, three bottles of white Pouilly Fuisse wine, one bottle of Amaretto De Sarnona liqueur, coffee, eight large bottles of Perrier water, one gallon of spring water, three quarts of orange juice, cold cuts of roast beef, turkey breast and ham, tuna salad, chicken salad, fresh fruits or vegetables, cheese, crackers and bread.

Still, grandstand stage manager Dick Garfat says some headliners in past years demanded considerably more.

He recalls K.C. & the Sunshine Band wanted the fair to provide limousine service from St. Louis to Springfield two years ago. Only the band members insisted the fair use three new white Cadillacs. Garfat informed their manager the fair had no white Cadillacs and only one limousine. Any other limousines would have to be rented from local funeral homes. The band rejected the fair's offer and rented white Caddies from a St. Louis firm.

Johnny Cash's contract called for a specially prepared filet mignon dinner with a linen and china spread in his dressing room in 1977. A similar order was placed by the Osmonds last year. They were served chicken cordon bleu and Beef Wellington by candlelight.

The biggest spread in recent years, however, was ordered by the Bay City

Rollers.

A rider to their $30,000 contract specified "a constant supply of refreshments including coffee, tea, soda, juices, sandwiches and cake."

Then, at show time, their order was for six bottles of orange juice, two bottles each of grape juice, apple juice and milk, two cases each of Coke, 7-Up and tonic, fried chicken, ribs, roast beef, ham, barbecue, turkey and seafood or a complete deli with all relishes and bread.

Some entertainers merely request a sit-down meal, leaving it up to the fair as to what is served. But such open requests are usually tagged with this phrase: "All franchised foods are unacceptable."

## WILLIE ON THE ROAD ~

One of this year's highest paid ($51,000) and most popular entertainers at the fair, Willie Nelson, travels with his own kitchen — a complete mobile unit. His chef, "Beast," prepared butterfly pork chops, Mexican-style beef, sausage, ham and a tuna-noodle dish for Nelson's crew of nearly 75. About 25 members of Garfat's stage crew were invited to the feed, too.

Nelson's rolling restaurant also was well-stocked with Lone Star Beer — 100 cases of it. Much of it was consumed during his 12-hour stay at the fair.

Among Nelson's requirements for "special stage equipment" was two large garbage cans for empty beer cans. Both were nearly full before the end of his first show.

## JUNIOR BLOWS A SALE ~

A woman shopping for an economical used car responded to a State Journal-Register classified ad that offered an aging Chevy for sale. Her phone call to the owner's home, however, was answered by a 7-year-old boy. Mom and dad weren't home, he told the woman, but he said he knew all about the car that was for sale.

"Does it have the big motor?" the woman asked.

⌣

"Oh, yes," the boy boasted, "it has a real big motor."

"Does it use a lot of gas?" the woman asked.

"Yeah," he said innocently. "I know it does because my dad says we gotta get rid of that gas hog."

## PASSING THE BUCK ~

A couple of kids were given Susan B. Anthony silver dollars. While playing with the coins in the yard, one kid threw his Suzie Q at the other kid and lost it in the grass. He enlisted the aid of his father, but it couldn't be found.

"You'll just have to pray to St. Anthony that it turns up," the father told the 6-year-old boy.

"Is that her husband?" the boy asked.

## WATER CLOSET ~

A man who took in a show at the Prairie Capital Convention Center last week hiked up to a restroom during intermission.

Beyond the main entrance, which was marked "MEN," were two doors. Neither was signed. He presumed the door to the restroom was straight ahead and was proceeding in that direction when the other door flew open and a 7-year-old boy stalked out.

"All they give ya is a bucket to go in!" the youngster muttered to no one in particular.

That made the man wonder. Is that the door to the restroom and are there no fixtures? He entered to make sure. And sure enough, it wasn't a restroom. It was a janitor's closet. There was the bucket the boy was talking about and evidence that the boy really had mistakened the bucket for a toilet.

# 1980

## WHO WAS THAT UNMASKED MAN? ~

A limousine was sent to Capital Airport to pick up actor Clayton Moore (better known as The Lone Ranger) Friday. Moore appeared at White Oaks Mall in connection with a weekend benefit for cerebral palsy.

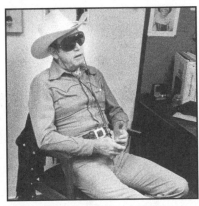

*Clayton (The Lone Ranger) Moore*

Airport police escorted the limo to the rear of the terminal building, where the driver parked to wait for his famous passenger. Minutes later, an important looking gent was guided to the limo.

"It's nice to meet you, Mr. Moore," said the driver as the gent climbed into the back seat.

But it wasn't Moore. It was Joe DiMaggio. DiMaggio was escorted to another car.

## SMART-ALECK 'KID' ~

A woman checked into a local hospital the other day.  She listed her age as 91.

"Who's admitting you?" a hospital clerk asked.

"My mommy and daddy," she replied.

Doubtful as that was, the hospital staffers shrugged it off. Then, the next day, an elderly man and woman showed up at the hospital to visit the 91-year-old woman. You guessed it. Her parents.
"Mommy" is 104. "Daddy" is 105.

## 'WILL' POWER ~

The state of Illinois is 10 bucks richer, thanks to the generosity of a Missouri woman.

State Treasurer Jerry Cosentino received the money this week in the form of a bequest from the late Florence Tulley of St. Louis. Her will provided for $10 to go to each of the eight states bordering Missouri.

The St. Louis lawyer who handled the estate said the will gave no explanation of the unusual bequests. The woman, however, was not wealthy.

Interestingly enough, she didn't leave a penny to her home state of Missouri.

## STEAL CITY! ~

The Amtrak conductor who announces "Steal City" when his passenger train pulls into Springfield is Harold Feger, a Springfieldian who's been railroading the past 35 years.

Steal City, as we noted some time ago, is a pun on the legislative process here. But, now we learn, Feger's sense of humor smacks at other cities on the Amtrak line, too. Feger's familiar calls include:

JOLIET — "Stone City" (There's so much rock there and, besides, that was the city's original name.)

PONTIAC — "Chief City" (Referring to the Indian, naturally.)

BLOOMINGTON — "Home of the Living Dead" (Legend has it Bloomington is kind of a dead town.) Feger called it the "Home of the Dancing Mayor" when Bob McGraw was the mayor. (Hizzonor liked to dance.)

LINCOLN — "Watermelon Village" (Recognizing the fact that Abraham Lincoln christened the city with watermelon juice.)

CARLINVILLE — "Ambroseville" (In honor of a retired railroad conductor who resides there.)

ALTON — "Jack & Jill" (City of hills.)

## PARTY LINE ~
The 100th anniversary of W. C. Fields' birthday yesterday didn't go unnoticed by Linda McCoy. She threw a party in honor of the comedian at her north-side home.

While swapping their favorite W.C. yarns, guests picked through stacks and stacks of Fields memorabilia. Linda, whose interest in Fields prompted her to write a college term paper on him years ago, ranks him as one of the two greatest comics the United States has ever produced. Rodney Dangerfield is the other, she says.

One of his best lines, Linda says: "Anybody who hates kids and dogs can't be all bad."

Pointing out the Fields mind was before its time, she offers this quote: "Reminds me of my expedition into the wilds of Afghanistan. We lost our corkscrew and were compelled to live on food and water for several days."

## TEN WORDS OR LESS ~
A monster question was posed by 4-year-old Clay James.

"What is life?" he asked.

But before a grown-up could respond, he came up with his own answer.

〜

"It's a funny experience people have to go through."

## ERRAND BOY ~
Two cars pulled up to Thrifty's drug store at Sixth and South Grand the other night. Gov. Jim Thompson and a plainclothes policeman were in one, two plainclothesmen in the other. Thompson, with a security man on his tail, went into the drugstore and made a purchase. He bought a box of crayons.

## PRO & CON ~
One guy in the "Movement Against the Draft" (MAD) demonstration downtown Wednesday was waving this sign: "Hell No — I Won't Go."

A well-dressed older gent confronted him:

"You apparently don't appreciate living in this country," he commented.

"Yeah, I do," the protester replied. "That's why I don't want to go to some other country and get shot."

"Why not?" the gent countered. "A lot of men have so people like you can complain."

## LAUGHING GAS ~
A couple of guys thought they had a good thing going at Lindner's Shell Service at Jefferson and MacArthur. They'd pull up at a self-serve island, load up with gas and turn back the tumblers on the pump to $1 or $2. It was the cheapest gas in town — while it lasted.

Station employees were onto the scam, however, and were keeping a sharp eye out for their thieving customers. The pair drove in again a few days ago when the lone employee was busy. But he noted how fast and how long the gas pump ran, and then showed a purchase of only $1 — less than a gallon.

Then the pair asked for a car wash. The attendant directed them in and started the automatic washer. He waited.

When the car reached the halfway point and was surrounded by whirling brushes, he stopped the conveyor belt and called police. He turned it on again when officers arrived.

Four squad cars had the car wash surrounded when the gas thieves — now in a clean car with a full tank of gas — reached the end of the line.

## IF THAT WOULDN'T FROST YA! ~

A woman awoke Saturday morning to find the water pipes in her mobile home frozen. So, no water for cooking, washing, brushing teeth, etc. But there was plenty of fresh snow outdoors. She could use the snow to at least brush her teeth, she decided.

She grabbed a small pan, dashed outside, scooped some snow into the pan and put it on the stove to melt while she turned to another chore. Returning to the stove a few minutes later, she found evidence a little dog had already used the snow.

Needless to say, she didn't brush.

## NICE GUY FINISHED LAST ~

Once upon a time in Springfield, there was a man who liked to "crash" funeral processions. It was the mid-1960s. He barged into the line of cars and harassed mourners by, among other things, making faces at them.

Someone finally traced his license number and went to authorities to press charges. But they were talked out of it.

The crasher, they were told, happened to be a real nice guy and an upstanding citizen, and an effort should be made to protect his good reputation.

Who was the man? John Wayne Gacy.

## SMILE, SENATOR ~

A man cruising I-55 — admittedly beyond the speed limit — tells of being passed by a state senator.

"He passed us like we were standing still," the man said.

He told his wife, who was behind the wheel, to put the pedal to the metal and see how fast the lawmaker was going. For the next 30 miles, the senator's car stayed in the 70 to 80 mph range, he says. The man then told his wife to pull out and pass. As she did, he whipped out a camera and snapped pictures of the senator. At that point, he says, the senator slowed to about 65 mph.

"That's not true," the senator counters. "I was cruising, but I wasn't doing that kind of speeding."

"Oh, yes he was!" his accuser contends.

"Well, he passed me," the senator points out, adding that that's proof the other car was speeding more than he was. "If I'm speeding, that doesn't justify him speeding."

"That's right," the man admits. "But he makes the law. He should be the first to abide by it."

The senator says he remembers the man.

"I wondered about him. I thought he was joking around."

Did the senator know his picture was being taken?

"Yes. I smiled for him."

Would the senator like to place an order?

"Yes," he says. "I'll take an 8-by-10 glossy for my office wall."

POSTSCRIPT: Sorry, senator, but every one of the pictures were one big blur. Completely out of focus. You were simply going too fast, according to the photographer.

## HOME SWEET HOME ~

They were told not to "fight city hall." But they did, and they won. Ottis Finley received official word of their victory yesterday. It was quite a relief. Now they can keep their modest little home at the corner of 10th and Phillips, having beaten back the city's attempt to seize it in the name of urban renewal.

What his 68-year-old wife describes as "pure hell" began two months ago, when representatives of the city Community Development Department dropped by to inspect her home. A letter stating the city's "intent to purchase" the property followed.

The Finleys made it clear from the start they didn't want to sell the house, their home for the past 32 years. Finley, a retired painter, is 83 years old and has been in failing health for some time. For one thing, he has heart trouble, so the news that he was about to lose his home was particularly unnerving to him. In addition, Mrs. Finley's 89-year-old mother — who is going blind and is bedridden — lives in the home, which was paid for long ago. The Finleys make do on meager Social Security benefits. They pay their bills — taxes included — on time. They don't bother anyone and can't understand why the city started pushing them around.

The city, in the process of acquiring a number of older homes in the neighborhood, wanted to relocate the Finleys, tear down the house and sell the land for redevelopment.

"Why do you want to take our home away from us?" Mrs. Finley asked one city representative.

"Oh, we're not taking your home away," she was told. "We're just going to relocate you."

The prospect of being driven out of the their home made Mrs. Finley a "nervous wreck."

"I cried and cried and cried," she says. "I couldn't sleep. I just got sick with worry. That made Ottis get worse. I've really been worried about him."

Finley spends the day in his big easy chair in front of a picture window in the living room. Because he can't lie down any more, he sleeps in the chair, too.

"He wants to live his days out here, in this house," Mrs. Finley says. "This is our home. They just don't understand that."

The process of acquisition rolled on. Inspection visits by city agents, appraisers, official letters, etc.

"I begged them to leave us alone," Mrs. Finley said.

"Don't fight it," she quotes one city agent as telling her. "It won't do you a bit of good to fight it. When they (government) make up their mind to do something, they do it."

Word of the Finleys' plight finally reached friends, who volunteered to take up the fight. That was two weeks ago. Yesterday, the Finleys received a letter from Willis Logan, community development executive director, stating the city has dropped plans to acquire their home. Although the letter says "budgetary reasons" forced the city to throw in the towel, Logan says the hardship factor is the real reason.

"Stop, don't go any further. . . leave her alone," Logan told his staff when state Rep. Josephine Oblinger informed him of the situation.

The city has encountered budget problems with the program and might not be able to go through with the acquisition anyway, Logan says. But "the fact they are old and sickly is what disturbed me most. That's really why we dropped it." The city was following procedure set by the federal government, said Logan. But no one should have told the Finleys they couldn't fight it.

Finley spends a lot of time reading his Bible.

"You know," he said after hearing the good news, "the Bible says prayer changes things."

Has he been praying?

"You betcha!"

## LIGHTS OUT! ~

"The savage in me just came out," says state Sen. John Knuppel, explaining his tangle with Chicago television reporter Rich Samuels in a Senate committee hearing room.

〜

Knuppel's temper flared after a WMAQ-TV camera crew set up floodlights in the Judiciary Committee hearing room. He asked Samuels to turn off the blinding lights until they were needed. Knuppel, who has cataracts, says Samuels first turned his back on him. Knuppel's second request was met with Samuels' explanation that he is not a member of the camera crew's union and wouldn't be allowed to operate the lights.

"Well, by God, I don't have to have a union card," Knuppel said. "I can turn them off."

He hopped over a table and kicked over one of the lights.

Samuels and the senator engaged in a heated argument. Samuels invited Knuppel to join him for a little violence outside and that's where they were about to go when Knuppel was restrained by his colleagues.

"Most of the reporters around here are very reasonable," Knuppel said later. "But these guys came in and threw their weight around. It was his arrogant attitude that set me off."

Like the senator said: "I react differently than the average person."

## 'I TRIED TO GET AWAY!' 〜

It sounded like a good deal — training employees to fly airplanes. So, John Harms, owner-operator of a flying service based at Virden, Ill., took the job.

"It looked like easy money," as Harms, 45, put it.

That was less than two years ago. Today, he starts serving a two-year sentence in federal prison, standing convicted of conspiring to smuggle drugs into the United States. But things could be worse. At least he's alive, he says, reflecting on his harrowing experiences with a multimillion-dollar international drug smuggling ring known as "The Company."

Harms technically entered a plea of nolo contendere to the reduced charge after turning state's evidence — as did most of his co-defendants — in the sensational case, which unfolded four months ago when a federal grand jury in Indianapolis indicted 23 persons involved with The Company.

The indictments followed a 23-month probe involving scores of investigators who traveled more than 50,000 miles in 12 states to build the case. The Federal Drug Enforcement Administration alleged the ring smuggled more than $40 million worth of drugs into the United States from Colombia, South America. Forty-four vehicles, ranging from dump trucks equipped with snowplows (for clearing isolated landing strips used by the ring) to luxury cars (Mercedes Benzes, Lincolns and Cadillacs), plus the ringleader's ritzy Florida home, were seized when federal agents moved in to shut down the operation.

Authorities say Harms' first association with the ring was limited to buying some of those vehicles under fictitious names. Purchases were made from agencies in several states. Soon after, the ringleaders presented their plans to train pilots to fly bigger planes so much larger drug shipments could be made.

"I only agreed to train pilots, not to fly drugs. I never did fly any drugs."

Harms' first and only mission was with three other members of The Company, flown from a Fort Lauderdale airport.

A few hours later, as they searched in vain for a makeshift airfield in a jungle near Santa Marta, their DC-4 was buzzed by a Colombian jet fighter. They were fired upon. (More than 100 bullet holes were found in the plane.) The jet then guided them to a landing at a Colombian military field. They were placed under arrest by armed soldiers, strip-searched and jailed on charges of violating Colombian air space. All four eventually ended up in the "Ging," a notorious jail in Barranquilla where the movie "Papillion" was filmed.

"The place was full of rats, huge rats, and they were fearless," Harms recalled. "It was infested with bats, too."

The four finally were given conditional release, under guard, to raise $25,000 to pay their fines. Not long after that, they were kidnapped by a rival drug gang. After large sums of money were supplied by The Company a few weeks later, they were freed one by one and smuggled back to the United States.

"There were many times we'd given up all hope of ever getting out alive," says Harms who, by that time, was in ill health.

Realizing he'd gotten into a lot more than he bargained for, Harms left The Company and moved his family to the Hawaiian Islands, where he went to work for a legitimate flying service.

"I tried to get away from them, but they kept after me," Harms said. "They threatened to kill my wife and kids if I ratted. That kept me quiet for quite a while."

Then some of The Company members started talking. Harms decided to talk, too. Then the indictments came down, and Harms was arrested in Honolulu. Harms entered the "no contest" plea to protect his pilot's license.

## AD LIBS ~
• Gov. Jim Thompson says he'll be in his temporary office at the Illinois State Fair on a daily basis to listen to citizens' complaints. It'll be interesting to see just how many people will stand in line that long.
• Thompson intends his fairgrounds office to be a "rest area" for fairgoers. In other words, during the run of the fair, Illinoisans will find the seat of state government in a "restroom."
• The city's new ordinance banning fireworks only goes so far. It won't keep politicians from shooting off their mouths.

## GOLF BAWL ~
A golfer teeing off on the 11th Street side of Bunn Park Golf Course Sunday morning apparently made a really lousy shot. He was so teed-off about it, in fact, that he threw his golf club so hard it flew into the street and struck a passing car. It knocked a hole in the car's grill.

The driver of the car, who was on his way to church, said he was just thankful the guy wasn't bowling.

## POLITICAL YOKE ~
Congressional candidate Dave Robinson made the mistake of leaving his brand-new campaign car unlocked in front of his campaign office. Someone turned it into an omelet.

It was a vicious egging. The vandal opened the door and plastered the windows from the inside with rotten eggs. Ditto for the air-conditioning system, which now gives off a cool stench.

To add insult to injury, campaign aide Tom Serifin discovered the mess when he sat in it.

## SALES PITCHEROO! ~

A Springfield man who was approached by some of those cultists peddling magazine subscriptions last week — before police ordered them to hit the road — says one young woman tried to sell more than magazines to him.

She first gave him the pitch to buy a magazine, but when he declined she proposed marriage to him. She happened to be seven months pregnant. Her pitch for marriage was that she needed a father for her child.

The man already has nine kids, plus 56 grandchildren and 15 great-grandchildren. He's 80 years old.

"I need a 20-year-old pregnant woman like I need a hole in the head!" he said in declining her proposal.

## PLEASE DON'T FEED THE LAWMAKERS~

The hectic days at the end of the legislative session left a lot of Statehouse visitors in awe, as usual. Among other things, some citizens who dropped in to witness last-minute activities in the House found themselves more interested in the legislators' appetites — and what it took to satisfy them — more than anything else.

Besides the usual bill of fare (coffee, cold drinks and sandwiches) catered to lawmaker's desks, some sank their chops into such finger-lickin' favorites as fried chicken and pizza. On one occasion, legislative aides lugged crates of bananas desk-to-desk until it seemed like everyone was peeling and chomping on bananas.

One spectator quipped: "It was just like going to the zoo."

## AD LIBS ~

• The city has a plan to tap the Sangamon River for drinking water.

〜

Sounds fishy, doesn't it?
• Bars could whip up a new drink. River water on the rocks. Call it a Carp Cocktail.
• It could be served with a maraschino cherry and an old tire.
• Utilities Com. Paul Bonansinga says the next step is to test the river water to "determine its bacteria, organic compound and pesticide levels." That's the polite way of saying it.

## BABY-SITTING TROOPER ~
Things go better with Coke. Just ask Paul Haley.

He was headed home when a tire on his car blew out atop the overpass at Interstate 55 and Sangamon Avenue. It was hotter than blazes, of course, and Haley soon realized he had more than a disabled car on his hands. He also had his 6-month-son, Paul III. Junior was not only uncomfortable. He was hungry. Haley could tell by the way the baby was screaming. Haley reached for the baby bottle. It was empty.

Then he saw flashing red lights in his rear view mirror. It was a state trooper who stopped to offer assistance. Haley explained his biggest problem was his hungry son and showed the trooper the empty baby bottle.

"Can he drink Coke?" the trooper asked.

"Sure," Haley said.

The trooper calmly filled the bottle with a Coke he happened to have. Then he took the baby to his air-conditioned squad car and fed him the Coke while Haley changed his flat tire.

## GOOD OLD BOYS ~
Singer Ray Price ran into an old pal, songwriter-singer Hank Cochrane, when he played the Illinois State Fair here a couple of weeks ago. And it was some reunion.

Cochrane, who's touring with Willie Nelson, laid over in Springfield with the rest of the Nelson entourage while Willie made a quick trip to the Democratic National Convention to sing the national anthem. Cochrane, taking advantage of Price's itinerary, which called for him to be picked up by limousine, spent the day arranging an embarrassing red carpet welcome for Price.

He scoured the lesser known used car lots until he found the junkiest automobile in town. It was a Lincoln Continental — full of dents and covered with rust, but drivable. He paid full price for it: $200. Cochrane picked up a few cans of spray paint — the ugliest colors available — on his way back to the fairgrounds. He gave the car a fast and sloppy paint job, painting " Ray Price Music Co." in big letters on both sides.

He then arranged for a police escort across the city, to the Holiday Inn East, where Price was waiting for his limousine. Price, after the initial shock wore off, got in, and police escorted the old rattletrap, per Cochrane's instructions, through the busiest sections of the city on the way back to the fair.

As Cochrane put it, he wanted to embarrass Price as much as he could. But word is Price enjoyed every minute of it, especially since it was at Cochrane's expense.

Cochrane didn't junk the car when the gag ended. At last report, he was southbound in the clunker, headed for Nashville.

# CIRCUS CITY ~

Ringling Bros. and Barnum & Bailey Circus drew 42,257 to the Prairie Capital Convention Center Labor Day weekend. The circus played to a sellout crowd of 6,800 people on opening night and to near-capacity crowds for most other performances.

Renowned animal trainer Gunther Gebel-Williams, who wowed circus-hungry Springfield, personally supervised the traditional "animal walk," which drew 10,000 spectators, and then starred in all eight circus performances. It was the first time in 35 years The Greatest Show On Earth played Springfield.

*Toby McDaniel, aboard elephant, leads Ringling Bros. animal parade.*

## AD LIBS ~

• If the referendum to slash the number of seats in the Illinois House from 177 to 118 passes, 59 lawmakers are going to learn firsthand what's it's like to drive 55 mph.

• Outspoken Anita Bryant finally has been squeezed out of her lucrative job with the Florida Department of Citrus. After hawking all those oranges, that is the "Tangs" she gets.

• Presidential candidate John Anderson unveiled his campaign platform. It's 8 feet square and 11 inches high.

• Like all campaign platforms, it's made out of used lumber.

## CRIME PREVENTION ~

There were several break-ins at Larry's Home Tavern on the city's north side. Then owner Larry Smith put this sign in the front window:

"Warning. After Business Hours This Building Is Protected By a .357-Magnum Three Nights A Week. You Guess Which Three."

No intruders since.

## IT'S THE E-E-L THING! ~

Twelve-year-old Cindy Woodward returned home from summer camp at Knox College to tell her folks camp was great, but she sure was hungry. Questioning by her father brought out the fact she hadn't eaten dinner on the last day of camp.

"Nobody ate," Cindy said. "They served eel."

"Eel? They couldn't have served eel," her father countered.

"They did," Cindy contended. "Everybody was really mad."

Her father dropped the subject.

A few days later, the Woodwards went out to eat. Woodward ordered veal parmesan. Cindy turned up her nose.

"Yuk!" she said. "That's what they had at camp — eel parmesan.

## AD LIBS ~

• Gov. Jim Thompson skipped town in order to avoid Jimmy Carter. Now Carter wants to have Thompson arrested on a fleeing and eluding charge.
• There are others, however, who think the more appropriate charge would be leaving the scene of an accident.

## BIG SPENDER ~

Everything usually comes out in the wash, they say. So it was at Holiday Inn East this week. Wanda Williams, who works in the motel laundry, picked up a pillow case and a billfold fell out. It was crammed with $100 bills — several thousand dollars worth.

The billfold was traced to a man attending a convention there and was returned to him intact. He promptly gave Wanda a cash reward — $5.

## CHECKOUT LANE ~

A woman shopping with food stamps was at a supermarket checkout counter when the clerk informed her she could not use the stamps to purchase the dog food she had in her cart. With that, the woman calmly gathered up the dog food and handed it to one of her kids.

"Here," she said, "take this back and get a ham instead. He likes ham just as well."

The kid did as he was told and, presumably, some lucky dog was treated to a ham dinner that night.

# 1981

## BANK ROBBED/CITIZEN MUGGED ~

The armed robbers who hit the Bank of Springfield on Stevenson Drive a
few weeks ago used a stolen car in their successful getaway. It was a 1972
Ford Torino owned by Jay Guggenheim. He eventually got it back, but,
like many other law-abiding citizens whose vehicles have been stolen and
used in the commission of a crime, he was left holding the bag — and not
a bank bag.

Guggenheim awoke early one morning to find his car had been stolen. He
reported the theft to police immediately. About five hours later, the bank
was robbed. Police found the car later in the day, only two blocks from
the bank. The motor was still running. Police, suspecting it might have
been the bank robbers' getaway car, had it towed to a compound for routine processing.

Meanwhile, Guggenheim, who is partially disabled and unable to work,
was in dire need of his car to get the doctor's office. He checked with
police frequently to see when the car would be released. During that time,

investigators asked him to go to police headquarters to look at mug shots as they attempted to find suspects in the bank robbery. Guggenheim made two such trips, both times by taxi, which cost him a total of $16 in fares. He expected to be reimbursed. He wasn't.

More than two weeks after the robbery, police notified him he could retrieve his car from the tow company. When he arrived, he discovered he would have to pay a towing and storage bill of $70. He balked. Eventually, the tow bill was cut to $40. He agreed to pay and seek reimbursement from the police department later.

Guggenheim has just been denied that request, according to a letter from Police Chief Howard Rogers. The police department realizes the theft of the car and the time Guggenheim was without its use was "extremely inconvenient" to him, the letter said, but such cost must be borne by the citizen, not the public. Guggenheim also must pay for the damage the thieves did to his car. They knocked out the whole ignition mechanism. Since the car is so old, he carries only liability insurance. Considering the taxi fares, tow bill and damage, Guggenheim estimates he's out at least 200 bucks — a big part of which he thinks the police department should pay.

## NEWS THAT WASN'T ~

News travels fast and far these days. Like this story about the Springfield political scene, as it appeared recently in an Australian newspaper:

"Boy, they sure play local government politics hard in the states.

"The mayor of Springfield, Illinois, was stricken by a heart attack during a council meeting. The council voted 19 to 18 to wish him an early recovery. I wonder if the mayor cast an absentee vote."

Fact is, of course, there was no such happening — in this Springfield, anyway. Mayor Mike Houston, although he takes a licking on occasion, keeps on ticking.

Whatever, that version was published and 12-year-old Erin Roscetti of Springfield has a newspaper clipping to prove it. It came from Suzanne Brion, a pen pal in Murray Bridge, Australia.

## MOTHERHOOD (WINKED) ~
Several women were shopping in a store at White Oaks Mall but didn't buy anything. Upon leaving, they were intercepted by the store manager and ordered back. One of the women was told to hand over the socks she stole.

"What socks?" the woman asked.

"Those socks under your top," the manager said, pointing to a sizable bulge.

The woman hastened to tell him that she'd never stolen anything in her life, and hot socks had nothing to do with the bulge in her dress. She happened to be six months pregnant.

She was told to "carry on."

## OINK! OINK! ~
Across the front of Virden, Ill., hog equipment dealer Louis Dysson's pick-up truck: "I'm Rootin' for Your Business."

## HIGHWAY PATROL ~
A motorist heading into Springfield late at night on Sangamon Avenue was passed on the I-55 overhead by a speeding car bearing official license plates. He caught up with and gave the driver (apparently a state Department of Conservation officer) a piece of his mind.

"Why don't you have to abide by the same laws I do?" he asked, noting that the officer didn't appear to be on any kind of emergency run.

"I'm in a hurry," the driver of the official car growled, explaining further — in four-letter lingo — that he was answering a call from Mother Nature.

## SPRINGFIELD ON ICE ~
A car, its emergency flashers flashing, moved slowly along South Grand Avenue early Monday evening. A woman was behind the wheel.

And behind her, squatting in the trunk, was her husband . . . holding tight to a rope . . . at the end of which was a dolly . . . on top of which was a refrigerator.

## WHO CARES? ~

A woman on welfare phoned the Department of Public Aid to report that her ex-husband, who's more than $1,500 in arrears on child support payments, is back in town.

Since that money technically is owed to the state, she thought authorities probably would like to catch up with him. But she didn't get that impression from the woman who answered the phone.

After hearing the woman's reason for calling, the public aid employee — without covering the phone — yelled to a co-worker: "This woman wants to rat on her ex-husband for child support. Who does she talk to?"

The call was referred to another employee, who treated the matter much more seriously.

## PLANT LIFE ~

A seminar sponsored by the Illinois State Nurseryman's Association and the University of Illinois produced this yarn, which ISNA executive director Jim Hayward accepts full blame for passing along.

Taxonomist Floyd Swink of Lisle, Ill., told of the twit from Chicago who had a thing for mountain laurel, a flowering shrub. He kept planting it, and it kept dying.

"Why can't I grow laurel?" he asked a botanist.

"Well," the botanist explained, "laurel isn't hardy here."

## LOSE/WIN PROPOSITION ~

The Pontiac prison murder trial, at long last, is off and running after taking more than five months to seat the jury. Predictions are that the trial itself won't take that long.

The horde of defense attorneys — who have repeatedly accused Sangamon County trial Judge Ben Miller of, among other things, racial prejudice — resorted to a variety of stall tactics throughout the pretrial stage, which actually began in May, when the case turned into a full-time job for Miller. The key tactic, of course, was to flood the court with pretrial motions. Miller had to hear and rule on more than 400 defense motions, many of them as voluminous in size as they were ridiculous in content.

One of the motions, seeking dismissal of the murder charges against all 10 defendants, claimed each defendant is "New African by birth" and therefore are "citizens of the Republic of New Africa, a nation held captive and colonized by the United States and various European nations."

Consequently, the defense argued, Illinois courts have no jurisdiction in the case. That one and all of the other defense motions lost. But, as one court observer hastened to add, the lawyers are getting paid by the hour.

## TRASH MASHER ~
A guy poking through a trash bin at Sangamon State Univeristy found hundreds of Illinois Department of Transportation documents. He reported his find to DOT, and the files, which were safety responsibility forms that carry a confidential classification, were traced to a part-time DOT employee.

Instead of running the documents through a shredding machine, as he was required to do at DOT, the part-timer had — as far as he was concerned — found an easier way. He hauled several cases of the classified papers to the campus and tossed them in the trash.

DOT has since dumped him.

## BELIEVE IT OR NOT ~
There's never been anyone more skeptical of those highly touted clearing-house cash giveaways than Tony Stockus. But he's a believer now. He just collected $50,000 worth of prizes from a mail-order catalog.

"I still can't hardly believe it, but, by golly, I've got this beautiful new car to prove it," Stockus exclaimed Wednesday with a thump on the steering wheel of the 1981 Ford Granada just delivered by Landmark Ford. "It's too good to be true — but it is true."

The $9,000 car and $5,000 cash topped a long list of prizes received from the New York-based Independent Judging Organization Inc., when declared Stockus the grand prize winner in the United States Purchasing Exchange's "Houseful of Prizes" Sweepstakes.

Stockus, who retired six years ago after a long career with city and state government (he's been Republican precinct committeeman in his North 19th Street neighborhood for 32 years), had sent entries to the contest the past two years. He was first advised of being a "potential" winner in a letter from the firm in November. While most everyone else scoffed, Stockus followed directions and returned the enclosed questionnaire. Another letter arrived three weeks later, confirming he was a winner and listing the prizes.

"I called my wife Joanne at work and read it to her. She made me read it again. She couldn't believe it either," he said.

It wasn't long before delivery trucks started arriving at the Stockus home almost daily. Among other things, they left a washer-dryer set, a color TV, bedroom furniture, range, piano, gas grill and trash compactor.

## REASON TO KICK THE HABIT ~

It's pretty obvious that most business firms in Springfield have a no-nonsense attitude when it comes to shoplifting. Shoplifters, it sometimes appears, are prosecuted more vigorously than bank robbers.

Convictions have been obtained in the local courts against young and old for pilfering the most piddly things: a candy bar . . . a package of Twinkies . . . a two-bit ballpoint pen . . . a can of shaving cream. Even mitigating circumstances are sometimes ignored and the accused is subjected to full-scale prosecution.

Such was the case a few weeks ago when a supermarket, adhering to the company's prosecute-one-and-all policy, pressed charges against a 70-year-old woman. She was accused of stealing a package of cigarettes.

An employee testified in court that he saw the woman put the cigarettes into a shopping cart shortly after entering the supermarket. A few minutes later, he told the court, she removed one cigarette, lit it and put the package in her coat pocket. He kept her under surveillance until she completed her shopping. She paid for $20 worth of groceries at the checkout stand, he said, but never took the cigarettes out of her pocket.

~

Employees confronted her as she left the store, at which time she apologized and offered to pay for the cigarettes.

No dice. She was escorted to a storeroom to await the arrival of police. She was charged with stealing merchandise having a value of 70 cents, excluding tax.

The woman, responding to questions from her attorney, told of having been a regular customer at the supermarket for years. She was trusted, she testified, by other employees who knew her.

A few weeks before her arrest, she recalled, she found herself $1 short of being able to pay for her grocery purchase. The cashier told her to take the extra groceries and pay the difference later. She returned to the store with a dollar the next day.

"I intended to pay for the cigarettes when I picked them up." she testified. "I put them in my pocket out of habit when I smoked one and simply forgot about them."

The judge sided with the defense, finding that the element of intent to commit a crime was lacking. He cautioned the woman to "be more careful" in the future and handed down a verdict of not guilty.

## BINGO! ~

It had been 35 years since a girl at Sacred Heart Academy lost her boyfriend's class ring, but she never forgot. About a month ago, as the old school building was being readied for demolition, she asked Chuck Anderson, job superintendent for R.D. Lawrence Construction Co., to try to find the ring.

She took Anderson right to the spot where the ring had slipped off her finger and dropped through a crack in a wooden stairway when she was a senior back in 1946. He pulled off a board and started looking.

"At first, I found an old penny, a lot spitballs and wads of chewing gum but no ring," Anderson said.

Then, as he was about to give up, he brushed a hunk of lint aside and there was the ring — exactly where the woman told him it would be.

## TALK ABOUT 'HOGGING' THE ROAD! ~

Allen Entwistle had a heck of a time getting his hogs to market the other day. He loaded a pair of 200-pounders into his pickup truck and headed out from his farm near Riverton.

A mile or two later, he realized he should have taken time to put on sideboards. That's when he discovered one hog hanging over the side, scrambling for all it was worth to escape. Entwistle kept driving with one hand, while reaching back with the other, trying to push the hog back into the truck. He was having little success — and then he noticed the other one about to bail out.

He slammed on the brakes, throwing one hog into the side ditch. While he was chasing that one down, the other one jumped out. It was during the morning rush hour and traffic was heavy.

Entwistle finally corralled the animals and got them to the sale barn. He got rid of them there, but not without having to explain why they were so beat up.

## HOSTAGE STANDOFF ~

A baby sitter gave this ultimatum to the mother of a child she was caring for: "No cash — No kid."

A Sangamon County sheriff's deputy responded to a call from the child's mother in Dawson last week. She reported her child was being held hostage until the baby-sitting bill was paid. The deputy met with both parties at the Dawson post office to negotiate a settlement.

The mother had cash in hand. The baby sitter had the child in tow. The exchange was made peacefully.

## FOOD STAMP ACT ~

A tax-paying, working mother of four stared as two young women ahead of her went through the checkout counter at a local supermarket.

One purchased $80 worth of groceries. Large quantities of candy, soft drinks, doughnuts, cookies and popcorn were among the junk foods that accounted for more than half of what she bought. She paid with food stamps. The other woman, outfitted in the most exclusive brand name fashion jeans, bought only $25 worth of groceries. That included a considerable amount of junk foods such as peanuts, candy and cake. She also paid with food stamps. However, she paid cash for a package of cigarettes.

The working mother, of course, paid cash for her groceries — limited to things like bread, milk and meats — and left the store just in time to see one of the food stamp recipients drive away in a late model Buick and the other in a 1979 Cadillac Eldorado.

She got into her old Chevy and drove off in disgust.

## ILLINOIS STATE CIRCUS ~

Balloon-A-Gram received an order to deliver a bouquet of 50 balloons and a 50th birthday card to Rep. Phil Collins while he was on the House floor. A gal decked out in top hat and tux, with the balloons in tow, gave it a good try. But she was refused admittance to the House chambers.

Someone quipped they probably didn't want any more of a circus atmosphere than there already was.

## DON'T TOUCH MY BUNS ~

It was about 7 o'clock Monday morning. Street department aide Scott Denham, who had worked with cleanup crews through the night following the close of LincolnFest, was using his last ounce of strength to clear a Sixth Street gutter of debris. As he started to pick up a half-dozen hot dog buns, a woman leaned out of an upstairs apartment window and yelled at him.

"Hey, you! Leave those alone. They're for the birds."

Denham thought she was, too.

## DISORDER IN THE COURTROOM ~

There was more action than usual in a Sangamon County courtroom when Judge Ben Miller sentenced burglar Robert Spice the other day.

Miller had handed Spice an eight-year prison term and was preparing to

⌐⌐

leave the bench when Spice started scuffling with the two officers whose duty it was to return him to the county jail. A table and several chairs were knocked over as they struggled with their prisoner, trying to apply handcuffs. Miller, concerned that Spice might escape, quickly doffed his robe and rushed to the center of the courtroom to assist the officers. However, they were able to subdue Spice without Miller's help.

As order was restored, Miller climbed back into his robe, reconvened court and sentenced Spice to an additional six months for contempt.

## DEAD LETTER FILE ~
Copies of this bogus letter to Ann Landers are being circulated among state employees:

"Dear Ann,
"I have a big problem. I have two brothers. One works for state government, the other was put to death in the electric chair for murder. Also, my mother died from insanity when I was 3 years old. My two sisters are prostitutes, and my father sells narcotics to grade school students. Recently, I met a girl who was just released from a reformatory where she served time  for smothering her illegitimate child to death, and I want to marry her. My problem: If I marry this girl, should I tell her about my brother who works for the state?"

## FAIR 'FOOD' ~
No one has become more of a fixture at the Illinois State Fair than Gov. Jim Thompson. But there are a few who still don't recognize him. Such was the case when a young man assigned to the fair's security force briefly blocked Thompson's path to the grandstand stage.  He was on his way to present awards to winners of the tractor pull.

"Where's your pass?" the kid asked Thompson.

"I don't have a pass," Thompson admitted.

"How'd you get this far?" the kid pressed.

"He's got a pass," the guv said, pointing to "George," the Hulk-sized state trooper with him.

Then what happened?

"The kid was about 3-foot-2 and George is about 6-foot-7," Thompson said. "George ate him for breakfast."

## CAN'T SAY THAT IN A SALOON ~

Three women from Franklin Life Insurance went to the state fair Tuesday, after stopping in at Franny's Tavern on the way. While in the tavern, Midge Mellinger dropped a quarter. It hit the floor and rolled under some guy's foot.

"Don't anybody move!" she yelled, as she dove to retrieve the coin.

That was a poor choice of words, she quickly realized. For a minute, several people thought it was a holdup.

## DARN IT, ANYWAY! ~

The postman delivered a bill from the Springfield Clinic to the Joe DeMarco residence.

"What's this for?" DeMarco asked his wife as he ripped open the envelope. "We don't owe them."

The bill was for $545.

"Can't be," he said.

Then he read the "services rendered" column.

"Delivery of a baby boy."

"Now I know they've got the wrong guy," sighed DeMarco, who is way into his 70s.

DeMarco, who retired from the Springfield Police Department more than 15 years ago, laughed as he related the story.

"I just wish I owed it," he said.

## KID STUFF ~

A mother was briefing her 9-year-old on the student exchange program and mentioned some of the kids would be from Taiwan. She was interrupted with this enthusiastic declaration: "I know about them. That is where they make everything."

## PAGING SATCH ~

The gold ring awarded to baseball legend Satchel Paige upon his induction into the Hall of Fame 10 years ago was one of several things taken in the burglary of his room at the Downtown Motel here more than two years ago. He didn't expect to see the ring again. But Satch is in for a surprise.

*Satchel Paige*

Police just recovered the ring and turned it over to Redbird baseball team owner A. Ray Smith, who'll see that it gets to Paige in Kansas City.

A northsider, who happened to remember reading a newspaper report of the burglary, saw a man wearing the ring the other day and informed police.

The man, who said he found the ring in his yard more than a year ago, quickly surrendered it to the officers.

## THURSDAY NIGHT LIVE ~

Channel 20 news director Don Hickman opened his 6 o'clock newscast Thursday night with a story on the merger of electronic fund transfer banking systems, touted by the industry as a giant step forward in the banking business. His introduction to the story was to be trailed by, as they say in the electronic media, an on-the-spot report direct from the Statehouse press room.

But, due to a technical goof, it was Hickman who ended up on the spot. Instead of a videotape of the bankers' news conference, the TV screen was filled by a picture of a masked man wielding a gun inside a bank.

Obviously the wrong tape. Back to you, Don.

## SCHOOL DAZE ~

A teacher who'd been having trouble with an unruly boy in her class stopped by the boy's home after school to speak with his parents. The boy greeted her at the door.

"They was here," he told his teacher, "but now they's gone."

"Where," the teacher demanded, "is your grammar?"

"She's taking a nap," he said.

## SHOW BIZ ~

A fresh-baked cake and a supply of cold milk to wash it down was delivered to Prairie Capital Convention Center dressing rooms when the rock band The Tubes arrived for a concert last month. But the band members didn't eat the cake. Instead, their road crew used it and the milk to wash down the dressing room walls. And the ceiling. And the floors.

Supposedly the cake fight was an effort to relieve tension, a way of blowing off steam. Convention center staffers weren't impressed.

Word soon got around that the musicians would have to pay for having the mess cleaned up, so the road crew mopped up the worst of it. Center employees still had to finish the job, and their bill was handed to the concert promoter.

The cake had been requested by the band. They wanted the cake so much, in fact, that it (as well as many other foods and drinks) was part of their contract.

Entertainers usually add such contract riders specifying select food and beverage items. But some rock groups — depending on their popularity — stand alone when it comes to the quality and quantity of their order.

Rocker Christopher Cross, for example, tacked on a three-page list of refreshments and foods to the contract for his August appearance at the convention center. In addition to select food items, including one whole smoked turkey, sliced ham, deli tray, fresh fruits and assorted cheeses (for after-dinner snacks), the band's demands included:

Three cases of soft drinks, two gallons of bottled spring water, 24 bottles Perrier water, three quarts tonic water, three bottles Chenin Blanc wine, three cases Heineken beer, two cases Budweiser, two cases Miller Lite beer, one quart 80 proof vodka, one quart of gin, three gallons fresh orange juice, one quart grapefruit juice, one urn of coffee, etc.

Four more cases of beer were ordered for later that night.

## IQ TEST ~

The Rubik Cube have you stumped? Do what one sharp Springfield business executive did.

He toyed with the maddening puzzle for months — without success. Then he left it on his desk overnight.

Next morning he found it in perfect alignment — testimony to brilliant work by the janitor.

## COKE COP ~

The B&G Cafe was the target of an "undercover investigation" conducted by a plainclothes Coca-Cola agent a few weeks ago.

Posing as a customer, the agent ordered a "Coke." He no doubt was able to tell simply by taste that he was served RC or Pepsi instead. But it's believed that — in cloak-and-dagger style — he secured physical evidence and subjected it to laboratory analysis.

Restaurant owner Steve Kapshandy later was approached by a representative of the Coca-Cola company's Atlanta office. He accused Kapshandy of substituting other cola brands when customers ask for Coke.

Kapshandy was lectured on loose use and abuse of the Coke trademark. When people order Coke, they must be served Coca-Cola or told that product is not available and he must so instruct all employees, he was told.

"That's the law . . . you can be sued," Kapshandy quotes the Coke man as saying in a very serious tone.

～

"Well, I think about 90 percent of the people who ask for Coke only want a cola product, don't you?" Kapshandy argued.

"Absolutely not!" the Coke man countered. "They want our product."

Recognizing the odds, Kapshandy apologized and promised to take every step possible to make one thing perfectly clear to his customers — that Coca-Cola isn't available at the B&G.

These two signs are now conspicuous in the restaurant:

"We Are Proud To Announce We Do Not Serve Any Coca-Cola Products!!!"
"We Do Serve Pepsi-Cola and RC Cola."

## DRIVER OF THE YEAR(S) ~
Police stopped a local man for a traffic violation the other day and discovered his driver's license had expired — in 1952.

## SIGN LANGUAGE ~
On the Holiday Inn East marquee: "Welcome Visually Impaired."

# 1982

## BALLOON DETAIL ~

A traffic checkpoint was set up near Bruns and Jefferson, shortly before the magic hour on New Year's Eve. Motorists were checked for their state of sobriety.

Some drivers were asked to display their drivers' licenses. Some were ordered to stand at the roadside and blow up balloons. None were arrested.

That's because those doing the checking apparently weren't law enforcement officers. No one was the wiser at the time, and there were no inquiries or complaints to area police agencies.

## WILD KINGDOM ~

A woman in Laketown was surprised to see an owl perched on the steps at her front door a couple of days ago. It was broad daylight. She noticed it was sharing the steps with a sparrow. How nice, she thought, then she saw feathers flying.

The owl ate the sparrow.

## PAUL 'GOES HOME' ~

The death of a man here a few weeks ago left an indelible mark on residents and employees at Ryerson Center, the rehabilitation facility operated by the Sangamon-Menard Alcoholism & Drugs Council.

His name was Paul. (Ryerson residents refer to each other by first name only.) Like many others at the center, Paul was a transient.

He ran away from home, in Macon, Ga., when he was 15. That was 36 years ago. He drifted from job to job, city to city, working as a truck driver, cabbie and common laborer.

Somewhere along the way, he ran afoul of the law. Something to do with stealing a car. No one seems to know the details, but he admitted serving a long prison hitch.

The brightest spot in his life — the one thing he seemed proud of — was his stint in the movies. He had once been a "walk-on" in Hollywood.

Paul entered Ryerson Center for alcoholism treatment late last year.

"He made a real strong commitment to sobriety," a staff member recalls. "That was most important to him, of course, and he encouraged others."

He successfully completed detoxification and rehabilitation programs and had barely settled in the center's halfway house when a doctor detected cancer. Paul was given two weeks, three at most.

Now, he had one goal. He wanted to make peace with his mother before he died.

Ryerson counselor Mike Brown called the Rev. Eugene Costa. All they had to go on was Paul's family name and that he last saw his mother in Macon in 1945.

A stroke of luck. The first Catholic church Costa called was in the family

～

parish. A priest there located Paul's mother almost immediately. She contacted Ryerson Center.

But in the meantime, Paul's condition had deteriorated rapidly, forcing him from his "home" at Ryerson into a hospital. "Smitty," another Ryerson resident, stayed at his bedside for three days straight — until Paul died.

Paul's mother took him back. She arranged for burial in Macon.

## TOO CLOSE FOR COMFORT ～

Virginia Judge Robert Welch, presiding in the Richard Harrel murder trial at Quincy early this month, thought jurors might have to be sequestered for the night before reaching a verdict, so he ordered a room for each juror set aside at the Hotel Quincy.

But the jury kept at it, yielding a guilty verdict about 2 o'clock in the morning. Welch then announced the hotel accommodations were available and, since jurists would have to return that afternoon to determine whether the death penalty was applicable, he gave them the option of staying at the hotel or going home.

Since most of the jurors were Quincy area residents, they decided to go home for the night. But one woman elected to stay in the hotel rather than travel back and forth to her home at Camp Point. Welch, who was 90 miles from his home, had no choice but to stay overnight.

In reporting the outcome of the trial, a reporter for a Quincy radio station put it this way: "After the jury returned the guilty verdict, a lady juror and Judge Welch spent the night at the Hotel Quincy."

The judge laughed when chided about the startling radio report. But for the record, he and the juror were in separate rooms.

## IT PAYS TO ADVERTISE ～

This offer appeared among State Journal-Register want ads yesterday:

"Post Holes For Sale - Stacked Free - 787-2070." Jim Walker, who placed the ad, was flooded with calls.

⌇

"Sorry, but I'm sold out," he told many callers. "I ran out early this morning."

Walker, who's retired, says he just wanted to "break the monotony" — for anyone who wanted to bite, as well as himself.

## HOT SEAT ~

The announcement of a substitute act — singer Gary Morris for the group Nightstreets — was made just before Morris went on stage for the first show at Sangamon State Univeristy Saturday night. That didn't please a Tammy Wynette fan seated near the back on the main floor.

*Tammy Wynette*

"I oughta go and get my money back right now!" he blurted.

He kept griping. When the time came for Tammy to appear, she didn't. Her entrance was delayed several minutes.

"She ain't here!" the grumbler went on. "I guarantee you she's not here."

About that time, Tammy took the stage. A lengthy hair-drying session was blamed for the delay.

She proceeded to make several introductions from the audience, one being her daughter, Jackie — who was seated next to the guy who'd done all the grumbling.

"Oh, my God!" he sighed, sinking into his seat, as Jackie stood to be recognized.

## HOT DOG! ~

A springer spaniel, family pet at the John Sullivan home, was being ushered to the back door when its extraordinary talent as a hunting dog was discovered. It stopped in the middle of the kitchen and "pointed" a frozen turkey on the countertop.

## COPS CLOWN AROUND ~

A couple of clowns got the raspberries from two men as they stepped into an elevator at the Holiday Inn East late Wednesday night.

Behind the clown faces were Ansar Shriners John Weston and Harold Loveless, part of a troupe that entertained at the Illinois Adult & Continuing Educators Association convention. Weston was dressed as a hobo. Loveless wore an old-time cop uniform.

There were some wisecracks about the the "cop."

"He's a real cop, ya know," Weston told them. "So am I."

"Sure you are," one guy quipped.

At that point, Weston whipped out his badge. He happens to be a U.S. deputy marshal, which his hecklers readily recognized.

"We may look like clowns," Weston told them, "But we're on an undercover operation."

The two guys got off the elevator, convinced they just ran into two peculiarly dressed plainclothes cops at work.

## HOSE LINE ~

A city police officer gave chase when he saw a car run over three fire hoses near McCreery and Clear Lake while firefighters fought the four-alarm fire at Goff Linen Services.

It wasn't the typical police pursuit. The officer was on foot.

He caught the car and ticketed the woman driver. It no doubt added to the excitement of the evening for the gang of kids she had in the car. But she wasn't so impressed. She drove away muttering something like:

"Well! I'll never come to a fire in this city again!"

## KID STUFF ~

Three-year-old Douglas Welk watched closely as neighborhood kids planted a garden. His interest centered on the sowing of carrot seed. He was shown the picture of a cluster of carrots on the package.

"Do you know what these are, Douglas?" Lindsay Neal asked.

"Hot dogs!" he snapped.

## FAMILIAR RINGS ~

A "phony" map making the rounds outlines AT&T's new names for its regional holding companies. New England states fall under "Yankee Bell." Washington, D.C., and surrounding states are designated "Liberty Bell" properties. Southern states form "Southern Belle." Midwestern states are dubbed "Cow Bell." The Plains states comprise the "Sioux Bell" system, Texas and Oklahoma are operated by "Taco Bell" and California-Nevada is "Tinker Bell."

## 'AMMO' MAN ~

A clown walked into Sgt. Larry Buhl's office at Camp Lincoln and handed him a bouquet of 39 balloons. It was his 39th birthday.

Minutes later, the balloons started exploding. They'd been loaded with firecrackers.

All the noise attracted a lot of attention. Buhl happens to be in charge of ammunition.

## FOUL BALL ~

A few nights ago, precisely at midnight, two cars stopped at Fifth and Iles. A teenager, armed with a baseball bat, hopped out of one — a white car with vanity license plates. He took three hard swings, through an open window, at the teenage driver of the other car — a yellow vehicle.

Someone who was watching asks: "Do the parents of these children know they play night baseball?"

## WAY WITH WORDS ~

Exercise maniac Richard Simmons was preparing to go to the Illinois State Fair's Lincoln Stage for his opening show Sunday when he learned a crowd of nearly 3,000 awaited his arrival. He was flabbergasted.

⌐⌐

"Oh, I'm nervous," Simmons blurted. "I'm gonna throw up!"

## TIPPING THE SCALES OF JUSTICE ~

It's no wonder that Clarence Eugene Wilson, acquitted here this week of the 1970 murder of an Oblong police chief — his fifth trial in the case — chose to represent himself in court. (Technically, he was "assisted" by a local attorney on order of the court.)

Wilson, contending all along he was the victim of miscarriages of justice, came away from his fourth trial — in "notoriously corrupt" Williamson County, as he puts it — particularly bitter toward the system, and with a story one might expect to see in the movies.

Recalling his first court appearance there, Wilson says the presiding judge told him: "It takes a little while for the constitutional law to filter down to Williamson County." All pretrial motions by the defendant were then denied, and the judge appointed a public defender of then-questionable character to represent Wilson.

The lawyer dozed throughout the trial, Wilson complained. He was found guilty, but the conviction later was overturned and assigned to Sangamon County for a new trial. It wasn't long after the Williamson County trial that the lawyer who was accused of misrepresenting Wilson there was convicted on felony drug charges and sentenced to prison.

## ANTI-SMOKE WEAPON ~

When a couple of gals sat down to lunch in a local restaurant, a man behind them fired up a cigar. His smoke drifted straight ahead, directly into their faces.

Besides having to put up with foul odor, one woman happened to be allergic to smoke. She decided to fight back. She borrowed a spray bottle of perfume from her companion, pointed it over her shoulder at the smoker and fired.

Apparently the guy got the message. He snuffed the cigar.

Perfume is a very effective weapon, she says. Besides giving the offender a subtle hint, it has a get-even quality. Imagine, she chuckles, what might happen when some guy like that gets home and has to explain the fragrance to his wife.

## BING CROSBY UNEMPLOYED? ~

A suspicious claim for unemployment compensation was filed against Mick & Mary's tavern-restaurant at Thayer. It was the claimant's name that made it suspicious.

He claimed to be Bing Crosby.

"That ridiculous!" said restaurant owner Steve Stanhoven, replying to the state Department of Labor. "Bing Crosby never worked here. His brother Bob didn't, either. But I sure wish they had."

Crosby claimed to have been employed by Stanhoven in early 1981. As soon as Stanhoven received notice of the claim, back in April, he urged the agency to investigate for fraud.

"It was pretty obvious somebody was ripping off the state and me too," he said.

Stanhoven finally received a reply from the state last week. To his astonishment — and the surprise of Labor Department officials — there really is a Bing E. Crosby who qualified for unemployment compensation in Illinois. He once worked in the Joliet area and now resides in Louisiana.

However, Crosby never did work at Mick & Mary's.

The mix-up was traced to an error in the Social Security number of someone else who was once employed by Stanhoven. And the wrong Social Security number turned out to be Crosby's.

The name was definitely suspicious, says a Department of Labor spokesman. But so are a lot of others.

One such name: Richard Pryor. Another: John Doe. Those names appeared recently on the list for unemployment compensation. Funny names, all right, but legitimate.

〜

## SHAGGY DOG TALE ～

A broken dog chain and pry marks on the door of a southwest-side residence enabled a sheriff's detective to draw this scenario:

A burglar was at work late Monday night in the 2900 block of South MacArthur Boulevard. As he tried to pry open a door, the resident's dog, chained in the back yard, detected the intruder and sprang into action. But the dog reached the end of its chain before it reached the burglar.

The chain didn't hold, though. No wonder. The dog weighs in at 142 pounds.

There was no evidence (blood, etc.) to indicate that the dog ever made contact with the guy prying on the door. But it obviously influenced him to leave the job site. Likewise, there's nothing to indicate that the burglar isn't still running for his life, with the big dog in hot pursuit.

Like the burglar, the dog is missing, too.

There's no description of the burglar, but the dog, which answers to the name of "County," looks like this: 2 years old, short, light brown hair with two white-tipped paws, a white-tipped tail, and wearing the proper tags. When standing on his hind legs, he's 5 feet tall.

## THIEF WITH GREEN THUMB ～

It was shortly before dawn's early light. A man, carrying a potted plant, was descending the stairway at a home in the 1000 block of West Monroe. He was spotted by a woman. She ran to phone police. He ran back upstairs and put the plant back where he got it.

Then the police found his car, searched it and found it full of potted plants. "Hot" potted plants.

He was arrested for petty theft. He's been branded the "petty potted plantsnatcher."

## RELAX ABE - IT'S A JOKE ～

NBC-TV "Real People's" Byron Allen, interviewed on the "Today Show" yesterday, singled out one of his favorite film clips from the cast's cross-country train tour this summer. It showed him as a black Abraham Lincoln greeting the big crowd that met the special 25-car Amtrak passenger train in downtown Springfield. Allen shouted to the crowd from the train's rear platform: "Y'all are free!"

## TRAFFIC STOPPER ~

The flashing red lights on a city police car parked along South Sixth Street prompted motorists to slow down. But that wasn't the officer's intent. He was running radar.

It wasn't until after business had slumped for awhile that he realized he'd neglected to turn off his red lights after arresting the last speeder.

## COME ON, OFFICIER, I GOTTA GO! ~

A woman who was pinched for speeding on the city's west side this week found it to be quite a "moving" experience.

The past two days had been perfectly rotten, she said, recounting her bout with flu. She suffered the usual symptoms, diarrhea included. That's why she was in a hurry to get back home Tuesday afternoon.

As she buzzed along West Lawrence, a city policeman clocked her car at 44 mph in a 30 mph zone. He pulled her over.

"I was beside myself," she says. "I didn't have any time to spare. I jumped out and ran back to the police car."

She told the officer she was ill and had to get home fast. And she told him why.

"I've got to get to the bathroom!"

The patrolman asked for her driver's license, then released her. But that didn't end it. He followed her home and waited outside while she raced into the house to attend to more urgent business. When she emerged a few minutes later, he handed her a speeding ticket.

"I didn't deny I was speeding," she says, "but I thought I had about as good of an excuse as anyone could have."

Aware that a lot flimsier excuses are often accepted from speeders, she thinks it was ridiculous to receive a ticket under such circumstances.

She says she really wasn't bluffing. She had been caught in the same predicament the day before, didn't drive fast enough and didn't make it home in time.

## UPON REFLECTION . . . ~

There's a lighter side to just about everything, concludes crime victim Ray Dickerson, the 76-year-old blind man who — along with his 82-year-old wife — was taken to a desolate east-side area and robbed a few weeks ago.

Although he still hasn't fully recovered from the harrowing experience, he's able to joke about one phase of the investigation that followed.

Dickerson, who retired from state government in 1973 after 41 years as a social service worker, didn't give in easily to his assailant. In fact, he didn't give in at all.

It took three or four minutes for the robber, even though he was much younger and stronger than Dickerson, to pry a wallet from Dickerson's clenched fist.

Because of Dickerson's blindness, he obviously couldn't identify the suspect in a police lineup. But one officer asked him if he might be able to point out the robbery by voice recognition.

"No, I'm afraid not," Dickerson said. "But if you let me shake hands with him, I might be able to identify him."

## SHY AND SLY ~

A well-dressed middle-aged couple appeared to be lost in the convention center parking ramp Sunday night. A young man approached and asked if he could be of assistance.

"Well, uh, no," the gentleman replied, still appearing confused.

The young man stood by.

~

"Well, uh, yes," the gent finally said.

The young man asked if he was going to the show (the nude musical "Oh, Calcutta") at the convention center next door.

"Well, uh, ah, uh, yes,"

He proceeded to direct the couple toward an exit, pointing out that was the shortest route.

"Thank you," the man said, leading his female companion in that direction.

However, the young man saw them change course soon after. He watched as the couple turned, walked two blocks south, one block east, then back to the convention center and enter.

## ALL IN THE FAMILY ~
Illinois State Police last week pinched three members of one family for speeding — all in less than three hours and within a couple of miles on the same highway.

Two troopers were assigned to a short stretch of Illinois 127 near Butler in Montgomery County, designated as a high accident rate area. They were using radar.

First, they clocked Nancy Eickhoff driving 64 mph in a 55 mph zone. About 2½ hours later, her brother, Larry Eickhoff, was clocked at 81 mph in the highway's 35 mph zone in Butler. Minutes later, their father, Charles Eickhoff, was stopped for driving 67 mph in a 55 mph zone.

Because of the excessive speed involved, Larry is the only one who will have to appear in court. He says he'll plead guilty, as will his sister and father. "They got us!" he said.

## PRESIDENTIAL CONFIDENTIAL ~
The official announcement of President Ronald Reagan's scheduled trip to Illinois Agriculture Director Larry Werries' farm near Jacksonville next Wednesday didn't come until yesterday. It had been confirmed with key

officials here nearly two weeks ago but, under a threat that the presidential visit would be canceled if word got out too soon, they kept it hush-hush.

Still, word got out.

At about the same time the visit was confirmed, Reagan staffers reserved nearly 50 rooms at the Holiday Inn in Jacksonville. The mere fact that the reservations were made for the "White House" let the cat out of the bag. There was an unofficial announcement of the president's coming to motel bar patrons that night.

## McBURGER INC. ~
Dorothy McDonald owns "Having Second Thoughts On Clothes," a consignment shop on South Second Street. And the manager of the shop is Joan Hamburger.

## WHERE THERE'S SMOKE ~
A teacher walked into a girl's restroom at Springfield High School and saw cigarette smoke drifting from one stall. Confident she had caught a student breaking the school's cardinal rule against smoking, she marched up to the door and barked: "All right, you, come out of there!"

The door opened slightly.

"It's just me," whined the young woman inside, who happened to be a teacher.

(Postscript: Restrooms in all Springfield public schools are "No Smoking" zones. In fact, students aren't permitted to smoke anywhere in a school building or even on school grounds. Faculty members, however, are allowed to smoke in rooms designated as teacher lounges. This teacher had retreated to the girls' restroom to puff because there was a capacity crowd in the smoke-filled teachers' lounge.)

## SHELL OIL AND 'COAL' CLASH ~
The city lost one of its unofficial historical sites this week.

The Shell Oil Co. closed its gas station at Sixth and South Grand, the

*Shell picketed in Springfield.*

main target of picketing by the defunct Coalition Of Area Labor nearly two years ago. Shell dealer Tom Dietrich said he was unable to renew his lease because the oil company decided he was not selling enough gas.

However, Dietrich said his overall business, which included a considerable amount of automotive repair, was profitable and provided him and his employees with a good living. He had been a Shell dealer for almost 16 years and had operated the station at Sixth and South Grand since 1969.

But his long association with Shell was no concertino.

"I was just a number (to Shell)," he figures. "I had a profitable business, but it wasn't profitable enough so far as Shell is concerned."

Dietrich did have a chance to buy the station, but he couldn't afford Shell's asking price.

Reflecting on Jan. 7, 1981, the day his station was surrounded by 100 COAL pickets, Dietrich says: "They really knocked our socks off."

He, as well as other Shell dealers who saw many of their customers driven away by the pickets over several weeks, sustained substantial losses.

Dietrich never did recoup his loss and, he says, all of the gas customers he lost during COAL's boycott movement did not return. COAL is "partially to blame" for Shell pulling out, he is convinced.

## DRY RUN ~

The emergency medical dispatcher at fire department headquarters received a report of a "man down" on the front porch of a residence at 1101 N. Walnut St. An ambulance was dispatched. So was the fire department's Emergency Squad 1 and Engine Co. 3.

Two minutes later, the first firefighters to reach the scene reported back that the man was A-OK. He wasn't ill. He hadn't fallen. He had laid down to paint a hard-to-reach spot on the porch step.

## BONKERS AT THE BANK ~

A bank with a Playboy bunny? Yep! But it was a "he" in "she" clothing. Mike Hughes, loan officer at Sangamon Bank & Trust, played his role to the hilt: black leotard, pantyhose, wig, bunny ears, bunny tail, etc.

Don't laugh. He tied with three other bank employees for first prize in the Halloween costume contest. Every employee, in fact, dressed up for the bank's haunting observance Friday.

The goal was fourfold: to combat the growing negativism about Halloween; boost employee morale; demonstrate that bankers aren't as stuffy as some people think they are; and, last but not least, entertain the youngsters.

Several teachers at nearby grade school took students to the bank for treats and to show off their costumes.

For the bank, there were big dividends. It was one of the biggest business days ever. Bank officials have already decided to celebrate Halloween again next year.

## COMMUNITY 'DRIVE' ~

It's been more than a year since the fiery crash that nearly took the life of 19-year-old Donna Nieman.

With second- and third-degree burns over nearly half of her body, she was confined to Memorial Medical Center — a long way from her Hillsboro, Ill., home — for six months. Much of that time, she was in critical condition.

Since then, she's been hospitalized off and on for reconstructive surgery on her face and hands. To date, Donna has undergone surgery 38 times, and there will be a lot more over the next several years.

During her earlier hospitalization, she was deluged with get-well cards.

More than 2,000. Time passed, and  hometown response slacked off — until three weeks ago.

That's when "Donna Nieman Day" was declared at Wilma & Bob's Dairy Queen in Hillsboro. Owner Bob Hefley announced he would contribute all proceeds that day to Donna, hoping there would be enough to pay for the "electronic hand" she would need.

It turned out to be the biggest day Helfley's business has ever had. He raised $3,653 — almost twice the goal he set.

"The whole town turned out," said Hefley. "We ran nearly two hours behind on most orders all day long. Most people waited, though. They knew where the money was going."

Donna happened to be back in the hospital that day.

"I kinda thought everyone had probably forgotten by then," she said. "But when I heard about the turnout, I really felt good."

Hefley assures her that no one forgot. He and his wife "wanted to do something" soon after the accident, which occurred less than a block from the DQ, at the edge of  Hillsboro. But, he said, Donna's family asked that he wait until the money could be earmarked for something specific.

"The credit doesn't go to us," Hefley insists. "It goes to the people of Hillsboro."

Despite the facial disfigurement and loss of fingers on both hands, Donna says she feels fortunate to have escaped without injury to her eyes. And she is thankful that she sustained no brain damage from the smoke inhalation.

"I know I was very lucky there," she says. "Doctors don't know to what degree I'll be able to recover use of my hands. But I'm hopeful that future surgery will fully restore my facial features."

Donna doesn't remember anything about the accident.

She was a passenger in a car driven by her boyfriend, Jerry See, now 21 and a senior majoring in medical technology at Southern Illinois University.

A car slammed into the rear of their car, which burst into flames.

At this point, Donna boasts: "I do know this — Jerry saved my life."

He was thrown out on impact, but ran back to the flaming car and pulled Donna out. He suffered minor facial burns in the rescue.

## TERRORIZING A TODDLER ~

It was shortly after midnight when a man leaving the Town & Country Bowling Lanes spotted a 2-year-old girl walking around the parking lot. It was cold and damp out. She was "petrified," the man said.

Assuming he had found a lost child, he approached to take her in tow. But a man and woman, identifying themselves as the little girl's parents, suddenly appeared.

Turned out she wasn't lost. She was being "disciplined," the parents said. They explained they had pretended to leave her there.

"We wanted to make her think we were gone," they said, adding — get this — they were "teaching her a lesson."

## BOAT DOC(K)TOR ~

There's a guy on the west side of town who has a kayak. The other night, he decided to perform some year-end maintenance.

Since it was a little chilly outdoors, he carted the kayak into the living room. It was close quarters — the kayak measured 16 feet long and the living room 17 feet.

Not long after he went to work, he ran into trouble. He got half of himself stuck inside the kayak.

Some time later, his wife returned home to find the big orange fiberglass boat in the living room, the beam from a flashlight bouncing around the inside and a pair of legs hanging out. She tried to help her husband wiggle out. No luck.

She suggested Vaseline. Forget that, he said. Too messy.

She suggested calling the fire department. No way. He didn't want the embarrassment of having firefighters pry him out of his own boat.

He twisted. She pulled. He wiggled. She tugged. Finally, they hit the right combination and out he came.

"Don't tell anybody about this," he told her.

## NEVER-NEVER LAND ~

The first-grade class at Concordia Lutheran School, along with teacher Pam Billotte, toured the Executive Mansion the other day. Six-year-old Michael Hovey gave his mother a full report: "Mom," he blurted, "the governor must really be rich. He's got the biggest Christmas tree I ever saw, bigger than dad's truck (a semi).

"The lady told us about a dumb waiter. You know, a man who fixes breakfast and gets on the elevator and takes it to the governor.

"Boy, was that a neat place," he went on. "Steve Adams wants to know if the governor mows his own grass! They also got a dog named 'Guff.' "

Mrs. Hovey interrupted: "You mean Guv?" (The dog is named Guv.)

"Well," Michael replied, "whatever his name is don't matter 'cause he looks like Lassie to me."

# 1983

## ANIMAL CRACKER ~

Amid fears that some hunter couldn't resist blasting one of the albino deer at Sangchris State Park during the past hunting season, there also was concern that the rare animals might simply be accidentally shot. The fact that some hunters shoot at anything that moves revived a story about a couple of guys who mistook farm animals for deer a few years ago.

When one of them attempted to register the "deer" he bagged, conservation officers couldn't believe their eyes. He had shot a goat — not a deer. He didn't know the difference.

Neither did his hunting buddy. He shot a goat, too.

## HORSE LAFF ~

The "littering" problem confronting the Springfield Police Department's mounted patrol really hit home the other night.

A squad car pulled up outside the convention center as the governor's inaugural ball got into full swing.

The door opened and out stepped Field Commander Don McCarty. McCarty quickly realized he wasn't on solid ground. Then he spied the mounted patrol, standing guard nearby. Immediately, McCarty knew what he'd stepped in.

He won't soon forget it, either. Fellow officers won't let him.

One, for instance, keeps reminding McCarty that he now stands out in the department because he's the only guy with one green shoe.

## BON APPETIT ~
It just happens to be the name of a cook at a local restaurant, but when a waitress sends an order to the kitchen, she hollers, "Order up, Chuck!"

## FOLLOW THAT T-SHIRT ~
Springfield police broadcast an alert for a man wanted for aggravated assault Thursday. According to description details, he's the kind of a guy who should stand out in a crowd.

He was last seen wearing orange pants and a blue T-shirt bearing this declaration: "I'd Rather Eat Cow Chips Than Listen To Country Music."

## HIZZONOR RIDES IN STYLE ~
A Lincoln Continental spotted on Springfield streets the other day was conspicuous with its "M" license plates, which identified the car as belonging to a municipality.

That municipality is Colp, Ill., a village of only 280 population located a few miles west of Carbondale. Behind the wheel was Frank Caliper, mayor of the town. How can a small town afford to furnish its mayor with a luxury car?

"We've got a lot of money down here," Caliper barked. "And my village board gives me what I want!"

But he hastened to add: "I'm just kidding."

The car is registered to the village, Caliper said, but he hinted that it wasn't purchased with taxpayers' money. Although he declined to be more specific, he declared the arrangement is "legitimate." He's sure of that, he says, because people have questioned it before and "it's all been checked out."

Colp is the "richest little city" in Illinois, Caliper declares. He isn't kidding about that. The village has no indebtedness and has a surplus of $50,000 in the treasury. Caliper says that was achieved by "doing our own work on things."

For instance, if there's a water line problem, he fixes it. He's a plumber. The town saves in other ways. Caliper is Colp's one-man police force.

He admits the town isn't as prosperous as it used to be. A number of coal mines have closed. Until recently, Colp had nine taverns. Only two remain. That's resulted in a considerable loss in sales tax revenue, and the village has lost the liquor license fees.

There's one thing Caliper is particularly proud of. Never has Colp applied for a federal grant.

"We accept revenue sharing money, but we don't want anything else from the federal government," Caliper says. "We don't want the federal government getting a hold on us."

Caliper has been mayor of Colp for 48 years. He claims the distinction of being the youngest man ever elected mayor in Illinois. Now, at age 72, he's preparing to retire at the end of this term. That will give him 50 years in office and, he hopes, a mention in the Guinness Book of Records.

## TAKES HIS WIFE EVERYWHERE ~

A man standing on the corner of Sixth and Jefferson flagged down a police car and asked Patrolman Ron Pickford for a ride. But first, he said, he wanted to pick up his wife at the bus depot.

"She's in my suitcase," he told Pickford.

He went on to explain that she had passed on and was cremated. Her ashes were in a box, and the box was in the suitcase.

⌒

Later at the bus depot, the man picked up the suitcase and "introduced" Pickford to his wife. He recalled how his wife didn't like to travel when she was alive.

"But I take her everywhere now," he said, "and she don't complain at all."

## MAIL BAG ~

From Stephen Cullison of Hillsboro: "Regarding the village of Colp and its mayor, as a former assistant state's attorney of Williamson County where Colp is located, I could not help but be amused. It (Colp) is probably the most proverty-stricken, rundown town I have seen in the state of Illinois.

"Colp originally started out many years ago in the days of 'Bloody Williamson County,' when blacks were not allowed to live in the other coal mining towns. When the owners of the old Colp No. 9 mine brought in blacks to attempt to break the United Mine Workers, they had to build a company town for them to live in, since they were not allowed to even set foot in nearby towns. Although the Colp No. 9 mine has been closed for many years, the village and its remnants remain. A majority of the population of Colp are descendants of those Negro coal miners who were brought in to break the United Mine Workers union.

"Although the town was once famous throughout southern Illinois for its many bars, clubs and other risque establishments, there are now only about two taverns and not even a gas station left. Many of the houses are deserted. Many others do not appear to have been painted since Frank Caliper first became mayor. Most of the streets are unpaved, just made of dirt, gravel or cinders. There appears to be virtually no city services whatsoever.

"Although Caliper claims to be a one-man police force, in my 2½ years with the Williamson County state's attorney's office, I never knew of him to take any action whatsoever in the capacity of a policeman.

"The village of Colp apparently cannot even afford to gravel the streets, let alone buy a vehicle for the mayor."

## COLD-BLOODED GUNMEN ~

The two gunmen who robbed the religious book store on the city's east side Wednesday were disappointed when the cash register yielded only about $200. That's when they decided to rob Berean Book Store employees and customers. They were less than polite.

"Let's kill everybody right now!" one told the other.

There were pleas for mercy;

"Oh, no, no, no."

"Please, oh no."

"Oh, don't do that."

One employee, 72-year-old Anna Simpson, apparently didn't move fast enough when ordered to walk around a counter and join others who were being held at gunpoint. One man aimed his gun at the floor and fired.

The bullet ricocheted and struck her in the right leg. Despite the wound, which fractured a bone, she remained on her feet until after the gunmen fled minutes later.

## NAKED CITY? ~
A police radio dispatcher sent a patrolman to a Springfield home Wednesday with some very interesting instructions.

"Stand by while a woman removes her clothes," the officer was told.

He radioed back, asking the dispatcher if she meant for him to stand by while the woman removed personal property from the residence. He got a big 10-4 on that.

## HEAT OF DEBATE ~
Sometimes state legislators talk too fast and loose. A sampling:

State Sen. Leroy Lemke of Chicago recently argued the merits of a bill that would make certain statements by rape victims inadmissible at trial. Making some statements privileged, Lemke contended, would make it difficult to determine the "truth and velocity" of the witness.

Sen. Adeline Geo-Karis of Zion slipped while boosting her bill to disallow psychiatric exams for rape victims. Such exams are unfair, she argued, "because they aren't required of robbery victims, or of burglary victims, or of murder victims."

*Illinois General Assembly.*

## TO PEEL OR NOT TO PEEL ~

They're a bit thin-skinned at the Illinois Department of Revenue when it comes to strip-o-grams.

A verbal memo sent through the ranks at the tax processing center last week put employees on alert, although many interpreted it as an order banning the "baring" of congratulatory messages. However, a department spokesman called it "a verbal recommendation to discourage" the activity.

Actually, few strip-o-grams have been delivered in Revenue offices, but it's said they have proved "disruptive or embarrassing."

Balloon-grams are something else, and apparently tolerable. But if employees persist in ordering strip-o-grams, an official ban will probably be imposed.

The spokesman, pointing out that such carryings-on don't project a proper image of the department, puts its this way: What would grim citizens think if they walked in to pay their taxes and saw revenue employees watching a strip show?

(For one thing, they might think the stripper was just another hard-pressed taxpayer giving the tax collector the shirt off her back.)

## NO FISH STORY ~

There's been many a snake in the grass, but this one was in Mark Butchek's pants.

Twelve-year-old Mark was with his dad, Mike, at a fishing hole near Salisbury, Ill., the other day, when something took his attention from the business at hand.

"A-a-a-a snake!" Mark said.

As he ran to Mark's aid, Mike picked up a brick to use as a weapon. But he saw no sign of the snake. It had already slithered back into the pond, Mark told him, and none too soon.

Mark had been sitting on the bank when the snake climbed onto his shoe, under his pants cuff and up his leg. Mark didn't move a muscle. The snake stopped at his knee, made a U-turn and crawled out.

## QUOTABLE ~
Longtime WVEM deejay and dance band emcee Bill Lawrence, who died Tuesday, always left his listeners with this:

"The road to success is always under construction."

## AD LIBS ~
• Gov. Jim Thompson says he's mad at state legislators. Welcome to the crowd, guv.
• But legislators are just trying to put Thompson's tax increase in a pretty package. That's not an easy task. How do you gift-wrap a turkey?
• Thompson has threatened to keep the legislature in session all summer. That's cruel and unusual punishment — for Springfield.
• They're only trying to preserve Abraham Lincoln's laundry woman's house now. But more historical goodies are just around the corner. Who did Abe's ironing? Who darned his socks? Who mowed his lawn? Where did they live and can their homes be designated historical sites?

## NEWS TRAVELS ~
A central Illinois woman, who was in Alabama a couple of weeks ago, found a Springfield dateline on a story in The Huntsville Times. The headline on the story read: "Salons Get Down To Bare Essentials."

She figured she'd catch up on the latest action in the Illinois legislature. The governor and honchos in the legislature had held a closed-door meeting. Then, she was shocked to read, it wasn't really a meeting. It was more of a "smoker." The state's top officials went into hiding to receive a strip-o-gram.

"Actually, I was surprised to hear our elected officials were working so hard," she quipped.

## I'VE WON? OH, SURE! ~
One of the millions of people who have responded to clearinghouse sweepstakes come-ons is George Tapscott's wife. In fact, she put his name on one of her entries.

Like most everyone else, they figured they'd never win. Then, the phone rang at the Tapscott home in Pleasant Plains a few weeks ago.

A woman asked Tapscott if he had any plans for the week of June 24. He said no. She said that was good because he'd have to make a trip to New York to pick up the $100,000 cash prize he'd won in the sweepstakes.

There was silence.

"Are you still there, Mr. Tapscott?" she asked.

"Yeah," he replied, "and a herd of buffalo just went through my back yard."

"You really don't believe this, do you?" the woman pressed.

"Do you believe me about the buffalo?" Tapscott retorted.

"No," she said."

"You just answered both questions," Tapscott fired back.

The woman continued her pitch, instructing Tapscott to be prepared to be picked up by limousine at a specified time, fly to New York and be escorted to the firm's office to collect his winnings. Although he thought the whole thing sounded perfectly legitimate, Tapscott remained unconvinced.

Then, the appointed time came and went. No limousine. Tapscott says he made no preparations to go to New York, but "I was at home and could have been ready to go in a few minutes."

"I wasn't believing a word of it," he says, "but at the same time, it was something you couldn't really ignore. I'll tell you this, my neighbors who had heard about it were a lot more enthusiastic than I was."

Just like Tapscott suspected all along, the phone call was a prank. He's learned the sweepstakes promoter doesn't notify winners by telephone. They send letters via registered mail. He's also learned he's one of many victims of such prank calls.

"I've never won anything like that," he says. "I'd certainly like to, though."

Tapscott, who runs a trucking business at Pleasant Plains, admits he had visions of being able to retire on the $100,000. But he'll just keep on truckin'.

## WATCH FOR FALLING . . . ~

Stories about kids falling from the top of bunk beds are legendary. So, when 7-year-old Tim Stuckey went to a church camp at Lake Springfield last week, his mother made sure he got a bottom bunk. Her logic backfired, though.

The kid on the top bunk, who was older and bigger than Tim, fell out. Tim was sitting on the concrete floor, tying his shoe. The other kid landed on top of him. Tim went home early — with a broken ankle.

## LITTLE DARLINGS ~

A 2-year-old bailed out of his stroller in a store at White Oaks Mall. His mother forced him back in.

"You dingbat!" he yelled at her. "You dumbbell!"

That startled another kid in his mom's tow nearby.

"What's a dingbat?" he asked excitedly. "What's a dumbbell?"

∽

## AD LIBS ~
You know it's hot when:

- Dogs don't get within 2 feet of fire hydrants.
- "Brown-out" describes lawn color instead of a power outage.
- The golf course is vacant at 1 o'clock in the afternoon.
- You only have to mow the lawn every six weeks.
- Ice water is considered an entree.

## GREATEST WASTE ON EARTH! ~
There's more to a circus than always meets the eye, although it some-times meets the nose. Manure, for instance. And 21 elephants plus scores of other animals leave Ringling Brothers with a heap of that — more than 20,000 cubic yards a year.

But the task of disposal has been simplified. Ringling gives away most of it. Free! First-come, first-served. Just take your bag, bucket, tub or pick-up truck to the animal compound.

This is no ordinary stuff. Circus publicist Art Ricker touts it as "mineral-rich, premium-quality fertilizer." After all, he says, it comes from animals on a rich and varied diet, consisting not only of hay and grains, but apples, carrots and other vegetables, too.

"Circus manure is pure and unadulterated," says Ricker, resorting to ringmaster jargon. "Generated in gargantuan proportions by the quadruped performers of The Greatest Show On Earth."

## EYEWITNESS NEWS ~
Sangamon State University professor Bill Miller was lecturing his public affairs reporting class the other day when a masked gunman burst into the classroom, a small conference room in the Stratton Office Building.

Students were startled. No cause for alarm on Miller's part, though. It was his annual surprise exercise for students, testing their knack for observing and reporting action firsthand.

He's been pulling the prank for 10 years with never a hitch. But this time, it backfired. As the holdup man demanded that Miller hand over his wallet, and pretended to take a poke at him, Miller lost his balance and fell to the floor. Instant pain. Something had snapped.

The assailant ran out the door with two students in hot pursuit. By the time Miller could scramble to his feet and dash into the hallway to call the thing off (fortunately, he'd alerted secretary of state security guards of the hoax in advance), someone was calling for police and an ambulance. The gunman (it was a toy pistol, of course) was Luke Carey of the Statehouse information service staff, who holed up in an adjoining room until things calmed down. Miller cracked a rib.

## PLEASE DON'T SQUEEZE . . . ~

The Springfield School Board got hung up on a delicate matter Monday night, and it wasn't teacher contract negotiations. It was toilet paper. What brand to buy was the question at hand.

A lengthy debate centered on the price quoted by the current supplier and the merits of that product's durability. Board members strained for the proper words to describe certain failures that have been experienced.

Samples were actually passed around the room for touch tests. That prompted a variety of wisecracks.

One spectator suggested the school district chuck it all and equip restrooms with Sears catalogs.

The proposal by the current supplier — $16,000 for T-paper and paper towels — ultimately was accepted.

## FLASHLIGHT MAKES GREAT CLUB ~

There's a refreshing twist to a local crime story first reported last January. That's when a 75-year-old woman clubbed a burglar over the head with a flashlight, then stood guard over the intruder until police arrived.

Since the man had broken into a home, he was charged with residential burglary, the recently enacted felony that carries a mandatory 4-year prison term. A second felony charge, criminal damage to property over $300 was added because of the damage he did to two doors.

⌒

Evidence presented at his preliminary hearing a few days later established probable cause for the charges, and his trial date was set. But the case was continued three times by defense motions, then again by the state. Finally, a bench trial just ended.

The state's case in a nutshell: The victim was awakened at 1 a.m. when an alarm on the front door sounded. She grabbed her flashlight, confronted the burglar in the living room and ordered him out of the house. When he didn't obey, she beat on his head with the flashlight until he fell to the floor. ("I don't know how many times I hit him," she says, "but enough that it ruined my flashlight.") She then pushed him out the door and phoned police, who found the guy on the front porch.

"Not guilty," said Circuit Judge Jerry Rhodes, in ruling on the residential burglary charge. However, he did find the defendant guilty on an amended count of criminal damage "under" $300.

Oh, yes, there was an additional penalty. Rhodes ordered the defendant to go out and buy the best flashlight he could find for the woman. He did.

## LOTTO (PIGEON) FEVER ~

A bird in the garage — especially one that picks winning lottery numbers — is worth cleaning up after. So says the Springfield man who lets his pigeon do the picking when he plays the weekly Lotto game.

Upon being promised anonymity, he explained his believe-it-or-not Lotto system. (His request to remain nameless stems from a deep-seated fear of being bombarded with inquiries from other lottery hopefuls demanding to know which numbers his bird picks.)

It all began the day he met the pigeon, which he found grounded on a south-side street several weeks ago. One wing was broken. He took it home and put it in a cage. And he talked to it.

"If I hit the Lotto tonight," he told the pigeon, "I'll name you Lotto."

He hit for $21, so he started calling the bird Lotto. Then he came up with the "pigeon system" — putting two bingo-like boards on the garage floor, at the bird's disposal, you might say. A few days later, he does a little scraping. BINGO!! The magic numbers appear. He plays them in the next lotto game.

"Hit the hot ones!" he keeps telling the pigeon.

The bird has yet to make the guy a millionaire. But he has won several small prizes, including $35 for selecting four of six Lotto numbers in one game. To date, the bird is credited with winning a total of $373.

POSTSCRIPT: While the guy doesn't want his name published, he is willing to disclose that he's employed by Illinois Bell.

"You can just refer to me as a ding-a-ling at the phone company," he says.

## TEACHING HISTORY —BY MEMORY ~

A festive mood prevailed at Lincoln Land Community College Friday. Students and faculty threw a party in celebration of Amanda Hahn's birthday. She's been a student at LLCC several years.

Birthdays usually don't get such recognition, but Amanda happens to be special. She is 83 years old.

A couple of years ago, she earned a teacher's aide certificate. She's taking two classes — art and American history — this semester.

Amanda isn't just recognized as the oldest student on campus. Her personal contributions in the classroom have proven invaluable to classmates, as well as instructors.

Take the time Halley's comet was being discussed in one class. She remembered when it was last seen — in 1910 — and gave an "I Was There" account.

On another occasion, in a history class, the topic was World War I. She recalled having lived through that historical period. Amanda gave a firsthand account of the day that war ended in 1918, and how people on the homefront reacted.

"She just loves this place (LLCC)," said one student. "And we feel the same about her."

~

## SOAP SUDS ~

A group of elderly women panicked when the lights went out in their neighborhood Tuesday afternoon. Not because they're afraid of the dark — because their television programs were knocked out.

One woman, in her 80s, grabbed the phone and aired the group's frustrations to this corner:

"We just got through watching 'Days of Our Lives' and were ready for 'Another World' when the lights went out. Here we sit with no television. Now we don't know who's sleeping with who. We're losing out on our sex life."

## GET YOUR GOAT, DEAR? ~

The deer check station at Hillsboro, Ill., turned in this report the other day: 96 bucks, 54 does, 1 goat.

True, swear eyewitnesses at the police-fire station in the Montgomery County seat, where Department of Conservation employees set up shop. Some guy brought in a goat he'd shot.

Not true, says DOC's Richard Andrews, who heads the central Illinois region for deer counts. He says it sounds like "beer talk" to him. Although Andrews admits he can't prove it didn't happen, he'd bet it didn't.

This story surfaces every year, he says. It has some hunter shooting a cow, a donkey or a goat. Usually, it's some dummy from Chicago.

No, Hillsboro sources counter, it happened. This guy, whoever he was, hauled in the carcass and reported it as a deer kill.

The goat did have horns, which the hunter probably mistook for antlers. But no question about it, they say, the guy was convinced he'd bagged a deer.

## HOW TO FIGHT TAXES: ~

One of the thousands who protested tax assessments to the Sangamon County Board of Review in recent months called it a "frustrating and unrewarding" experience.

He says he was told his home was assessed higher than similar homes in the neighborhood because it was "exceptionally well kept." That prompted him to take pen in hand. He composed this list of guidelines that, he thinks, should foil the assessor every time:

1) Never paint the exterior of your home. Nothing beats peeling paint for giving that unkempt look that is so necessary in avoiding an excessive assessment.

2) Allow your lawn to grow into weeds. A few tin cans carefully placed among the weeds will give just the right decorative touch.

3) Give attention to the little details that give the impression of a run-down property:
      Place cardboard over an unbroken window pane.
      A rusting appliance on the front porch adds a nice touch.
      An automobile without wheels and windows in the front yard is the ultimate statement.

4) Enlist the support of your neighbors.
      With a bit of community effort, you may be able to downgrade the whole neighborhood enough to qualify for urban renewal.

Only in this way can you fight a system that encourages deterioration and then uses tax monies for rehabilitation.

# 1984

## TAXPAYER BITES TAX COLLECTOR ~

It's a financial loss, but a moral win, for Lee Bormann who fought Big Brother in the courts for more than six years. That $1,000 he's getting in an out-of-court settlement won't begin to compensate Bormann for his time off the job, travel expenses and legal fees incurred in his challenge of the method that Sangamon County used in collecting delinquent property taxes. He's satisfied, though.

"I made my point," says Bormann, "I thought the county overstepped its bounds and denied me my constitutional rights. I think it's obvious I was right all along."

Bormann began battle in 1977 when then-county Treasurer Fred Tomlin sent a raiding party to Bormann's south-side home to either collect delinquent property taxes or seize personal property in lieu of payment. Bormann, contesting the tax as unconstitutional, refused to pay. He also refused to unlock his garage and hand over the keys to his automobile, which was parked inside. That did it — the raid was on!

As the raiding party swung into action, Bormann grabbed his home movie camera and started recording the action. A friend picked up the sound with a tape recorder.

A sheriff's deputy pried the lock off the garage door. A tow truck was used to pull the car out, then haul it away.

"I see this as a grave injustice to everyone," Bormann declared at the time. He then announced he would file a lawsuit.

"He's got no chance at all," said Tomlin. "I think our collection program is legally right."

But, Tomlin added: "It takes a courageous man to test the system."

Bormann — acting as his own attorney — filed suit in federal court, contending the seizure of his car was illegal because the raiding party carried a warrant issued by a tax official — not a judge. Eighteen months later, U.S. District Judge J. Waldo Ackerman ruled Bormann essentially was right.

Then, nearly a year later, Ackerman ruled that the county officials who were defendants to the suit did not intentionally or recklessly violate Bormann's rights; therefore, they wouldn't have to pay the hefty punitive damages he sought. Bormann, still acting as his own attorney, pursued the case to the U.S. District Court of Appeals in Chicago. He lost.

Then, in 1982, he filed an amended suit in federal court here, seeking damages from the county itself. As that case neared trial, he hired an attorney, a settlement was negotiated and the county board — while contending the county admits no liability — approved payment this week.

## KIDS WHO CARED ~

Helping a friend with a flat tire cost Eleanor Auerbach her purse. A kid ran up and grabbed it from the front seat of her car. It contained $21, her driver's license and other valuables. She chased the thief for four blocks, then lost him.

That was three weeks ago. Neither the purse nor its contents have been recovered.

A few days ago, someone stole her billfold at St. Joseph School, where Auerbach, a widow, is employed in the maintenance department. She lost only $4 this time, but the new driver's license she'd just been issued was in the billfold.

Then came good fortune — on Friday the 13th, oddly enough.

First, Auerbach was informed that a student at McClernand School nearby had found her new driver's license and returned it.

Then she was called before a group of St. Joseph students and presented $118.75, which had been donated by the student body. The collection was suggested by students David Holmin, Robert Kavish and Paul Rapps to reimburse Auerbach for her losses and as an expression of concern to a dedicated school employee and friend.

"We heard about the two crimes in three weeks," one student told her, "and we thought that was just too much."

"I was so surprised," Auerbach said later. "I didn't know what to say. So I just cried."

## STREETS OF SPRINGFIELD ~

Three drivers stopped at Second and Edwards streets to permit a man to cross last Wednesday during the noon hour. As the man walked across, a pickup truck passed the stopped vehicles on the right side.

When the driver of the truck spotted the pedestrian, he hit his brakes, went into a skid and hit the man. As the pedestrian rolled about 20 feet along the street, the truck jumped the curb and came to a stop.

The pedestrian scrambled to his feet, picked up his hat and walked over to the truck. He shook hands with the driver and walked away.

## AD LIBS ~

• Heeeeeeere's "Nicorette!" the new nicotine chewing gum for smokers. They say the gum is pretty effective — but it's hard to light.
• Biggest drawback appears to be its peppery, spicy taste — kinda like chewing old cigar butts.

⌒

• It comes in buff-colored, flat squares. Yes, it's the world's first nude gum.

## ROVING EYES ~

It was love at first sight. But not true love. After all, the lady doing the ogling happens to be happily married.

She was in a checkout lane at a local supermarket when, as she tells the story to friends (hubby, too), she noticed the man ahead of her. Tall, extremely handsome, immaculately dressed, an absolute knockout, according to her.

She really gave him the eye — both barrels. (So did the cashier.)

She followed his every move as he picked up his groceries and strolled to the door. She quickly paid for her purchases and sprinted to the door, thinking she might catch one more glimpse of her Prince Charming in the parking lot.

Just as she started out the door, she realized she'd forgotten something: her groceries. She rushed back to the checkout counter.

"You really went for that guy, didn't you?" the young woman behind the counter teased.

"I've never seen such a handsome son-of-a-gun," the woman blurted.

"I felt the same way," the cashier confessed, "but I couldn't leave my cash register to go after him."

## FULL 'MOON' ~

Two men were traveling along Ninth Street, near Carpenter, during the wee hours when another car pulled alongside. Two young men in that car, apparently itching for a fight, started yelling at the others.

The men in the first car tried to ignore their agitators. But, as they neared Adams Street, one guy in the other car backed his backside out the window and "mooned" them.

∽

The guy barely had time to hoist his pants before he was arrested for disorderly conduct.

The moral of this story is: It's not nice to insult two plainclothes police detectives.

## POTSHOT ~

Taking cover behind his parked car during a sniper attack Monday afternoon on Douglas Avenue was John Reilly's reaction to a shot he heard — not a shot he felt. Although the force of one rifle bullet spun him around, it was a half-hour later before Reilly realized he was wounded.

"Boy, I was lucky," Reilly exclaimed later. "But I feel so sorry for that young man and his family. To think, he was only 18 years old."

Reilly, who retired 10 years ago as City Water, Light and Power's real estate superintendent, spotted the gunman as soon as the shot rang out.

"I saw the gun sticking out the window and it was aimed right at me," Reilly said. "Seeing that made me think one thing: Oswald!

"I ducked down fast. I figured he was going to shoot again. I don't think he did, though."

Reilly waited until he saw the gunman pull in his rifle and close the window. Then he rushed into his elderly mother's home, a couple of doors from where the sniper was holed up.

It was there, when he took off his coat, that he saw the blood. As he was assisted by a police officer, he realized he'd just had a close brush with death.

He would have taken the bullet in the chest if it hadn't been for a comb in his left shirt pocket. It deflected off the comb and grazed his left arm. About 20 stitches were required to close the gash.

Reilly says he's none the worse for wear and warns his golfing buddies he'll be back on the links soon. But he expects to be allotted an appropriate handicap — say, one stroke per stitch.

## POLICE STORY ~

The state trooper who narrowly escaped death at the hands of his kidnapper Sunday forgot something when he left home for work that morning. His gun. But Trooper Craig Hudson realized his holster was empty by the time he checked in at district headquarters. So he didn't go unarmed for long.

Trooper Terry Ward, duty officer at the state police post that morning, loaned his gun — a 9mm automatic model that is standard issue to all troopers — to Hudson. Conversation between the two touched on the fact that "nothing much was going on" (typical for a Sunday morning), and Ward suggested Hudson return home and get his gun.

In the meantime, the post received a report of a stalled car on the Lake Springfield bridge, a short distance away. Hudson was directed to assist the motorist before going home.

Within a few minutes, Hudson had helped the motorist restart his car and was directing him back into I-55 traffic lanes when he saw a pickup truck run off the highway and slam into another stalled car nearby. Thinking the driver was either drunk or had suffered a heart attack, Hudson immediately radioed for assistance and ran toward the truck to render aid.

As he reached the truck, a door flew open and a man, later identified as a 26-year-old Springfield resident, jumped out and aimed a .45-caliber automatic at the trooper. He held the gun against Hudson's head. It was loaded and cocked. Hudson was forced into his squad car and ordered to drive to St. Louis. The guy later lowered his gun, but Hudson, whose borrowed weapon was still in his holster, was unable to draw. But after he turned onto the entrance road to the state police command post, the guy raised his gun again. Hudson grabbed for it and there was a shot.

It barely missed the trooper's head.

Hudson told of "feeling" the bullet fly past his face. It hit the driver's side of the windshield.

In the ensuing scuffle, Hudson got his assailant's gun, removed the clip and threw both across the road. Seconds later, the trooper found himself staring down the barrel of another gun and went for his gun. The would-be kidnapper put his gun back in the waistband of his trousers.

Meanwhile, since Ward was the only other trooper within a reasonable distance, he had responded to Hudson's call for assistance at the accident scene. He reached the scene quickly, but found no trace of Hudson's squad car. Then he recalled having seen a state police car going across the interchange bridge seconds earlier. Ward turned across the median and sped back. When he caught up with Hudson's squad car, the two were scuffling.

Ward fired one shot from his shotgun — his handgun, of course, had been loaned out. He fired that blast into the ground, not at the gunman. Then he joined Hudson in trying to take the guy into custody.

Three other officers arrived soon after. And it took all five to subdue the wild man, who police said was armed with three guns and four knives.

## AD LIB ~
How about that radio weather forecast Monday?

"From 6 to 12 inches of snow."

That's like predicting a temperature range of "from 20 to 80 degrees."

## GATOR COUNTRY ~
Alligators have been spotted on the city's southeast side — at Humphrey's Meat Market, to be exact. They're not on the loose — they're in the meat case. It's in answer to requests from customers, says Elsie Humphrey.

"Seems like a lot of folks all of a sudden have developed a taste for alligator. It's fresh from Louisiana," he says, "completely dressed and ready to cook."

How do you cook an alligator?

"Very carefully," Humphrey jokes. (Actually, alligator meat is cooked similarly to chicken.)

## OFFICER'S LAST SHIFT ~

The police radio crackled this message about 9 o'clock Thursday night:

"Sangamon — 209. Chalk me up. I'm 10-8, 10-41."

It was Pleasant Plains Police Chief L.G. Roberts, in his usual cheery voice, telling the Sangamon County sheriff's dispatcher he was "in service" and "on duty." Less than an hour later, another officer discovered Roberts dead in his squad car, parked along a Pleasant Plains road. His death was attributed to a heart attack.

*Pleasant Plains Police Chief*
*L. G. Roberts*

Roberts, 54, has long been dubbed the "Pistol-Packin' Preacher." Besides being the police chief, he ministered at Richland Baptist Church.

The personable Roberts was well known for his own style of communicating, too.

For instance, Roberts had a standard reply to police radio dispatchers who would ask if he needed a backup after he had stopped a vehicle.

"No, thanks," Roberts would radio back, "Ol' Bessie (his service pistol) and me will take care of it."

## COMMUNITY CARE ~

Thanks to several west central Illinois businesses and individuals, funeral expenses for the Walter Johnson family will be minimal. And, because of a huge public response to last week's tragic fire, those costs have already been covered. As expressions of "sympathy and courtesy" over the deaths of the two Johnson children:

— Aunt Pam's Flowers of New Berlin provided a floral arrangement for the casket.
— Henry Whitehurst-Menard Livery of Petersburg provided the hearse.
— Lockett Ford of Ashland provided transportation for the family.
— Wanda Huff of Virginia provided music for the funeral.

— Harry Lee Campbell of Virginia charged half the usual fee for a grave opening.
— Bill Buren at Perfection Vault Co. in Woodson contributed labor and equipment.
— Facilities and staff services were donated by Massie Memorial Home at Ashland.
— The Rev. Norman Downs, pastor of Ashland Church of Christ, assisted the family throughout the week, then conducted the funeral.

Quantities of food, clothing and household furnishings have been collected for the family. And nearly $7,000 in cash — donated by hundreds of people in several central Illinois counties — has been sent to Contact Ministries for the Johnsons.

## VCR GOES BANANAS ~

The harried mother of four preschoolers attempted to slide a cassette into the family video recorder. She made several attempts. Each time the recorder spit out the cassette. One look into the recorder told her why the cassette was unacceptable. A banana was in the way.

Yes, a banana. A real banana. And, by this time, a smashed, mushy, rotten banana.

She knows one of the kids put it in there, but she doesn't know which one. Nobody will squeal. Fearing the worst, she rushed to Young's Inc. to see if the recorder could be salvaged. Turned out it only needed a good cleaning. However, the banana was a total loss.

"It's funny now," she says, "and I can laugh about it. But I was furious when I found that gooey mess."

Something else helped calm her down. She heard about someone else's kids who stuffed caramels into a video recorder, and they melted. That one was beyond repair.

## HOT AGENDA ~

This week's session of the Sangamon County Board could be referred to loosely as a "strip-a-thon." No one needs to be reminded that the board entertained — and passed — the tough anti-nudity ordinance. But that was just one of three "strip" actions. The board also heard, and denied, a zoning petition that would have permitted a privately operated airstrip near Dawson. And there was another zoning request from John Weiss who operates a woodworking business at New City. It passed. Part of Weiss's handy work is "stripping" furniture.

## QUOTABLE ~
Word had just come down that Congress voted against prayer in public schools, and WGN's Uncle Bobby Collins declared:

"Well, kids, that means that if they catch you on your knees in the class-room, you'd better be shootin' craps!"

## GOOD NEIGHBOR ~
A man who shouted and beat on the back door of a near-north-side home the other night frightened the daylights out of a woman who happened to be alone at home at the time. She feared the worst: that he was trying to break in.

She called police first, then a neighbor. She told the neighbor what was happening and asked him to turn on his floodlights. He assured her he would do more than that.

"I'm coming right over," he told her.

The neighbor loaded his shotgun, stuck a loaded .38 in his pocket and ran out the door. But by the time he got there, two squad cars had already arrived. And officers already had the intruder in tow, leading him around the house. The neighbor decided to make his presence known to the offi-cers anyway and, in what he terms "a spirit of camaraderie," he walked up to them. That was a big mistake.

Playing their flashlights on him, police ordered him to drop the shotgun. He suddenly found himself spread-eagled against a fence. He told them he had a gun in his pocket and he was relieved of it, too.

Then came the questions:

Why was he running around with guns?

〜

"I was going to help my neighbor," he told them.

Trying to take the law into his own hands?

"No," he countered, adding he was merely trying to help a neighbor who was in danger.

One of the officers snapped back with something like, "I can't stand that — somebody taking the law into their own hands."

"You're not listening to my side of the story," he argued.

"I'm going to arrest you," the officer declared.

"This is like something you'd see on television!" he sighed in disbelief.

He was handcuffed and hustled to a squad car for the trip downtown.

Meanwhile, the real troublemaker was turned loose.

He had convinced police he was only seeking refuge in the woman's house. He claimed to have been running from four other men who had accused him of slashing the tires on their car a couple of blocks away. He said he didn't.

Police charged the friendly neighborhood defender with unlawful use of weapons and jailed him. He was bailed out soon after by a relative.

Figuring he'd never be able to make his point with police, he hired a lawyer and prepared to fight the charges in court. But, some weeks later, after he told a close friend of his scrape with the law, someone called it to the attention of police brass. Deciding the whole thing was an "overreaction" by the arresting officers, a police department official asked the state's attorney's office to take appropriate action.

Charges were dropped.

## CAROUSEL GOVERNMENT 〜
It was like getting off a merry-go-round. That's how Judy Edwards of Girard felt when she retired from Illinois state government Friday. She

worked for 21 years in what is now known as the Department of Central Management Services.

Nothing seemed to stand still during that time. For one thing, her division shuffled from one department to another — four times in two decades — from the Department of Transportation to Department of General Services to Department of Administrative Services to the present agency, CMS. Most, if not all of the maneuvering, was attributed to "cost cutting" measures.

Then there was the telephone, or telephones. Although her office phone number remained virtually the same until 1979, when her division moved from Third and Ash streets to the Stratton Office Building, it has since been changed 13 times. That includes five changes in the past two months.

"And all that," she says, "was in the same office."

Edwards not only had to keep up with agency name changes and play musical telephone numbers, she also had to keep track of immediate bosses. She counted 27 in the 21 years. And 22 of them came and went in only 14 years.

## 'SEIZER'S' PALACE ~

The palatial new Illinois Department of Revenue building — which carries a $69.9 million price tag — will boast many luxuries: a huge glassed-in courtyard, a tropical garden, a waterfall, an indoor stream, $633,215 worth of landscaping, etc. But an art collection costing $250,000 is apt to get the most attention.

The focal point of that is a giant aluminum sculpture, a creation of Northern Illinois University professor Bruce White. (It's already in position, inside the main entrance.)

White calls it a whale. However, others fail to see any resemblance and are calling it other things, and not in the complimentary department.

White's work of art did cost a whale of a lot, though — $100,000.
That left $150,000 for assorted pieces of art.

Incidentally, the state has a formula to determine the amount of such expenditures: one-half of 1 per cent of the total construction cost. And art work is acquired only for "suitable" structures. For the taxpayers, fortunately, such facilities as prisons, parking ramps and maintenance sheds do not qualify.

Another "luxury" for the building is still in the planning stage and, so far, hasn't been mentioned. That's a day-care center for children of Department of Revenue employees.

## OPEN HOUSE CLOSED ~

A lot of hard work and long days by Allan and Shirley Katz went into redecorating a house on Winch Lane that they're going to sell. By the time they finished late last Sunday morning, and were ready for an open house that afternoon, they were exhausted.

Shortly before noon, they retreated to their motor home, parked in the driveway, to freshen up. Shirley decided she would take a short snooze. Allan assured her he would stay awake.

Several hours later, she awoke and found him asleep. It was after 5 o'clock, and their open house was history. They don't know if they had any buyers or not.

## MINUTE QUIZ ~

Illinois legislators levied the soda pop tax because:

(a) It's a good way to penalize downstaters for not living in Chicago.
(b) They suddenly realized uncola was untaxed.
(c) They know kids guzzle plenty of pop, and their philosophy is that little squirts should pay taxes, too.
(d) There's nothing else left to tax.

## GO DIRECTLY TO JAIL ~

A policeman stopped a car near 17th and Ash streets last Saturday morning. After questioning the driver briefly, he radioed for another squad car. Minutes later, the motorist was handcuffed, locked in a police car and taken to jail. Then came the routine booking procedure: search, mug shots, fingerprinting, the works.

⌢

Another criminal taken off the streets? Not quite.

The motorist, 19-year-old Julie Fisher of rural Rochester, was jailed on two petty traffic charges — speeding and driving on an expired driver's license. Now, back to the scene of the crime.

Julie, on her way to work at a south-side supermarket, was stopped for speeding. She was clocked at 41 mph in a 30 mph zone. She doesn't contest that.

Then the officer asked for her driver's license. She discovered she had left it at home. He checked secretary of state records and learned it had expired July 10. That was news to Julie. She explained that her billfold (her driver's license was in it) was stolen last year and that she was issued a new license. She assumed that license would be good for three years. Now she knows it was only a duplicate and carried the same expiration date as the original.

That, the officer decided, was serious enough to put her in jail. So, off she went to the "graybar hotel."

Nearly an hour later, after being booked, she called her boyfriend. He went to the jail and posted the $50 cash bond required for her release. Meanwhile, her mother had received two phone calls from her employer who wanted to know why Julie had not reported for work.

"I told them she was on the way," Mary Ann Fisher said, "but it really scared me when they called the second time. I could imagine the terrible things that could have happened. I was frantic."

She drove into Springfield, following Julie's usual route, and found her car abandoned on Ash Street. She finally talked to a man across the street who saw police stop her daughter. He told her Julie had been taken to jail.

"She isn't a criminal," Mrs. Fisher said. "She was speeding. Her driver's license had expired, but she didn't know it. I can't understand why it's necessary to put someone in jail for that.

"I'm sure this is a discretionary thing as far as the officer is concerned. He sure went to the extreme."

## CONSCIENCE CLEARED ~
A guilty conscience plagued Harry Moody for 52 years. No more.

Moody, a 77-year-old retired Springfieldian, had gone to Los Angeles that many years ago. It was 1932. He had just graduated from the University of Illinois. It was during the Depression, of course, and Moody had no hope for employment. It was also the year of the summer Olympics in L.A., and he wanted to take in some of those events in the worst way. But he was short on money.

He had only $18 in his pocket. An adult ticket cost $12. A child's ticket was $8. Moody decided to fudge a bit . . . er, uh, economize. He slipped in on a child's ticket.

"I felt guilty about it then," he admitted the other day. "And I've felt guilty all these years."

Then, a few weeks ago, Moody and his wife returned to L.A. for a vacation. It was time for the Olympics again. He was outside the Coliseum and saw Jessie Owens' daughter carry in the torch for the opening ceremonies.

That was a "real thrill," he says. "I'd seen her father in several of his gold medal events."

Of course, Moody's guilt over his venture to the 1932 Olympics peaked again. But then he happened to catch L.A. Mayor Tom Bradley in a television interview, and heard Bradley admit he climbed over the fence to get into the Olympics the same year. Bradley, 14 years old at the time, didn't even pay.

"I decided right there that I don't need to feel guilty any more," Moody says. "Not after hearing him admit to that."

## QUOTABLE ~
An elderly gent answered a knock at the door. It was a young woman.

"I'm collecting for the Lord," she declared, shaking a contribution can under his nose. "Can you give $5, brother? Remember, this is for the Lord."

The old fellow dug into his billfold and extracted a five-spot. He handed it to the woman.

"Bless you," she sighed. "I'll take this to the Lord."

Her donor had second thoughts.

"Just a minute, young lady," he said. "How old are you?"

"I'm 19," she answered.

The old man grabbed the $5 bill out of her hand.

"Well, I'm 87," he said. "I'm bound to see the Lord before you do, so I'll just give it to Him myself."

## SHOW STOPPER (LITERALLY) ~

The state fair Grandstand stage apparently isn't the most appropriate place in the world for a legislative function — particularly when several thousand country music fans are there, waiting for the legendary Willie Nelson to perform. That's the impression drawn from crowd response last Thursday night when the "warm-up" act turned out to be Jim Thompson and The Statehouse Boys.

Thompson, who had been holding the bill exempting pickup trucks from safety inspections for a ceremonious signing, took to the stage with other state officials minutes prior to Willie's entrance. It didn't turn out to be the historic occasion the governor probably dreamed it would be.

"How many of you own pickup trucks?" Thompson bellowed to the crowd.

There was only a slight buzz among Willie fans.

"Do you think it's fair that cars don't have to be inspected but your pick-ups do?" the governor pressed.

Again, there was some mumbling from the audience. A few yelled "Hell, no!"

"Well," Thompson shouted into the microphone, "would you like to do something about it?"

Outside of a "Hell, yes!" here and there, reaction was still cool.

Finally, Thompson signed the bill. He quickly introduced Secretary of State Jim Edgar and accompanying legislators, then split.

By this time, there was considerable crowd reaction. Booing.

Like somebody said, it's a good thing Thompson confronted Willie Nelson fans, not a Hank Williams Jr. crowd.

## COURT DAZE ~

A "flasher" drove around a west-side neighborhood where several schools are located one day last winter. But he ended up flashing the wrong person — an off-duty city police officer. He was arrested for indecent exposure. The case didn't go to trial until this week.

Defense attorney Mike Costello told the jury in closing argument there wasn't a shred of evidence that his client was guilty.

State's Attorney Bill Roberts, who handled the prosecution, summed up the evidence by reciting a Latin phrase he recalled from law school days. Then, before realizing just how applicable it was to the defense, he gave jurors this translation: "The thing speaks for itself."

Evidently so. Guilty as charged, said the jury.

## AD LIBS ~

• The EPA will hold a hearing here on the ban of leaded gasoline. Don't miss it, folks. It isn't often that government proposes to get the lead out.
• The hearing will be held at city hall. As long as they're there, they might as well kill two birds with one stone and ban hot air, too.

## WATCH THE SPEED LIMIT ~

A middle-aged man staggered into city police headquarters Saturday night. Gesturing toward the parking lot across the street, he asked the desk sergeant if his car would be safe there. Explaining that he once had been convicted of drunk driving, he declared he was too drunk to drive that night.

⌣

Stumbling toward the door, he whirled around with an afterthought.

"Can I be arrested for walking home drunk?" he asked.

"Only if you go over 30," the sergeant replied.

## WHERE'S THE FIRE? ~

Jeweler Pat Shaughnessy was driving down 11th Street, on his way to work, when he spotted a fire. He stopped and ran into Lu's Home Tavern, grabbed a pay phone and dialed the operator. He asked her to relay his call to 911.

"Where are you?" she asked.

"On 11th Street," Shaughnessy replied. "No," she countered, "I mean what city are you in?" (She was in Champaign.)

When he was switched to the 911 operator, Shaughnessy told her a house in the 1200 block of South 11th Street was on fire.

"What kind of structure is it?" she asked.

"Well," he responded, "it's a two-story now — but if you don't hurry up, it'll be a one-story."

## STREET SEEN ~

A sign on the back of a garbage truck in Springfield proclaimed: "YOUR GARBAGE IS OUR BREAD & BUTTER."

## CAT TALE ~

A woman stopped off at city hall to pay her utility bill Wednesday. But she didn't have the bill with her.

"Where is your bill?" a CWLP cashier asked as the woman offered her money.

"Oh, I didn't bring it," she replied.

She proceeded to explain how it had slipped off a table, onto the floor and that her cat — well, let's just say her cat is paper-trained and simply did what it thought it should do. And, in this case, the paper was the utility bill. The cashier laughed.

"If you don't believe me," the woman snapped, "I'll bring it in so you can smell it."

The cashier assured her that would not be necessary.

## ODE TO LEAVES ~

The continuing saga of leaf burning in Springfield inspired a reader, who prefers to remain anonymous, to pen this verse. Sing it to the hit tune, "To All the Girls I've Loved Before" (apologies to Willie and Julio, of course):

"To All the Leaves I've Burned Before"

To all the leaves I've burned before,
I can't burn them anymore
It's been such a drag
To put them in a bag
To all the leaves I've burned before.

To all the leaves I've burned before,
I put them in my bottom drawer
If burning them was wrong
I dedicate this song
To all the leaves I've burned before.

The winds of change are always blowing,
And ev'ry time the leaves stay
The winds of change continue blowing
But they won't blow them away.

To all the leaves I've burned before,
I won't bag them anymore
I'll fill the air with smoke
And make my neighbors choke
To all the leaves I've burned before.

# 1985

## RONALD REAGAN'S 'FOREMAN' ~

The story about Jacksonville Mayor Helen Foreman being one of President Ronald Reagan's high school teachers at Dixon has received national play in recent weeks. First noted in a State Journal-Register feature article last November, after Foreman was appointed mayor at age 80, the story later circulated via Associated Press wires. It then caught Reagan's eye, and he responded with a letter to Foreman this week.

"I'd like to say I taught her about everything she knows but, since she was one of my high school teachers in Dixon, just the reverse is true," Reagan wrote.

Foreman taught biology at Dixon in the mid-1920s. Reagan was in one of her classes.

"I taught him biology in the year of the evo-

*Jacksonville Mayor Helen Foreman*

lution trial in Tennessee (1925)," she said in the SJ-R story. "When I see these clips of Reagan telling his crowd that evolution is just a theory, it's straight out of what I had to say.

"I was not so much older than Ronald Reagan when I taught him."

Foreman graduated from college only a few months before starting her Dixon teaching job in 1925.

"If he (Reagan) can run the country," she summed up, "I can run a small city."

Besides fame, the AP story has proven beneficial to her current campaign for election. She's receiving campaign contributions from fascinated readers across the country.

## CHICKEN REEL ~

Buckhart tavern owner David Stover is still reeling from the nationwide publicity his "Chicken Bleep Contest" attracted last week. "Needless to say, I was taken aback," says Stover, who was still being pursued by the media over the weekend. (He even had a call from the David Letterman show.) "It really got out of hand," he said.

At first, when columnist Mike Royko penned a moving tribute to the fowl game of chance (a chicken did its business on a number board and patrons wagered nickels and dimes on which numbers it "bombed"), Stover saw the humor. But when the question of illegal gaming activity cropped up, and the Sangamon County Sheriff's Department started asking questions, he decided things had gone too far. Stover says he was "really disappointed" when the media started playing that angle.

"The last thing I wanted was for people to think I was running a gambling joint," Stover said. "It was just good clean fun. And besides that, it ended nearly two years ago."

He's convinced the deputies he had contact with weren't too concerned, noting that some good-natured puns were exchanged during their meeting."

"I'm sure they didn't consider it any big deal."

In retrospect, Stover thinks the real story has gone untold.

"The story is that we're preserving a little history here," Stover says. "Even though it's an old falling-down building, my tavern and the little town is a picture of rural America past."

Buckhart, a small crossroads community several miles east of Rochester, and only 1 mile west of the Christian County line, claims only two other commercial interests (the elevator and the Buckhart Sand & Gravel Co.), and about a dozen homes. The tavern building, which originally housed a hardware store-gas station, is more than 100 years old. After evolving into a grocery store, it became a tavern.

"Sometimes, some of our customers bring their fiddles, banjos and guitars. We just sit around and pick — and tell lies."

Stover says the chicken gimmick was simply something for patrons to have fun with.

"No one ever put down more than a quarter, and we always paid out twice as much in prizes as we took in."

Stover says he called a halt to it when his lawyer told him that, technically, he probably was violating some law. Now, after the publicity blitz, Stover might reconsider the whole thing.

"I'm thinking about bringing the chickens back, if I can be sure that however we do it will be within the confines of the law," Stover says. "We'll have to wait and see, though."

Meanwhile, he's preparing to build a new tavern, next door to the present building. When it's ready for business, he'll tear down the old building, which he says is beyond repair. But, whether or not he brings back the Chicken Bleep Contest, he plans to capitalize on its notoriety.

"My new tavern will resemble a big chicken house, and I may put a giant chicken sculpture out front," Stover says. "I'm not sure about the name, but I may call it the Buckhart Chicken Ranch."

## THE HOOPER BLOOPER ~

A cigar-smoking, smooth-talking, middle-aged gent — saying he was out to buy prime farmland — pulled a fast one on several Springfield real estate agents before he blew town.

He scored a hit at one realty office after introducing himself as Mr. Hooper. (He told other Realtors he was Mr. Hill.) He asked to see a farm that had been advertised in the newspaper that day. It was pointed out that the farm was 60 miles away, in Montgomery County, and that it was being advertised for private sale by owner. Besides, it was dark outdoors, and he wouldn't be able to see anything at night. The man persisted. Friends in Hot Springs, Ark., where he claimed his horses are stabled, had highly recommended the realty firm. Swinging his briefcase, he demanded immediate attention.

"He was not well-dressed at all," the saleswoman recalls, "but he did have an awfully nice-looking briefcase."

So she called a male associate and explained the situation. He suggested she send the man to his office.

"I can't go to his office," the guy said flatly. "I'm driving a truck and it's dirty. It stinks real bad."

Both realty agents had already detected a peculiar odor to the whole thing, but decided to string along — especially after the guy dropped the name of a prominent St. Louis attorney and said he was prepared to write a check if they could agree on a purchase price that night.

An appointment for a late-night showing was made with the farm owner. Then the two realty agents and their client climbed into a Lincoln Continental and took off for Hillsboro.

The man talked all the way — about raising horses, having been a truck driver, his experiences in the U.S. Navy, his wife's access to government surplus, etc. But he talked most about his horses, and how some of them were racing that very night. He suggested they might like to place a bet on one of them.

Thanks, but no thanks, the realty agents said.

They stopped at a Hillsboro restaurant for a quick dinner and the man excused himself to make a phone call to a racetrack. He returned minutes later with good news: His horse had won the last race and made him $2,000 richer.

There was still time to bet on the sixth race, he told them. He'd phone in the bets. All they had to do was place their bets with him. It was too good to pass up, the agents decided. One bet $10 and the other bet $40.

Then on to meet the farm owner. A purchase price was agreed on. Arrangements were made to draw up a contract the next day.

Returning to Springfield about midnight, the agents offered to drive their client to his hotel. He declined, saying he'd hop out at their office, where his truck was parked. But there was no truck in sight.

That put the agents on renewed alert.

The man got out of the car and hurried off — on foot — toward a motel a couple of blocks away.

When it came time to close the deal the next morning, Mr. Hooper didn't show up. It was later learned he had checked out of the motel bright and early that morning. And he appeared to be leaving town — in a hurry.

"I don't know what he got out of the others," sighed the local saleswoman, "but, boy, did we get clipped! He took us for 50 bucks, dinner and a round trip to Hillsboro."

## END OF THE LINE ~

There was a long noon-hour line at the cashier's stand in the cafeteria at the Illinois Department of Transportation. But that didn't intimidate one young DOT executive.

He marched to the head of the line and handed her his money.

"You'll have to go to the end of the line," she told him.

He insisted that she take the money.

〜

"No," she said, "you must get in line like everyone else."

Still, he protested: "Apparently you don't know who I am!"

"Yes," she countered, "I know who you are and you have to go to the end of the line."

She won out. He went to the end of the line and waited his turn. The cashier won cheers from scores of DOT employees.

"I wonder where she's working now?" someone asked, assuming she was axed for inhumane treatment of a stuffed shirt.

Never fear. She's still cashiering in the DOT cafeteria. She is employed by a catering firm that runs the food operation there, and she doesn't have to play the game.

## SYMPHONYGOERS 'SPANKED' ~

You could not have heard a pin drop when the Springfield Symphony Orchestra began playing after the intermission at Sangamon State University auditorium the other night. There was too much whispering, coughing and shuffling in the audience.

After playing a few bars, conductor Kenneth Keisler froze his baton. Suddenly, the hall became deadly silent. He laid his baton on the music stand and turned to confront the audience.

"I mean not to offend," Kiesler said to the startled crowd, "but this is a very quiet piece of music and I must have quiet!"

While many concertgoers stared at each other in disbelief or puzzlement, he made an about-face, raised his baton and, after waiting a good 30 seconds, continued. One symphony fan summed it up this way: "He conducted both the orchestra — and the crowd — very well."

*Kenneth Kiesler*

## AD LIBS ~

• PCB-tainted fish have been found in Lake Springfield, confirming reports about night anglers catching channel catfish that glow in the dark.

• The fish have only themselves to blame. They shouldn't have been drinking the water.

• Health officials warn people not to eat carp from the lake if it weighs more than 10 pounds. No problem. What you can't chew, you can't eat.

## TALK INTO MY TIE ~

In the early 1950s, WTAX radio carried a locally produced feature called "The Hidden Microphone." Bill Miller, now a professor at Sangamon State University, was the man behind that mike. (Actually, the mike was concealed behind Miller's tie.)

It's the 1950s at WTAX again, periodically over the next several weeks. Morning man Bruce Bagg is replaying some of the old Miller tapes.

Miller, in true Allen "Candid Camera" Funt tradition, would hide a mike under this tie, run the cord down his pant leg and hook up to a tape recorder manned by an engineer some distance away. (Yes, Virginia, that was pre-Electronic Age.) Miller mostly preyed on merchants.

A clerk at Pease's candy shop was among his victims. He captured some prize comments while proceeding to sample virtual-

*Bill Miller at WTAX in 1950s.*

ly every kind of candy in stock. He devoured nearly a pound of candy that day.

He once put on a shoe repairman by introducing himself as a political candidate, asking the cobbler to "wear down" the soles of his new shoes so they would resemble those worn by presidential candidate Adlai Stevenson.

⌇

"We had a lot of fun," Miller recalls, hastening to add that he did get himself into some tight spots.

One such situation occurred when Miller strolled into the old Senate Theater at matinee time. He found only a couple of people in the whole theater. One, a man, occupied an aisle seat. Telling the man that was his favorite seat, Miller asked him to move over. He did.

Then an accomplice of Miller's sat next to the man on the other side. As they passed popcorn back and forth to each other, whispered and annoyed the guy every way they could think of, he jumped out of his seat.

"What's your game, anyway, mister?" he demanded, convincing both pranksters that he was ready to take them on.

Miller's accomplice whipped out a $5 bill and suggested the guy enjoy some more movies on them.

"All I want is my 64 cents back!" he shouted.

Miller drew a lasting impression.

"I'll never forget that the price of a matinee movie back then was 64 cents," he laughs.

It was all for naught. That skit was never aired. Miller wasn't able to obtain a signed release.

"We couldn't have aired it anyway," Miller says, "because of all the foul language the guy used."

The series was extremely popular, but ran little more than a year. By that time, Miller was finding it difficult to sneak up on anyone. He — or his voice — was recognized too easily.

But the thing that really put "The Hidden Microphone" out of business was a new law enacted in Illinois: the law against electronic eavesdropping.

～

## HERZZONER'S WIT ～

"Good Morning America" host David Hartman interviewed Jacksonville Mayor Helen Foreman about her Reagan connection. Did she ever think he would grow up to become president?

"No," said the mayor. "He was a perfectly normal, bright kid who was more interested in sports and getting the lead in the high school play."

And, was age a political issue in the 80-year-old Foreman's campaign for election?

"I handled that rather neatly, I thought," she said. "I used the same response Reagan used — that I did not hold the youth of my opponent against him." She found Hartman a "really nice person" who is familiar with central Illinois. (His wife is Maureen Downey, a 1962 graduate of Springfield's Sacred Heart Academy.)

"They treated me royally, and I had great fun," the mayor says of her brief stay in New York City. "I rode around in a limousine all the time.

"I was getting to think how nice it would be if the city would get me one here. But I'll pass on that. Our budget couldn't stand it, and my conscience wouldn't let me."

## KID STUFF ～

A member of the younger generation has a name for those automatic bank teller machines. He calls 'em "money pukers."

## STATE OF CONFUSION ～

The first batch of "Build Illinois" lapel buttons — hundreds of 'em — are hot off the punch press, but too hot to handle. All have been rejected. It's not that the product was inferior. It's the manufacturer's stamp on the back of the buttons that didn't sell.

That inscription: "Made in Indiana."

Agreeing with aides that you can't build Illinois by having things made in another state, Gov. Jim Thompson ordered the foreign-made goods dumped and new buttons ordered from an Illinois manufacturer.

The order was originally placed with an Illinois firm, but that company subcontracted the job to an Indiana corporation.

## LOTTERY WINNER LOSES ~

A Riverton man has been playing Lotto since the game began. Faithfully, week after week, he checked off the same combination of Lotto numbers. He never missed a game. When the winning Lotto numbers were announced a few weeks ago, he knew he'd finally done it. His lucky numbers came up. He called everyone he could think of to give them the good news. But he spoke too soon. Later in the day, he discovered he hadn't won. His numbers were drawn, all right, but there was no way he'd get the jackpot. He didn't get a Lotto ticket that week.

Here's what happened.

Since he had been ill, he gave his Lotto numbers to his son and asked him to pick up the ticket for him. But his son, the story goes, didn't go straight to a lottery ticket agent. By the time he did get there, he forgot which numbers his father told him to play.

He substituted his own numbers. Needless to say, they weren't the right ones.

His father reportedly has just about recovered — as well as forgiven — but he's still reluctant to talk about it. And he prefers to remain anonymous.

He didn't give up on Lotto, though. He's still playing the same "lucky" numbers every week.

## ROBIN HOOD TERRITORY ~

The new "Sherwood Forest" theme just adopted for Hillsboro's city campgrounds leaves no stone unturned.

In carrying out the theme, the lake patrol has been dubbed the Sheriff of Nottingham's Posse and the eatery is Maid Marian's Canteen. Roads, walkways and other facilities on the grounds are being named for Robin Hood's men.

Guess what they named the toilets? "Little Johns."

## MANSION 'SMOKER'? ~
A belly dancer in the Executive Mansion? What's going on in there?

Questions like that have been popping up since The State Journal-Register reported that a belly dancer's costume was stolen out of a truck while the dancer performed in the mansion Sunday night.

But don't get excited folks. Belly dancing isn't a nightly event at Gov. Jim Thompson's official residence. It happened to be Greek Night. It's a big bash, held annually at the mansion. A band and the belly dancer, all from St. Louis, provided the entertainment. A thief broke into their equipment van outside and made off with her costume.

One more question that's come up:

If she was dancing in the mansion at the time her costume was stolen, what was she wearing? Another costume, of course. She had a spare.

## LEAVE IT TO SENATOR SAM ~
A bit of dubious wit popped up on the Senate floor in the waning hours of the Illinois legislative session. Sen. Charles Chew was introducing an Abraham Lincoln look-alike. He was extolling all of the Great Emancipator's virtues, how he freed the slaves, etc.

Sen. Sam Vadalabene interrupted to quiz the Lincoln character:

"Mr. Lincoln," he drawled, "do you think, that if you'd have met Charles Chew, you would have freed those slaves?"

## OH, BOY! OH, BOY! ~
It was some birthday cake that was delivered to Springfield insurance agent H. B. Hollis' office Thursday, in observance of his 79th. (He's been in business 54 years.) One of his insured, Mary Ann Brammer, baked the cake in the shape of a bikini-clad, shapely miss.

"It's something else," Hollis exclaimed, "I've never seen anything like it. It's too nice to cut."

Hollis took it home and put it in his freezer.

## FIRING LINE ~

One of the amateur marksmen at the Southfork Sportsman's Club's annual shotgun shoot last weekend was a strait-laced telephone company employee. He blasted away 10 times at the clay pigeons. He missed every time.

An instructor offered assistance. Comparing the shotgun to a garden hose, he explained that it was important to "lead" the target.

"Squirt the water ahead of the target," he said.

The guy said he understood.

"OK," the instructor said, "from now on, for all practical purposes, your shotgun is a garden hose."

Resorting to that method, the guy fired three more blasts. He missed again. He turned to the instructor and said with a poker face: "I'm not doing any better with this hose than I did with the shotgun."

## SAFETY 'PEN' ~

A Springfield woman bemoans the seat belt law with rhyme.

No matter what
Your size or cup,
The law says you
Must buckle up.
The shoulder strap
I struggle into
Lifts and separates like
No bra could ever do.
Pregnant I
Must never be
For then this belt would never
Reach 'round me.
Seat belts are not made
For the plump and stout,
By the time I get in
It's time to get out!

## MOUTHS OF BABES ~

Just like Art Linkletter has always said: Kids say the darndest things. But when it happens to be Gov. Jim Thompson's 7-year-old daughter Samantha doing the talking, and the subject is the Illinois State Fair — something near and dear to the guv — the utterings are priceless. Samantha spoke her mind on opening day at the fair when WSSR-FM reporter Tara McClellan spotted her alone in the governor's limousine, parked near the radio station's remote headquarters on the fairgrounds. Going through channels, McClellan obtained permission from the governor, then embarked on a lively interview.

Selected excerpts as broadcast:

"Where's your mom?" McClellan asked .

"She's up in Chicago — working," Samantha replied (like her dad doesn't).

"What food do you like best at the fair?"

"I brought my lunch today, so I don't know." Samantha said.

"What did you think about the Chinese exhibits?"

"I didn't go in 'em because they're always boring. Every year they're boring. Even with the talking robots they're boring!"

"What are you and your dad going to do today, go on some of the rides?"

"Uh-huh. We're going to go on all of them — except the ski ride 'cause it's boring! If there's a ride that's really, really fun, that goes upside down and all that stuff, I might go on that five times and get sick."

"Why would you want to do that?"

"I don't know."

## BELTED! ~

One-size seat belt does not fit all, a middle-aged Springfield woman laments.

~

"Mine was designed for someone at least 6 inches taller than my 5-foot-2 frame," she says. "I know because the strap crosses my face.

"Of course I can hook it under my chin so that it presses on my neck and runs up beside my ear. In this position I can't turn my head enough to check traffic as I back out of my driveway, pull out of a parking place or make a turn. Nor can I reach anything on the dashboard.

"One day I released it and the buckle flew up and hit me in the face. Good thing I wasn't wearing my glasses."

Surely, any judge would buy that defense.

## ENTER AT YOUR OWN RISK ~
The report of an open door at a southwest-side residence one night prompted police to investigate. On the chance that a burglar might be at work inside, two officers entered the darkened house. Meanwhile, personnel at police headquarters started tracking down the owner of the home. A few minutes later, the officers radioed back that they were unable to find any intruders. In fact, there was no sign of forced entry. Someone apparently just failed to close the door.

That got a big 10-4 from headquarters, where a dispatcher had just talked to the homeowner, who said the door had been left open on purpose. Seems the house was infested with fleas, forcing the occupants to abandon the place three days earlier.

The officers, who had been in the house for about 20 minutes, looked at each other. Then they looked down.

Both were covered with fleas.

They were ordered to go home immediately, throw their uniforms in the washing machine and take showers. Both squad cars were fumigated. That, and a lot of scratching, did the trick.

## LINCOLN LITTER ~
The Lincoln Home (excuse the expression) "came up" in Johnny Carson's monologue Tuesday night. Picking up on an Associated Press update of

"Project Garbage" — i.e., anthropologists sifting through chicken bones, eggshells, broken dishes and assorted treasures Abraham Lincoln discarded in a well behind his home — Carson quipped that an L. L. Bean catalog was also found there.

Then, noting the garbage would be a little old by now, he said, "Springfield must have a lousy pickup schedule."

The main reason for nosing through Abe's garbage, of course, is to see if it might shed light on his lifestyle in Springfield. Some of the stuff has been sent to laboratories for a thorough going-over. Tests of bone remains and plant matter, for instance, could provide clues about the presidential palate: what cut of meat he preferred (was he a leg man when it came to chicken?), etc.

One project anthropologist, Floyd Mansberger, said he's not repulsed by scrounging through another man's garbage or even his privy. There, he said, you might find stuff that falls out of a man's pockets when he drops his drawers.

"Archaeology," as he puts it, "is the study of garbage."

## AD LIBS ~
Live Aid, Farm Aid, AIDS Aid. Let's not stop now. How about a concert for:

— People who have gas: Rol Aid
— Hired housekeepers: Maid Aid
— Ladies who've chosen the single life: Old Maid Aid
— Squaredancers: Prom-N Aid
— English sailors: Limey Aid
— Unscrupulous used car dealers: Lemon Aid
— Musicians: Band Aid
— Athletes: Ban Roll-On Aid

## DUCK'S REVENGE ~
State Division of Criminal Investigation agent Terry Lucas went duck hunting. He and a buddy shoved off in a boat and waited.

Quack! Quack! Quack! Three ducks approached. Both hunters aimed for

⌣

the sky. Bang! Lucas fired one blast and whirled around to shoot again.

Kerplunk!!

As the kayoed boxer would say, the lights went out. Lucas had scored with his first shot, and the dead duck, plummeting earthward, hit him in the head.

He agrees, he should've *ducked*.

## MORGANNA AND THE COAL MINER ~

A Divernon coal miner had a dream several months ago, and it just came true. Mike Aden, a foreman at Freeman United Coal Company's Crown 2 mine near Litchfield, was thumbing through an old issue of Playboy last spring when he ran across a photo spread of Morganna, better known in the sports world as "The Kissing Bandit." Having just read about USA Today's "sports fantasy" contest, he started dreaming.

His fantasy, Aden decided, was to pitch a major league baseball game. Between pitches, the buxom blonde would run onto the field, throw her arms around him and give him a big kiss.

"I always wondered what goes through these guys' heads when that happens to them," Aden said.

His fantasy won. Aden, 39, was flown to Columbus, Ohio (Morganna's hometown), two weeks ago and told he could live out his fantasy. However, since baseball season was over, the whole thing had to be staged.

Aden suited up in a uniform provided by the local AAA team and went to the mound. A team member filled in as catcher. When he started pitching, Morganna rushed up and delivered a kiss.

Cameras were rolling and picked up all the action. But photographers wanted to be sure, so they called for a retake.

"Do all the retakes you want, fellas," Aden told them.

Over, and over, and over — Morganna charged again and again.

⌒

"I got at least a dozen kisses," Aden says, "although they weren't all retakes. I sneaked in a few."

So, what was it like?

"Like I'd died and gone to heaven."

That was two weeks ago. Has Aden recovered?

"I'm still smiling," he beamed.

# 1986

## TONGUE TROUBLE ~

The following is not tongue-in-cheek. It's tongue-on-fence, and that's the truth.

Jefferson Elementary School principal's assistant Luke Gleason, lamenting that one never knows what to expect next, rescued a second-grader whose tongue froze to a steel fence rail when temperatures plunged below zero Monday.

"I don't know exactly how she got into that fix," says Gleason, "but there she was. I couldn't believe it."

He quickly decided his first course of action should be to prevent panic, if possible. Although he wasn't quite convinced, Gleason assured the girl she had nothing to be alarmed about, that he would be able to set her free posthaste. He told another student to go inside and tell a teacher to send out a glass of warm water.

~

"To me, that was the obvious thing to do," says Gleason, again pointing out his inexperience with such an emergency. "If that didn't work, I was going to call experts."

But it worked, and the girl suffered only minor pain. Although Gleason can't explain how the girl ended up plastered to the fence rail, the incident sparked a memory of his youth. He doesn't know how or why, but he once became very attached to his bicycle on a cold winter day: His tongue froze to the handlebars.

## AD LIBS ~
• Can you believe it? Americans have to be told to leave Libya. That's like having to coax people out of a fireworks factory that's on fire.
• President Reagan is slapping an embargo on Libya. That's terrorism American-style.

## STATION BREAK ~
Gubernatorial candidate Adlai Stevenson was in the last gasps of his "State of the State" retort at the Capitol Monday when a Chicago television-type pulled a microphone cord to the edge of the crowd to stage an on-the-spot news report. Locating the preferred camera angle, he crouched, gained a throttle-hold on the mike and — in a typical Ted Baxter style — started the countdown.

Cut!
Take two.
Cut!
Take three.
Cut!

Something wrong with the sound. It wasn't getting through. A cameraman trudged through the crowd and quickly resolved the technical problem.

"You gotta turn the mike on," he told the flustered newsman.

## COPS 'N' ROBBERS ~
Montgomery County State's Attorney Barbara Adams, in summing up a felony theft case against Willard Mahr and Jolene Wright there last

Friday, told the jury that the Springfield couple "met their match" when they picked on Hillsboro, Ill., businesswoman Deanna Laurent.

She chased the pair up Main Street, shouting "You're not getting away with this!" after they stole merchandise from her downtown clothing store.

Adams' assessment was correct. Testimony by Laurent and her employees convinced jurors beyond a reasonable doubt, and they returned guilty verdicts against both defendants. But that was just Act I.

After the verdicts were announced, Mahr and Wright lit into Sheriff Jim Moore and two deputies. During the courtroom fracas, Mahr reportedly had one deputy's revolver halfway out of the holster. Finally, the lawmen gained the upper hand, applied the cuffs and hauled the couple off to jail.

Once again, Mahr and Wright met their match in Hillsboro.

## A JUDGE TURNED GREEN ~

A vibrant chapter — probably a whole book — of Springfield history has passed with the death of retired circuit judge and Irish clan "mayor" William Conway. He died at age 86 after being hospitalized for several days.

Conway's public tributes to St. Pat no doubt overshadowed his 37-year career on the bench. For sure, courthouse corridors haven't been the same on St. Patrick's Day since Conway's retirement a decade ago. His antics made it the brightest and lightest day of the year for the local criminal justice system. Conway decked out his office and himself — suit, shirt, tie, socks, shoes, spats — in green, treated one and all to green cake and punch, then paraded office to office throughout the building.

*Judge William Conway on St. Patrick's Day.*

He's remembered for equally colorful observances of the day on the third floor of the old city police headquarters building where he reigned as magistrate for 20 years.

Conway had his ups and downs in political circles, and he had his critics in general. But many a parent, whose sons ended up in his courtroom in the old days when the law was somewhat flexible, credited Conway with getting their kids on the straight and narrow for life. Many times, after sizing up a young man in trouble, Conway took the mother or father aside to discuss what a promising military career awaited their son if he so chose. He painted a picture: neat haircut, neat manners, neat uniform; how proud of their son they would be.

They, in turn, pep-talked the defendant. The alternative — going to jail — almost always was rejected.

Then, there were the more sensational cases.

One day in 1947, Conway looked down from his bench into the eyes of legendary fan dancer Sally Rand and Georgia Sothern, one of the

renowned striptease artists of the era. Both were charged with disorderly conduct. The two beauties had been hauled in after a disturbance in the Leland Hotel, triggered when Miss Sothern caught her husband in Miss Rand's room. Incidentally, the Rand fan dance was the big attraction at the Illinois State Fair at the time.

Sally readily admitted to the cozy scene. Furthermore, she told Conway, she "had nothing to hide."

All was resolved in due time. Charges later were dismissed for lack of prosecution. Miss Sothern obtained a divorce and Miss Rand obtained a hus-

*Sally Rand*

band, who just happened to be Miss Sothern's ex.

## IT'S GET-EVEN TIME ~

The race was on for Springfield High Schoolers to get their musical, "Anything Goes," on the road.

Kevin Mayes pitched in to do his part in rounding up props and materials. He hopped into his car between classes the other day and headed for Ace Hardware, a few blocks away, to pick up a couple of gallons of paint.

⌒

That was no problem, he says, but getting it back to school was. He recounts his traumatic experience:

"A gentleman in the right lane decided to move into the left lane, disregarding the fact my 1963 Rambler was already there. I was forced to slam on the brakes and pray for the best. The cans of paint on the seat, however, didn't stop — and smashed into the dashboard, popping the lid off one. Suddenly antique white was on my clothes, window, seat and even the dice hanging from the rearview mirror."

Paint ran 1 inch deep on the floorboard.

Then the Rambler died as the perpetrator sped away.

Fortunately only one gallon spilled.

Mayes has a message for the guy who's to blame for his Rambler's interior paint job: "Watch out, the other can has your name on it!"

Like the musical, he says, anything goes!

# DR. COP ~

A not-so-funny thing happened to a Petersburg, Ill., couple on the way to the hospital the other day: They were pulled over by a state trooper. Speeding along Illinois 29, near Capital Airport where the limit is 45 mph, they were clocked at 65 mph. Emergency flasher-lights on the couple's car were blinking, a good indication, they thought, that they weren't out for a Sunday drive.

The trooper stopped them anyway.

The man behind the wheel hopped out and told the trooper he was in a hurry because his wife was about to have a baby. Since that's one of those silly excuses anybody could come up with, the trooper marched up to the car to see for himself.

"He wanted to make sure I was pregnant," said the flustered woman who was in the car. "It didn't take me long to convince him. I was having a contraction at the time."

⌐

Before waving the couple back into the race with the stork — with a few words of caution, of course — he offered some fatherly-doctorly advice. Since this is your first child, he noted with authority, there's little to worry about. You're usually in labor for 10 to 12 hours, he said.

So much for the advice. Ninety minutes later, in the hospital, the couple became proud parents of a bouncing baby boy.

They may have been guilty of speeding, joked the new mother, but the trooper was guilty, too — of practicing medicine without a license.

## JET NAG ~

A charter flight from Springfield to Las Vegas three weeks ago was described as "beautiful" going out, but a "nightmare" coming back. After three days of fun in the gambling capital, 343 pooped-out people climbed back on board their L-1011 jet and settled back for the flight home. It was to have been a three-hour trip. It took 26 hours.

One passenger recalled "a nice takeoff," looking out the window and snapping a picture of Lake Mead, just outside Las Vegas, as the plane climbed. A half-hour later, she looked out the window and snapped another picture — of Lake Mead.

"Uh-oh!" she exclaimed.

It then became obvious the plane wasn't gaining altitude or distance. Not only that, there was the odor of something burning. Then came a message from the pilot.

"A little problem with the landing gear," he announced.

"Uh-oh!"

After cruising awhile longer, the pilot advised he was dumping 5,000 gallons of fuel.

"Yep," he said, "I guess we're going to land back in Vegas due to mechanical problems."

As the big jet glided in, passengers peered out the windows to see the runway lined with ambulances and fire trucks.

"Uh-oh! Uh-oh!"

No problems, though. Safe landing. Passengers got off the plane and were bused to the Hacienda Hotel, where they were provided a thick-carpeted room, plenty of pillows and a complimentary buffet. Six hours later (12 hours after the original takeoff), they were bused back to the airport, informed that repairs had been accomplished and they would be boarding the previously crippled L-1011. Five people expressed their fear of flying at that point and took a taxi to the bus station.

Takeoff time was set for a half-hour past midnight. As the hour approached, a two-hour delay was announced. (This time, the delay was due to poor visibility in the Springfield area.) Finally, takeoff, without further incident. Before most passengers knew it, the plane was on final approach to Capital Airport. Down went the plane, down went the landing gear (cheers), then up went the plane and up went the landing gear.

"Uh-oh!"

After circling 20 minutes, the landing was aborted. Too foggy.

Airports in Chicago, St. Louis and elsewhere in Illinois were fogged in, too, so it was on to Milwaukee.

Other than running low on fuel, and running into an air traffic jam in Milwaukee, the plane landed safely during the wee hours.

Once again, passengers got off the plane for a short layover. Fifteen more abandoned ship. That afternoon, the weather cleared and the charter returned to Springfield, 23 hours late and 20 passengers short.

## AD LIBS ~
• A pilot program for all-day kindergarten in Springfield, eh? Fact is, nine out of 10 kids don't want to be a pilot.
• Schools where the all-day classes will be held will be designated day-care centers.
• School officials say the curriculum will consist of "academic" activities

in the morning and "enrichment" activities in the afternoon. Enrichment: That's teacher talk for Twinkies, Ding Dongs, milk and nappy-poo.

## BINGO? YOU BETCHA! ~

The wagering on bingo was small potatoes compared to what was at stake on the side at one local bingo hall the other night.

A group of women who apparently were bored with the B-11, O-71, I-22 ritual stepped up the action by betting on who would hit the first bingo. At first, it was dollar bills on the table, then five-spots, as the fun grew more and more serious. Then a security officer blew the whistle.

After all, it's against the law to gamble in a bingo hall.

## IF IT WEREN'T FOR BAD LUCK ~

Talk about a run of bad luck. Darlene Willhite was driving her kids to school on the west side one morning last month when a car pulling off Glenwood, onto Washington, plowed into the front of her car. Seconds later, another car slammed into the rear of her car.

She and her kids (they were wearing seat belts) escaped with minor injuries. Her car sustained more than $1,000 worth of damage.

That was phase one of what she calls a "bad day." Next came a traumatic experience in a hospital.

On her way into Memorial Medical Center that afternoon, she stopped at a restroom. While occupying the stall, Willhite suddenly became aware that she was not alone. A pair of white shoes and pant legs were visible outside the stall door. Although she couldn't tell, she assumed they were occupied by a female. As the seconds dragged on, she hoped it was a female — a friendly female. It was not to be. It was a man.

"Give me your purse!" he barked.

"What?" she said.

"Throw out your purse — now!"

She complied. He dumped the contents on the floor and sorted out the valuables — $300 in cash, a diamond watch worth $775, a checkbook and credit cards. Why did it have to happen that day, she said to herself. She never carries valuables like that in her purse.

"If you know what's good for you, you won't come out," her assailant warned as he made his getaway.

She waited as long as she could.

"Then I went nuts."

While off work, recuperating from her injuries, she got another shocker. Neither of the two motorists who hit her car has insurance.

## ALL YOU CAN EAT ~

There'll be an unofficial alternative to the official Physical Fitness Day in Springfield this year: "Fatness Day." That is according to a gag memo trailing the Physical Fitness Day memo now circulating in state government offices.

"All these people that are so wrapped up in this 'fitness' kick, it's enough to make me sick!" screams the memo author, a "Mr. Donut" who serves as inactivity coordinator for the alternative movement. "Phooey on all that sweating and huffing and puffing and jogging! Down with fitness!"

His memo goes on to detail the day's events:

The 1st annual Employee Fatness Day will be held at the smorgasbord of your choice.
Prizes and ribbons will be awarded to the largest eaters and the least active non-participants.
Fatness Day is co-sponsored by the Greater Springfield Institute of Gastronomical Awareness and Hostess Twinkies.

"Let's all get involved in this great eat-a-thon," says Donut. "Being healthy is okay, but those people can't be happy. I mean, c'mon, they gotta have dreams about Heath Bar Blizzards, chili dogs, triple-decker sandwiches and all-u-can-eat specials.

"Get serious! What better way to spend the day than to pig-out nonstop, pass the Alka-Seltzer and complain about seeing the last chicken wing or candy bar disappear."

## TATTLETALE ~

Among those locked up in recent bail benefits for the March of Dimes and American Cancer Society was AT&T public relations manager Larry Kearney. Kearney's last trip to the play pokey was witnessed by his 3-year-old son, who watched wide-eyed as uniformed police officers took his father into custody. He then saw his mother post his father's bail.

Soon after, the family went to Morris, Ill., Mrs. Kearney's hometown, and attended a church service there.

The pastor's announcements at the conclusion of services included comments about a church delegation working with people in jail.

"Daddy!" the 3-year-old blurted out loud, "He said jail. That's where you were!"

Every head turned.

"I turned purple," says Kearney, pointing out that he was in his wife's family's domain and he was a total stranger. "What else could I do? I certainly couldn't explain it."

## HOODWINKED ~

The grandiose opening of gangster Al Capone's so-called secret vaults, broadcast live in a two-hour nationally televised special Monday night, may have gone bust. But preparations indicated everyone involved was set to go for the gold. Virtually every arm of the legal system, including a forensics expert from the Chicago crime lab, was on hand and ready for action. Even "body bags" were at the ready.

Springfield demolition expert Dennis Komac, who headed the two-man blast team, says that end of it went "as planned," despite several major change orders only 20 minutes before air time.

By the way, that antique plunger that program host-ringmaster Geraldo

Rivera pushed to trigger the big blast was all show. Komac and partner Jerry Janik detonated the dynamite with electronic gear off-camera.

While only dirt and a few old gin bottles were found after the walls were blasted away, it could have been a somewhat different story. A rep from one Chicago radio station, knowing Komac would be first into the vault after the blast, offered him $5,000 if he would smuggle in and then "find" a T-shirt or bumper sticker bearing the station's call letters. He turned it down.

"Boy, they don't miss a trick up there," he said.

# FORE! ~
Patrolman Emmett Cleghorn spotted a burglary suspect on the street and made the pinch. Turned out the guy was wanted for the ultimate crime: stealing a doctor's golf clubs.

Talk about compounding a felony, he smashed the rear window in the doctor's Porsche to get to the golf clubs.

# VICTOR UNPLUGGED ~
The venerable Victor Borge, playing a concert at Sangamon State University two weeks ago, apparently vented some personal frustration with one of his laugh lines to the matinee crowd. He called Moammar Khadafy an SOB, only he used all three words.

*Victor Borge*

Borge's son, who acts as his stage manager, reacted with surprise: "He's never said that before!"

# HOT AIR ~
Mayor Mike Houston, although bushed after one of the longest days of his life Friday, spoke that night at the American Business Women Association's spring conference at the Hilton. It was a bad day from the start, Hizzoner noted as he began his address.

First, he went to get the morning papers. Not there. There was no letup throughout the day; a city council meeting, etc., and finally the historic compromise in the lingering discrimination suit against city government. After all of that, Houston headed for his engagement at the Hilton.

On the way in, he told his audience, he dashed into the men's room to scrub up. After washing his hands, he turned around and pushed the button on the blow dryer. That really ruined his day, he said, as he read this graffiti on the air machine:

"THIS IS YOUR MAYOR SPEAKING!"

## SAY AH-H-H-H! ~
This sign adorns the rear of Larry Richard's motorcycle.

"EAT SWEETS — MAKE MY DAY"

Makes sense, Richard is a dentist.

## OH, BOY!!! ~
A local used car salesman got a big surprise while at work on his birthday Friday. Friends sent him a double-header strip-o-gram.

He enjoyed every minute of the show until the two strippers, who he thought were Debbie and Louise, turned out to be Bob and John.

## HERE'S LOOKIN' ATCHA! ~
When Angie Meiron removed her contact lenses the other night, she couldn't find the little case she keeps them in. So she filled two glasses with water. She dropped the right lens into the glass on the right and the left lens into the glass on the left. She figured they'd be safe that way and that they wouldn't get lost or mixed up.

Wrong! Sometime during the night, her father got up for a drink of water.

All Angie knows is that one glass turned up empty and one contact is missing.

## BATTERY-POWERED CORONER ~
It was a bitter pill for Cass County Coroner Richard Pugh to swallow.

Preparing for his daily dose of medicine, Pugh laid a pill on the kitchen counter about the same instant he decided to change batteries in his hearing aid. In the process, he mistakenly picked up the small disc-shaped battery, popped it into his mouth and washed it down with a glass of water.

"I realized right away what I'd done," Pugh says. "I shouldn't have tried to do two things at once."

He chased it with a glass of milk. No repercussions. But Pugh's getting a lot of ribbing about trying to get a cheap charge.

## HOME SWEET HOME ~
The impending closing of Lincoln's Home for restoration got a dig from David Letterman Wednesday night. Noting that a new air-conditioning system will be installed with the project, Letterman quipped: "In keeping with the Abraham Lincoln tradition, if you can't free the slaves, you can at least make them comfortable."

## DEAR 'JOHN' ~
The U.S. Postal Service is on the "move." A ceremonious occasion the other day in the bowels of the downtown Federal Building proved it.

Gathered for an early-morning dedication of new construction were post office officials, including Postmaster J. Earl Holmes, plus the rank-and-file.

Pertinent remarks were uttered, and a bright pink ribbon was snipped to formally christen the facility: a brand new restroom for women employees.

## FOREIGN EXCHANGE ~
To promote the "Buy American" theme, the International Association of Machinists Union gave away several American-made products via a free raffle at the Illinois State Fair. Top prize was a "Made in USA" Norge washer-dryer set. It was won by a Japanese woman.

## KID STUFF ~
A little boy and a neighbor lady talking:

"Mike," she asked, "what grade are you in now?"

"Second grade," he replied.

"And how old are you?"

"Seven," Mike said, adding, "I had to take the first grade over."

Then, with a straight face, he hastened to explain.

"I made straight A's the first time. They just wanted me to take it over to see if I could do it again."

## COLOR IT RED ~

During the 1940s, Red Skelton was President Franklin Roosevelt's official emcee for White House occasions. Reminiscing on those days while in town last weekend, he told this tale:

Back then, the White House had a rodent problem — a rat problem, to be specific. A rat on the run in any room usually was no real cause for alarm.

But there were exceptions, like the time FDR hosted the king and queen of England at a state dinner. Skelton was the emcee.

*Red Skelton*

During the course of the dinner, a big rat crawled across the queen's foot. Skelton, remembering Eleanor Roosevelt's knack for saying the right thing at the right time, recalls the first lady's remark to the queen, who had frozen in fright: "Big SOB, wasn't he?"

## ELECTION DAY —PLUS ONE: ~

• The day many of the harder-campaigning candidates run to the nearest hospital and put their mouths in traction.

• Still other candidates are reporting for surgery. Cosmetic surgery, to be exact. They're having their noses restored to the length they were before the

⌒

campaign. (In political circles that procedure's known as a Pinocchio Tuck.)

• Many of the losing candidates will be charged with DUI — Defeated, Unemployed and Indebted.

## HAIRLINE ~

A woman was nearing the last spoonful of chili at a local eatery when she spotted a long blond hair doing the dead-man's float. It wasn't hers. She's brunette.

"Everything OK?" she was asked by the cashier minutes later.

"Well, no," she said, figuring she should be honest. "I found a hair in my chili."

"Really?" the cashier asked. "Did you sent it back?"

"No, I was almost finished eating when I saw it."

"Is it still there?" the cashier pressed. "Could you show it to me?"

She returned to the table, fetched the hair and took it to the cashier.

"That's a hair all right," he admitted. "Sorry," he said in the same breath, "That will be $2.48."

She's wondering if the hair was supposed to be in the chili, and if she's lucky she wasn't charged extra for it.

## JUST(ICE) IN TIME ~

Convicted of mail fraud and lying to government agents, ex-state Rep. Larry Bullock shed some tears and begged for mercy as he was sentenced by a federal judge in Chicago. It was a far cry from the hard-hearted attitude he had when, as a first-term legislator in 1980, he shrugged off all responsibility when a 16-year-old House page wrecked Bullock's car while running an errand for the lawmaker.

The teenager was working to earn college tuition when Bullock summoned the youth to the House floor, handed him the keys to his new Buick and

~

ordered him to get it gassed up. Minutes later, a few blocks from the Statehouse, the boy ran a red light, broadsided a pickup and knocked it into a car. Two people were hurt. Bullock had no insurance. He shirked all responsibility, telling the boy's mother it was up to her and her insurance company to pay damage claims, which amounted to several thousand dollars. He even held her responsible for the damage to his uninsured car. Eventually, her insurance company honored all claims except for $200 under a deductible clause. Bullock sicked his lawyer on her for the $200.

The lawyer, in going after every dollar he could get for Bullock, said of the woman's dilemma: "That's one of the hardships of raising kids."

Judge Milton Shadur virtually ignored Bullock's plea for mercy. Scolding the former legislator for using public office to "feather your own nest," he ordered Bullock to prison for six years.

# 1-800-SANTA-R-US ~

The "Ho Ho" hot line allows kids to talk to stand-ins for Mr. and Mrs. Santa Claus at Dirksen House Healthcare. Nursing home residents manning the North Pole substation phone talk to kids of all ages, offering Christmas cheer to the callers and at the same time making the holiday season happier for themselves. More than 2,500 calls were logged last year. Among them:

"Have you been a good boy all year?" Santa asked.

"No."

"Why not?"

"Because I'm a girl!"

An appearance-conscious little girl said:

"Bring some hair for my daddy, because he's bald."

Santa asked a little boy who called what he wanted for Christmas.

"You should know. I told you at the mall on Saturday."

## MOM KNOWS BEST ~

As Barbara Farb drove down Fifth Street past the Executive Mansion the other day, her 10-year-old son Kelly sized up the iron fence and lush landscape.

"Is that a cemetery?" he asked.

"No," his mom replied, "that's the governor's mansion."

"They're digging over there," he countered, zeroing in on the garden construction project. "Looks like they're burying something."

"Could be," mom quipped, "the legislature's in town."

## CHRISTMAS DREAMS ~

It's time for our annual peek into Santa's mail bag.

Dear Santa
Since the thing I want is ultimate, it's the only thing I want. It's a twin-size waterbed. If you decide not to give it to me, send me the money.
Your friend, Ryan

Dear Santa
Bring me everything in the whole wide catalog.
Adam

Dear Santa
I want to know if you can help me with something. I want you to get me in touch with my girl friend from the first grade. You can give me her phone number, or address so I can write her letters.
Your friend and life pal, Brian

Dear Santa
I'm sorry I haven't been so good this year. I don't know what came over me at the mall. I probably won't get anything, right? Well, this is what I want even though I won't get it but I am sorry for what I did. Now since I told you I won't get what I want, this is what I want even though I won't get it.
Love you, Brandy

## CHRISTMAS EVE FEVER ~

Twas the night before before Christmas and all through the Statehouse
Politicians were stirring; don't you wish you were a mouse?
Some were confident, others were in doubt
In hopes U.S. Attorney Bill Roberts would not find them out.
Others were nestled all snug in their hotel beds
While visions of pork barrel projects danced through their heads.
When out on the Statehouse drive there arose such a clatter
Lobbyists out-ran legislators to see what was the matter.
To the new thermal-pane windows they flew like a flash
And tore open the draperies like they were looking for cash.
The moon on the breast of the new fallen snow
Gave luster to all the lame ducks below
When what to their wandering eyes did appear
But a big black limo pulled by Democrat reindeer.
Out jumped a big, tall fella — so lively and slick,
They knew in a moment it sure wasn't St. Nick.
It was Jim Thompson of governor fame;
He looked up and shouted and called lawmakers by name.
"John Davidson! Lee Daniels! John Hallock!
"Mike Madigan! Penny Pullen! Howard Carroll and Phil Rock!
"To the top of the Hilton! To the top of the Dome!
"Let's pack it up and all go home!"
Then in a twinkling they heard a big rumble.
It was obvious Big Jim had taken a tumble.
As they drew in their heads and were turning around,
Down the elevator shaft he came; it made a horrible sound.
He wore tattered blue jeans and looked country-pure
His Nikes were tarnished and caked with manure
"I've been out at the fairgrounds. I'm on the verge of a fit
"I just can't wait 'til Willie does his ninth straight bit."
A bundle of state jobs and contracts he had flung on his back
This may not be the real Santa Claus, but he sure has the knack.
His eyes — how they twinkled!
His dimple — how simple!
His droll little mouth was drawn up in a bow
And cottage cheese on his sleeve was white as the snow.
The stump of a pipe he clutched tight in his teeth
Smoke choked the room; you could barely breathe.
A gent stepped forward and identified himself

He was Dr. Bernard Turnock, state director of health
"There's no smoking here, guv! Cool your fuel
"So we can all enjoy a healthy yule."
Thompson looked down, blinked his eyes and said,
"I'm (cough!!) with ya, Bernie, you've (cough!!) nothing to dread."
He spoke nary another word but went on with his work,
Filled legislators' stockings, then turned with a jerk
And laying his fist to a newspaper columnist's nose,
He turned tail; back up the elevator shaft he rose
He sprang to his limo, to his chauffeur gave a shout
And away they all flew, toward the nearest state route.
That's where he was last seen, in a burst of speed
Like some legislators, speed limits he did not heed
but we heard him proclaim as he sped away
"Merry Christmas to all — that includes you, too, Adlai!"

# 1987

## SOUPLINE ~

It was the biggest Christmas yet for Litchfield, Ill., pharmacist Mike Makuta. He handed out 3,000 cans of Campbell's chicken noodle soup to customers — plus others who got wind of the annual giveaway — at the Litchfield Medical Pharmacy. Makuta gave away more than 2,000 cans a year ago after we mentioned the giveaway. People need only walk in during the month of December and ask for soup, no purchase required.

"I thought I was going broke last year," he says. "But it went over even bigger this year. People remembered and passed the word. "

Makuta realizes soup makes a rather odd Christmas present, but he's convinced it's a healthy gift. He's long touted the "medicinal" benefits of chicken noodle soup. And he practices what he preaches: He eats at least one can a day. He started the soup handout as a gag several years ago. It's become the pharmacy's trademark. Makuta claims the recent publicity prompted offers from bologna manufacturers, who want him to give away samples of their products.

⌐͡

"I had to refuse all requests," he says, pointing out a conflict of interest. "I have my own line of 'baloney' I hand out."

## FINAL SALUTE ~

"The secretary of war desires me to express his deep regret that your husband, Corporal Myron Berger, was killed in action on Eight October in France."

That terse Western Union telegram was sent to Edith Berger, 3027 E. Carpenter St., Springfield, Ill., in 1944. Torn, wrinkled and stained, the telegram was found among some of the World War II casualty's personal effects which, as unclaimed property, ended up on the auction block at a Van Nuys, Calif., storage company last month. It was in a worn brown paper shopping bag, along with faded family photographs, newspaper clippings, letters and medals — a Purple Heart and Silver Star — the Army corporal was awarded. But bidders showed no interest in the sack. It did not sell.

"Myron Berger, you deserve better — so much better," Van Nuys Daily News columnist Dennis McCarthy wrote. "You gave your life for your country."

McCarthy poured over the contents of the sack with Howard Suer, president of California Moving & Storage Co.

"Your legacy as a fighting man was almost lost forever — thrown out with leftover trash nobody else wanted," he said in a personal tribute to the fallen soldier.

There is evidence in the sack that Berger's widow requested more information from the Army. A letter from his commanding officer told her Berger was a scout for a rifle squad and that he was hit by sniper fire in the village of Moivron, France.

"Although dying and although the enemy continued to fire on him, he warned his squad of snipers, located their well-hidden position and continued to fire on the enemy until death overcame him," his commander wrote.

"By his gallant action, he created a diversion that enabled his squad to outflank and eliminate the snipers without further loss. His heroic determination to seek out, engage and destroy the enemy, even at the cost of his life, upholds the finest traditions of the United States infantryman."

Suer has scoured company records in a futile effort to trace a relative.

"I'm holding on to these things for a while," Suer said Wednesday. "I'd like very much to find some of his family."

Suer and McCarthy reached the same conclusion: It isn't right that the memory of this life wind up in a paper bag in some warehouse — forgotten and unclaimed.

## CORPORAL CONNECTION ~

The legacy of World War II casualty Myron Berger will live on. Distant relatives of Berger have been located in Springfield and are in the process of recovering the soldier's personal effects, which were discovered in a California warehouse last month.

Charlotte Blumle, a niece of Berger, expects to receive the war medals, papers, letters and photographs next week. She hopes to find information that might help trace Billy Walch, the son of Berger's widow, who remarried after the war and moved to California.

"I'll sift through everything," she said. "Maybe there'll be something to give us an idea where he could be found. We haven't had contact with him for about 15 years."

California moving company executive Howard Suer discovered the items when unclaimed property was auctioned, and set out to try to find a Berger relative.

"I'm really glad it turned out this way," he said Tuesday. "These things, which may be all that is left of a war hero's life, should not be lost and he should not be forgotten."

## PARENT TRAP ~

The parents of a teenager, upon returning home late one Saturday night, observed their son's car parked at the edge of the driveway. That told them he had ditched his wheels and was out with friends. Because of the late hour, they decided to wait up for him. The clock struck one . . . then two. He didn't show. Concern — and tempers — were on the rise.

Three o'clock came. Then 4 o'clock. He was still missing. Mom and dad were still waiting. Somewhere around 6 a.m. he walked into the kitchen — straight from his bedroom. That's where he'd been all along. His parents hadn't thought of looking for him in his room.

"Don't you know you're supposed to get up and report to us when we come home?" his dad kidded.

"Why?"

"You should know how hard it is for kids to raise parents these days!"

## SPLAT!!! ~

The Illinois Department of Conservation has opened a mail order T-shirt shop. One of four designs available has this imprint over the state map: "State Parks Are For The Birds."

It's topped off with a big white blob on one shoulder — evidence that Illinois birds are right on target.

## POSTAGE DUE ~

The mailman delivered a letter with a ballpoint pen enclosed to Del Angelo last week. The letter was mutilated, the pen was smashed. Couple of days later, Angelo received another letter with buttons enclosed. The envelope was a mess, the buttons appeared to have been dropped in front of a steamroller.

The pen and the buttons were in protective wrappings. Both were marked "Hand Stamp."

"The post office must have thought it said, 'Hand Stomp,' " Angelo quipped.

Both envelopes bore a message from the main postal station in St. Louis, expressing regrets for the brutal handling.

⌐

"I'm not sure," Angelo says, "but I think the post office down there is part of the St. Louis Zoo."

## BANK ON IT! ~

State Treasurer Jerry Cosentino must have a Rodney Dangerfield complex these days. He isn't getting much respect from bankers. Bank credit card interest rates have nose-dived in recent days, ironically, just as Cosentino started making good on a campaign promise to pull state funds (millions of dollars) out of banks he contends have been gouging charge card customers. But bankers deny he was any influence. Just coincidental to the clamoring by Cosentino, they claim.

"I've never received any credit for anything I've ever done in this office," says Cosentino. "But they know and I know."

## DREAM ON, DECATUR ~

Abe in Decatur, Ill.? That thought crossed Decatur Herald & Review columnist Dick Icen's mind this week:

"If Abraham Lincoln had decided to remain in Macon County and practice law in Decatur, we would have utopia in Soy City. Decatur would be the repository of Abe's home and body and the millions of tourist dollars that have fallen over the last century into cash registers in Springfield.

"Having cast his lot with Decatur, Honest Abe and the Long Nine would have moved the Capitol here from Vandalia, not Springfield, leaving to us the plunder and tribute of the rest of the state to pay indecent salaries to yuppie bureaucrats and overstuffed elected officials.

"While attending to leisurely lunches at elegant restaurants surrounding the Capitol, we might all wonder why the people of Springfield seem so different, so much more — how can this be put kindly? — rustic, parochial, defeated by life?

"Alas, Abe ended up in Springfield and the rest is history."

NOTE: Abe often said, "Oh, I remember Decatur. I spent a week there one night." T. M.

~

## SECRET TABLE SERVICE ~

The security blanket for Vice President George Bush at the convention center on Lincoln's Birthday was a bit much, some thought.

As 1,800 luncheon guests (who had to clear checkpoints and be seated earlier that morning) are now aware, the Secret Service insisted that Bush make his entrance, deliver his speech and be whisked away before the meal was served. But few knew of some of the other security measures.

For instance, a long list of dignitaries at the speaker's table — from governor on down — couldn't have knives and forks until Bush's motorcade departed. Secret Service orders.

## PAPER CHASE ~

A Meter Molly was preparing an overtime parking ticket for a car near Sixth and Adams early Wednesday when the owner of the car yelled from across the street:

"Wait a second, I'm going to move it."

She looked up, then slapped the ticket on the windshield and ran around the corner. The race was on. Eager to find out why she didn't give him a chance to move the car, and why she ran away, he pursued her. He caught up with her two blocks away.

"Why did you run?"

"Once I put a ticket on the windshield (remember now, she hadn't got that far), you got the ticket," she said.

"That's not how I understand the policy," he countered.

Since he was stuck with the ticket, the guy decided to go on about his business. By the time he got back to his car, there was another ticket on the windshield — from the same Meter Molly.

## FINGER(ED) FOOD ~

A couple in a local restaurant watched as a tray of food for a nearby table was placed on a serving stand. A waitress then scanned the tray and apparently inventoried the french fries on each plate. Deciding they hadn't been distributed equally, she picked up a couple of fries, figured out which plate was short and dropped them there. After several such moves, she decided the portions were equal and proceeded with the serving.

## CAPITAL CITY ~
Police were dispatched to a local tavern Saturday night where the bartender wanted to throw out a Christian who was attempting to convert some of the patrons.

## NAH! WOULD SAVE TOO MUCH MONEY ~
"Stop building new prisons," says Murray Thompson, "there's a cheaper way. Use old coal mines instead. Put criminals in a real hole. Call it Hell." Thompson points to cost-effectiveness: "With only one way in and one way out, you'd only need one guard."

## PHONE LINES ~
The phony alert broadcast Wednesday morning by a WNNS DJ, who warned listeners to cover their telephones because the phone company was going to blow out phone lines, was believed by many.

Golden Mirror beauty salon employee  Susan Miller heard it and alerted owner Tom Fileccia. Not realizing what day it was, they tied plastic bags around the receivers of nine of the 10 phones in the beauty shop. A customer who inquired about the bagged phones later in the day tipped them off that they were victims of an April Fool's joke.

## AD LIBS ~
• Original, uncut, blow-by-blow, long-winded versions of Springfield City Council meetings are to be broadcast on the local cable network. Just what we need: more violence on television.
• Meetings will be taped for broadcast later. But in the event of a big brouhaha, regular programming may be pre-empted. We can here the announcer now: "Pet of the Week will not be seen tonight so we can bring you the following special program, "Little City Hall on the Prairie."

## SUPERMARKET COMEDY ~
A woman described as "immensely pregnant" was checking out at a local

~

Jewel supermarket. She was told to stand by, that a bag boy would carry the groceries to her car.

"Take this out for the lady," the clerk instructed the bag boy. "We don't want her to have that baby here."

"Sure," the kid quipped, "we carry out, but we don't deliver."

## GET WELL CARD ~

Heart surgery patient Cecil Fairfield, who underwent a triple bypass at St. John's Hospital last weekend, is proving an inspiration to other patients as well as hospital staffers. He's making a splendid recovery, as well as some sort of local medical history for his age.

Fairfield is 85 years old. Heart surgery is rarely performed on people over 80. When doctors suggested the procedure, he didn't flinch.

"I want to be here to celebrate my next birthday," he said, giving the go-ahead.

He'll be 86 in September, and his 19 children (another was a Vietnam war casualty) will help him celebrate, just as most of them have been at the hospital to support him through the ordeal.

## TOO GOOD TO BE TRUE ~

A Springfield man and his get-rich-quick scam have been put out of business by postal inspectors. Calling it one of the oldest con games known, the feds shut down Finney Enterprises, which ran a series of sucker ads in local publications.

"EARN $50-PLUS DAILY STUFFING ENVELOPES," said the ads. A self-addressed stamped envelope to a local post office box would get this pitch: "Send me $10 and I'll show you how it's done."

Those who sent in $10 then received this response: "Do the same thing I'm doing. Advertise like I do and (presto!) you're making money stuffing envelopes."

This guy boasted he was raking in $100 to $300 a day until postal authorities closed in.

❧

## MEMO TO JOHNNY CARSON: ~
There's an old outhouse along the fence line off I-55, about 40 miles south of Springfield with your name on it.

"H-E-E-E-E-R-E-'S J-O-H-N-N-Y" is painted on the side visible to passing motorists.

## GOVERNOR SNUBBED ~
Four-year-old Justin Bergen of Milford was tagging along with his mother, Kathy, on a tour of the Statehouse last week when he bumped into a tall stranger — Gov. Jim Thompson.

"Hi!" said the guv.

"I don't talk to strangers!" said Justin.

## TAMMY ANOTHER IMELDA ~
The scandalous saga of former PTL kingpins Tammy and Jim Bakker swept former Springfield hotelman Lacey Brooks, now executive director of Heritage USA's religious theme park's plush Grand Hotel, into the national spotlight last week.

And Brooks' quip, in reference to Imelda Marcos, added still more intrigue to the story.

PTL's new regime was conducting a news conference at ministry headquarters when questions arose about the opulent top-floor suite often occupied by the Bakkers. Brooks was asked to conduct the news corps on a tour and told to "answer any and all questions" about it. As he led 40 reporters and photographers through the 12-room, 3,000-square-foot suite, attention was drawn to a chandelier-lit closet 50 feet in length. He explained that, until recently, it was full of the Bakkers' clothes — mostly Tammy's expensive garb. And all of the empty shelves were once filled with her shoes.

"What did that remind you of?" a reporter asked.

"That lady over in the Philippines," Brooks replied.

∽

But, he says on reflection, "Tammy didn't have as many shoes as Mrs. Marcos did." He estimated Tammy's shoe collection at 700 to 800 pairs. Shortly after the Bakkers took flight, their personal belongings were shipped to their Palm Springs mansion.

A safe was among the things they left behind. Tammy is often seen dripping in diamonds, but hopeful PTL officials found the safe empty. Besides gold-plated fixtures in seven bathrooms, a white grand piano and lush furnishings, walls were covered with expensive paintings, testimony to "Jim's love for expensive things," says Brooks.

It's fancy digs all right, but Brooks says he has seen other hotel suites as good or better.

The Heritage Grand has four stretch-limos and four Lincoln Continentals used to shuttle VIPs to and from the airport at Charlotte, N.C.

However, Brooks says the fleet will soon be reduced by 50 percent in an effort to reduce operating expenses.

Publicity about the scrumptious "Bakker" suite is prompting inquiries from would-be guests. Brooks says a lot of people simply want to live one night like the Bakkers lived. No reservations have yet been accepted from those willing to fork over $2,000 a night, but Brooks expects to accommodate some of the requests.

Otherwise, the suite will be maintained for VIPs, like heads of organizations that hold conventions at the hotel. For them, the suite will be complimentary.

"That's good for business," says Brooks.

## AUCTION OR A WAKE? ~

Is there life for an old casket? Auctioneer Jim Woodward proved there is, unloading a used (for something other than burial) oak coffin at a sale last Saturday night. It attracted a curious crowd, he says, from people who wanted a peek inside to a woman who barked at her husband, "Get away from that thing!"

Several bidders went for it.

A tavern owner wanted it for a Halloween decoration. A grocer had visions of setting it up in his produce section to display fruits and vegetables. Best bid was $110 by Larry Duhs, owner of Plaza Furniture & Variety Mart, who isn't sure what he'll do with the casket.

"I was going to put a glass top in it and use it as a 'coffin' table in the family room," Duhs quipped.

His wife nixed that idea.

## HAT CASE COVER-UP ~

Springfield's phantom hat-masher will get away with his misdeed: that mysterious assault on a downtown bar patron three weeks ago. City police officially closed the case Wednesday after the victim had a change of heart and refused to press charges.

He was the guy wearing a cowboy hat at the Campaign Headquarters tavern — not far from the Statehouse — when some bozo approached him from behind, told him he hates cowboys and mashed the hat while it was still on the victim's head. He then knocked the cowboy to the floor and smacked him in the face.

Although police had a description (white, 6-foot-2, 240 pounds) and the license number of the assailant's dark blue 1984 Chevrolet, they hadn't been able to track him down. The Chevy turned out to be a state-owned car. The trail led to the Statehouse, and that's where it ended.

Police ran into roadblocks from the beginning. When they first tried to trace the license, some bureaucrat contended it was a "confidential" plate assigned to a state senator. Police persisted. Then it was confirmed it is registered to "Senate Operations, Room 403, Statehouse." Senate staff members, while contending all vehicles were accounted for on the night of May 5, refuse to reveal who drove the car in question.

Unmarked state cars are assigned to "the respective leaders" in the Senate (Senate President Phil Rock and Minority Leader James "Pate" Philip) "for their personal use" when they are in Springfield, according to Senate Secretary Linda Hawker. However, she would not say which cars or which license plates are assigned to whom. She says it is difficult to keep track of who drives the cars at any given time because they are fre-

⌣

quently used by Senate staffers and pages. For instance, a senator often turns the car keys over to someone else to run errands.

Why the "straight" license plates and "confidential" license registration listings?

"I think ranking people deserve that courtesy," Hawker said. And, she explained, that protects staffers and pages when they're running official errands, like out to a restaurant to pick up pizza or chicken. That way they aren't subjected to the ire of tax-paying citizens who think that would be misuse of state vehicles.

And, obviously, an unmarked state car with straight license plates comes in handy for someone who doesn't want to be conspicuous when he goes on a binge at midnight.

## 'LOUD' ROBBER ~

There was an easy answer to the robbery in the Easy Answer bank booth at Sixth and Cook streets three weeks ago. An automated video camera in the booth recorded the crime in progress.

A man wearing a loud Hawaiian shirt jammed what felt like a gun (turned out to be a pair of vise grips) into the ribs of a physically handicapped man and slammed him against the wall, then took the $52 the man had just withdrawn, credit cards and car keys. So police had a good description of the holdup man.

Police arrested a man on drug charges the next day. That man happened to be wearing a loud Hawaiian shirt. Same guy. He was charged with the robbery.

## VIP GARBAGE ~

The temporary exhibit of Lincoln Home furnishings at the Illinois State Museum (while the home is closed for renovation) includes more than the family's furniture.

Samples of Abe's celebrated garbage — exhumed in archaeological digs at the site of his trash pile and privy — are displayed amid the fine antiques like a monarch's jewels; strategically positioned on crimson fabric and encased in clear plastic. (A security guard watches from a few feet away.) Alongside fragments of the Lincolns' glassware and crockery are steak, fish and rabbit bones. That, says the sign, tells us something of Abe's lifestyle (i.e., he wasn't a fast-food junkie.)

Only the type of bone is noted. Whether they are from Abe's own plate, or are the remains of meals downed by the missus or the kids, historians do not indicate. And whether the family dog got to gnaw on the bones before they were trashed, we'll never know.

Another sign notes that the archaeological dig also revealed facts about Abe's "personal hygiene." Fortunately, museumgoers are spared that evidence.

## TALK ABOUT LOUSY LUCK ~
Spring Crest Drapery Store owner Eric Shaver has had his share.

Shaver's latest flub occurred a few weeks ago. He had just completed a job at a Springfield home and was backing his truck out of the driveway. He failed to notice an extended portion of the house. He smacked it, doing considerable damage. Luckily for him, the homeowner — a lawyer — had a sense of humor.

Then there was the time he was driving across the middle of Town & Country Shopping Center parking lot. A nice, bright day, no cars blocking his vision. He hit a light pole, head on.

But here's the topper: Several years ago, in the winter, Shaver drove to Bloomington during the early morning hours to hang draperies at a carpet store. It had snowed. He pulled into the parking lot, jumped out onto the blanket of white and disappeared.

A manhole cover apparently had been swept away by a snowplow the night before. Enough snow fell afterward to hide the hole. Shaver found himself at the bottom of the sewer. He was unhurt but he was in over his head. Ice on the rim of the sewer prevented him from getting a good grasp and hauling himself out. No one was around to hear his calls for help. In time, he was able to chip away the ice, then hoist himself out.

## BURP! ~

It happened years ago but the story is still being told, and the kid involved — now a young man — apparently will never live it down. Folks were filing out of a local church following Sunday morning services. The pastor was at the door to greet folks.

A 4-year-old boy, in line with his parents, studied the situation. He observed that everyone had a handshake and comment for the reverend.

"Can I say something to the preacher, too?" he asked his mother.

"Sure you can," she replied.

The line inched along. Finally it was the boy's turn, and he stretched out his hand to the preacher and blurted, "When you're outta Schlitz, you're outta beer!"

## SMOKE SCREEN ~

As predicted when the state Health Department hung up the No Smoking sign for that agency several months ago, the anti-smoke order has had a trickle-down effect. The latest to hop on  the "ban" wagon is the Department of Transportation. But smokers there are being herded into — of all places — the employee cafeteria.

Yes, the cafeteria now serves not only smoked salmon, smoked sausage and smoked turkey, they have smoked bread and butter, smoked vegetables, smoked salads, smoked Jell-O, smoked pudding, etc.

So when you see nonsmoking DOT employees put on gas masks, you know where they're going. To lunch.

## INSTANT TERROR ~

It was super-hot the other day when Frank Melchiorri was driving his pickup truck through a rather infamous part of town. He heard a "pop." Very much aware he was near a high crime area, he assumed what he'd heard was a gunshot. He crouched as low as he could and still maintain control of his truck. Then he realized something was oozing through his shirt. He reached back. He felt something warm and wet.

〜

"I've been shot!" he said to himself.

He kept driving until it was safe to pull over and stop. He leaned up, expecting to see the back of the seat covered with blood. It was soaking wet all right. And it was sticky. But it wasn't blood. It was soda pop.

A can of Seven-Up had rolled under the seat, heated up, fizzed up, and exploded.

## BANANA 'SPLIT' ~

Upon returning to Capital Airport via limo after a wrestling show, Hulk Hogan was confronted by some young fans. Several boys tagged after him as he headed for his plane. Hogan, lugging a big bag of bananas, handed each of the boys a souvenir — a banana. That didn't quite satisfy one 7-year-old. So Hogan autographed the banana before he split.

## POT SHOT! ~

Portable Sanitations Systems owner Phil Pennington of Springfield, losing bidder on the state fair's contract for portable toilets, charged that his competitor, Johnny-On-The-Spot of St. Louis, wasn't so Johnny-On-The-Spot when it came to service.

However, fair officials quickly disposed of Pennington's allegations, saying the Missouri business firm made a "good-faith attempt" to live up to the contract. So, Johnny isn't on-the-spot anymore.

## THEFT CASE A SHOE-IN ~

The headline was a grabber: "Springfield man gets seven years in prison for stealing a pair of shoes." Eyebrows went up, here and elsewhere. News services picked up the story and wired it coast to coast. A lot of readers, including a man in San Francisco who called here Wednesday to express "concern" about the heavy sentence muttered the same question. Seven years for one lousy pair of shoes?

Yes.

But.

〜

There were other things Judge Raymond Terrell considered in sentencing Anthony Burrows.

Assistant state's attorney Leo Zappa says the key to the seven-year term is the "accumulative" factor. Stealing the shoes wasn't Burrows' first brush with the law. He's well known to both the police and the judicial system.

Although Burrows is only 25, he was already a three-time loser. He was sent up for two years on a felony theft conviction, later for five years for burglary and the last time he got three years for felony theft. He'd been out of prison only a short time when he was arrested for stealing the shoes from a car parked near Memorial Medical Center in April. Burrows also has been convicted of several misdemeanors, ranging from theft to criminal trespass to motor vehicles.

"Add it up," says Zappa. "He's a habitual criminal. Technically, we could have asked for an extended prison term, more than the maximum seven years."

Defense attorney Bruce Locher finds fault with both Burrows' convictions and his sentence. He has filed a notice to appeal. Zappa sums up what he calls a good case:

"The shoes in question were the same lace-up Italian leather Sears-brand shoes stolen from the car. A witness saw the car being ransacked by a barefoot man, identified as the defendant, who fled with a bag. Minutes later, police nabbed Burrows running down an alley a few blocks away. He was wearing the shoes, untied. The theft victim positively identified the shoes. If it's appealed, I think the conviction will stand and the sentence will be found appropriate."

Whatever, the case may prove to be a deterrent to criminals who consider plying their trade in Sangamon County — particularly shoe thieves.

## INCREDIBLE, EDIBLE SPAM 〜

A World War II veterans group meeting here this weekend will ceremoniously salute Spam, the "miracle meat" that contributed so much to the war effort. But the salute will be a dubious one. After all, millions of soldiers forced to eat various concoctions of Spam for months on end grew to hate the stuff. To this day, to most vets, Spam is a four-letter-word.

An agenda item for the reunion of Veterans of the Solomon Islands, head-quartered at Econo Lodge, reads like this: "Slicing of Spam with Samurai Sword."

At the prescribed time, the presiding officer will attack a block of Spam with a Samurai sword, a genuine Japanese weapon that's a prized sou-venir. Bite-sized bits of Spam will be served on crackers (to help kill the taste) prior to lunch.

"It's for reminiscing purposes only," Solomons veteran C. F. Marley of Nokomis, Ill., is quick to point out. "It's not because we like Spam. I don't know any veteran who likes Spam. We had to eat so much of it during the war."

Spam, which was introduced by Hormel in 1937, became a staple for the armed services because it didn't require refrigeration. Army cooks dis-guised it every way possible: breaded, buried in pineapple, shredded in gravy, ground in soup and pasta dishes, etc.

"It didn't make any difference," says Marley, "you always knew it was Spam."

Of course, Spam was the butt of many jokes:

"Spam is ham that didn't pass the physical."

"Spam is a meatball that didn't go through basic training."

It was dubbed by many on the battlefield as "Mystery Meat" and hound-ed by rumors of how strange animals and stranger animal parts wound up in the little tin cans.

"But like it or not," Marley admits, "Spam played an important role in the war, and we won't forget that."

The veterans have made their tongue-in-cheek tribute to Spam a perma-nent part of their annual reunions. It's only a coincidence that Hormel is currently touting the 50th anniversary of the canned meat that will not die. Hormel has a sense of humor about its own product. Hormel Luncheon Meat Trivia includes this statistic: "Spam kills 3.7 million hogs a year."

Hormel can afford to laugh. Spam corners 75 percent of the ham-like food market, with 3.6 cans of the pickled meat being consumed every second. That's 90 million pounds a year.

## OLYMPIC MATERIAL ~

The personalized memo pad says "From the Rocker of Sam Dorman." Don't let that fool you. Dorman, at 81, is far from being tied to a rocking chair. He's a retired railroad clerk, but he's better known in Springfield as an athlete. He returned from the U. S. National Senior Olympics, held in St. Louis recently, with a fistful of medals: a gold for the 1500-meter walk race, silvers from the 400-meter run, half-mile and 3-mile bicycle races, and bronze for the 100/200-meter runs.

## SAME NAME —THAT'S ALL ~

A police car closed in on a woman driving down a south-side street and the officer signaled her to pull over. After informing her she was driving with an expired license plate sticker, he returned to his squad car to write a citation.

Time dragged on, says Selvarine Jones of Springfield, who was on her way home from work at the time. She watched anxiously through her rearview mirror. He finally returned, but with another officer instead of a ticket.

"Ma'am, did you know there is a warrant for your arrest?" he asked her. That was news to her.

"What for?" she asked.

He said something about a theft charge pending in another county. He told her she was under arrest and ordered her out of the car. As she was being handcuffed, she tried to explain they had the wrong woman. She was dumbfounded.

"Is this one of those Jail-N-Bail pranks?" she asked, "Is this some kind of joke?"

Assuring her it was for real, the officers asked Jones if she wanted to specify a wrecker company to tow her car.

"That's nice," she thought, "Beggars can't be choosy, but people under arrest can."

There she was, handcuffed, in the back of a patrol wagon, about to be hauled off to the county jail for something she knew nothing about. She kept trying to convince the officers there was some mistake.

"Well, you could be right," one officer admitted.

Next thing she knew, she was being searched in the prisoner intake room. Then a computer spit out details of the charges against her in St. Clair County. Onward to jail.

"It seemed like this nightmare would never end."

Then, as she was about to be mugged and fingerprinted, she was shown the computer printout. Although the wanted woman also was listed as "S. Jones," and matched her description and date of birth, she quickly spotted the error that led to the mix-up. Police had erred on one digit of her license number. That's what fingered her as a fugitive. She was quickly returned to her car which, oddly enough, had not yet been towed.

"Well," one of the officers confessed, "you were right."

Now, what about the expired license plate sticker? After all the hassle, would police have the nerve to cite her for such a petty violation?

You betcha! She got a ticket. It'll cost her 50 bucks.

## FINGER-LICKIN' GOOD? ~
There are some interesting entrees on the Sangamon State University cafeteria menu. According to the student newspaper, SSU News, "Southern Style Fried Children with Mashed Potatoes" is being served.

## AD LIBS ~
• So Pat Schroeder decides to stay out of the Democratic presidential

race. There goes a great campaign slogan: "We Cry Harder."
• Just think what a crying jag she'd go on if she ran and lost.
• It wasn't easy for her husband, Jim, either. He must have had visions of becoming First Man.

## VETERANS GET THEIR 'DEW' ~

The famed skytroopers of World War II — soldiers in white camouflage who, with rifles strapped across their backs, skied across snow-covered mountain slopes under enemy fire — open their Midwest reunion today with a new name. But the name change came strictly by accident. Formally, the veterans organization is the 10th Mountain Division Association. In corresponding with the Springfield Hilton during the preliminary planning stage, the group referred to itself as the "10th Mountain Div. Association."

Later, when the vets met with the hotel's director of convention services, Meryl Judd, to iron out details, she popped this question:

"Now how could this group be connected with Mountain Dew?"

She had mistaken "Div." for "Dew," laughs Donald List of Mason City, Ill., one of the reunion planners. It was explained that the 10th Mountain Division has nothing to do with Mountain Dew. But it was too late. Reservation and regulation forms all listed the group as the 10th Mountain Dew Association.

"This has gotten to be quite a joke," says List. "We're getting a lot of laughs out of it."

The Pepsi-Cola Bottling Co., which produces the soft drink, is getting in on the fun. It's donating Mountain Dew for the 150 vets who are attending the reunion. With 3,000 dues-paying members, the 10th is the largest non-active duty Army division. National reunions are held and members return to Italy every few years to visit the mountainous battlefields. The unit spearheaded the final push into the Po Valley in Italy, which ended the war.

## AD LIBS ~

• They say this new "smokeless" cigarette doesn't burn tobacco. It must

burn old tires.
• It's said to still be in the "research stage." In other words, they haven't been able to get one lit.
• And it doesn't produce any ash, which sure will knock the tar out of the ashtray business.

## KID STUFF ~

On a shopping trip to Penney's recently, Carla Doedtman and her kids, 4-year-old Jeff and 6-year-old Sarah, ran into four Springfield Cardinal players at an autograph session.

Sarah wanted to know what an autograph is. Mom explained, then told her she could stand in line for one if she wanted to.

"Are we for the Cardinals?" she asked.

"No, Dad's for the Cubs," Carla replied, "but it would be fun to have the Cardinal autographs anyway."

Sarah got in line. Jeff stayed with his mother. When Sarah returned with an autograph, Jeff asked in all seriousness, "Did they stink?"

"No," said Sarah.

"Oh," he countered, "then they must have gotten themselves cleaned up because the Cardinals stink!"

His mom quickly figured him out.

"He's been taking his dad's comments literally."

## VOICE IN THE WILDERNESS ~

Webber Borchers, the feisty former state representative from Decatur, Ill., who waged many a battle in the capital city, is in the forefront of opposition to changing the name of that city's Broadway Street to Martin Luther King Jr. Drive.

Borchers, 80, says he's trying to preserve history. Broadway, he explains, was the route used by Army regiments marching to troop trains that carried them to the Civil War, and Abraham Lincoln's train stopped at Broadway when he was headed for inauguration in Washington. Borchers proposes that Lake Shore Drive should be renamed for King.

Borchers, often called Decatur's "old soldier," once boasted during a legislative battle, "I'm not afraid of anything!"

This proves that!

*Webber Borchers*

## AD LIBS ~
• The hearings on Supreme Court nominee Robert Bork, in which Sen. Joseph Biden has been so prominent, haven't been all for naught. Watch for a new television sitcom called "Bork and Windy."
• Bork's chances of confirmation are about as good as a gallon of grease going unused at an Illinois chili cook-off.
• Workers at the Lincoln Home restoration project found Lincoln-related documents and assorted junk inside a wall of the house. Better than finding bugs.
• Apparently Abe didn't believe in wastebaskets.

## BIG GIRL ON CAMPUS ~
Plop, plop! Gee whiz! A live cow goes to Springfield High School? Yes. But only for a day.

"Beulah" will be big girl on campus during the noon hour today as the student body revs up for Saturday's homecoming football game and dance. She'll be the "caller" for a "bovine bingo" game the student council is sponsoring to help defray homecoming expenses.

The cow will be turned loose on the football practice field to do what cows are known to do. Kids bid — a buck a shot — on precisely which areas of the field Beulah will leave her mark. When the whistle blows and Beulah is led away, game officials will put on their boots, hold their noses and venture into the wastelands to match locations of the pasture patties to numbers held by students. Winners get free tickets to the homecoming.

## CAT TALES ~

"Morris" the cat lived the good life in Springfield, having the run of one of the Hilton Hotel's best suites for three nights. He would have been given the presidential suite, says the hotel sales director David Gerig, but it was occupied . . . About 30 guests greeted Morris at a champagne reception in his honor. He received a dozen roses and was the hotel's guest of the day. Gerig says the four-legged celebrity attracted more attention than any big-name entertainers who've stayed at the Hilton . . . A "barn" cat named Charlie Chaplin won the coveted Morris trophy at the Feline Fanciers show. He's an 18-month-old long-haired, orange and white cat co-owned by Sue Price and Helen Roundtree of Springfield. They say Charlie was born in a barn and lives in a barn.

## PUTTIN' ON THE DOG ~

Election hoopla reminds Smokey Joe Miller of the old hound dog that sat next to the barn and howled day after day.

"What's wrong with your dog?" a traveling salesman asked the farmer.

"Nothing," the farmer replied.

"What kind of dog is he?"

"A politician dog," the farmer said.

"A what?"

"Well, you see," the farmer explained, "he's sittin' on a thistle and it hurts. He's like those politicians. He'll do a lot of howlin' but he won't do anything about it."

## CAPITAL FUNISHMENT ~

Memorial Medical Center speech specialist Maggie Cullen was testing a second-grader's language abilities. "What do you like about school?"

"Studying capitalism," he said.

What a challenging curriculum for a second-grade class, she thought.

⌒

"Exactly what is capitalism?" she pressed.

"Oh, you know," the boy replied, "when you make the letters of the alphabet big."

## DASH OF SALT ~

A couple dining Monday night at Bianco's Little Supper Club was overheard talking about buying a bottle of tequila on the way home. Just before they left, they asked the waitress for a large slice of fresh lemon to go. She happily complied,  sealing it in a little plastic bag. She didn't even charge for it.

Minutes later, as Shirley Bianco cleared their table, she discovered the salt shaker was missing.

"Yep," she says, "They stole the salt shaker so they could make their margaritas. I'd have been glad to give them a bag of salt, too, if only they'd just asked."

## I SPY ~

There's a new dollhouse in Mandy Hurt's future, only she isn't supposed to know. It was purchased during an early Christmas shopping spree and hidden in the garage.

Just the other day, 3-year-old Mandy and her grandmother were thumbing through a Christmas toy catalog.

"Look, Grandma!" Mandy exclaimed, "there's a dollhouse — just like the one in the garage!"

## CUSTOMER SERVICE ~

A boy took a video cassette recorder to a local department store the other day. He told a clerk the VCR was a gift from his mother, but it wasn't the brand he wanted, so he would like to have a refund.

"No problem," the man said, more than a little bit suspicious. "What's your mother's name?"

He volunteered the name without hesitation.

"Just a minute while I go to the office and write up the refund," the clerk told him.

He went straight to the phone and called police. Minutes later, the boy was arrested. The VCR was hot. It had been stolen from a south-side residence. The name the boy had given was that of an employee of the department store. The clerk recognized the name and knew her home had been burglarized. He also knew she didn't have any children.

## HE SINGS 'EM HIS WAY  ~

'Tis the season when pest-control engineer Mark Netznik gets his kicks. He likes to sing Christmas songs. But he sings them his way. He doctors up the lyrics. Netznik serenades folks wherever he goes in the line of duty for Sentinel Insect Control, which services a  number of downtown government office buildings and he breaks for coffee almost every morning at Gold-N-Glow Donut Shop and entertains customers there with his ditties. Among his parodies:

*Rudolph the red-nosed rodent,*
*And his little mousey friends.*
*Once they get in my poison,*
*You know they're gonna get the bends.*
*Out they all came one evening,*
*And got into my rodent cakes.*
*And let me tell you, kiddies,*
*They all got bad bellyaches.*

Netznik's repertoire of 12 such ditties, another of which is "Silent Bug, Dead  Bug," are committed to memory and he's prepared to burst into song anytime, anywhere.  All relate to the variety of bugs and other pests he fights daily.

"It loosens people up and takes the edge off my job," Netznik says.

# 1988

## ONE FOR THE ROAD ~

The car was packed for a trip to Cedar Rapids, Iowa, for the holidays, and Laura LaCombe set her cup of coffee in a plastic holder as she started the engine.

"Mommy!" spouted her 3-year-old daughter, Abbie. "You mean you're gonna drink and drive?"

## HAIRY TALE ~

It started out as a social call.

Ken Griffith stopped by a friend's home Tuesday night. In the dark, it was difficult to distinguish one duplex from another, and there were a string of them. But he assumed he had the right one. He knocked. No response. Hearing voices, he knocked again. No response. One voice was that of a child. So he decided on a different approach. Humor.

"Open the door or I'll huff and puff and blow your house down," Griffith growled.

Still no response. He knocked awhile longer before giving up and returning to his car. Then, as he started to back out of the driveway, someone peered out the living room window. He waited.

"Next thing I know, a man wearing only shorts and socks ran out the door and started yelling at me," Griffith said. "He had a butcher knife. He was really upset. He thought I'd said I was going to blow his house up. He accused me of terrorizing his family."

It was obvious at that point that Griffith had the wrong house. He later called police to report the incident, just in case the man had complained. He had.

## HIGHWAY PATROL ~

A state trooper who pulled over a car south of Springfield may be thinking of applying for hazardous duty pay. Behind the wheel was Secretary of State Jim Edgar's wife, Brenda. Her license plate sticker had expired. She received the usual $50 ticket and is paying without protest. She quickly renewed her license plate sticker, too.

Brenda, who handles the mail on the home front, doesn't recall ever receiving a license renewal notice from the secretary of state's office. But — to keep peace in the family, no doubt — she's assuming she did receive one, that it went unnoticed in the pile of holiday mail and got lost in the shuffle.

## SYMPATHY CARD ~

It's likely that Secretary of State Jim Edgar's wife, Brenda, didn't receive a notice from the secretary of state's office to renew her license plate sticker, says a sympathetic Springfield woman.

"She's being kind when she says she probably did receive a renewal notice and it was overlooked," said the woman. "I know I didn't get one. I'm very careful in handling the mail and I know I didn't receive it. So it does happen."

A police officer reminded the woman of her expired license sticker a few days ago. She, too, was ticketed and paid a $50 fine.

"I think the secretary of state's office is to blame in my case and probably hers, too," says the woman. "Of course, I can say that because my husband isn't secretary of state."

## BIRTHDAY GIRL ~
Today, Feb. 27, 1988, is Anna Maggio's 100th birthday. Enjoying good health, she still handles kitchen chores and other household duties. She did have to go to hospital the other day — but just to visit her grandson.

## PASS THE GAS MASK ~
There'll be an extra added attraction — or distraction, depending on one's perspective — at a Department of Corrections public hearing on the proposed prison site at Taylorville, Ill. In an effort to pack the high school gym Wednesday night, the town meeting has evolved into a social wingding of sorts. Among other incentives, everyone who shows up early will get a free bowl of bean chili. Planners predict a crowd of more than 3,000.

"I don't know about anybody else," gasps one Taylorville wag, "but I don't want to be cooped up for hours with that many people who've been eating chili. Count me out!"

## PIG TALE ~
Channel 20 newsy Robin Beckham was as dazzled as the kids were with the farm animals at the Farm Bureau's petting zoo. Just like with the kids, it was her first close encounter with cows and pigs and such. She couldn't resist holding one of the cute little squealing pigs. But she quickly handed it back to the farmer, asking why she wasn't forewarned of the little porker's physical capabilities. Suffice it to say Robin had to make a quick trip to the dry cleaners.

## NO-SMOKING SECTION ~
There's a price to pay, as U.S. Rep. Dick Durbin is finding out, for the fight he waged to pass the law that snuffs smoking on shorter airline flights. (The law takes effect next month.)

〰️

First, shortly before Christmas, Durbin was snubbed by the R.J. Reynolds Tobacco Co. He was passed up when sampler boxes of Nabisco products were distributed to members of Congress. (Nabisco owns RJR.) That attracted considerable press at the time, and it was hinted that Durbin was not intentionally slighted. But the word on Capitol Hill was that Durbin was the only member of Congress who didn't get a box of goodies, making the message loud and clear.

Then, about a month ago, former Springfield Chamber of Commerce exec Bill Browning, now in a similar position at Wilkes-Barre, Pa., decided to "have a little fun." Without telling anyone who it was intended for, Browning obtained one of the Nabisco gift boxes from the corporation's local accounting office, then asked U.S. Rep. Paul Kanjorski of that district to present it to Durbin, preferably on the House floor. Kanjorski accepted the box, indicating he would carry out the mission. That was weeks ago, and Durbin has yet to see it. In fact, neither he nor his staff had heard about it until our inquiry. Browning either didn't know or didn't consider that Kanjorski was one of 193 reps who voted against the Durbin bill, which squeezed through by only five votes. Apparently Kanjorski didn't see the humor.

However, there was no discrimination this week when the National Association of Tobacco Distributors delivered a box of Irish mints to members of Congress. Whether a miscue or not, Durbin did receive a box of the NATD's candy.

Postscript: Durbin's anti-smoking measure has drawn positive and negative response. But the Democratic congressman's highest praise came indirectly from — of all places — a closed-door Republican House/Senate conference two weeks ago. The subject at hand was AIDS, and Surgeon General C. Everett Koop was asked to name the country's biggest health hazard. He said smoking. When asked what he would like Congress to do, he referred to Durbin's bill and called it the "best thing so far."

## LIGHT OPERA 〰️

Three glass doors and frames were removed at a main entrance to state Department of Revenue headquarters, allowing a work crew to get a large hydraulic lift inside. Carpenters then installed a temporary wood frame and door. An electrician was then launched by the lift machine into wasted space — the three-story-high atrium — to replace bulbs in 72 light fixtures. When that task was completed, the entrance was unboarded, the lift removed and the glass doors were rehung.

Now, people with inquiring minds want to know, how many taxpayers' dollars does it take to screw in one light bulb? Exactly $66.66. The total project, contracted out to a private electrical company, cost $4,800. Incidentally, the state provided the light bulbs.

That's the first time the bulbs have been changed since the building opened, and they're expected to last about four years. Of course, when they have to be changed again, the same costly procedure will have to be repeated. Most of the cost is attributable to leasing the hydraulic lift (at $35,000, the state considers it too expensive to buy one) and the union electricians required to screw in the bulbs.

Obviously, designers of the $70 million building didn't take bulb-changing into consideration. They didn't provide an entry large enough to accommodate such machinery. By the way, after four years, the huge atrium still leaks.

## KILLER 'SAVED' ~

A drug-crazed man armed with a hammer terrorized a neighborhood on Springfield's near south side nearly 13 years ago. He attacked every man, woman and child in his path. When his rampage ended, in the Thrifty drugstore at Sixth Street and South Grand Avenue, eight people had been bludgeoned. Two of his victims died. Another suffered permanent brain damage.

A self-admitted drug addict, 25-year-old Francis "Frank" Sherry later pleaded guilty to two counts of voluntary manslaughter and six counts of aggravated battery. He was sent to prison for 10 to 30 years. Sherry, now 38, was paroled three months ago. Now a resident of Marion, where he is employed as a laborer, he just returned to Springfield May 1 to tell his story.

Sherry, with his wife at his side and the widow of one of his victims present, told the South Side Christian Church congregation of his conversion to Christianity while in prison.

"I pray you might forgive me for that heinous crime and atrocity against

∽

this city and against you," Sherry said. "Back then I wasn't saved. I didn't know anything about being a Christian. As a youth, I was rebellious. You couldn't tell me a thing. I had a pretty good education and upbringing, but I was a rebel. I thought I knew it all."

Sherry said he "launched out into a world of drugs and rock music" after entering military service.

"Every drug out there, every single one, and every liquor and every beer and every wine, I used to indulge in," he said. "I had absolutely no morals. I would steal. I stole from my own family. I would lie. I was evil. All I wanted to do was grow my hair long and run the streets and take dope and do my own thing. I was hooked. I was a drug addict. I went from one city to another. I fell right into it here."

Sherry moved into a second-floor apartment near Second and Scarritt several months before that fateful day: Aug. 4, 1975.

"On (that) day I was taking PCP (the animal tranquilizer phencyclidine, the most prevalent drug on city streets at the time)," Sherry recalled. "It was an awful day. Satan whispered in my ear to kill. I was obedient. I followed this thing out. Flowers, plants that were in my house, our cat, even. Anything that was alive, that's what I attacked — with the intention of killing. I'm not trying to get out of this thing, but I believe I actually was possessed."

Sherry said he doesn't recall details.

Police reconstructed the crime this way:

After trashing his apartment and beating his cat to death in the kitchen, Sherry, armed with a hammer, went downstairs and clubbed two men who were doing remodeling work. He then went around the corner and beat another man with the hammer. He drove to the drugstore and attacked five people there. One of the victims disarmed Sherry. He was cutting his wrists with a broken bottle when police caught up with him.

A few weeks after Sherry was jailed, he had a visitor. Florence Dace, whose 74-year-old husband Tom died of head injuries inflicted by Sherry, went to the county jail to meet the killer face to face. She gave her late husband's Bible to Sherry and told him he should read it. Sherry recalled that meeting.

"Jesus loves you, Frank," he quoted her as telling him. "I'm a Christian. My husband was an elder in the church and was doing great work for the Lord. Scripture says we must forgive or our Heavenly Father won't forgive us."

Sherry credits Mrs. Dace with starting him on the road to Christianity.

"This lady was really living for the Lord," Sherry told the church congregation. "How else could she do that after I had murdered her husband?" He says he started reading the Bible.

"I got 10 to 30 years," Sherry said. "That was a miracle of God, to get a light sentence."

He encountered other men in prison who had committed similar crimes but got much longer sentences, he said. Sherry singled out young people for this warning.

"Let me tell you something," he said of his prison experience. "You never want to go to prison. It's an awful place. It's literally a survival test. I saw people carried out. People were killed there. People were knifed. People were beaten."

Sherry thanked both Mrs. Dace and South Side Pastor Bob Green for encouragement and guidance over the years.

"I'm here to tell you the Lord changed my life dramatically," he told the congregation.

Mrs. Dace followed Sherry to the pulpit.

"It took me a long time to make up my mind to go see him (in jail)," she said of Sherry. "I still had the burden on my heart. But somebody had to go, and I guess that somebody was me."

## PIGEON DROP ~
The state of Florida, in launching its lottery a couple of weeks ago, paid

homage — loosely speaking — to a Springfield pigeon. Floridians were introduced to "Lotto," the one-winged pigeon that has been randomly picking Jim Tureskis' lottery numbers for the past five years.

"You won't believe it," the Florida Times Union told its readers. "It's a pigeon drop, of sorts."

The story went on to tell how Tureskis, a Springfield telephone cable repairman, snapped a long losing streak when he gave the bird the chore of selecting lottery numbers. He found the wounded pigeon on a south-side street in 1983. One wing was broken. He adopted it, came up with the lottery system and named it Lotto. Tureskis' system works like this:

He puts a number board in the bottom of Lotto's cage. Lotto goes about his business for a few days. Then Tureskis scrapes the board clean, taking note of the numbers Lotto bombed. He then plays those numbers in various combinations in the next Lotto game. Lotto, who we had last reported on in 1984, still calls Tureskis' garage home, and he's still picking numbers. Tureskis has yet to win the big one, but he once was within one number of being rich and famous.

"We're still trying for the million dollars," Tureskis said this week.

Lotto is appreciated for more than his gambling sense.

"He's probably one of the best pets we've ever had," says Tureskis' wife, Joanne. "He struts around here and over to the neighbor's yard. He likes their birdbath."

Tureskis says they've both become attached to the bird.

"Other than having to cover my car with a blanket every night," he says, "Lotto is no trouble."

## CYCLIN' GRANDMA ~

Take a good look, the driver of that shiny new Harley "hog" you see tooling around Springfield this weekend may not be the black leather-jacketed motorcyclist you'd expect on such a mean machine. It just might be 62-year-old Hazel Kolb of New London, Mo., president of the 68,000-member national HOG (Harley Owners Group) organization. She arrives today for a get-together of the Motor Maids, a 600-member national motorcycle club for women only.

Hazel will be among Motor Maids running the parade lap at motorcycle races at the state fairgrounds this weekend. She just traded her 1985 Harley-Davidson, which had more than 50,000 miles on it, for the new one.

"I've ridden 300,000 safe and happy miles in the last 20 years," she beams.

The grandmother of four, Hazel fulfilled her late husband's dream of riding the perimeter of the United States in 1979, which took her more than 16,000 miles. In 1985, she rode to every state capital: 28,000 miles. That earned her the title "Motorcycling Grandmother" and appearances on the Johnny Carson and David Letterman shows. Her autobiography, "On the Perimeter," is in its second printing.

What do the grandkids think about Grandma gallivanting all over the country on a motorcycle?

"They're just as proud of me as I am of them," she says.

## SHOELIFTER ~

Soon after the South Bend White Sox baseball team, in town for a series with the Springfield Cardinals a few days ago, left the El-Bee Shoe Outlet in Capital City Shopping Center, manager Greg Gietl found a pair of old tennis shoes. Then he discovered that a pair of new tennis shoes was missing. He phoned the team manager at a nearby motel to relay his suspicions. Someone with the team must have a new pair of white Nike shoes, size 9½, and no sales receipt, he said.

The manager was genuinely concerned. That kind of conduct would not be tolerated, he said.

Ten minutes later, one of the players — extremely nervous — returned to the shoe store and asked Gietl to let him pay for the $44 shoes. With an understanding that the team manager would take appropriate action, Gietl accepted cash payment instead of calling police.

⌣

"Let's hope he's better at stealing bases than he is at stealing shoes," Gietl quipped.

## AD LIBS ~
You know it's a drought:
• When your lawn has a better tan than you do.
• When you only have to mow the yard every eight weeks.
• When crabgrass dies.

## LESSON LEARNED? ~
Three teenagers were confronted by a man trying to peddle a brand-new VCR when they stopped for a traffic light Wednesday night. He asked only $60. He had a commercial VCR packing box, its contents cellophane-wrapped.

"Just like at the store," one of the kids later explained to his parents. Heckuva deal.

They couldn't cough up $60 between them. But they were able to pool $38.

"Good enough," the man said, grabbing the money and handing them the VCR box.

After driving away, they unwrapped their bargain VCR, which turned out to be three bricks. Unlike the victim who was robbed of $100 at gunpoint by a man selling VCR equipment Monday night on Martin Luther King Drive, the teens — bugged by guilty consciences — didn't report their experience to police. There was little doubt the VCR was stolen. They knew that. And, they know what happens to people caught with stolen property.

## POLICE STORY ~
A motorcycle roared into the wild blue yonder when a Jerome police officer signaled the teenage driver to pull over. With the squad car on their tail, the young cyclist and his passenger raced through stop signs on Cherry Road at 65 mph, cut across a shopping center parking lot and went down an alley at high speed. In a last-ditch effort to end the chase, the officer turned on the squad car's loudspeaker and grabbed the microphone.

 ᓄ

"When he comes out of the alley, shoot him!" he said, simulating a broadcast as if police officers were laying in wait at the intersection ahead.

It was a ruse, of course. But a split-second later, the motorcycle screeched to a stop and both boys jumped off with their hands in the air.

"Don't shoot! Don't shoot!" they yelled.

## KID COMES CLEAN ~

A west-side woman was busy cleaning out a closet when her 3-year-old daughter, Maggie, decided to go for a swim. She asked if she could fill the kiddie pool.

"No," her mother replied. "There's a water shortage, and you can't use water for things like that."

Maggie went out to play in the back yard. Later in the day, a police officer knocked on the door. He told the woman she was in violation of the city's water conservation policy. To her surprise, the sprinkler hose was on full-blast. It had been on for some time, because the ground was soaked.

"I understand," she told the officer, "but my 3-year-old daughter must have turned on the hose. I didn't."

About that time, Maggie ambled around the corner, water bucket in hand. Obviously, she was still trying to fill the kiddie pool. It had been a slow process, trying to fill the little bucket with spray from the sprinkler hose. The officer, convinced Maggie's mother wasn't trying to pin a bum rap on her 3-year-old daughter, confronted the little girl. He knelt in front of her. First, the officer had to keep a straight face. That wasn't easy. Maggie, standing there in all her innocence, was clad in underpants, a winter coat and her sister's soccer shoes. (Remember, she had been helping her mother clean out the closet.) And, a pacifier was wedged in her mouth.

"You must not turn on the hose . . ." the officer began.

Maggie appeared to be impressed. She eventually confessed. She had turned on the hose, not her mother.

Still, there was a violation, the officer explained, handing a ticket to Maggie's mother.

## TRESPASSING TOURISTS ~
A family tour of the Lincoln Home produced this exchange.

"Where is Mr. Lincoln?" one of the boys asked his father.

"He's dead," the father replied.

"Where is Mrs. Lincoln?" the boy pressed.

"She's dead, too," he was told.

"Well," the boy exclaimed, "if Mr. and Mrs. Lincoln are both dead, what are we doing in their house?"

## THE LONGEST HOUR ~
A sidewalk construction crew sliced through electrical feeder lines at the state Department of Transportation. Everything — lights to telephones — was knocked out. Power was off about an hour but — except for one DOT employee — it wasn't a major disaster. The power outage left him stranded in an elevator. He was on his way to the restroom at the time.

## DEER (DOUBLE) CROSSING ~
A humane act by a young Springfield man almost landed him in jail. But, because his "heart was in the right place," the Department of Conservation is going to let him off with a $50 fine.

"It was a really disappointing experience," says Mark Wohler, a student at Eastern Illinois University.

Wohler and a friend were returning to the campus when a car ahead of them struck a deer on Illinois 121, just west of Sullivan, Ill. Two elderly couples occupied the car that hit the animal. Wohler stopped to assist.

"They were freaking out," he said. "The deer was in bad shape. Its back and legs were broken. It was jerking around and bawling. Those people didn't know what to do."

〜

Wohler happened to have his squirrel hunting gun, an old .36-caliber flintlock rifle, in the car. He loaded it and, after several misfires, shot the deer in the head. It died immediately.

Assuming the animal should be turned over to authorities, Wohler and his companion unloaded their books and clothes, removed the back seat and — after a heckuva struggle — put the deer in the back of Wohler's Volkswagen. They drove to the Moultrie County sheriff's office and reported the incident, thinking they could unload the deer and be on their way. But deputies told them they would have to wait until a Department of Conservation officer arrived.

"They believed our story, but said the DOC officer would have to handle it." said Wohler. "However, they did find it hard to believe a deer could be stuffed into the back of a VW."

About an hour later, the DOC officer arrived. That's when Wohler discovered he was in trouble. Although he, too, believed Wohler's account of how and why the deer was killed, the conservation officer said "we just can't let you walk out of here." He informed Wohler he could be jailed, and his gun and car impounded. He could be cited for offenses that carry fines totaling $150.

But, he said, because Wohler thought he was doing what was right, and college students usually don't have money to spare, he would just give him a $50 ticket. That he did. Wohler was charged with "killing a road-hit deer without permission from a law enforcement officer." But to show Wohler his heart was in the right place, the conservation officer postdated the ticket so the $50 fine wouldn't have to be paid until after Christmas.

"Now, what do I do with the deer?" Wohler asked, preparing to depart.

"It's yours," said the DOC officer.

So, Wohler took off for Charleston with his friend and the dead deer. He found help and an empty garage later that night, dressed the animal, packed the meat in ice and drove back to Springfield. A friend helped him process it. He missed two days of classes.

⤳

"I think I got at least $50 worth of meat out of it," says Wohler, "but I have a lot of work to make up at school. It wasn't worth it, though. Everyone, even the conservation officer, was super nice through the whole thing. But the experience was very disappointing.

"I thought I was doing the right thing, what had to be done. I'm a hunter, although I don't hunt deer and I've always tried to obey the law and avoid something like this. It's no wonder people don't want to get involved any more."

## WATCH FOR FALLING GEESE ~

A Springfield man went all the way to Missouri on a goose-hunting expedition, then didn't bag a single goose. But a goose bagged him.

He was taking his turn at the top of the goose pit, waiting for a good shot. That's when a hunter in another pit scored a direct hit. The mortally wounded goose plummeted earthward and hit the unsuspecting Springfield man square in the head. He tumbled down the steps and into the pit — knocked out cold. At first, his buddies though he'd suffered a heart attack. As he regained consciousness, they saw the dead goose and figured it out. He escaped with only a headache.

He eventually got a shot at a goose, but missed. However, he didn't go home empty-handed. He got to keep the goose that bagged him.

The intrepid hunter, who's trying to remain anonymous (he's well-known in the auto parts trade), is described by friends as "rather accident prone." He's been "wounded" twice within the past two years.

On one occasion, a wild shot by another hunter hit him in the leg. Another time, he was at a public auction and an elderly man asked him how to cock a BB gun that was offered at the sale. As he offered instructions, the man shot him in the foot.

## MARIJUANA, PIRANHA; WHAT'S THE DIF? ~

The view of Rend Lake, along Interstate 57 north of Benton, didn't look inviting to 9-year-old Miranda Wilkins as the family headed back to Springfield after a trip to Tennessee.

❧

"I don't think I'd like to swim in that," she said.

"Why not?" her father Chuck asked.

"Could be marijuana in it," she replied.

"Marijuana?" her father pressed.

"You know," Miranda innocently explained, "those little fish that eat up people."

# 1989

## BATHROBE BIT(E) ~

The bathrobe that Mary Ann Gobble gave to Marian Epps for Christmas was a perfect fit. But the extra little goodie in the pocket wasn't.

After Marian slipped into the robe, she put her hands into the pockets and pulled out a surprise — somebody's false teeth. She accused Mary Ann of pulling a prank on her, but that wasn't the case. Mary Ann says she bought the robe at Penney's and only gift-wrapped it. A clerk confirmed that particular style of robe doesn't come with teeth.

Best guess, says Mary Ann, is that someone had tried on the robe in the store and decided to give their choppers a rest at the same time.

## GOOD SAMARITANS ~

Springfield investment broker Ken Tyler and his wife Joyce, killed Sunday night when their small plane crashed near Capital Airport, befriended many a stranger. In most instances, few knew because the couple preferred anonymity. One was chronicled in this column eight years ago. But there was no reference to the Tylers. That's how they preferred it.

A young woman had been raped and robbed on a near-west-side street. She approached them. They didn't hesitate to get involved. It was a frightening experience for them as well as the victim.

〜

Tyler and his wife were getting into their car, parked on South MacArthur Boulevard, on a cold February evening in 1981. That's when the woman ran out of the darkness, gasping that a man armed with a gun had just raped her and threatened to kill her. Tyler helped her into the car.

"She was hysterical," Tyler said. "She got down low in the back seat, trying to hide."

While Joyce tried to comfort the woman, Tyler — not knowing where the gun-toting rapist might be — drove off and headed for police headquarters. They stayed with the woman until police had the situation well in hand. But that didn't end their involvement.

Tyler posted $500 reward for the rapist's arrest. And he and his wife kept in touch with authorities, as well as an eye out for the victim's welfare, as the investigation progressed.

## DEER TRACKS 〜

The Springfield college student who put an injured deer out of its misery in Moultrie County six weeks ago "did the right thing," says Lt. Gov. George Ryan and Ryan puts his money where his mouth is. He paid the $50 fine for Mark Wohler, who pleaded guilty to killing a road-hit deer without permission from a law enforcement officer.

Ryan, among scores of sympathizers who offered to pay the fine or finance a court challenge, enclosed a check when he sent a letter to Wohler. Besides the deluge of mail and phone calls supporting Wohler, scores vented their wrath on the state Department of Conservation. Wohler, who attends Eastern Illinois University (an institution close to Ryan's heart) at Charleston, says he apparently is technically guilty. But he believes he was the victim of an overzealous conservation officer.

He and a friend were returning to campus when a car ahead of them, occupied by two elderly couples, struck the deer on Illinois 121 west of Sullivan. He assisted them and shot and killed the seriously injured deer. Then he loaded the dead animal into his car and took it to the Moultrie County sheriff's office. A conservation officer later said he believed Wohler, but had to issue a ticket.

"I understand the law and the reason for it," says Wohler. "Someone could shoot a deer illegally, run over it with a car and then report it as an accident. But that wasn't the case.  Even though the officer told me he believed me, he still gave me a ticket.  He didn't treat me right."

## SAY WHAT? ~
An elderly Litchfield, Ill., couple had just returned home after picking up a new hearing aid for the mister. His wife decided to put it to a test.

"How is it?" she asked.

"Three-thirty," he said.

## DAZE OF THEIR LIVES ~
Just in case the veterans of Gen. George Patton's 4th Armored Divsion have forgotten their World War II days, they're about to be reminded.  Vets from 18 mid-U.S. states will gather here in May for their annual reunion.

Springfield will be hosting the group, which will headquarter at the Lincoln Plaza Hotel, for the first time. To take the troops back in time, hotel manager Dave Gerig will set up a typical battlefield mess hall on the parking lot.  Gerig, himself an Army vet, says  he'll feature typical WWII delicacies like K-rations (if he can find any) and Spam. Breakfast will consist of the infamous chipped-beef-gravy on toast ("SOS" in Army slang) for breakfast. And there'll be real Army field coffee. The recipe for that delicious brew: dump coffee into bucket of boiling water, allow grounds to settle to the bottom and pour.

For even more realism, the old soldiers will be provided with authentic Army mess kits, and there'll be no chairs to sit on.

## TRY, TRY, TRY AGAIN ~
It was a long haul for an elderly Springfield man who set out to renew his driver's license a few weeks ago. A license examiner flunked him on his first behind-the-wheel test in mid-December.  He failed again two days later.  He returned to the Klein Street examining station a third time. Again he failed the test. But he just barely failed.  A week later he tried again, and failed. But just barely.

He returned later the same day and was retested. He passed!

Minutes later, with his new driver's license in hand, he climbed into his car and drove away — sideswiping five parked cars.

## CB'ERS CORNER KILLERS ~

It isn't unusual for motorists equipped with citizens band radios to help law enforcement by reporting stalled cars, traffic accidents, suspicious characters and traffic offenders — especially drunken drivers. Occasionally, a CBer proves invaluable in a major criminal case. That's what happened after two gas station employees were robbed and shot — one fatally — at Farmersville, Ill., last summer. State police say the assistance of an Arkansas man and woman who saw the killers in the service station, then kept police informed via CB radio of their flight up Interstate 55, enabled troopers to make arrests quickly.

The play by play:

After a nightlong drive from Arkansas, 23-year old Susan Birrell pulled into the Shell station at Farmersville and parked near the front door. Her companion, Rick Stinebaugh, remained in the car as she walked toward the door. A man inside, later identified as Tuhran Lear of St. Louis, opened the door for her. She first thought he was an employee, but then saw a man's body in a pool of blood on the floor. She saw a second man, who turned out to be Randy Lee Thomas, also of St. Louis, behind the counter.

"I realized something wasn't right," Birrell said in testifying at Thomas' murder trial in Hillsboro, Ill., a few days ago.

She began to back away.

"Come back in here," Lear ordered.

Birrell kept walking toward her car, even though Lear lifted his shirt, showing her he had a gun in his pants waistband. She got into the car, told Stinebaugh what she had seen, and they drove away. Heading for the interstate, they looked back to see Lear get into a tan car, pull up to the front of the gas station and pick up Thomas. Stinebaugh grabbed his CB and radioed for help.

Another CBer responded and instructed him to switch to Channel 9 so he could communicate with state police directly. Stinebaugh, now north-bound on I-55 with the murder suspects following, broadcast descriptions of Lear and Thomas, plus their location and direction of travel. State police relayed that information via the ISPERN radio channel that links patrol cars from all agencies. It was now 6:48 a.m., 18 minutes after Birrell first encountered the killers.

Trooper Patrick Keen, who had stopped a motorist for a traffic violation in the northbound lanes, cut back across the median and started following the suspect's car. Trooper Robert Haley, also southbound, saw the car about the same time. He crossed the median to join Keen.

By that time, Keen was monitoring Stinebaugh's CB messages. He asked Stinebaugh, who had just pulled into the parking lot at state police district headquarters near Lake Springfield, for more details. Stinebaugh stayed in his car and continued to relay information to Keen. Trooper Kenneth Mullen, waiting just south of district headquarters, pulled in behind Keen and Haley. The trio of troopers moved up on the suspects' car, turned on their red lights and pulled it over.

Thomas and Lear were arrested at 6:55 a.m., only 25 minutes after the shootings and only 19 miles from the scene of the crime.

## FAMILY FIRST ~

Taylorville, Ill., Mayor Dick Adams likes his job, but he likes his family better. That's why he isn't seeking re-election. Adams wrestled with the question for weeks, right up to the filing deadline.

"I like the job very much," he says after nearly four years as mayor. "I was really having trouble saying no."

Then one night at home a few weeks ago, he overheard his son talking on the telephone. Someone called and asked for the mayor.

"My dad's at a meeting," 3-year-old Jordan told the caller, unaware his father was downstairs.

*Taylorville Mayor
Dick Adams*

"He's never home. He's always at meetings."

That cinched it.

"I decided I had better get my priorities in order," says Adams. "I decided right then that I wouldn't run."

## SPOON LICKIN' GOOD ~
A 4-year-old girl, lunching with her mom at Pizza Hut on Wabash Avenue, returned to the food bar alone to help herself to dessert. She zeroed in on the chocolate pudding. She filled her little dessert dish and was about to put the spoon back, but apparently decided she should tidy up first.

She licked the spoon up and down on both sides, then — obviously proud of her penchant for neatness — stuck it back into the pudding bowl and marched back to her table.

Several customers who witnessed her little ritual alerted a waitress, who quickly fetched a new bowl of pudding.

## FUN HOUSE ~
It's next to impossible to crack up House Clerk Jack O'Brien — the Illinois legislature's "resident Maytag repairman" — when he's performing in perfunctory session (reading bills aloud, often for hours on end, before an empty House to fulfill a constitutional requirement). So, it was a rare feat when members of the O'Brien clan finally tripped him up, making him lose his place briefly, last week.

Countless attempts by Statehouse jokers — particularly House pages — over the years to break the monotony for O'Brien proved futile. Even the time a page mooned him. He didn't even flinch.

## POSTAGE DUE ~
Eighty-year-old Gus Sutter, Raymond's elder rural delivery mailman, is one in a million. Actually, he's one in 800,000. That's how many employees the U.S. Postal Service has, and Sutter has been on the job longer than any of them. To put things in perspective, Calvin Coolidge was president and it cost two cents to mail a letter when Sutter started his career.

Sixty years, 11 presidents and 13 postal rate increases later, Sutter is still driving his 80-mile mail route. He isn't bored.

〜

"You're out there where there's no pressure. You're out there with nature and you see things, watch things grow, talk to people," he said Saturday when postal workers helped him celebrate his 80th birthday at the Raymond Post Office.

He'll take time off next month to go to Washington where he'll be honored for his government service, then it's back to the rural route. Retire? Sutter says he isn't planning on it.

## BIBLICAL CHARACTER ~
A Sunday school lesson left 5-year-old Moses Dyer a little mixed up. He was really ticked by the  time he got home.

"My Sunday school teacher talked about me all day," he complained to his mother, "and I didn't do any of the things she said I did."

## MIZZONER-THE-MAYOR ~
Ever-quotable 84-year-old Jacksonville Mayor Helen Foreman, who'll retire with the swearing-in of newly elected Ron Tendick Monday night, was asked about her plans.

"It'll be interesting to see what's on Monday night TV," she quipped.

For the past five years, Foreman has spent Monday nights at council and committee meetings.

## MOTHER'S DAZE ~
A high schooler, reciting memories of mom, told this one at a mother-and-daughter banquet.  She was briefing her mother on track practice, she said, explaining that the coach had concentrated on high-knee exercises that day.

"Oh!" her mother replied. "Now just what does that do for your heinie?"

## BEAN BIT ~
"The first case of product tampering occurred in 1926," Smokey Joe Miller reveals. "Four people who lived on the same block found big hunks of pork in cans of pork-n-beans. A man  working on the production line in a canning factory in Newark finally admitted to the misdeed. He was fired

and the company promised consumers it would never happen again. It hasn't."

## SMOKE SCREAM ~

If R.J. Reynolds' mailing list is any indication, one of the country's biggest "smokers' rights" movements is going to the dogs. An invitation to a smokers' rights rally sponsored by the tobacco giant was mailed to Ms. Z. Bitter on Windsor Road. Full Name: Zipper Bitter.

Zipper's a dog.

Zipper, described as a wire-haired fox terrier, is not an advocate of smokers' rights, according to family spokesman, Janet Bitter.

"I think she'll RSVP that she will attend (the Springfield meeting Tuesday night) and will be bringing several friends," says Janet. Zipper's friends, of course, are other dogs in the neighborhood.

## DOG-GONE! ~

Central Illinois Public Service executive Sam Poe claims that this Lost & Found notice, on the wall at Coney Island restaurant, refers to his dog:

"LOST: Dog with three legs, blind in left eye, right ear missing, tail broken, answers to name of Lucky."

## CONGRESSMAN AT THE BAT ~

"True, there are more serious subjects for Congress to be discussing," an aide to U.S. Rep. Dick Durbin admits, "but things had been serious long enough, and Durbin's 'baseball bat' speech provided the comic relief House members needed.

"They went ape!" Durbin spokesman Steve Blakely said, referring to in-House reaction to the oratory, which came after three days of debate on the military budget. "We're hearing from all over the country, and the response has been overwhelmingly positive."

Only a handful of negative remarks have reached Durbin. One took him to task for "comparing" the American flag to baseball bats. Well, not quite.

*Congressman
Dick Durbin*

Durbin began his 60-second speech:

"Mr. Speaker, I rise to condemn the desecration of a great American symbol. No, I'm not referring to flag burning; I am referring to the baseball bat."

The wooden baseball bat appears to be "doomed to extinction" because major league baseball may adopt the aluminum bat, he said.

"Baseball fans have been forced to endure countless indignities by those who just cannot leave well enough along. Designated hitters, plastic grass, uniforms that look like pajamas, chicken clowns dancing on the baselines. And, of course, the most heinous sacrilege — lights in Wrigley Field. Are we willing to hear the crack of a bat replaced by the dinky ping? Are we ready to see the Louisville Slugger replaced by the aluminum ping dinger? Is nothing sacred?"

He continued.

"What is next? Teflon baseballs? Radar-enhanced gloves?

"I do not want to hear about saving trees. Any tree in America would gladly give its life for the glory of a day at home plate.

"If we forsake the great Americana of broken-bat singles and pine tar," he concluded, "we will have certainly lost our way as a nation."

Durbin gets full credit for his remarks.

"It was his idea, and he wrote it," Blakely said. "He surprised everybody." Durbin had been moved by a Sports Illustrated article citing the increased popularity of aluminum ball bats.

## PICKIN' ON THE WRONG GUY ~

A pair of pickpockets working the St. Louis airport terminal crowd one day last month must have figured Walter Marcussen would be a pushover. He surprised 'em.

Marcussen, a former Menard County sheriff (1951-58) who now lives in

Springfield, had just seen his daughter off at a TWA gate and was riding a moving walkway through the concourse, when he felt a hand in his back pocket. Too late — the guy had already lifted his wallet.

The thief quickly pitched it to an accomplice headed the other direction.

"Get that guy . . . he's got my wallet!" Marcussen yelled to another man.

As the pickpocket leaped over the handrail, Marcussen grabbed him by the neck and decked him.

"I caught him just right," said the 79-year-old Marcussen.

He planted his foot on the thief's neck and held him on the floor while the other man chased down the guy with the wallet.

Meanwhile, someone had pulled a security alarm. Cops were there within seconds. Both thieves were arrested. When their pockets were emptied, police found four stolen wallets. One contained $600. Marcussen had $129 in his.

"That's the biggest haul we've made yet," one pickpocket boasted.

It was enough loot to hold them on felony charges.

The thieves, 27 and 32 years old, had been fired by an airline recently. They told police their crime spree had been inspired by a book they had read: "How to Pick Pockets."

## DIGITAL DIG ~

The Illinois State Fair parade was nearing its destination when Gov. Jim Thompson, wife Jayne, daughter Samantha and comedian Jim Varney drew dubious recognition from one spectator — the single digit salute.

It was rendered by a 6-year-old boy. Jayne and both Jims caught it but played it cool, in hopes First Daughter's attention had been focused elsewhere. Nothing was said until the parade ended.

"Dad!" Samantha blurted. "Did you see what that kid did?"

⌐ↄ

"Uh, whaddya mean . . .?"

"He gave us the finger," she declared. "If I was his mom, I'd have turned him over my knee and spanked him."

## DWARF TOSSING TOSSED ~

The public outcry over dwarf-tossing in Springfield caught Deja Vu night-club management by surprise, all right. But that's just the half of it. What really amazed club managers was the widespread media interest — particularly from distant radio and television stations. While much of that was Chicago-based, inquiries came from throughout a 200-mile radius.

Dozens of reporters and photographers (mostly TV cameras) wanted to cover the first dwarf-tossing competition Wednesday night, the club manager said. If all had been admitted, he added, there wouldn't have been much room left for customers.

The club was besieged with phone calls when it was announced the dwarf-toss had been canceled. Most of the estimated 150 callers voiced disappointment, according to the manager.

The cancellation prompted a DJ at Chicago radio station WLS Thursday morning to blast city and state officials, and anyone else who had condemned dwarf-tossing. And it inspired WLS program producer Tom Johnson (once with WTAX here) to volunteer to substitute for the dwarf if another toss is ever scheduled.

Thanks, but no thanks, said Deja Vu management.

## 'PEEP-LE' ~

A West Coast producer scouting New Salem State Park for shooting sites for the new movie "Joseph and Emma" (location work is scheduled in the Springfield area in October) obviously was not a perfect stranger to these parts. For one thing, he had heard of "The Great American People Show" staged in the park's outdoor theater every summer.

Commenting to one of the locals who was showing him around, he said he'd really like to see "The Great American Peep Show."

## FACIAL IN THE CROWD ~

Among customers at the cosmetics counter in Hills department store Monday afternoon was ukulele-plunking legend Tiny Tim. He stocked up on several makeup items (mostly blush).

Sporting a loud green jacket and his trademark scruffy sneakers, he graciously accommodated admirers with autographs for nearly a half-hour.

The falsetto-voice singer was part of the "Rock 'n' Roll Reunion" that was the Illinois State Fair's Grandstand offering Sunday night.

## GASOLINE ALLEY ~

A drastic jump in pump prices overnight — from 87.9 to 98.9 cents per gallon at one gas station — primed Smokey Joe Miller when he got a fill-up.

"What happened?" he ribbed the cashier. "Did the Exxon Valdez hit another rock?"

## SKELETON CREW ~

Two guys driving through downtown Springfield in a silver Toyota mini-van Thursday morning drew plenty of strange looks and a few gasps. Behind the wheel was Dr. Ed Trudeau, a physical medicine specialist at Southern Illinois University School of Medicine. In the passenger's seat was a human skeleton.

Trudeau and friend had just made an educational appearance before grade schoolers at Cathedral School and were heading up Sixth Street, back to the hospital. Since the back of the van was full, Trudeau positioned the skeleton upright in the front seat. The skeleton appeared to have startled most pedestrians and motorists who spotted it, but a security guard at the hospital gate took it in stride as Trudeau drove in.

"Glad you got him here in time," Sgt. Don Dalton drawled.

## BUS STOP ~

A motorist stopped alongside a city school bus Thursday morning at Monroe and Old Jacksonville Road. As he waited for the traffic light to change, several wet specks hit the windshield. He thought it was starting to rain.

Then he looked up to see two bus windows open and kids leaning out. They were spitting on cars. He figured maybe they were on their way to reform school.

## STORM WARNING ~

This bit of advice is taped to the wall next to the service counter in the Sangamon County clerk's office — where altar-bound couples apply for marriage licenses:

"Marriages Are Made in Heaven — So is Lightning and Thunder."

## SHORTCUT ~

'Tis the season when, as far as many a motorist is concerned, any space will do when they need a place to park. Even in front of a fireplug. And that can be hazardous to an automobile.

One motorist in Springfield learned the hard way. He left his car next to a fire hydrant and went shopping. While he was gone, fire broke out in a nearby business and firefighters needed the fireplug.

His car was parked so close to the hydrant that firefighters couldn't bend the hose around it. So they opened both car doors (fortunately they were unlocked) and stretched the hose through the vehicle to the fireplug.

## HOUSE OF CLAUS ~

The nightly bedtime story for 5-year-old twins Mike and Dan O'Keefe had just ended, and they were being tucked in.

"Can I ask you a question?" Dan asked his mother, Mary.

"Sure. What's your question?" she said.

"Where does Santa Claus live?"

"At the North Pole," she replied.

"Well," Dan declared, "that's what I've been telling all the other kids. But they say he lives at the mall."

## 1990

## SIZE-WISE ~

The stick 'um measuring tape on the door frame at Rax restaurant, an anti-crime tool police provide to businesses to help employees obtain accurate physical descriptions in stickups, has been embellished. Some wise guy has added instructions on how employees should react to crooks who fit these size categories:

6'5" - Run!
6'0" - Call 911.
5'8" - Might be trouble.
5'4" - Don't worry.

## STRANGE BEDFELLOWS ~

Occupying three banquet rooms in a row at Holiday Inn East the other day:

1 - A stop smoking class.

2 - An R.J. Reynolds Tobacco Co. delegation.
3 - The Illinois Lung Association.

And there was no riot.

## OH, WAITER! ~

A woman was enjoying her lunch at a Springfield restaurant the other day until her teeth banged down on something as hard as a rock. Just a bone fragment, she thought. She checked to make sure. It wasn't a bone — it was a tooth. A decayed tooth, at that. She knew it wasn't hers. She wears dentures. She complained.

## PEE-YOO! ~

The new conceptual art exhibit at the state museum in Springfield — the sweaty T-shirt part — may stir up more of a stink than the artist intended. One man who viewed the exhibit called it "disgusting" and an "insult to the public." At the very least, he adds, it's a waste of valuable museum space.

Museum art director Kent Smith says the offbeat exhibit intrigues and appeals to most viewers' sense of humor, while others simply make sarcastic comments.

That part of the second-floor exhibit, which began a three-month run Monday, consists of dozens of dirty T-shirts, each emitting the scents of real sweaty people. (Friends of Chicago artist Laurie Palmer personally perspired in them per her request.) They're scattered on tiers of shelves and, should the odor in the room not be repelling enough, a machine pumps fumes from synthetically re-created sweat into the air. Although the museum prefers otherwise, art connoisseurs can pick up the T-shirts and take a good whiff if they're so moved — and some are.

"It smells like a locker room, all right," Smith says of the exhibit. "But I don't think it's as bad as a high school locker room."

The area is sealed off with plastic sheeting (resembles a construction zone) to prevent the foul odor from spreading to other areas of the museum, so the rest of the exhibits smell much better.

## HOLD THE LINE ~

"Car telephones are dangerous and ought to be banned," Vicki Huff says after seeing a motorist — talking on his mobile phone at the time — run over a dog in front of Grant Middle School Wednesday morning. Huff says the well-dressed man driving a luxury car could have avoided hitting the dog if he hadn't been preoccupied with the phone call.

"He was concentrating on his phone conversation, not his driving," she said. "It could have been a child instead of a dog."

After witnessing the incident, she turned around and followed the car. She honked her horn until he pulled over several blocks up the street. He continued with his phone call for 15 minutes, then confronted her.

"He told me he didn't know he had hit the dog, that he was on an important phone call," Huff says. "When I pointed out the damage to his car, he said he wasn't worried about that or the dog, that the phone call was worth more than a damned dog.

"I really read him off."

Huff points to laws regulating tinted windows and requiring seat belts.

"We should have a law against car phones, too," she contends. "They're dangerous — not to mention ridiculous. That's why we have phone booths."

## JUST WHAT THE WORLD NEEDS ~

Among the notices on a state office building bulletin board:

"For Sale:  Pit Bull Puppies - 3 Male, 3 Female. 782-1800."

And which state agency answers that phone number? The Department of Insurance.

As one wag put it: "Anybody who gets one of those will need insurance."

## RESTAURANT BEAT: ~

A motorist pulled into a fast food drive-through lane and placed his order.

"Is that to go, sir?" the girl at the window asked.

"No," the guy quipped, "I'll just park here and eat it on the driveway."

## HUMBLE OR WHAT? ~

The abundance of crime and incompetence in today's society inspired Rochester, Ill., poet laureate Vernon Harris to write, "Portrait Of A Perfect Man."

*With my confidence unshaken, there's no chance that I'm mistaken,*
*for I've never made an error in my life.*
*I am righteous in my habits — I don't even shoot at rabbits —*
*and I try to covet not my neighbor's wife.*
*Other people fight and bicker, and I guess time passes quicker,*
*but I'm far above such petty little deeds.*
*I am cultured, suave and quiet, and too honest to deny it,*
*and it's frightening where my perfection leads.*
*While my fellow men are lazy — some are careless, others crazy —*
*I am always trying hard to get ahead.*
*I have marvelous endurance, and a lot of life insurance,*
*and I go where even angels fear to tread.*
*While I'm debonair and charming, all this goodness is alarming,*
*for I've never known just how it feels to sin.*
*So forgive me if I stumble, and my spotless image crumble,*
*as I question where the rest of you have been.*

## 'EXCEPTIONALLY' FRIENDLY GUYS? ~

The legendary crash test dummies Vince and Larry were big hits in the St. Patrick's Day parade, particularly with one 6-year-old boy. Seated in the back of a convertible, the dummies tossed candy and bumper stickers while promoting seat belts. As the convertible rounded a corner near the end of the parade route, the little boy ran up and held out his hand. Vince handed him some candy. The boy was in awe.

"Hi, Vince! Hi, Larry!" he shouted, tagging alongside the car.

The dummies waved to him.

"You guys go everywhere together, don't cha?" he exclaimed.

Vince and Larry shook their heads yes.

The boy stared for a few seconds, then blurted:

"Are you guys gay?"

## MAYBE, MAYBE NOT ~
A 5-year-old boy watched intently as his mother selected a sexy nightie for a bride-to-be, whom he knows. He knows the intended groom, too, and obviously didn't want him slighted.

"Aren't you going to buy something for him?" the boy asked his mother.

"Oh, he'll enjoy this," she replied.

With a puzzled look, he asked, "You mean he's gonna wear that, too?"

## FAST LANE TO PRISON ~
The wheels of justice jumped into high gear after a Florida woman was picked up for hitchhiking along Interstate 55 in Montgomery County last week. For Diane Garletts, 28, the court process was faster than a speeding bullet: arrest to prison in three days flat.

Garletts' arrest came soon after state police Sgt. Ron Williams ticketed her for walking along an interstate highway. She tore up the ticket, and threw the pieces on the ground. Williams slapped the cuffs on her. She broke loose and ran across the highway.

A motorist picked her up and turned her over to the trooper. Williams locked her in his squad car. She kicked out the windshield, then attacked his red lights and police radio.

That was just for openers.

Upon reaching the Montgomery County Jail, the 5-foot-1, 118-pound woman cursed and fought jailers. When dinner was served, she dumped her tray of food, whipped off her jail uniform and used it to wipe up the mess.

The next night, she turned in a false fire alarm, then stripped and greeted firemen in the nude. She later broke the small window in her cell door. She showered Judge John Coady with obscenities during her first court appearance, encouraging State's Attorney Kathryn Dobrinic and public defender David Grigsby to quickly agree on a negotiated plea to criminal damage over $300 (breaking the cell door window, which cost $305) and criminal damage under $300 (the squad car) — felony and misdemeanor charges, respectively. Garletts was promptly sentenced to a year in prison.

Sheriff Jim Vazzi wanted her out of his jail as soon as possible. It was almost noon on Friday. When Department of Corrections officials at Dwight informed him that Garletts would have to be checked in before 2:30 p.m. that day or stay in his jail until Monday, he put her in a squad car and took off.

"She was still ranting and raving," says Vazzi. "She thought her sentence was pretty stiff."

Vazzi won't say how fast he drove to meet the check-in deadline at Dwight, but he covered the 178 miles in 2½ hours.

"I did exceed the speed limit, but there was very little traffic," he said.

Garletts, it turns out, had been dumped by a trucker on I-55. The trucker left her with only the clothes she was wearing — a T-shirt and skimpy shorts — and penniless. Montgomery County authorities say she has a rap sheet 14 pages long and has been arrested for similar shenanigans in several states coast to coast.

## LAST LAUGH ~

A woman who placed fresh flowers on grave had been gone only a few minutes when thieves struck.

She got mad, but also decided to get even.

She put on rubber gloves, mixed poison ivy with some new flowers and put that little arrangement on the same grave. She checked a few minutes later. Someone stole that, too. She hopes the thief itches forever.

## TOW TRAP ~

The engine died as Kelly Chisam, with five kids in the car, drove along Spring Street just north of Cook at mid-morning. She was barely able to get out of traffic and coast into the Ideal Lounge parking lot — that infamous tow-away zone. She had the kids pile out and went to a gas station across the street to call the motor club.  When she returned minutes later, her car was gone.

She asked a man in the parking lot about it. He suggested it might have been stolen. She asked if she could use his phone to call her husband.

"He said no and told me to go to the gas station," Chisam said. "I told him I just did that and when I came back, my car was gone."

She soon was alerted to the fate of her car by passers-by.

"Almost everyone who came along told me my car had been towed away," she said. "Two people told me mine was the fourth car that had already been towed that morning. I couldn't believe it. This place wasn't even open for business yet. But people kept telling me this goes on all the time at this parking lot, that the tow truck waits across the street and swoops in as soon as someone leaves their car."

Chisam eventually contacted her husband and confirmed the car was being held by Sager Towing Co. on the far northeast side. It would take $55 to retrieve it, and only cash would be accepted.

While waiting for her husband to pick her up, she saw a man park in the lot and leave. She watched the tow truck move in and timed the operation.

"It took less than a minute for them to hook up this car," she says. "The guy came back before they could get away. He had to pay before they would let him have his car."

On the way to the tow company, the Chisams stopped at home to scrape up a few extra dollars.  It took $3 worth of pennies to round out the $55 they needed.  When they handed the coins and bills to a man at Sager, he told them he wouldn't accept the pennies. An argument ensued.

Meanwhile, the couple's kids were getting restless. She told the guy they wouldn't leave until he took the money and they had their car. Her husband telephoned police. It got noisier and noisier.

Finally, the man gave in and accepted the pennies. But not until after the Chisams counted out every last cent for him.

## AX FINALLY FALLS ~

The 20-year prison term federal Judge Richard Mills slapped on rock 'n' roller/art thief/drug peddler Myles Connor was music to Jack Spinney's ears. Spinney, whose daughter's savage murder 15 years ago has been one of four killings linked to Connor, says news of Connor's sentencing overwhelmed him.

"I though it was great," Spinney said from his Boston-area home Monday. "After all this time, I can hardly believe it."

And the irony of it all, Spinney adds, is that Connor had to come to Illinois before justice took its course.

"If that (Connor's sentencing last week) had been here in Massachusetts, he would have walked right out the door. I wish we had a judge like him (Mills) here. We don't have anything close.

"It wasn't as much as I wanted, of course," Spinney said of the 20-year term. "He deserves a lot more. He deserves to die."

In a letter to Mills, in anticipation of the sentencing, Spinney — well aware that the death penalty legally didn't apply in the Connor case — was a little less pointed.

"Would you please do what the Commonwealth of Massachusetts has failed to do or been afraid to do? Put this miserable creature behind bars for all the time that is within your power," Spinney wrote. "This man's record is replete with offenses that shock sensibilities and stun propriety. His only redeeming feature, if it can be called that, is his ability to sing to rock audiences and compliant district attorneys. A parasite like Connor could only survive with the complicity of those charged with enforcing the law in Massachusetts."

⌐∽

Spinney referred to Connor's "connections" with Norfolk County District Attorney William Delahunt over the years.

"Delahunt played games with Connor, letting him off time after time," Spinney says, "because he had aspirations for higher office — state attorney general or governor. He didn't consider our feelings or the Websters' feelings (Susan Webster and the Spinneys' daughter Karen, both 18, were repeatedly stabbed with a carving knife and screwdriver). Delahunt did all he did for Connor for his personal advantage."

Spinney said that, since Connor's sentencing, he has received calls from jurors who convicted Connor of participating in the double murder.

"They feel Connor's sentence in Springfield vindicates them in a way," Spinney says. "They're more sure than ever now that they were right in the first place."

A high court in Massachusetts threw out the conviction. Connor later was acquitted in a second trial, prompting Boston Herald columnist Howie Carr to write: "He was acquitted by 12 individuals who should have formed their own band under the name "The World's Dumbest Jury."

"I sure agreed with that," says Spinney. "Seven of the 10 clowns that testified for Connor were straight out of jail. And Connor's mother was brought into the courtroom in a wheelchair pushed by his sister, and she testified. Lies and sympathy swayed that jury."

Extensive news coverage of Connor's criminal exploits over the past two decades, and with his reported cozy relationship with Delahunt and top brass with the Massachusetts state police, made his name a household word in the Boston area.

"I feel good because Connor won't see the outside for awhile. He shouldn't be able to hurt anybody else for awhile," said Spinney. "But, he is a manipulator, so nothing would surprise me."

## SACKED FOR JUNK COMMENT ~

A television interview with a gift shop clerk, which aired on the Channel 20 news one night last week, cost the clerk her much-needed job. The woman, a senior citizen who had held the summer job for nine years to

~

supplement her Social Security, didn't please her boss when she referred to select kiddie merchandise as "junk." That reference came near the end of the interview, after she talked about many quality items in the store but most of those comments, she says, were edited out.

"I didn't mean it that way, I meant no harm. It was so unintentional," she says. "That (junk) is what we've always jokingly referred to it as."

She's needs a new part-time job.

## SHORE DUTY ~

The first American to set foot on Japanese soil following the surrender that ended World War II was a Springfieldian. Bill "Ossie" Oswald, a retired contractor, claims that distinction. That fact, along with recollections of two years at sea and nine major engagements in the Pacific Theater — Iwo Jima included — will be the basis for a book Oswald intends to write.

Oswald was a chief boatswain's mate aboard the destroyer escort USS Waterman, which led a three-ship scouting force into Tokyo Bay on Aug. 29, 1945, right after the Japanese surrendered. After sailing past the charred remains of the Japanese fleet in Yokosuka Naval Base, the Waterman, destroyer escort USS Weaver and light cruiser USS San Juan stood by through the night, then docked at a small town south of Tokyo. The Waterman docked first.

"I was the first guy off the ship," says Oswald.

He manned the lines and tied down the gangway. Armed with duffle bags full of cigarettes, soap and candy bars to use in lieu of Japanese currency, Oswald and several crewmen ventured into the town. Not only did they encounter no resistance, they found Japanese civilians most hospitable. He calls it a liberty he'll never forget.

## PREYING ON THE ELDERLY ~

Two elderly victims of a cowardly mugging on the city's east side shortly after midnight Sunday say they were "too trusting" when four men offered to guide them to a highway on the outskirts of Springfield.

~

"We though they were nice people who wanted to help us," says a 74-year-old Effingham County woman who, with her husband, also 74, fought their attackers. "We were lost. All we did was ask for directions."

Instead, they were misdirected, then attacked and robbed. And their car was stolen.

Shortly after leaving St. John's Hospital, where they had been visiting his critically ill sister, they realized they'd made a wrong turn. Pulling into a supermarket parking lot at Ninth and Converse, they approached a car occupied by four men and asked for directions to Illinois 29.

"The driver said he was going that way and we could follow him," the woman recounted. "So we did."

After the cars stopped at about three intersections, two young men jumped out of the car in front and jumped in the back of the couple's car, explaining they would provide directions from there. But after driving down side streets and a dirt road, the couple knew they'd been duped.

"Then they jumped us," the woman said, as soon as they stopped at the intersection of Cressey and Monroe streets.

One reached over, grabbed the keys out of the ignition and jumped out of the car. As her husband got out and started scuffling with him, the other jerked open the passenger door, grabbed the woman by the hair and started pulling.

"I braced one foot against the door and kicked him with the other," she says.

Meanwhile, the other man had picked up some kind of a stick and was clubbing her husband. A blow to the side of the head knocked him to his knees.

"Please give us the keys so we can go home," the woman pleaded, still trying to fend off the other man.

The assailants then demanded the couple's money. The woman pulled a $5 bill out of her billfold and told them that's all she had. She offered the

⌐

money to one of the men in exchange for the car keys. He wanted more. After rummaging through her billfold, he demanded she hand over her wedding rings.

"No," she told him, "I'm not giving up my rings."

"You're pretty tough, aren't you?" he shot back.

"You better believe I am!" she replied.

He didn't get the rings.

About that time, a man rode up on a bicycle.

"He was even bigger than the other two," the woman recalls. "From the way they talked, I'm sure they knew each other. But I don't know where he came from, or if he was one of the four men in the car."

As the argument over the money continued, the man on the bicycle volunteered to mediate. He said he'd hold the $5 until the car keys changed hands. She handed him the money. Then the guy with the keys jumped into the car and roared off. The guy on the bike took off, too — with the $5. The couple went to a nearby residence on Monroe where a woman called police. There are only scant descriptions of three of the men involved. No one has been arrested. The victims' car, a 1985 tan-colored, four-door Chevrolet Caprice, Illinois license BN 3202 — last seen southbound on Cressey Street — has not been found.

"We're really lucky," the woman said Tuesday. "We just have bruises. We could have been killed."

## CULPRITS ARE WOMEN ~
A tip to Crimestoppers has cracked that cowardly mugging of an elderly couple. One unidentified woman was arrested. Police will charge her with robbery. A warrant for a second suspect, also a woman, was being sought. That's right: two women — not men, as the 74-year-old victims believed.

"It was so dark you just couldn't tell for sure," the elderly woman now says. "I kinda wondered afterwards, but my husband said they had to be men."

Police found the couple's car — heavily damaged — on the city's southeast side. Tires and wheels, windshield wiper blades, license plates, battery, dome light and fuses were missing. Headlights were cracked, and everything in the glove compartment and trunk was stolen.

Also stolen was the elderly man's billfold, containing nearly $200. He had slipped it under the front seat when the attack began.

## ELDER POWER ~

A tasty brand of applesauce tempts a 71-year-old woman to stop frequently at a Phar-Mor drugstore. She always buys the biggest jar. That's all she had in the little plastic sack when she strolled across the parking lot to her car the other day. She clutched the sack in one hand and her purse in the other.

As she started to open her car door, a man leaped toward her and grabbed for the purse. She drew back with the sack and let fly — smacking him in the side of the head with the jar of applesauce.

She scored a direct hit, knocking him to his knees. She was ready to go another round. But the thief had had it. He scrambled to his feet, yelled obscenities at his intended victim and fled across the parking lot.

"He saw this old gray-haired woman and thought I was easy picking," says the woman, known to acquaintances as "Smitty."

He was dead wrong.

"I'm just glad I didn't buy potato chips," she quipped.

## HEAT STROKE ~

One wag who takes the weather forecaster's summer temperature multiplier seriously suggests a change in terminology.

"Instead of Heat Index," he growls, "they oughta call it the Furnace Formula or the Hell Factor."

## LUNCH BREAK ~

A woman confronted her boyfriend during the lunch hour in one of

Springfield's classier restaurants the other day, whipped out a pair of undies she'd found and made it crystal clear they didn't belong to her. She ended her tirade by throwing them at him. She missed her mark and they landed very close to a horseshoe sandwich a local judge was about to enjoy.

## AD LIBS ~

• Atlanta will host the 1996 summer games, marking the first time the Olympics will be run on biscuits and gravy.
• It's one way the U.S. can get even with Saddam Hussein — make Iraqi athletes eat grits three times a day.

## A SHOPPING WE SHALL GO ~

Still stumped on what to give that special someone for Christmas? Not to worry. A variety of brand-new gift items has just been introduced by some obscure manufacturers. So, for that gal or guy you might think has everything, how about . . .

CRA-Z-BOY EASY CHAIR/RIDING MOWER: Recline and vibrate in the living room while watching your favorite television game show or shift gears, lower wheel assembly, drive out the front door and mow the lawn without getting off your duff. Smooth-running, 4-horse, solar-powered motor and Teflon-coated rotary blade.

OOZY SEMI-AUTOMATIC SANDWICH SHOOTER: Load with desired ingredients and fire at will. Create the sandwich of your dreams in seconds: submarine, meatball, peanut butter and jelly, egg salad, Dagwoods, etc. Double-barreled model makes twice as many sandwiches in half the time.

FATAL SASSOON HOME APPLIANCE: Something every member of the family can use. All attachments and first-aid kit included. Use as a toothbrush, hair dryer, blender, insect sprayer, weed whacker, fire extinguisher or chain saw.

ENGLISH WEATHER AFTER-SHAVE: The fragrance of a cowboy's saddle and a whole herd of sheep.

OIL OF OVERLAY: Soothes chapped skin. Recommended by nine out of

⌐

10 highway construction workers.

VEGETABLE CAKE: Finally, an alternative to fruitcake. Chockful of garden-fresh carrot, radish, celery, potato and turnip chunks, blended with pure honey and oats, baked to a golden brown and iced with rhubarb marmalade. It weighs less than fruitcake, and so will you.

CELEBRITY DIPSTICK: Oil-measuring rod fits any domestic or foreign car. Decorator colors. Hand-carved handles are heads of appropriate famous people: Madonna, Cher, Jim Bakker, Roseanne Barr, Donald Trump, etc.

GEEK SNEAKERS: High-top, high-heeled tennis shoes in neon-colored stripes. Extra-wide steelbelted radial soles. Gives new meaning to the expression, "hot foot."

ELECTRIC HANDKERCHIEF: Low voltage. No-iron. Kills germs on contact. Works on same principle as backyard bug light. Great for outdoorsmen. Blow your nose via remote control. Transmitter sold separately.

B-29 HOME CEILING FAN: Four-thousand horse motor. Speeds up to 800 mph. Cool off in seconds and dust at the same time.

TAMMY FAYE BAKKER MAKEUP KIT: Includes wire brush, putty knife, 2-gallon bucket, spray gun and 9-inch roller.

BIODEGRADABLE SOCKS: Teens will love them. Never have to take 'em off. Wear 'em 'til they disappear.

NUCLEAR-POWERED BBQ GRILL: Hamburgers and steaks sizzle in seconds. Cook in the dark. No lights required. Glows in the dark. Lead apron sold separately.

FRUIT OF THE LOOPS BRIEFS: Colorful bikini shorts for men. Stripes and polka dots. Wear as underwear or starch and use as catcher's mitt.

"ROAD KILL" BOARD GAME: Each space on board secretly scented. Roll dice, drive down highway number of spaces specified, trying to avoid wild animals that pop up along the way. When landing on space marked "Road Kill," scratch and sniff, and try to guess the species you hit. If you fail, return to the nearest crossroads. Do not pass up a McDonald's and do not collect $100.

# 1991

## ANNIVERSARY SCHMALTZ ~

Oak Terrace Retirement Home residents Beatrice and Anson Emmerling, who just celebrated their 71st anniversary, owe it all to a bumblebee. They were both in New York. Anson, recently discharged by the Army after World War I, was working as an electrical engineer. Both were commuting by train daily to Schenectady. He had spotted her and tried to get an introduction.

A girlfriend pointed out Anson one day and told Beatrice he was saving the seat next to him for her. She thought it was a joke, but checked it out anyway. She walked down the aisle and, as she passed Anson, he slid over to the window. She sat down. Neither spoke.

A few minutes later, a bumblebee — her worst fear in life — flew through the open window and landed on the book she was reading. She jumped to her feet. Anson to the rescue: He grabbed her arm and she sat down and resumed reading.

He asked her where she thought she was going to run to when the bee buzzed her. That broke the ice. Eleven months later, they were married. Funny thing about that bee business, says Beatrice. Once they were married, her initials changed to B.E.E.

# FOR THE LOVE OF ~

Popping the question was no small feat for Southern Illinois University med student Kevin Meyer, but that was by design. Meyer, of Quincy, mapped his strategy for weeks before executing the elaborate plan that led to his proposal — on hands and knees in a parking ramp — to Petersburg native Jill Fore, a student nurse at St. John's Hospital.

To catch Jill off-guard, Meyer enlisted the aid of two friends who are sheriff's deputies. Capitalizing on her unpleasant experience with car burglars a few months earlier, Meyer staged another break-in with the off-duty deputies. A detective summoned Jill to the hospital security office about noon that day. He told her that her car had been burglarized. That was the bad news.

The good news was that police had caught the culprit with the loot as he ran from the scene. She was asked to accompany the officer to the parking ramp and identify what had been stolen. As she was driven into the ramp, she saw a squad car, red lights flashing. Then she looked at her brand new car; trunk lid and hood up, doors wide open and broken glass on the concrete floor.

"She freaked out," Meyer said later.

Trying to calm her, the deputies showed her the fuzzbuster and cassette tapes they had recovered from the burglar. She confirmed they were hers. However, she was told, the burglar was refusing to surrender something else that belonged to her. So would she confront him and identify that item?

"Yes, I want to see what it is," she said in a threatening tone. "My brother is a lawyer. I'll call him."

Officers escorted her toward the squad car, where she could see the form of a man in the back seat. As she neared the car, the man, who was handcuffed, jumped out. It was Meyer.

⌒

"Honey," he began, dropping to his knees and thrusting a ring box at her, "I got caught trying to steal your heart, so I'll just ask for it. Will you marry me?"

It took a while for her to recover.

"I can't believe you did this!" she blurted.

Meyer was waiting.

"But you haven't given him an answer," one of the deputies reminded her.

"Yes!" she said."

## HORSE LAUGH ~

It was a losing proposition both ways when Dolly Angelo went to an off-track betting parlor for the first time. She lost, and so did her horse. Sizing up the card for the second race, she put $2 on Champagne Ruler, strictly because the horse's name had a ring to it. She was chided by friends for not being more scientific.

"Oh, I know," she sighed. "If I bet on it, it'll probably drop dead."

Say no more. Before the first horse crossed the finish line, Champagne Ruler keeled over.

## BIRTHDAY BLUES ~

Springfield comic Barry Martin, playing the national improv circuit, croons part of his routine. He sings of his traumatic experiences at the 30th and 40th birthday plateaus. From his "Over 30 Blues" number:

*It's amazing what turning 30 does.*
*Sometimes I look real bad.*
*Saw my reflection in the mirror,*
*And I thought it was my dad.*

From his "Over 40 Blues" on the flip side of a mini-cassette he hustles in the clubs:

*Well, I was driving down the highway,*
*Just happy to be alive,*
*When, for no apparent reason,*
*I was doing 35.*
*You find as you get older,*
*There's lots of things to learn.*
*You always leave your blinker on,*
*In case you want to turn.*

## BEATING A 'DEAD' HORSE ~

If horses could talk (apologies to Mr. Ed here), "Champagne Ruler" probably would be quoting Mark Twain about now: ". . . the report of my death was an exaggeration."

Yes, despite confirmed reports of his untimely passing while on the run at Fairmount Park last week, Champagne Ruler lives. And he wins. He not only finished that race alive, he returned to win in the third last Saturday night.

It was "Loogootee Kid" that keeled over in the race, and merely looked dead. A glimpse of the motionless horse was all that off-track betting parlor patrons, Dolly Angelo among them, got and they assumed the worst. Likewise with the wagering crowd and officials at trackside. Loogootee Kid didn't flinch. He looked dead enough. But minutes later he was upright and trotted off. Dolly had money riding on Kid, too. She just got her horses mixed up, thinking it was Champagne Ruler that went down.

"That's what everyone thought," she recalls, pleased to hear that neither horse ended up at the glue factory.

She's more confident in Champagne Ruler now than ever before, and can't wait to get back to the betting parlor.

"He came back from the dead," she said. "As far as I'm concerned, he's one lucky horse."

## MAILBAG ~

From Gerald Fritz of Springfield: "I read with interest your article explaining the shrinking of Sangamon County's new jail due to the Department of Corrections' new standards lowering from 10 to eight the number of inmates required to share a shower. Inmates' daily schedule is something I'm really not familiar with, but wonder if it is busier than members of the armed forces. During World War II, we were busy from about 4:30 a.m. until lights-out meeting mess schedules, work details, field training, shot lines, laundry trips, barracks and ground cleanup, just to name a few.

"I'm sure many GIs will remember being able to manage a daily shower in a 62-man barracks equipped with six showers. Some tent cities had even higher population ratios.

"Based on six shower heads, our ratio was 10-plus 'barracks inmates' per shower — busy schedules not withstanding! It's hard to believe that a ratio of 10-to-1 can't be worked out to avoid cruel or unusual treatment that warrants such a requirement. Perhaps DOC should hire some grizzled old 1st sergeants as consultants to help figure it out."

## AD LIBS ~
• The biggest news all week from 56-year-old CNN correspondent Peter Arnett was that he's going to return to the United States and marry his 23-year-old newscaster girlfriend. What? And give up his cushy public relations job with the Hussein administration?
• Time will tell how brave Arnett is. If he's really gutsy, he'll skip out without paying his Baghdad hotel bill.

## DILEMMA FOR VOTERS ~
Springfield artist William Crook Jr., a candidate in the park board race, may not have the most campaign signs around town but his slogan probably will grab the most attention.

"CROOK — A NAME YOU CAN TRUST."

## WIND SOCK ~
Springfieldians, blown-dry Wednesday by gusts up to 71 miles per hour, didn't have to be told winds were near hurricane-force. You know it's really windy when:

• Police stop garbage cans for speeding.
• Chickens fly.

• Motorists on the interstates drive sideways.
• You see campaign signs for Springfield aldermanic candidates in Chicago.
• Pedestrians cross the street at break-neck speed, and without moving their feet.

## ALL HANDS ON DECK ~

A general alarm was sounded throughout the news media in Milwaukee when the grisly remains of killer Jeffrey Dahmer's crime spree were discovered. Reporters and photographers turned out en masse.

At the Milwaukee Sentinel, for example, virtually every available writer was put on the story — 15 reporters the first couple of days.

But veteran scribe Lee Aschoff, who covered police news for The State Journal-Register in Springfield in the 1970s, wasn't on the Sentinel team. It was sort of an image thing. He is the Sentinel's food editor.

However, since he serves in that capacity and no doubt would be interested, fellow reporters informed him of the contents of Dahmer's refrigerator. Besides the human body parts, there was mustard, potato chips and beer.

## CAKE BAKER HELPER ~

A decorated cake entered in state fair competition by a 4-H'er attracted a lot of attention, especially from one woman among the spectators. She baked it. She let the judges know it, too, and the 4-H'er had to forfeit the ribbon she'd won.

Not only did the woman bake and decorate the cake, she had taken the order when the girl telephoned the supermarket bakery the day before. Then again, she wasn't really surprised to see the cake. The girl had provided specific instructions on what size it had to be, etc. It had to be "perfect," she told the baker, because it was going to be entered in the 4-H cake decorating competition.

"It was an unfortunate thing," said a 4-H official, "but it provided a positive experience. We hope she learned a lesson."

## FUNNY SIDE UP ~

The priest who eulogized retired professional umpire-tavernkeeper Larry Ellis, who suffered a fatal heart attack at the Illinois State Fair, invoked the Ellis-style humor. Noting he was certain he had Ellis' permission, he told this joke:

The church burned down one Saturday and there was a rush to find a place for Sunday services. Ellis, promising to clean up the place, volunteered the use of his tavern. Deciding that was better than nothing, the priest accepted. Ellis spruced things up, but he neglected to remove his pet parrot.

"Ahhh . . . a new bartender," the parrot said when the priest walked in early Sunday morning.

"Ahhh . . . a new barmaid," said the parrot when the organist walked in.

And when the parishioners arrived, the parrot blabbed:

"Ahhh . . . the same old faces."

## MARION AND THE JAILBIRD ~

Sangamon County's oldest employee, Marion Stokes, will turn 91 Thursday. Since joining the civilian ranks of the sheriff's department in 1970, Stokes has served in a security position on the receiving dock at the courthouse. His duties have included supervising jail visitation and jail trusties on outside work details.

He vividly recalls one trusty detail in 1973. Stokes, then in his early 70s, was supervising two trusties on a trash-burning detail at the incinerator on the courthouse roof. One called him aside.

"He asked for a cigarette," Stokes recounts. "I gave him a whole package. Then he asked for a match. Then he said to me, 'I'll have to tie you up.'

"I said, 'What for?' He said he wanted to get away and he'd have to tie me up to keep me from hollering.

"I said, 'Have you lost your mind? You won't get away with it. You'll get in

⌐

trouble.' "

Stokes told the prisoner he didn't have to bother tying him up because "I won't holler."

"I can't take a chance," the man told Stokes.

The inmate, in jail for burglary, tied him up with electrical cord. Then he asked Stokes for a handkerchief, to use as a gag. Stokes told him he didn't have one.

"I really got ticked off," the wirey Stokes says. "But he was a lot bigger than me. (He weighs a little more than his age.) There wasn't anything I could do about it."

The trusty made a clean getaway. But not for long. He was captured a few days later.

"When they brought him back, he apologized to me," Stokes says sympathetically. "He had tears in his eyes."

Stokes' life around the courthouse and jail has been much less eventful ever since. Does he have any plans for retirement?

"No," says Stokes, known around the courthouse as the little man who's always smiling. "I gave my golf clubs away seven or eight years ago. If I retired, I'd just have to go out and buy a new set of clubs."

## 'ANIMAL' HOUSE ~

The old story about the trashing of Sangamon State University's presidential home may never die. Not as long as literary giants like National Lampoon magazine are willing to dig it up. That's what the October edition of the magazine, dubbed the "Politically Incorrect College Issue," has done. On page 60, in the issue's "True" section, is a capsule account of how former SSU prez Alex Lacy left his university-owned five-bedroom house when he resigned in 1984 amid an uproar over his five-year reign.

A work crew had to wear protective face masks while cleaning up chicken and pig manure in the basement of the stately, practically new house on West Lake Shore Drive, within sight of the main campus. Also in the huge pile of waste, which filled five 55-gallon barrels, were chicken feathers and 300 empty egg cartons. Only chickens roomed in the basement, though. No hogs. Hog dung was hauled in to accommodate Mrs. Lacy's hobby — molding pottery made from the manure. Much of the living quarters in the home also was left in sad shape: wall-to-wall carpeting stained by dog urine, crayon markings on the walls and potter's dust caked on university-owned furniture. That became the talk of town, but the university wouldn't reveal what it cost to clean up the mess and redecorate the house for Lacy's successor.

## QUOTING HIZZONOR ~

Springfield Mayor Nelson Howarth was witty as well as he was feisty. Two of his more memorable lines still find their way into Public Aid Director Phil Bradley's speeches.

Howarth on Springfield politics:
"Local politics is like walking through a sewer in your socks."

*Mayor Nelson Howarth*

Howarth on tourism:
"A tourist is more interesting than a bushel of corn, and a lot easier to shuck."

## GUIDELINES FOR GOBLINS ~

The official tip list for safe trick-or-treating doesn't quite cover everything. Let us expand.

• Residents who welcome Halloweeners should leave their porch lights on. Old grouches should turn off all the lights, hide in the basement and turn on the lawn sprinkler.
• Trick-or-treating should be limited from 4:30 to 9 p.m. Thursday, or, in ritzy neighborhoods, by appointment.
• Parents should escort youngsters. In some neighborhoods, they should wear camouflaged clothing, a bulletproof vest and carry a bazooka.
• Trick-or-treat in your own neighborhood — unless you live in East St. Louis.
• Accept only treats that are wrapped, i.e., bacon-wrapped filet mignon, etc.
• Do not accept Tootsie Rolls that aren't wrapped. Who knows . . .

• Beware of apples that bear teeth marks.
• Parents should check all treats their kids receive, i.e., eat all of the good stuff.

## WHEN THE CHIPS ARE DOWN ~

What should riverboat gamblers watch for when winds blow and rivers rise?

Small craps warnings.

## GREASEY SPOT ~

Junior high school-age kids concentrated on Greece in a geography class one day. Next day, the teacher asked if anyone remembered what country they learned about the day before.

"I do," blurted one boy. "It was Crisco."

## WHAT IF . . . ~

Christmas was fast approaching and we had:

No credit cards?
No wrapping paper?
No Scotch tape?
No postage stamps?
No peanut brittle?
No twinkly lights?
No fruitcake? (Yippeeeee!)
No malls?
No Claus?
No 'L'?

## KIDS AND CLAUS ~

Off we go to the North Pole to peek into Santa's mail bag:

Dear Santa,
I've been a good boy most of the year. I started kindergarten this year. I really enjoy it. I've got several girlfriends already.
Love always, Jesse

Dear Santa,
I would like to know, do reindeer have exhaust pipes? Do you have special carrots to make your reindeer fly and, if so, what do you put on the carrots?
(Recipe requested)
Nathan

Dear Santa,
I want a bow and arrow (etc.)
Unsigned
P.S. If you are real, please send this note back to me. Circle yes if you're real. Circle no if you're not real. If you are real, tell me how old I am.

# 1992

## LET'S LEGISLATE ~

There oughta be a law . . . state, federal or whatever . . . that:

- Makes fruitcake a controlled substance.
- Forces anyone who owns a junk car to keep it in their house.
- Pays $1,000 in punitive damages to shoppers who don't steal anything but are embarrassed when they activate the security alarm on the way out.
- Revokes the driver's license of anyone who won't turn right on red.
- Requires all women's apparel stores to provide comfortable seating — minimum one vibrating recliner-chair per female shopper escorted by a male — in a dimly lit, soundproof room located at least 50 feet from the nearest cash register.
- Limits each household to two cable television channels.
- Classifies the Salad Shooter as an automatic weapon.
- Requires restaurant employees to eat at their place of employment at least twice a week.
- Bans pink cars.

~

- Makes lying by a politician a felony.
- Requires the price be clearly marked on any item for sale in a retail, discount or wholesale store, or the item is free.
- Makes it illegal to display Christmas merchandise before the Fourth of July.
- Makes jailbirds pay room and board.
- Requires trap doors in the floor at the end of express checkout lanes in every supermarket. Anyone with more than six items — Zip!
- Makes negotiable any printed matter that resembles a check (and isn't a check) and is mailed in a window envelope.
- Requires weather forecasters to be at least half right.
- Bans any television commercial that is stupid.
- Requires the cashier at any checkout counter to remove the adhesive price sticker from every item purchased — with their teeth.
- Forces state lotteries to guarantee 50-50 odds.

## YOU (MAY) HAVE WON ~

It looked important enough: a window envelope stamped "First Class" and "Private Business Use." And in big, bold letters beneath the return address was this warning: "$2,000.00 FINE OR 5 YRS. IMPRISONMENT." In smaller print it continued, "or both for any person who interferes with or obstructs delivery of this letter or otherwise violates . . ." Inside was a fancy "Certificate of Guarantee" from T.A.C. in Atlanta, Ga., informing the addressee he was a guaranteed award recipient. He had won:

1. Luxurious 1992 Chrysler Lebaron!
2. Two round-trip cruise fares to fabulous Freeport, Bahamas!
3. $2,500 cashier's check!
4. His or hers genuine diamond dress watch!
5. Sony rack music center with 21-inch color TV or $1,500 cash!

To claim his premiums, the addressee was instructed to call a toll-free 800 number. He placed the call to what turned out to be Time Award Company. An excited, cheery voice on the other end launched into a non-stop spiel that, she said, is required listening for anyone who desires to claim a premium.

"Nothing to buy," she promised before the guy agreed to listen. But first she asked for his phone number and mailing address. He went along with that. Then she asked for the expiration date on his MasterCard. Hold the phone! How did she know he has a MasterCard?

"Well," she said when he balked, "that's really not required." She put him on hold.

"Congratulations!" she exclaimed upon returning to the line. "I have exciting news for you. You've won . . ."

She proceeded to list all five of the premiums listed on the coupon, adding that everything was his if he agreed to listen to a pitch on a brand-name skin product. Agreed. He was then informed he could take his pick of the premiums by agreeing to pay $498.50 to cover "promotional" fees. She pushed the cruise. It has a retail value of $550, she said. (He figured that would put him $51.50 ahead after paying the promotional fee.)

"How do I get to the ship?" he asked. "I'm 1,500 miles from there."

Airline rates to Florida are very economical this time of year, she pointed out. No thanks. She then pushed the diamond watches.

"I have a rare skin disease and I'm allergic to watches," he told her. "Besides, I don't care what time it is."

She added a home security alarm system to the list of premiums.

"Everyone needs an alarm system for their home," she stressed. "This has a value of $2,779. I know you aren't going to turn this down."

"Oh, yes I am," he countered. "I don't need a home security system."

"Why not?" she pressed.

"I have a gun!"

Click!

## SPEAK UP, SON! ~

Sixth-graders packed a room at Christ the King School to hear Mayor Ossie Langfelder. After a brief biographical sketch, Langfelder opened to questions. He asked the kids to speak clearly and loud enough for him to hear.

A boy sitting with several other students on the floor, directly in front of the mayor, raised his hand and mumbled something. Langfelder didn't hear the question, which drew a lot of giggles from students nearby.

"I'm sorry," said the mayor, "I didn't hear you. Please repeat the question."

Again, practically in a whisper, the boy repeated his question. Giggles again. Apologizing, the mayor told the boy he would have to speak louder. This time he was loud and clear.

"What do you think about breast implants?" he asked.

## SMOKE RING ~
Conversation in a conference room:

"Mind if I smoke?"
"Mind if I cough?"

## AUTHOR UNKNOWN — 'TIL NOW ~
The 1992 edition of Lincoln Library's young adult magazine, "The Write Stuff VIII," has 13 poems and 12 short stories by Sangamon County school students. Sampling from the lighter side:

Sacred Heart-Griffin High School student Mike Tretter dreamed up a story titled "Halitosus: A Breath of Stale Air." It's about a handsome mortal named Halitosus who one day encountered Listrina, goddess of oral hygiene.

"Leave before you make me sick!" Halitosus cried out. "This made her so furious that she punished him by giving him and all of his descendants foul-smelling breath."

"Halitosus' descendants," according to Tretter's tale, "are people in our world today that have horrendously bad breath."

## HAIR, NOW! ~
One wag who's leaning toward Ross Perot says it's the little things that count.

"I like a man who gets more than his money's worth in a haircut."

## 'GAGGING' THE JUDGE? ~

Once was the time a convicted criminal could expect a tongue-lashing from the sentencing judge; the idea being that anyone destined for probation or prison needed a rude awakening. No more — with rare exception.

In Springfield, U.S. District Judge Richard Mills is the exception. Mills' reputation for raking many who are convicted in his court over the coals, then throwing the book at them, precedes him. Now, that's getting him into trouble. Mills has been taken to the woodshed (again) by the U.S. 7th Circuit Court of Appeals for calling a repeatedly convicted illegal Mexican alien a "turkey."

Yes, Mills is known for dressing down a felon now and then. Some examples:

*U.S. District Judge Richard Mills*

"You're a parasite and you ought to be stamped out," he told Samuel Coran while sentencing the convicted drug peddler to 15 years in prison.

"You are rotten to the core," he told notorious con man Myles Connor, who got 20 years.

Judge Mills told career criminal Patrick Scroggins Jr. he's a "blight on society . . . not worth a tinker's damn."

But, says the higher court, Mills went too far when he called Ramiro Perez Lopez a turkey. Unbelievable but true, Perez appealed his sentence solely on grounds that the judge "spoke harshly" of him. He had pleaded guilty to illegally entering the United States after being deported for the umpteenth time. (Perez was driving a van full of illegal aliens when arrested.)

Evidence against him was overwhelming. A prison term was inevitable. The only question was how long he should be imprisoned for? When Perez appeared before Mills for sentencing last year, the prosecutor recommended 41 months. A court-appointed attorney (taxpayers paid Perez' legal fees all the way through appeal) representing Perez asked for 37 months, on condition the term be suspended and he be deported — again. However, Mills, after a long dissertation, gave Perez the max — 46 months. Perez wouldn't have received such a long term, according to the appeal, if Mills hadn't worked himself into a frenzy before passing sentence.

The appellate court dismissed Perez's appeal a few days ago. However, in its eight-page opinion the court also lashed out at Mills' courtroom "tirade."

"Judge Mills expressed disappointment that deported aliens re-enter the U.S. notwithstanding adjurations to keep out," wrote Appellate Judge Frank Easterbrook. "This court expresses parallel disappointment that a member of the bench is unable to contain himself at sentencing. Judicial officers unable or unwilling to respect norms articulated by this court ought not lord it over persons in the dock who have a different kind of recidivism problem."

(Whew!)

Easterbrook eventually admitted the appellate court is not empowered to reduce sentences "in light of the judge's intemperate remarks."

What set Mills off was the defense lawyer's suggestion that Perez be released as an economy measure — that is, it would be cheaper than keeping him in prison.

"Isn't it going to be cheaper to feed him and clothe him than it is to have all of our agents constantly running all over the country looking for Mr. Perez?" Mills asked the lawyer at the time. "What do we do with this turkey?"

"Well, it's going to cost us about $1,500 a month to take care of you," he told Perez. "Quite frankly, I think that's cheaper to the American taxpayer to at least know where you are.

"All I can say is that apparently Mr. Perez likes our prison system. He figures three squares (meals a day) and a roof, and yellow jumpsuits . . . That's all I can (conclude because he keeps coming back)."

Mills then warned Perez.

"As soon as you get released and get down to the border, wherever you're going to go across, don't turn around and look back. Just keep on going, because if you come back up here to this district and you're in my courtroom, I'm going to pipe you away for so long they're going to have to package air and bring it to you. You've already done this too many times, and we're not going to screw around with it anymore. No threat. Just a promise.

"You stay the hell off I-55. Period. At least you stay off it from Dwight down to Staunton. That's this district. I don't want to see you again."

Easterbrook labeled Mills' remarks "inappropriate in both style and content."

"A judge imposing sentence represents the sovereignty of the U.S.," he wrote. "Although he may impress the defendant with the gravity of the law and seriousness of the offense, he should make every effort to suppress his idiosyncrasies."

(Ouch!)

Senior Appellate Judge Harlington Wood Jr. wrote the concurring opinion.

"It gives no satisfaction to one having to review the work of a hard-working, experienced district judge, and then to state a critical assessment of it," Wood said. "Regrettably, this panel (which included Appellate Judge Michael Kane) had little choice."

Wood recalled that he and fellow judges have commented on Mills' courtroom discourses in the past. He pointed to a case in which Mills, at sentencing, called the defendant a "flake." Wood also criticized Mills for using "considerable slang" during Perez' sentencing.

"References were made to the penitentiary as 'the slammer' or 'pigeon hole.' The phrases 'screw around' and 'piping the defendant away' (were used)."

Wood opined that calling Perez a turkey goes beyond labeling the other defendant (a U.S. citizen) a flake.

"That term, applied to a Mexican national, lends itself to an interpretation which might give the unfortunate appearance of possible prejudice and bias against citizens of Mexico," Wood said. "It comes very close to a constitutional violation."

Bottom line: Perez stays in prison.

## BIRD BRAIN ~

There's never a dull moment at Coble Animal Hospital when an Amazon parrot named "Popeye" is around. A boarder for the last several weeks, the bird entertains staffers by singing the obvious:

"I'm Popeye the sailor man . . . Toot! Toot!"

He mocks anything and everyone, adding every word he hears veterinarians, receptionists and clients utter to his vast vocabulary. And if there is no conversation, he strikes up one.

"Hey! Hey!" he often yells. "Hey! Hey!"

"What?" Dr. Sara Kessler, resident specialist for exotic types, finally responds.

"Nothin'!" says the parrot.

Popeye also specializes in sound effects: a ringing telephone, beeping microwave oven, etc. He likes to hang upside down and fiddle with surgical instruments. Kessler says he's on the loose during business hours and has the run of the place. He's caged at night, and the cage door is locked because the bird knows how to unlatch it.

"Some of these species have the intelligence level of a 2-year-old child," Kessler points out. "So they're pretty smart. You've heard the expression, terrible twos."

Speaking of sound effects, some of those mastered by Popeye leave much to be desired, etiquette-wise. Recently he was within earshot when a kennel helper cleared his digestive track. So, now the bird belches, too.

## PHILOSOPHER AT WORK ~

Sure we have a choice in the upcoming election, Smokey Joe Miller contends. It just depends on whether you want a boil on your nose or on your behind.

## TURKEY TROT ~

The scolding U. S. District Judge Richard Mills took from the 7th Circuit Court of Appeals a few weeks ago for calling an oft-convicted illegal alien a "turkey" has drawn a tart response. In a four-page "memorandum opinion" filed with the circuit clerk, Mills chided appellate judges Harlington Wood Jr., Frank Easterbrook and Michael Kane for the "harsh tone" of their admonition of him for using slang when sentencing criminals.

Even though the higher court threw out the appeal of Ramiro Perez Lopez without so much as an oral argument — meaning the 46-month maximum prison sentence Mills imposed will stand — Mills said the tenor of Wood's remark about him holding no ethnic bias "requires clarification for the record." Mills wrote he is unaware of any other case where the question of ethnic bias was ever voluntarily raised by an appellate judge. Perez himself did not allege ethnic bias in his appeal; it could not have arisen in oral argument, since there was none; and neither Easterbrook nor Kane joined Wood "in such a tortured interpretation," Mills said.

Calling Perez a turkey was not intended — nor could it be construed — as an ethnic slur, Mills added. Defending his use of the term, he cited slang definitions from two dictionaries, i.e., "person or thing of little appeal, dud, loser, regarded as inept or undesirable."

In other words, if the shoe fits . . . However, Mills said he will heed the high court's "caution that such terms are to be avoided" at future sentencings. Mills then recalled a recent circuit study that "decried the decline of civility." He quoted the Committee on Civility's report as indicating 50 percent of responding judges identified written opinions as the major source of discord, and 83 percent felt the problem was greatest at the appellate level.

A set of proposed standards for professional conduct evolved from the study. Under the section captioned "Judges Duties to Each Other" were: 1. We will be courteous, respectful and civil in opinions . . .

2. In all written and oral communications, we will abstain from disparaging personal remarks . . . about another judge.

3. We will endeavor to work with other judges in an effort to foster a spirit of cooperation in our mutual goal of enhancing the administration of justice.

The majority opinion in the Perez ruling directed a variety of remarks at Mills. The opinion said Mills had his "dander up," that he delivered "a harangue about aliens who re-enter the U.S.," that he should "suppress his idiosyncrasies," that he seemed "unable to contain himself" and that some of his remarks were "intemperate."

Reviewing one paragraph of the opinion, Mills wrote: "Incredibly, the opinion compared the sentencing judge to a recidivist criminal."

Mills reiterated his acceptance of the admonition against using slang.

"But the unduly harsh tone of the admonition was unnecessary," he concluded. "The opinion's brutal style does not serve the interests of civility."

## GOAL OF THE GAME ~
One of Saturday's youth soccer games ended in a 4-4 tie.

"Did we win?" 5-year-old Erik Carlson asked his mother, Cathy.

"Did you have fun?" she countered.

"Yes," he said.

"Then you won."

## LIP SERVICE ~
Never underestimate the power of political rhetoric. Grandmother Helene Butcher had her hands full with young Matt, Jonathan and Ben, 3, 4 and 7, respectively, the other day. Out of the blue, Matt asked for a root beer. Since he has a bit of an accent ( a front tooth is missing), she didn't quite understand him.

"What did you say, Matt?" she asked.

∽

"Gwan-maw!" he snapped. "Wead my wips!"

## AD LIB ~

• High levels of lead have been found in many municipal drinking supplies, and the Environmental Protection Agency is going to crack down. Now, what agency is responsible for getting the lead out of Congress?

## HOME SWEET HOME ~

Nowhere will President-elect Bill Clinton's pledge for change be more obvious than around the White House. Among other things that will make the Clintons feel at home:

• Rose garden will become melon patch.
• Recycling bin for corncobs.
• Outhouse. A 10-seater, to accommodate Cabinet briefings.
• Pickup truck with gun rack in rear window replaces helicopter for weekend getaways to Camp David.
• Bald eagle on flagpole replaced by chicken — a live chicken.
• Henhouse out back.
• Mud flaps, fender skirts and squirrel tail on presidential limousine.
• Clothesline in foyer.
• Muskrat traps hanging on front gate.
• Hog wallow on front lawn.

## REMEMBER OUR 'VETS' ~

Serious conversation between two 7-year-olds at their day-care center.

"I'm off school on Wednesday," said Angie Tucker.

"Well, silly, everybody's off Wednesday," Rob Schaub countered. "It's Veterinarians Day."

## RECYCLE PLEA ~

Eighty-seven-year-old Nat Curran looks beyond aluminum, plastic, glass bottles and tin cans.

*Now that almost everything*
*Is gathered for recycling*

~

*Heaven heed my earnest plea:*
*Recycle me! Recycle me!*

## CABINET LEVEL ~

Cabinet appointments seem to be President-elect Bill Clinton's best-kept secret. To make sure his forthcoming announcement of who'll head what won't come as a complete surprise, we reflect on his campaign promise for change. Some Cabinet titles are undergoing slight revision and new titles are being added. The scoop:

Secretary of Labor — Murphy Brown.
Secretary of Treasury — Charles Keating .
Secretary of Defense — Dan Quayle (It's either that or back to the Dairy Queen.)
Secretary of Offense — Joan Rivers.
Secretary of Inferior Decorating — Leona Helmsley.
Secretary of Energy &  Natural Attributes — Dolly Parton.
Secretary of Aerobics — Jane Fonda.
Secretary of Hot Air — Rush Limbaugh.
Secretary of Grits — Julia Child.
Secretary of Sin — Madonna.
Secretary of Cats — Socks.

## 'TIS THE SEASON ~

Scratch the Illinois legislature's plan to put a live nativity scene on the Statehouse lawn this Christmas. Both Democrats and Republicans have searched high and low throughout their ranks. Can't find three wise men.

## STOCKING STUFFERS AND MORE ~

Barely two Christmas shopping days to go. Still trying to find something for that special someone?  Just arrived. Available in select stores:

• ROSEANNE ARNOLD EXERCISE VIDEO — For wide-screen TV only. Load the VCR and step back 500 feet. Destined to be a big hit. Measures 8.8 on Richter scale.

• OLD VICE AFTER SHAVE — Smell like a working man. Splash it on and get arrested.

• MONSTER VAC — 5,000-gallon capacity wet/dry vacuum, handy for big garage cleanups or flood control. Powerful 200-horsepower, six-cylinder motor with six-inch diameter hose. Whisks up everything in sight— full bags of trash, cats, dogs, kids, compact cars.

• GOLD DIGGER BOBBIE — Most elegant doll of all. Perfectly coifed blonde hair. Fifth Avenue wardrobe includes diamond-studded silk gown, full-length silver fox coat, real 44-carat engagement ring. Price: $66,000.

• "ELVIS-LIVE AT KMART" — Elvis Presley's new Christmas cassette, recorded live at the customer service counter. Rock with The King as he serenades Kmart shoppers with "I'll Have a Blue Light Special," "Here Comes Security, Here Comes Security," "I Saw Your Mama Kissing Santa Claus," "Hark! The Shopping Cart Rangers Sing," "Randolph the Lazy Stock Boy," others.

• BEADED SEAT CUSHION — New and improved. Hundreds of tiny, sharp lava rocks provide orthopedic-like support for any shape car seat. Guarantees driver will never doze at the wheel. Great in summer (store in freezer overnight). Greater in winter (heat over open fire and drape over cold leather seat). Reg. $9.95 each. Sale priced, two for $24.95.

• CHOCOLATE PIZZA PIE — At last, an alternative to fruitcake. Delicious blend of imported Swiss chocolate and Swiss cheese plus tomato sauce, Jimmy Dean sausage, home-grown mushrooms (well, they look like mushrooms) and anchovies on double-rich brownie crust with thick meringue topping. Available in freezer section. Three pack $29.95.

• OPRAH WINFREY BODYSLIDE — Complete aerobic exerciser, as NOT seen on TV. Firms flab. Burns fat. Use indoors or attach coasters and 10-foot rope, tie to rear bumper and exercise in the great outdoors. Standard model $29.99. Industrial strength model $79.99.

• THE SLAPPER — Amazing electronic voice-activated device. Just shout "HEY!" and invisible hand swats the kids, wife, dog, overbearing relatives, the crazy aunt in the basement, etc. They won't know what hit 'em.

• JUNK FOOD SHOOTER — Now that you've become an expert marks-man with the Salad Shooter, take aim with the .357 Magnum Junk Food Shooter. Set the selector dial for your favorite snack and squeeze the trigger. Out comes Twinkies, Ding Dongs, Snickers bars, Pop Tarts, Fruit Loops, Eskimo Pies, etc. Release the trigger when your plate is full. $59. "Ammunition" sold separately.

## A CORNY CLINTON CHRISTMAS ~
M-e-e-e-r-r-r-y Christmas! Ode to our president(s)-elect:

Tis early Christmas morn, and way down south
Bill says to Hillary, "Well, hush my mouth!
"By this time next month, we'll be long gone
"I'll be the Prez, mowin' the White House lawn.
"For the next four years, folks will have nothin' to fear
"I'm gonna put, this country in gear!
"Like that guy Nixon once said,
"I want to make that perfectly clear."

Two Republicans were hung by the chimney with care
George Bush and Dan Quayle — strung up by their hair.
"Socks" was still nestled all snug in his bed
Visions of the Rose Garden birdbath danced in his head.
Hillary in her hair net and Bill in his coonskin cap
Were just settling down to study a road map.

When out on the dirt road there arose such a clatter
Bill sprang from his rocker to see what was the matter.
To the living room window he raced at top speed,
Stuck out his 12-gauge and drew a bead.
Headlights could be seen through the early morning fog
Twas the U-haul they'd ordered, it'd run over their dog.
Hillary's screams would have woke up the dead
Trying to quiet her down, Bill said,
"Put a sock in it, darlin'. First we load up
"Then we'll bury the pup."

"Like the Hank Snow song says, we're movin' on!
"So drag all the furniture out onto the lawn
"C'mon, Hil, get the lead out!
"Don't just stand there and pout.
"Do you still expect to get that Cabinet post?
"Or would you rather stay in the kitchen and burn the toast?

〜

"Why, Hillary, my dear, did I throw you a curve?
"Guess I must've struck a nerve.
"You're the one who got me elected, so don't jump ship.
"Calm down, honey! That was just a quip."
"The time has come to leave this abode.
"Come on, Hil, let's hit the road.
"Hop into the truck, and hold tight to your knapsack,
"No, not up front — in back!
"It's gonna be a long, long way to D.C.
"Cause we gotta pick up Tipper and Al in Tennessee."

Away they flew to fortune and fame — and dames,
Bill whistled and shouted incoherently and called out funny names:
"Now Mario Cuomo! Now Pat Buchanan! Now Marion Barry!
"On Jerry Brown! On Elvis! On Curley, Moe and Larry!
"Up the interstate. Stop at the first mall.
"So Hillary can cash away, cash away, cash away all."
And Hillary yells at Bill as they drove out of sight,
"When we get to the White House, you can go fly a kite!"

## BESSIE AND BIG (BAD) BROTHER ~

Back to 1985, when the state of Illinois threw elderly Bessie McNabb out of her home so the government could build another parking lot. Bessie's effort to save that little two-bedroom cottage — her home for 56 years — made headlines. But she was no match for Big Brother (state government). She was finally forced out. Bessie died Friday at age 87 and has been buried at Camp Butler National Cemetery. Her plight proved to be an ugly example of government in action, one that Springfield should not soon forget.

After years of speculation that the state would some day wipe out the two blocks around her to build a visitors' reception center, Bessie was ordered to take $35,000 for her Lincoln-era house and get out. Media coverage that followed didn't cast the state in a very favorable light. For one thing, it was pointed out that the adjacent Boone's Saloon — whose owners were well-connected politically — would not be disturbed. While state operatives contended it would be too expensive to take the tavern, then-Gov. Jim Thompson tried to smooth things over.

"I don't want Bessie to think she's any less important than someone who

351

might have political connections," he said after a personal visit to her home. Thompson then added $2,500 to the buy-out offer and promised Bessie that he and key aides would personally help her with her move. (They never did.) Talk about timing, Thompson had just announced he would seek re-election.

Admitting she had no choice, Bessie finally accepted the $37,500, which was barely enough for her to negotiate the purchase of another house.

One year later, her old house remained intact. Demolition had been delayed because neighboring property owners chose to fight the state in court. In fact, Bessie's house was never demolished. A group called Springfield Preservation Ltd. saved it from the wrecker's ball. Two years after Bessie had been forced out, the house was moved to a vacant lot down the street and restored.

# 1993

## ONE RINGY DINGY ~

A patron of Shane's Tavern hung his jacket on the wall, next to the pay telephone. Not long afterward, an Illinois Bell installer stopped by to put in a new phone. He removed an old wall-mounted phone, installed the new one and left.

A little later, Ned Padget grabbed his jacket and headed for the door. He didn't get far. His jacket wouldn't let him. When the Bell man bolted the telephone mounting plate to the wall, the sleeve of Padget's jacket got in the way. It was fastened to the wall, too.

The installer was called back to the tavern to unbolt the jacket.

## THERE OUGHTA BE A LAW ~

If lawmakers really want to do something constructive, they can enact laws that:

⌇

• Make talking on a cellular telephone in a restaurant or church a felony.
• Empower shopping center owners to confiscate vehicles parked in the fire lane and sell them to the highest bidder.
• Establish a speed limit for fast food.
• Require a surgeon general's warning on fruitcake.
• Allow banks to install security cameras that shoot pictures *and* bullets.
• Make potato chip companies fill bags with chips instead of air.
• Ban any compact car small enough to fit into the trunk of a full-sized car.
• Restrict political campaigns to 48 hours and limit individual campaign contributions to two cents.

## CONVERSION CHART ~

Cantrall, Ill., second-grader Jonathon Mundhenke was discussing his report card with grandfather Dave Jostes. He had all A's except one, the exception being an A-plus.

"What's that A-plus mean?" Jostes asked.

"A dollar-and-a-half!" Jonathon replied.

## WAS ELVIS DRIVING? ~

Springfield police were alerted to red splotches on the floorboard of a car Thursday night. Looked like blood. However, after a closer look, an officer confirmed the substance wasn't blood. It was drippings from a jelly-filled doughnut.

An obviously sticky situation, but not enough to hang anybody. But no question about it, the cop concluded, the guy is guilty of being sloppy.

## PEE-YOO! ~

Talk about making a silk purse out of a sow's ear:

The restroom building at Douglas Park will be converted into a picnic pavilion.

## BUT TOUGH TO CHEW ~

"I can smell the meat a cookin'," as Illinois' infamous Secretary of State Paul Powell used to say. But he wasn't licking his chops over main courses like Southern-style Roast Opossum, Raccoon Stew, Woodchuck-in-Sauce and Beaver Tail — recipes in this month's issue of Outdoor Highlights, the Illinois Department of Conservation magazine.

"Even though some of the recipes may sound like menu listings from the Road Kill Cafe," staffer Cheryl Gwinn writes, "you will be pleasantly surprised if you try them."

Most of the recipes call for hefty doses of flavor additives, like mint leaves, onion, garlic, onion, Worcestershire sauce, poultry seasoning, more onion and salt water . . . and lots more onion. Hold on, you frontier gourmets. If that doesn't send you racing to the nearest supermarket for the other white meat, savor some of the instructions.

"Remove scent glands . . ."
"Rinse and repeat soaking process . . ."
"Rinse again and boil 45 minutes . . ."
"Dip in scalding water and pull out hairs . . ."

Drool over this helpful little hint:
"Opossums that feed out of garbage cans aren't too tasty."
No kidding, Dick Tracy!

So much for woodchuck, opossum and raccoon. Let's get to the real delicacy, beaver tail. Since everyone will want to run straight to the cookhouse, here's the industrial strength recipe for that:

Place the beaver tail in hot coals — a propane flame works nicely — until the black scaly outer skin puffs and blisters. Do this to the entire tail. Be sure to wear heavy gloves (not to mention a gas mask). As soon as the tail is cool enough to handle, peel off the outer layer of skin. Wash the tail and place in large kettle of cold water. Add salt, peppercorns, tablespoon of pickling spice and clove of garlic, if desired. Cook for about an hour and slice when tender.

Gwinn says beaver tail is a real conversation piece when it's served chilled on crackers.

We'd bet the conversation would begin with this:
"Please pass the smelling salts!"

## DIM WIT SPECIAL ~

A full-page memo printed on an Illinois Department of Transportation letterhead looks and sounds official enough, maybe because it appears to be typical government tinkering. Practically everyone swallows hook, line and sinker until they get to the last sentence — the punch line. So it goes:

TO: All Illinois Vehicle Owners
FROM: Illinois Division of Motor Vehicles
SUBJ: Automobile Dimmer Switches

1. Pursuant to the Illinois Department of Motor Vehicles Act No. 92-93, all motor vehicles sold in the state of Illinois after Sept. 1, 1992, will be required to have the headlight dimmer switch mounted on the floorboard. The dimmer switch must be mounted in a position accessible to operation by pressing the switch by the left foot. The switch must be far enough from the left foot pedal to avoid inadvertent operation or pedal confusion.

2. Included in the above act and beginning Sept. 1, 1992, all other vehicles with steering column mounted dimmer switches must be retrofitted with a floorboard-mounted dimmer switch of the type described above. The steering column dimmer switch must be disabled or removed from the vehicle. Vehicles which have not made this change will fail the forthcoming Illinois State Safety Inspection Program.

3. It is recognized that this will cause some hardships for the driving public. However, this change is being made in the interest of public safety. Illinois DMV Act 289-9937 will revert all Illinois motor vehicles to the prevalent dimmer system in use prior to the influx of foreign market vehicles.

A recent study entitled "Initiation Sequence in Illinois Night Time Highway Safety" by the Illinois Department of Motor Vehicles, along with the Illinois State University Department of Research, has shown that 95 percent of all Illinois night-time highway accidents are caused by a blonde getting her foot caught in the steering wheel while attempting to dim headlights.

## RECYCLING PAUL POWELL ~

The reintroduction of Illinois State Police motorcycle patrols stirs memo-

⌐

ries of ex-Secretary of State Paul Powell. One might say his illu$triou$ political career started on two wheels.

Somewhere around 1930, a young Powell, a resident of southern Illinois, pressed his state representative for a state job. Come on up, the lawmaker said from his Springfield office. Once here, recalls retired Auditor General Robert Cronson, Powell was escorted to state police headquarters, where he was immediately hired and sent to the motor pool. There, Powell was handed a helmet, goggles and gloves, and pointed toward a motorcycle.

"What am I going to do with a motorcycle?" Powell asked.

"Congratulations, Mr. Powell. You are now a motorcycle cop."

He quit on the spot and returned to his home in Vienna, Ill. Not long after, Powell announced his candidacy for state representative. In retaliation, he ran against — and unseated — the state rep who got him the motorcycle cop job.

## GOTCHA!! ~

It's usually the ultimate excuse for not showing up at work, but it was unacceptable at the Sangamon County Courthouse one day last week. A court security officer, with a little help from her mother, called in dead. All in good fun, of course. She thought it would make a great April Fool's Day prank.

It backfired. Supervisors confirmed the hoax before the security officer reported for duty. She was called on the carpet.

A superior capped his lecture by pronouncing a three-day suspension. It wasn't funny anymore. She was stunned.

April Fool! No suspension after all, she was told. Don't let it happen again.

## DRUM ROLL ~

Drummer Barrett Deems' 80th birthday prompted autograph collector Carl Jacobs to pen a request to the Springfield native, who now leads a big band in Chicago. Deems phoned Jacobs to say an autographed photo

*Barrett Deems*

was on the way. That gave Jacobs the chance to relive his high school days in the '50s and tell Deems how music teacher Ed Sasch was always talking about Deems' drumming.

"It's hell to get old like this," Deems told him.

"Yes," Jacobs replied, "I know — I'm 52 myself."

Deems countered: "I have underwear older than that!"

## KID STUFF ~

A standing order is often repeated for a 5-year-old boy in one Springfield household. "Don't play with your food!" His mother reminded him again the other day as he fumbled with a can of Pringles potato chips. Off the table it went, scattering chips all over the floor. He scooped them up, stuffed them back into the can, set it on the table and climbed back into his chair. Looking his mother straight in the eye, he asked:

"Wanna see it again in slow motion?"

## HERE COMES THE? ~

Cupid took it on the chin at the marriage license counter in the Sangamon County clerk's office last Friday. When two young men entered, an employee offered her assistance. The conversation went something like this:

"I want a marriage license," one man said.

"In order to grant a license, both parties must be present," the courthouse employee noted.

"We are," the man said.

Uh-oh!

Fully realizing the situation at that point, she pointed out that state law bans two people of the same sex from legally marrying in Illinois. Both were referred to the state's attorney for further interpretation, which didn't change things. The men, described by the state's attorney office as being surprised and irritated, left the courthouse without a license.

## LITTLE DOODLER ~
Four-year-old Holly Walden of Taylorville, Ill., demonstrated a creative art form. Wielding a black marker pen, she connected all the dots on the family's Dalmatian.

## 'UNKNOWNS' ~
Montgomery County authorities are seeing to it that an unidentified woman whose decapitated, nude body was found in a burning brush pile nearly three months ago will have a dignified burial. As police seek leads that might lead to her killer or killers, funeral services for the murder victim will be held next weekend.

"She is a human being," says Coroner Rick Broaddus. "We want to give her a decent burial, not a pauper's funeral."

Any number of others in the community, and beyond, feel the same way. Broaddus has received a number of cash donations to help with the expenses, plus offers of floral arrangements and notes of thanks from dozens of central Illinoisans. Litchfield funeral director and deputy coroner Terry Plummer, who removed the charred body after it was discovered in a park north of Litchfield, has had similar response. Ross-Plummer Funeral Home is providing a casket.

"It will be a nice casket," Plummer says, "We don't know who she is, but she's definitely somebody's daughter, maybe a sister, maybe a mother. She deserves this."

The Rev. Johnathon Kosec will lead the funeral service at Mount Zion Lutheran Church in Litchfield. Montgomery County sheriff's deputies and Illinois State Police investigators who are working the case will serve as pallbearers. A hillside grave site has been selected in a small cemetery outside Honey Bend, Ill., not far from where her body was discovered. A vault and a small grave marker have been donated.

"Maybe someone who knows her will turn up," says Broaddus.

But odds are not favorable. Police can provide only a scant description of the woman: white, late 30s, 5-feet, 4-inches tall, 120 to 130 pounds and dark brown or black hair.

"Eventually we might find a relative who will want to move the body to a family plot," Broaddus says hopefully. "A proper burial will enable them to do that."

Burial of an unknown is rare in central Illinois. Authorities say they haven't encountered a "nameless" victim in nearly 25 years.

The last was a young man who was hitchhiking along Interstate 55 south of Springfield in the fall of 1971. He was struck by a car and thrown into oncoming traffic. He was run over by a second car and a pickup truck before a motorist was able to

*Toby McDaniel (second from left) and Coronor Norman Richter (foreground at right) act as pallbearers for the "unknown hitchhiker."*

stop and drag his body off the roadway. He carried no wallet and no form of identification. Police found seven cents and a cigarette lighter in his pants pocket. He carried a small duffel bag containing one change of clothing. Police theorized that the victim, thought to be in his early 20s, could have been hitchhiking across country and likely was far from home.

After a futile effort to establish his identity, Sangamon County Coroner Norman Richter arranged for a brief service at Bisch Funeral Home. A florist provided a spray of red roses for the closed casket. A small potted plant was sent anonymously. Two women, who said they were attending the funeral because they were afraid no one else would show up, were among a dozen people who attended the brief service. Pallbearers included an 80-year-old man who served on the coroner's jury that ruled the death accidental, this columnist and Richter. The unidentified man was buried in the far reaches of Oak Hill Cemetery, in an area known as the pauper section. His grave is unmarked. No one has ever asked for assistance in locating the man's grave, according to cemetery administrator Jack Dickenson. And he has never seen flowers on the grave. Richter has received no inquiries about the man.

## DAZE IN COURT ~

Court reporter Jerry Wedeking, who retired Friday after 28 years in front of the bench, worked in the last three Sangamon County courthouses. That means his first assignment was in what is now the restored Old State Capitol. However, the rumor that he recorded Abraham Lincoln's "House Divided" speech there remains unconfirmed. Speaking of the old-old courthouse, Wedeking recalls one of his first trials there.

The late Judge William Chamberlain presided. Chamberlain was a stickler for being on time, so he was irked on the second day of proceedings when both attorneys were late. Taking the bench at the appointed hour, Chamberlain told those assembled that he would wait up to 10 minutes. Neither lawyer showed up by the deadline, so he ordered the bailiff to bring in the jury. Fifteen minutes later, one attorney, from Springfield, walked into the courtroom and looked around.

"He had the strangest look on his face," Wedeking recalls.

Chamberlain told him to sit down. He did. Silence prevailed for another five minutes, then the other attorney, from Taylorville, made his entrance.

"He looked even funnier," Wedeking says. "Obviously, he had to be thinking that they had started without him. And no doubt the Springfield attorney was thinking the same thing.

"There they sat, wondering what they had missed."

Both offered their deepest apologies. Surprisingly, Chamberlain did not read them the riot act. Worse.

"Call your next witness," the judge instructed.

Wedeking says Chamberlain made his point. He's positive that neither attorney was ever late again — at least not in Chamberlain's courtroom.

## SNOWMOWER ~

Thinking she might be able to walk off the jet lag that set in after a flight home from Europe, a young woman decided to mow the lawn at the family residence in Fox Meadows subdivision. Her mother helped her lug the mower out of the garage.

Having never tackled the chore before (the men in the family always did that), they studied an instruction pamphlet in an effort to learn how to start the machine. A half-hour later, after a lot of tugging, it still wasn't running. That's when a friend drove up.

"Oh, good, you're just in time to start the mower for us," one said.

"Mower? That's a snowblower!" the man roared.

## SCULPTURE CULTURE ~

It's been legend that when it came to the Illinois State Fair's professional art exhibit, if someone plopped a pile of dung from one of the cow barns in front of the judges they'd pin a blue ribbon on it faster than you could say, "Gag a maggot." No more.

That's not to say a couple of entries still do not meet that criteria; it's just that they don't seem to be getting blue ribbons anymore. Case in point: Provoking disparaging remarks and a few giggles from fairgoers this year is a marble/epoxy sculpture called "Two Acrobats." Chicagoan Slawek Murakski had the nerve to put his name on this one. The so-called acrobats are two nude fatsos. One's outstretched arms support the other as his loins (probably 100 pounds per) lurch toward the heavens. (Remember, now, these guys are in the buff.) Scary thought, huh? There's no blue ribbon on it. No ribbon of any color, in fact. It didn't win anything. (Gotta hand it to those judges.)

One other redeeming value: The sculpture isn't life-sized. (If it was, the floor of the Artisans Building would've caved in.) It's table-top size is somewhere around 18 inches high. But who'd have the gall to park this on their credenza?

## LETTERMAN THE WEATHERMAN ~

A transplanted Springfieldian caught The Associated Press goof while reading The Orlando Sentinel. Winona Burris says she knows darned well that television talk show host David Letterman and Rebecca Paul, who just kicked off Georgia's new state lottery, never worked together as weather forecasters at Channel 20 in Springfield, as the story said.

*Rebecca Paul*

"Even though I am now a senior citizen, I don't think I am so deep in senility that I would have forgotten seeing David Letterman regularly on Springfield television," says Burris, now a Florida resident.

Right. Paul was at Channel 20, but Letterman wasn't. However, they did once work together briefly at Channel 13 in Indianapolis. Quoting the wire story:

"She parlayed her fame (as Miss Indiana beauty pageant winner) into a job at a television station in Springfield, Ill., where she became the week-end weather girl, relieving regular forecaster Letterman, who later became a TV talk show host."

AP had the right combination, just the wrong city. Paul recalls those days at Channel 13 in the early 1970s. "I was hired to do weather on week-ends," she tells us.

Letterman was told to teach Paul how to pitch the weather. "He was kinda crazy then, too," Paul says of Letterman.

During one of his early demonstrations for Paul, he blurted: "Ladies and gentlemen, it's raining cheeseburgers in Greenfield (a suburb of Indianapolis)!"

## TEST PATTERN DAYS ~

The big flap over whether the television networks' area affiliates will drop off the Dimension Cable system has been bending 6-year-old Michael Santini's ear. He's been listening to the pros and cons via radio and television. One radio listener who called in and said, "We should go back to the good old days and forget cable," sent him scurrying to his mother.

⌣

"What were the good old days?" he asked.

"When Dad and I were young," she explained, "there were only three channels to select from, and the picture we saw depended on how good the antenna was."

Michael was amazed. He paused briefly, then asked, "Mom, when Dad was little, was the remote made out of wood?"

## HALLOWEEN-R-US ~

Mail-order merchandising has taken a bizarre twist, thanks to mass murderer John Wayne Gacy. A six-page flier now in circulation offers a variety of Gacy-produced or endorsed products from original oil paintings to books to autographed book markers. Dozen of items, including some that are earmarked for the "serious collector" (dead serious, obviously) are being marketed under the name "Jac Kas Productions" via an out-of-state art dealer. Gacy, convicted of killing 33 young men in Chicago in the 1970's, resides on death row at Menard state prison.

So-called serious collectors are tempted with a lock of Gacy's hair, priced at $100 (plus $3 for postage and handling). It comes, according to the flier, with a "letter of authenticity signed by J. W. G." Supposedly, there's a limited supply. (But we'd bet he's more than willing to grow more.)

Also for sale are canceled checks from the contracting company he owned, PDM Contractors, that bear various dates of the month Gacy was arrested. They're priced at $100 each.

Topping the serious list is Gacy's old portable color television set. It's described as a 13-inch RCA XL-100 in good working order. Gacy discarded it after purchasing a new one. It, too, comes with a letter of authenticity signed by Gacy and is priced at $300.

The book markers, $35 each, are inscribed: "From the personal library of John W. Gacy, Execute Justice . . . Not People!" Purchasers are guaranteed that each marker is personally signed by Gacy on death row at Menard.

"More Letters to Mr. Gacy," a new book of letters written to Gacy, is available, as is the first book, "They Call Him Mr. Gacy." Numerous Gacy paintings, including sick clown images, are available by mail order. Prices run as high as $235. Portraits costing up to $300 each are commissioned on request. All paintings are original, signed, numbered, registered and painted on death row, the flier states. And there is this disclaimer: "John Gacy will not receive any proceeds from sales."

The Department of Corrections is checking into that.

## MR. GACY, YOU'RE RENT'S DUE ~

The state is dunning John Wayne Gacy for room and board. Gacy has cost taxpayers $141,074 since he's been on death row, according to Department of Corrections officials, and they think it's time he started reimbursing the state for his keep. That's the amount sought in a suit filed Tuesday by Attorney General Roland Burris.

Gacy is suspected of profiting from, among other things, the sale of his "artwork" through a Missouri mail order firm. However, the extent of his profits and where he may be stashing them has yet to be determined.

Officials say the suit will enable the state to probe for any hidden funds. Inmates are allowed to accumulate limited funds in a prison account. Under a law enacted in 1982, the state can recover the costs of incarceration if an inmate controls lots of money.

"Murderers should not be able to profit financially as the result of their crime," Burris said in filing the suit. "If John Wayne Gacy has any money in this prison account or elsewhere, then that money should help defray the enormous expense of his incarceration."

Gacy, convicted of killing 33 young men and boys, is imprisoned under 12 death sentences and 21 natural life terms. He is liable for incarceration costs since the recovery law was enacted. According to DOC figures, the cost of keeping a prison inmate currently is $41.61 per day, or $15,187 a year.

## PICTURE THIS! ~

Response to my anonymous inquiry via telephone to Jac Kas Productions about Gacy's discarded television set, listed in a flier that apparently is being widely circulated, strongly indicated Gacy will share the profit on that item. It's being advertised for $300. A man who identified himself as "Sean" (a Sean Jackson is co-owner of Jac Kas Productions) was asked whether the price is negotiable. He quickly dropped to $250. We noted that that is a hefty price for a used portable color television set. Sean began a sales pitch, stressing that this TV is one of a kind, a collector's item and that it comes with a letter signed by Gacy guaranteeing that it was his personal property, used on death row. Gacy has replaced it with a new television set, and there will not be another in the foreseeable future. Neither will Gacy send out additional television sets from other death row inmates, misrepresenting them to be his, Sean said. Noting that the television set simply would be used for its intended purpose, not a trophy, we expressed no interest in the letter of authenticity. Sean suggested the letter could be framed and hung on the wall above the television. (Welcome to the World of the Weird, folks.) Would $250 be the lowest price acceptable? Sean said he would consider any offer, but would have to discuss it before accepting.

"I will split the money with him," Sean said, implying his partner in this transaction is Gacy.

## POP GOES THE MAESTRO! ~

No complaints have been heard about the hi-jinks of Illinois Symphony conductor Kenneth Kiesler at the orchestra's annual Halloween concert. Not even the last skit of the evening, in which the walls of an outhouse fell down, exposing Kiesler with his pants down and his red-and-white striped undershorts for all to see.

"If that flies," laughed one member of the audience, "then anything goes."

The bottom line, perhaps, would have been to lump that gag with Beethoven's second movement. Maybe next year.

## FIVE-STAR HOSPITALS? ~

Let's hope President Bill Clinton's health-care reform package will guarantee better hospital accommodations. Namely:
• Doctors with warmer hands.
• No-frill, $10-a-night rooms.
• Answering machines for patients' telephones. (Hi, there! I'm literally out right now! But I'll return your call as soon as I regain consciousness.)

∽

• More back rubs.
• Keno and nickel slot machines at nurses' station.
• Substitute burgers, fries and shakes for the beef broth, cold toast and rubber Jell-O.
• Musical bedpans that play "Moonlight Serenade."
• Hospital gowns with fewer flaps and more snaps.
• And a little PEACE AND QUIET at night!!!

## EVER STOP TO THINK? ~

There never seemed to be a crisis at the landfill until fast food was invented.

## GAGGING GOURMET ~

That infamous Thanksgiving Day dinner (Christmas, too) staple — failed turkey dressing — can be put to any number of good uses. Let us count the ways:

1. Substitute for window putty.
2. Fish bait.
3. Combine one ounce dressing and two quarts water, stir briskly. Instant wallpaper paste.
4. Speed bumps.
5. Industrial-strength glue.
6. Dry large lump, attach to log chain. Makes nifty boat anchor.
7. Wadding for musket loader.
8. First base, second base or third base.
9. Flatten extra-large serving. Use as doormat.
10. Hockey pucks.

## STREET TALK ~

Some of the local criminal element is getting a wake-up call. The street name for U. S. District Judge Richard Mills, who has a reputation for handing out stiff sentences, is "Father Time."

## ON THE WARPATH ~

A woman phoned a Springfield department store the other night, rattled off some numbers from a price tag and asked what kind of item it was. It's something from the intimate apparel department, she was informed. Seeking additional information, she was transferred to a sales associate there. She repeated the numbers on the price tag and asked the sales-woman to identify the item.

Since the woman had all of the appropriate numbers, the saleswoman assumed she must have purchased the item in question. So she identi-fied the item: a bra.

The woman wanted to know more. What color of bra?

The saleswoman asked her to hang on while she retrieved one from the display counter and matched lot numbers and price. Returning to the phone, she told the caller that that particular style of bra is white. Then the woman wanted to know if it was a "sexy" bra.

"No," the saleswoman said.

"Is there any lace on the bra?"

"A little bit, around the front where it is sewn together," the saleswoman replied.

By this time, the saleswoman began to suspect this was a prank call.

"What else is on the bra?" the woman asked.

"There's a little flower right in the middle, on the front of the bra," she was told.

"Well, what size is the bra?"

"It's a 36AA."

"How big is that?"

"It's a small, basic training bra," the saleswoman replied.

That's when the woman on the phone "lost it."

"That S.O.B.," she yelled. "I'm bigger than a 36AA."

⌣

She then volunteered an explanation of sorts.

"I came home and found this tag in my bedroom and I haven't been shopping there for a while," she ranted. "My husband's got some explaining to do!"

Click!

## SANTA'S ORDERS ~
As usual, Santa's up to his whiskers in mail this time of year. He shares some jewels with us:

Dear Santa
I am four years old. I have been very good this year. I always help my mom at the grocery store. I don't leave the toilet lid up, but my dad does.
Love, Zachary

Dear Santa
Hi! How are you doing? Please stay warm so you don't catch the flu. It's going around, you know. I naturally want every and anything which is in my reach.
Love and Hugs, Kimberleigh
P.S. Sorry about that little incident at the mall. I just freaked out. I really do love you!

Dear Santa
Have you ever wanted something so badly one minute and not as badly the next? Well, that is how it is with me about wanting a puppy for Christmas. I'm almost positive that the (other) dogs would adjust. I'm not sure how long it would take. I know you're thinking all puppies grow into dogs. I know that. It's just that I think one more dog would make it click. Please don't bring a herding or hunting dog. I read they go nuts if they can't herd or hunt.
Your friend, Lydia.

# 1994

## EATING HIGH ON THE HOG ~

Entertainment is offered at every table at VanTine's Feed Company, a popular Mason City, Ill., restaurant. Simply read the menu.

Patrons find plenty of humor mixed in with the spiced-up bill of fare, which is printed on the place mats.

"An Experience in Country Dining and — New This Year — Indoor Plumbing," the menu boasts.

Some sage advice, compliments of father-son proprietors Richard and Kent VanTine, follows: "Van's secret to good eating while on the lam — never stop at places where the name starts with Mom's."

The restaurant is best known for its smorgasbord, but the full menu is available. One dish on the "Long-Time Favorites" list is called the "Fowl Ball." That's two pieces of chicken, fries and salad.

Then there's the "Double Burger & Fries."

"We've sold over 4 million burgers," the menu claims. "Do you realize that represents over 12 pounds of ground beef!"

On the sandwich list:

Carp-On-A-Stick (Seasonal)

One other seasonal special is listed. Rhubarb Meringue Pie.

More of the VanTine menu humor:

"We aim to cheat the other fella and pass those savings on to you."

"We've got the pork chop sandwich that choked Linda Watchmacallit. See your waiter for details."

"Yes, we charge extra for Roquefort, Sour Cream, Carp Gravy, White Meat, Cheese, Tomatoes and Lettuce. But restroom facilities are free."

VanTine's Feed Company is a one-of-a-kind. Just read the bottom of the menu:

".....For Other Locations See Reverse Side....."

The back of the place mat is blank.

## STROKING PICASSO ~

Chicago police, federal agents and practically every cop agency in between snapped to attention when a Picasso painting was stolen from an art gallery in the Windy City. So did outspoken Springfield artist Rocky Schoenrock. Schoenrock says call off the costly nationwide search for the $500,000 work of art, which he thinks was a desperate attempt to depict a shark's head.

"On second thought," he notes, "it could be a chicken."

*Rocky Schoenrock*

As his contribution to mankind, he has volunteered to pro-

〜

duce a replica of Picasso's "Tete" ("Head") and donate it to the art gallery. He would charge a mere $12.50, packing, postage and tax included.

That would be on cheaper paper, he adds. High-quality poster board would run the cost up to $14.50.

## WHEN I MET HARRY 〜

Springlike weather is a welcome change for Harry Taylor. Not that the cold and snow really bother him; bundling up and shoveling snow has been the least of his worries for several years now. Harry hung up his snow shovel, so to speak, in 1989. He was 100 years old then. He didn't actually hang up his shovel. Somebody stole it. He decided he had shoveled his share by then and didn't buy a new one.

"If somebody needed it bad enough to steal," he said, "they could shovel the snow themselves."

A few months after that, Harry gave up the upstairs apartment he had occupied for years in the New Berlin business district. Except for relying on a nearby restaurant for meals, he was still on his own. He was still voting at age 100. And, at 98, he was still helping out on the farm, cutting weeds out of bean fields. On really hot days, he could work two hours at a time before taking a break. Harry still had a driver's license at 100, but just as a souvenir. He quit driving — voluntarily — two years earlier.

He took up residence at St. Joseph's Home in Springfield in 1990. Now 104 he is content with soaking up attention from admiring staffers (who love his sense of humor) and reminiscing about the old days with niece Agnes Ridder and her husband, John, who are frequent visitors. Harry vividly recalls many milestones, from boyhood escapades to the gas station he operated in New Berlin. On one of his devilish days on the farm, he put a goat in an upstairs bedroom. He considers that one of the craziest things he ever did.

"I didn't have to push. It went up on its own," he chuckles.

It was funny until his mother found out.

"Oh, I got in trouble. I don't remember exactly how, but it was impressive at the time. I didn't do it again."

373

~

Such yarn-spinning earned him a nickname.

"I call him 'Uncle Remus' because he's always telling stories," says John.

Harry's first venture away from home was during World War I. He enlisted in the Army and was assigned to a logging camp in Washington state. He was twice "wounded" in action. Both times he suffered foot injuries when his ax slipped. Between several farming ventures (with a team of mules in the early days), driving a delivery wagon, managing a lumberyard at Litchfield, and selling billboard advertising, cars and farm implements, he ran the Shell gas station in New Berlin for 27 years. Back then, you could do more than stop in for a fill-up. His customers could play a nickel slot machine.

"A lot of people played, but I didn't make a lot of money with it — I played it too much," he confesses.

Harry also worked 15 years for the secretary of state's office. His job was to provide police agencies with license registration information, which in those days was manually culled from state records.

In addition to being a lifelong Republican and St. Louis Cardinals fan, he lists these personal preferences:

Favorite governor? Richard Yates, elected to his second term in 1901. (He was Harry's great-uncle.)

Favorite president? Teddy Roosevelt.

Favorite dessert? Ice cream.

What kind? "Cold."

Harry has a favorite ball cap. "I'm Only Grumpy When I Don't Get My Way" is inscribed above the bill.

That's ironic, because he never is grumpy, say nursing home staffers.

That's part of Harry's formula for longevity: Be nice to everyone and maintain a good sense of humor. Bachelorhood doesn't hurt either, he jokes.

He's one. But he likes the ladies. He's always open for a peck on the cheek and he gets plenty. How does he rate all those kisses from the nurses? "You've got to be somebody special," one nurse says.

"Good looks has a lot to do with it, too," Harry declares.

## HOOP DEE DOO! ~
Focusing on future Olympics, Dennis Komac has formed the meanest basketball team in the world. Erik Menendez, brother Lyle Menendez, Tonya Harding, Joey Buttafuoco and Lorena Bobbitt.

Of course, they'll need a coach: Bobby Knight.

## SNOW JOB ~
Hours of hard work by some kids in Thayer, Ill., were sabotaged by a group of teens. They knocked down the snow fort the kids had built.

A license number was provided to Police Chief Dan Skaggs, and he set out to track down the vandals. He eventually spotted the car, but the teens saw him first and high-tailed it out of town. Still wondering what he could charge them with (Criminal damage to a pile of melting snow?), Skaggs — knowing that the teens were from nearby Virden — took a short cut to a rural road and cut 'em off at the pass. He told them to return to the scene of the crime, and he followed.

Once there, he told them they had the choice of rebuilding the fort or going to jail. All four started piling up snow faster than you could say "Jack Frost." When the job was complete, he suggested they apologize to the kids and the mom. Done.

Skaggs, who by that time had recorded all of their names and phone numbers, then strongly suggested that they go straight home and inform their parents what they did — or he might just tell them himself.

## RESTAURANTMANIA ~
You know you've picked the wrong restaurant when:

• A sign in the window says: "Head Chef Wanted; No Experience Necessary."

- The hors d'oeurves are animal crackers — from real animals.
- You recognize the grill cook as the same guy on the FBI wanted poster at the post office.
- Your waiter is unzipped.
- You see the chef grab a plunger and race into the restroom.
- A man across the way finishes his liver and onions, pushes himself back from the table, lets fly with a big belch and starts buffing his dentures on his pant leg.
- You have to walk through the kitchen to get to the restroom.
- A big man at the table directly ahead is wearing beat-up cowboy boots, and when he crosses his legs, you notice that he stepped in something earlier in the day — and it wasn't chewing gum.

## WIDE LOAD AHEAD ~
A new survey shows that more than half of all joggers, if they could see themselves from behind, wouldn't.

## GACY: THE GRISLY CELEBRITY ~
Mass murderer John Wayne Gacy has basked in the media spotlight for more than 15 years, but never has he attained the celebrity — morbid as it is — that he enjoys now.

Setting his execution date made the difference. Phones at Illinois Department of Corrections headquarters here have been ringing off the wall ever since.

At first, calls came from news agencies nationwide. Then media queries rolled in from Japan, Australia, Germany, England, France, etc.

As Gacy's date with the executioner draws near, the calls from overseas have tapered off. But calls from U.S. media continue nonstop, agency spokesman Nic Howell says.

You'd think that every conceivable question about the man who killed 33 boys and young men has been asked by now. No way.

## CUT-RATE CRAZE ~
A woman who does all of her shopping at outlet stores was asked her husband's shirt size.

"He wears a 16-33 irregular," she beamed.

## COMMENCEMENT AT LAST ~

A one-class-at-a-time approach to higher education has worked for Dorothy Osborn. Finally, at age 83, she receives her bachelor's degree from Sangamon State University today. Does she know that makes her SSU's oldest grad ever?

"I'm afraid I do," she sighs.

It's been a long haul. Dorothy started working toward an associate's degree at Springfield College in Illinois in 1942. She also took classes at MacMurray College and then at Lincoln Land Community College, where she received an associate of arts degree.

"I would have gotten my degree earlier, but I couldn't afford to drop everything and go to school when I was younger." she says. "I almost gave up on getting a bachelor's degree, but I decided I'd be a fool not to. Besides, I wanted to learn about things."

A registered nurse who retired from the Illinois Presbyterian Home more than 20 years ago, Dorothy says she has really enjoyed her experience of pursuing an education. As for going to college at such an older age, she has a philosophy about that.

"Everybody should do something when they get older. Do something. Just be active."

## RESTAURANTMANIA ~

There might as well be a "Don't Eat Here" sign in front of a restaurant where:
• The menu features a catch-of-the-month.
• A big, long-haired cat that roams from table to table is a substitute for napkins.
• A sign in the window offers preferred seating for Mafia members.
• The fried chicken has webbed feet.
• The rustic decor features a high-pitched open ceiling, and pigeons roost on the rafters.
• The restaurant is called Mom's — and Mom is a man.
• You are required to tip before being served.

~

## NUTTY NUPTIAL ~

So, they really got hitched. Lisa Marie Presley really married Michael Jackson.

Mother Priscilla gave her blessing. No comment from Elvis, yet. Boy, if this doesn't bring him back, nothing will.

## SIGN LANGUAGE ~

As the family drove past a Springfield motel, 9-year-old Ben Butcher couldn't believe what he saw on the marquee.

"Welcome idiots?" he exclaimed.

Well, not quite. His mom set him straight.

The marquee actually said: "WELCOME IDOT."

She explained that IDOT stands for the Illinois Department of Transportation.

## CAMPAI(G)N QUIP ~

"I'm convinced that politicians are like dirty diapers," Eleanor Williams says. "They should be changed often."

## BUMP IN THE NIGHT ~

A Lincoln Correctional Center inmate's stay has been extended two years for hitting another prisoner in the head with a laundry bag. Convicted armed robber Erskin Sims of Chicago pleaded guilty to aggravated battery. After arguing with the other inmate the day before, he entered the victim's sleeping quarters and hit him. But two years?

The laundry bag wasn't empty. It had an iron in it.

## WHOSE CAT WAS THAT? ~

When Chris and Don Kramer-Nesbitt found a stray tomcat on their doorstep nearly two years ago, they took it in. The cat often went outdoors, but never left the yard of their Lake Petersburg home. But in early October, the cat came up missing. Chris and Don searched daily for two weeks before they found him a few blocks from home — dead. He had

⌁

been hit by a car a couple of days earlier.

"We were really upset, naturally," says Chris. "He was part of the family."

They took "Grunteouf" home and buried him.

Two weeks later, on Halloween eve, they returned home. It was dark. As they opened the door, a cat that looked like Grunteouf's twin — only on the scrawny side — ran past them and into the house. It went straight to Grunteouf's food bowl and ate like there was no tomorrow. They couldn't believe their eyes. This cat was the same color, same size and bore the same unusual markings as Grunteouf.

"It was bizarre," says Chris.

But it was Grunteouf, all right. He'd come back.

They have no idea whose cat they buried.

## GIFTS THAT FIT? ~

What to buy for that guy or gal who has everything else? Don't despair; here's a whole new line of merchandise that goes on sale at select stores today. Or order by phone. Dial 1-800-XMS-CRAP for overnight delivery.

• POPCORN POPPER-SPACE HEATER — Pop the new popcorn-with-a-bite in this amazing new kerosene-fired popper. Then flip a switch; popper converts to efficient space heater. No wood to chop, no ashes to haul. Just eat and heat.

• COONSKIN PAJAMMIES — For him or her. Stay cozy in the coldest winter climate without a blanket, or even a sheet. Footies with or without claws, detachable hood. (Not recommended for sleepwalkers who live in wooded areas.)

• SCREAM MACHINE — Be prepared. Small alarm mechanism fits in pocket, thin wiring affixes to forehead, runs down arms and legs. When mugger attacks, 10,000-decibel alarm sounds, alerting police and rendering assailant stone-deaf for life. Designer earplugs for alarm wearer sold separately; 12-V battery not included.

~

• REAL LINCOLN LOGS — Replicas of rails split by Abraham Lincoln. Build anything from fences to houses to outhouses. Triangular rails approximately 5x5x5 inches, 6-12 feet in length. Sold by the truckload. Stovepipe hat and fake beard sold separately.

• SMALL FRY FAST FOOD — Turn that dull playroom into a mini fast-food restaurant. Cola dispenser, milkshake machine, grill, deep fryer, cash register and starter supply of burgers, buns, fries, cups, wrappers, etc. Drive-up window sold separately.

• YAHOO RIDER WET/DRY VAC — Industrial sized 500-gallon tank, four-wheel drive with 240-horse V-8 engine, five-speed transmission. Ride this powerful machine as you clean the garage, vac a flooded basement or mow the lawn. Converts easily to golf cart with special attachments. Roll bar sold separately. $7,288.

• ELECTRIC GLOVES — Waterproof, fleece-lined poplin gloves with a flashlight in sixth finger. (Safety feature for hitchhiking.) Available in black, brown, navy, stripe or paisley. Includes 5,000-foot extension cord.

• CUDDLY TOOTHY PALS — Stuffed animals that bite. Bears, lions, birds, cats and dogs with real teeth. Rabies shot kit included.

• BIG BOY ERECTOR SET — Build a skyscraper in your back yard with this 813,296-piece solid steel and precast concrete erector set. Blueprints, rivets, building permit application and hard hat included. Excavating equipment and crane sold separately. Ages 35-up.

• BURPIE DOLLS — Dress Darbie and Len in second-hand clothes. Both emit loud belches when heads squeezed. Great fun for kids whose parents drag them to stuffy dinner parties.

• PANT SOCKS — At last, pantyhose for men. Acrylic-nylon-cotton blends for casual wear, formal occasions and the athlete. One size fits all. Full-body style with turtleneck top also available.

• KIDDIE KADILLAC KONVERTIBLE — Cruise your sidewalk in this sleek, sporty mini model. Front seat room for two, 12-V energy cube, four-on-the-floor, 0-60 in eight seconds, disc brakes, airbags, tape deck, leather interior and much more. Ages 4-6. $1,119.95.

∽

• ALL-PURPOSE TRENCH COAT — Heavy-gauge canvas provides maximum warmth in the winter, shelter in the summer. Pull two hidden zippers, coat opens to triple its size, becomes instant pup tent. Comfortably sleeps two. Collar-stays double as tent stakes. Tent poles sold separately.

• MICHAEL JACKSON MAKEUP KIT — Fifty-gallon drum of mascara. Bright purple tote bag free with each purchase. $19.95, two for $49.95.

• SURE-SHOT SALAD SHOOTER — Still a handy appliance in the kitchen, new and improved model features 4-hp gasoline engine. After dicing carrots and celery for salads, go outdoors and mulch leaves, small tree limbs. Good for shredding old newspapers and magazines. Attach special nozzle and shoot into attic. Presto! Six new inches of insulation. Spray-paint attachment available.

• MR. SMELLY BATH BASKET — Fifty-pound bar of Lava soap, wire brush, 2-liter bottle of Scope and 10 gallons of Old Spice.

• THE BOP-BRELLA — Keep dry and safe. Push-button umbrella that deploys at 280 mph. Wallops unsuspecting mugger. If assailant isn't knocked out, he can be bopped in the head with lead-weighted handle or impaled on the 6-inch-long steel point on end. If all else fails, pull hidden trigger. Ammunition sold separately/FOID card required.

• "REPOSSESSION" — A new perfume for the lady and cologne for men with the fragrance that leaves a trail that your creditors can follow. $9.95.

• LAST WORD IN CORDLESS PHONES — Not only cordless, this telephone has no buttons, no dials, no mouthpiece, no earpiece, no bell, no buzzer, no nothing. Hence, no bother. At last, the silent telephone.

• GAG YULE LOG — Play a trick on friends with fireplaces. Give them the smolder-forever, smells-like-something-died fire log. Each log individually handcrafted out of old fruitcake.

# 1995

## ROAD TO RUIN ~
New Year's resolutions for people in a self-destruct mode:

- Gain weight
- Start smoking
- Start drinking
- Never exercise
- Drive like you own the road
- Pack in the cholesterol
- Swallow when chewing tobacco
- Deep-fry everything
- Weekly Twinkie binge
- Absorb more TV
- Always frown
- Everyday, french fries for breakfast, french fries for lunch and french fries for dinner
- Wear black and jog in heavy traffic at night
- Gravy on everything

~

## NO SALE ~

A man's wine-colored velour house slipper was among a dozen or so drastically reduced items in a local department store bargain bin. House slipper singular; just one lonely house slipper. But it was the right one — for the right foot and for the guy the shopper had in mind.

However, as was the case with a couple of other things in the bin, the house slipper was minus a price tag. That should be no problem, he thought; a price could easily be determined and a tag attached. So, he took the slipper to the customer service counter and asked how much it would cost. He was told to wait while an employee was dispatched to find the slipper's mate and a price would be determined right away. But he only wanted to purchase the one house slipper, he hastened to explain. The clerk politely repeated herself; once the other slipper was found, she could quote a price for the pair.

"I'm only interested in the one slipper — not a pair," the guy told her.

"Well," she countered, "we only sell them by the pair."

"It's for a gift for a friend who only has one leg," the customer pressed. "He can only wear one slipper. He only needs one slipper."

(It's kinda like you and I have just one head, he thought to himself. We only need one hat.)

"But we can only sell a pair of slippers, not just one," the clerk insisted.

"Is that a store policy or a law?" the guy inquired. He was told it's store policy.

"Then, why was only the one slipper offered for purchase in the first place?" he asked.

"Someone must have separated them and put one in the wrong place," she guessed.

He requested to speak to the manager. She was immediately summoned from the back of the store. Quick action on the clerk's part, for sure. But it was pretty obvious she welcomed the opportunity to sidestep this guy who wanted to buy one house slipper for a one-legged friend. After hearing the slipper saga from the clerk, the manager — wine-colored velour house slipper in hand — approached the customer. She pretty much repeated what the clerk had said; selling a single slipper is against company policy.

However, she would be happy to initiate a search in an attempt to find the other slipper, and if it could be located, the store would notify the customer by telephone within 24 hours or so, and the store would put the slippers (there's that pair thing again) on "hold" until he could return to make the purchase. He agreed.

"But what if the matching slipper isn't found?" he asked.

"Then we still couldn't sell just the one slipper," she said.

(The guy started thinking to himself again: What's going to happen to this slipper if the mate can't be located? Ultimately, the trash can. Really, now, is it better to throw away one perfectly good house slipper than sell it for a couple of bucks and make a one-legged fellow a little more comfortable and happier?) Guessing the answers to those questions, he kept his thoughts to himself and headed home.

The phone call came a couple of days later. Just as expected: The mate to the house slipper had been found, the manager said, and the pair was available for $3.

"Thanks, but no," said the guy. "What would I do with the other one?

"I only know one guy with one leg. I'd just have to throw it away and if I did that, I wouldn't be able to sleep at night."

Every once in a while he's wondered if anyone ever bought that pair of wine-colored velour house slippers. Probably not, he has decided; they were so ugly.

## JAILHOUSE ROCK ~
There was a full moon Friday night — in the Sangamon County Jail's prisoner intake area, at least. A rebellious drunken driving suspect was being booked.

front of several jail staffers and police officers.

He'd been uncooperative from the time he was arrested, so — no surprise — he ignored commands to get back into his pants. Among those he harassed was a female correctional officer. She said she was so embarrassed that she thought even her ears turned red.

Finally, after one officer proposed to squirt his exposed zone with pepper spray, the guy put his pants on a lot faster than he took them off.

## TOO CLOSE TO CALL ~

The popular trend of downsizing business has caught on with  Scottsville, Ill., Mayor Roy Close. No, not in his official capacity — in his heating/air-conditioning business.

"It isn't that I want to take advantage of automation or get rid of the dead-wood," Close hastens to explain. "I am the sole owner of a business that has no employees."

It's sort of a lateral move. His son David is taking over so Close can devote full time to being mayor of the tiny hamlet (population 147 at last report) in northwestern Macoupin County. Now, as he puts it, since Scottville's riverboat casino project is in the hands of the political oversight committees, the town will move ahead on two more energetic undertakings.

"The first is to establish a Defeated Politicians Haul of Fame," Close puns.

"This would put our abandoned school building to use. The second is to bargain for a major league baseball franchise. Now that the baseball strike is in the hands of the politicians, we feel we are in a good bargaining position."

## SNIP, CRACKLE AND PLOP ~

The Great Flap in Washington over out-of-sight breakfast cereal prices may be for naught. Just wait until this new line of cut-rate breakfast-table treats hits grocers' shelves; watch the big boys — Kellogg's, General Mills, Post and Quaker Oats — scramble to roll back prices. Introducing:

• SHREDDED MEAT — Crispy beef, chicken and braunschweiger-flavored

- SHREDDED MEAT — Crispy beef, chicken and braunschweiger-flavored pellets shot from real guns. Great-tasting with milk and sugar. For a real waker-upper treat, double the sugar and substitute BBQ sauce for the milk.
- GOOP LOOPS — Multicolored gumdrops shaped like miniature dough-nuts. Drown in whole milk and you've got your calories for the whole day.
- GREAT NUTTY FLAKES — Crunchy kernels of wheat, bran and oats shaped like the heads of the country's most infamous politicians past and present.
- SPECIAL 'Z' — Corny flakes laced with Nytol. A bowl full at bedtime helps you z-z-z-z-z-z.
- CRISPY RICE CRITTERS — Tiny, tasty rice cakes shaped like snails, slugs, frogs and puppy dog tails.
- DYNAMITE STIX — Rolled oat bars with sausage gravy icing. For folks on the run. If they aren't, they can eat one of these and they will be.

## BURNING GRANDMA'S EAR ~

An unusually big airplane that passed low over Val-E-Vue subdivision on a landing approach to Capital Airport the other day interrupted an 8-year-old boy's play. He rushed into the house to tell his grandmother about the experience.

"Did you see that big plane?" he asked her.

"No, but I heard it," she replied.

"I was so excited I said a bad word," he exclaimed. "Know what it was?"

"No," she said, hoping that would be the end of it.

"Well, I won't say it. I'll just spell it," he warned her. "I said, 'Oh, c-h-i-t!' "

## BACK TO BASEBAWL ~

Major league baseball is back. Now for the real task. How to get the fans back into the ballparks. For starters, they could pitch some incentives, such as:

- Season ticket, $19.95.
- More spitballs.
- Replace ballpark organists with country-western bands.

- No postponement of games on account of rain. Mudball!
- Let fans instead of players shower after the game.
- Tuesday game rule for catchers: No glove, no mask, no shinguards, no chest protector, no clothes.
- Pitcher spits, batter walks. Pitcher scratches, game forfeited.
- New concession stand menu item: Popsicle-like treat called umpire-on-a-stick.
- Seventh-inning stretch and massage.
- Let a fan pitch last inning.

## PRODUCE SECTION ~

A 4-year-old tried to help as his mother shopped in the Rochester, Ill., IGA.

"Mom, look at this BIG peanut!" he blurted.

"Put that back," she told him. "That's not a peanut, it's a potato."

## SPRING CHICKEN ~

Overhauling the carburetor on his motorcycle cost Breckenridge, Ill., resident Joe Taylor double. In the process, he dropped a small spring. His pet rooster beat him to it and gobbled it up. Taylor made another trip to the parts store. He had to buy a whole new kit — again. And that cost him another 40 bucks.

## POODLE DOODLES ~

When something is missing, Sherwin Kroll can account for it immediately: The dog ate it. As a pup, the family poodle, Gigi, ate shoes, eyeglasses, pencils and the like.  Her biggest, most expensive and most memorable trick was chewing up both of Kroll's hearing aids. That cost him $1,600.

Now 4 years old, Gigi still gets into minor mischief around the Kroll household on Shetland Drive. Like the other day, when she ambled into the living room with a piece of thread hanging out of her mouth. Kroll guessed she had gotten into his wife's sewing basket. He pulled on the thread. Out came yard after yard after yard — of dental floss. Finally, still attached, out popped the spool.

Then, not long ago, he put $70 cash on the bedroom dresser. His wife was

Then, not long ago, he put $70 cash on the bedroom dresser. His wife was aware that the money was there. And then that it wasn't. She asked him what he did with it. Assuring her that he hadn't touched it, they immediately launched a search of the room. A $20 bill was found under the edge of the bed. They soon confirmed their suspicions that Gigi was now into eating money.

They waited until the next morning. After the dog did her constitutional, Kroll checked things out, so to speak. Sure enough, there was a bit of green something with a "10" printed on it. Arming himself with a pair of pliers and the garden hose, he retrieved the $10 bill. After more probing and hosing, he really hit pay dirt. He found two wrinkled, tattered, well-soiled $20 bills.

"It's amazing what a guy will do for money," Kroll quips.

"Why do we put up with this animal?" he asks. "She's our only child. (Their kids are grown and gone.) And, besides, she's the most affectionate and intelligent dog we've ever owned."

## RESTAURANTMANIA ~
You know you've picked the wrong restaurant when:

• Sign out front says: "You'll Never Guess What Makes Our Meatloaf So Tasty!"
• Soup of the Day is Cream of Quaker State.
• A goat in the kitchen is the garbage disposal.
• Blackbird pie features a real feathery crust.
• Waitress gives you extra napkins to sop up the grease.
• You have to use a knife to cut the gravy.

## BAD TASTE ~
You know corporate takeovers have gone too far when these brand-name products hit grocery store shelves:

• Old Spice salad dressing.
• B.F. Goodrich brownie mix.
• Pennzoil potato chips.
• Jergens soup.

~

- Amocola.
- Alpo summer sausage.
- Purex chewing gum.
- Sherwin Williams ketchup.
- Brillo sandwich cookies.

## WAR STORY ~

Fifty years ago seems more like a few days to Darrell Long when he thinks of the bloody World War II battle for the island of Okinawa, where that anniversary is being formally observed this week.

"I remember that like it was yesterday," says Long, a Marine corporal on a stretcher-bearer detail exactly 50 years ago.

While any number of hair-raising events remain fresh in his memory, he recalls one in particular. He was with several buddies, awaiting the next call to rescue wounded. To their surprise, Army Lt. Gen. Simon Bolivar Buckner Jr., a Chicago native who commanded the invasion forces, walked past. Despite being very close behind the front line, Long recalls that Buckner made little or no effort to hide his rank. A large pair of binoculars dangled from his neck. He was accompanied by his aide, Maj. Frank Hubbard Jr., walking up to a forward observation post.

"I remember someone saying, 'That brass is really asking for it,' as the general walked by," Long said in recalling the incident. "It wasn't five minutes later that artillery shells started coming in."

Shrapnel from one of the exploding shells hit the general in the chest. According to an Associated Press report at the time, Buckner and other officers were watching combat from the observation post on the forward slope of a ridge. Long was one of four Marines who responded to Hubbard's call for a stretcher. He held the plasma that was administered during the attempt to save the general's life. Hubbard ordered the stretcher-bearers to evacuate Buckner for medical treatment. Long says he will never forget how the major repeatedly barked his order to, "Get him out of here!"

"He was really hot," Long recalls. "It was too late for the general, but the major insisted we take him down (the hill)."

targets. Snipers opened fire.

"We'd have to duck down and drop the stretcher. He was a big man, and that made it harder than usual," Long says.

"When the snipers stopped, we'd start out again. Then they'd start shooting again and we'd have to take cover. None of us were hit, but we could hear bullets zinging all around us. It was close."

That was during the day; at least the stretcher-bearers could see where they were going.

"The worst was at night, you couldn't see anything. But when they yelled (for a stretcher), you went. Night orders were, 'Anything that moves, shoot it.' There was just as good a chance you'd get shot by your own guys as the Japanese."

Long didn't realize it until about a week later, but he turned 28 two days after the general was killed.

"That made me one of the old men on Okinawa. Most everybody around me was only 18 or 19 years old."

Long went on with the 2nd Battalion (nicknamed the "Silent Second") of the 8th Marine Regiment and other occupation forces to atomic-bombed Nagasaki, then returned to Springfield in the summer of 1946 and to his old job with the Railway Express Agency. He retired in 1975.

Long observed his 78th birthday Tuesday, an event that never fails to rekindle memories of Okinawa.

"You'd think after 50 years you'd forget a lot of these things, but you don't," he says. "I never will."

# ENDANGERED SPECIES ~
. . . of a different ilk:
• Home cooking.
• Quality time.
• Pride in ownership.
• Clean restrooms.

∼

- Real radio stations.
- Truth in packaging.
- Restaurants with dress codes.
- Skinny.
- People willing to start at the bottom and work their way up.
- Personal service.
- Peace and quiet.
- Patriotism.

## PROFESSIONAL GARAGE SALE ∼

Indications that a residential garage sale isn't just an ordinary, amateur operation:

- Open 24 hours.
- Shopping carts provided.
- Six checkout lanes.
- Full-service cafeteria with seating for 100 in back of garage.
- Fully staffed customer service center.
- If item desired is not in stock, will back-order.
- All major credit cards accepted.
- On-site appliance repair available.
- Blue-light specials every 15 minutes.
- Free gift wrapping and delivery.

## ONE-MAN-ARM-LEG SHOW ∼

Restoration of the century-old Gass family farm home near Lowder, Ill., a small community at the southwest tip of Sangamon County, is an ambitious undertaking for 62-year-old Jack Gass. Four years into the do-it-yourself project, he proudly points to his accomplishments with the 10-room, two-story house so far: plastering, electrical wiring, window trim, siding, etc. finished and he's done it all single-handed — literally.

Gass has only one arm. And he also has only one leg.

"I climb the scaffold. I handle 14-footers," says Gass. "It only takes one arm. I did have to hire someone to put up the scaffolding. I do just about everything else. I work slow but steady. I always did move slow, even on all fours."

Gass acknowledged a brief setback the other day. He had to call a short timeout after someone sneaked up to the house in the dark of night and sloshed yellow paint all over his lift-equipped van. Black paint was thrown on one side of the house.

"It didn't bother me," says Gass. "My niece's husband in Carlinville is a painter, and they cleaned the paint off the van. I can repair anything on wood and the (paint-splashed) window and awning."

He plans to start painting the house, where he resides with his brother, this fall.

The paint was among building supplies Gass had stored in the garage. He had the black paint for his two battery-powered wheelchairs. The yellow paint was for his lawn mower. (He also mows six acres of grass.)

Gass, as a Marine sergeant with the corps' 1st Division, served two years in Korea on what became known as the "Jamestown Line." Circulatory problems resulted in the amputations of his left arm and leg in 1991. He's been working on the house since.

"I gotta do something," he says.

## RESTAURANTMANIA ~
You've selected the wrong restaurant if:

- Food is free with $29.95 beverage.
- Patrons are required to check their wallets with cashier upon entering.
- Hostess ties you to your chair.
- Booster chairs are suspended from slow-moving ceiling fans.
- Customers are required to wear blindfolds until finished eating.

## GET ME OUTTA HERE! ~
The first day of school for a Tuscola, Ill., first-grader was an eye-opener — especially for the teacher. Routine indoctrination for youngsters that morning included stowing book bags, showing them where to put lunch boxes, etc. Then it was time for recess. Everyone knew what to do then.

After the fun and games, the first-graders marched back to their classroom. One little girl, apparently with kindergarten still on her mind, picked up her book bag and headed for the door.

"Where are you going?" her teacher asked.

"Home," she said.

Her teacher hastened to explain that first-graders stay in school all day.

"Well," the little girl spouted, "who in the hell signed me up for this?"

## NOSE JOB ~

A couple pulled up to self-serve pumps at a west-side gas station. He got out, grabbed the hose and leaned over to remove the gas cap. At that very instant, she reached over and turned on the car radio. Up shot the power antenna, which happened to be mounted on the rear fender, right above the neck of the gas tank.

Concentrating on the task at hand, he didn't see the antenna rocketing skyward. So he didn't have a chance to get out of the way. The antenna went up his nose.

He wasn't seriously injured, but it was a heckuva nosebleed.

## SEASON'S SQUEEZIN'S ~

Fall frolics you may not have heard about, until now.

• CENTRAL ILLINOIS CARP CARNIVAL — The state's favorite catch served up any way you want it: deep-fried in 100 percent pure lard, broiled, baked, stuffed, barbecued, scrambled or raw. Dead or alive. Miss Carp contest.

• BILLY GOAT RODEO/BURGOO — Goat busting, roping and riding. Sanctioned by Barnyard Rodeo Association. Guess what's in the burgoo?

• PUDDING, PANCAKE & POSSUM PICNIC — Homemade pudding flavors you've never heard of. Filling pancakes served 40 ways. Possums run over, dressed and cooked to order. Miss Possum contest.

〜

• ANNUAL ILLINOIS POLITICIAN ROAST — Real, live politicians roasted the old-fashioned way: basted and on a spit. Get your fill with a Demo-kabob or grilled Republican.

• CHICKEN-N-NOODLE DOODLE — Exciting chicken races. Kill, cook and eat what you catch. State championship noodle eating contest. Miss Noodle beauty pageant.

• POTHOLE & OLD TIRE BLOW-OUT — Chuckholes big enough to fish or swim in. See demonstrations of 101 ways to use old tires. Retread contest. Hottest bonfire in the world on Saturday night. B.Y.O.T. (Bring Your Own Tires).

• FIB-FIDDLE-FROG-FALSE TEETH FLING — Competitive events for all ages. Liar's contest, fiddle battle, nonstop bullfrog-jumping contest and a new twist on senior citizen track/field: "Denture Derby." New set of dentures for contestant who flings his choppers the furthest.

• CHOCOLATE CARNIVAL - Everything is coated in chocolate. Chocolate-covered corn-on-the-cob, chocolate burgers, chocolate chicken, chocolate french fries, chocolate cotton candy, etc. Hot fudge wrestling.

• POISON IVY PICNIC - Vinery crafts. Poison ivy floral arrangements. celebrity dunk tank filled with calamine lotion. Cash prizes for Biggest Blotches and Reddest Rash.

• YUGO DAYS - Spare parts swap meet. Demolition derby. Yugo owners story-telling contest.

## FLIP SIDE ~

Nature called during the wee hours at Lake Sangchris State Park. Lewis Smith of Taylorville, camping with his wife, Marguerite, in their mini-motorhome, started to descend a lean-to ladder from the upper bunk. About halfway down, the ladder flipped over, sending Smith to a rough landing on the floor below.

"I said a few choice words," he recalls, "but all I got out of it was a skinned leg." Telling the story to friends later, Marguerite put it this way:

"He would probably have paid two bucks for a ride like that at the state fair."

# A VETERAN SALUTES ~

Camp Butler National Cemetery always was near and dear to Wally Jackson, the balding, bespectacled, always-smiling World War II veteran whose postwar career concentrated on selling cars and working as a security guard on the state fairgrounds.

*Camp Butler National Cemetery, Springfield, Ill.*

Ever concerned about the slack crowds for Memorial Day and Veterans Day observances at Camp Butler, he wrote the following essay, expressing what he imagined some of the thousands of veterans buried there might have to say about the day that is dedicated to them.

It was originally published in this column in 1981.

☐ A civil war veteran opens the conversation:
"Things have changed a bit since I was laid to rest here in '64" says Ned Rebel. "This was nothing but an old campground with a prisoner-of-war stockade. I was with a passel of my buddies back then.
"Look! They're still with me. This is Jack next to me and that's Bill over there. We were all captured at Vicksburg. I was wounded. Some Yank put a Minie ball into my shoulder. A Yankee doctor dug it out. Boy, did that hurt.
"They put us all on a train with lots of guards and brought us to Yankeeland. After a time, that old Yankee bug done us in. Never did get to see my wife or kids. None of my relatives have ever come to visit. Guess they won't even know where I am."

☐ Another vet chimes in:
"Hi. I'm Billy. I went up San Juan Hill with Col. Teddy Roosevelt. Boy, did we give those Spaniards fits. And was the blowin' up of the Maine

somethin' to see.

"Always told my wife I wanted to be buried in Camp Butler. So here I am. And she's right here next to me."

☐ The chatter continues:

"I'm Tommy. I fought in the war that was supposed to end all wars. It didn't.

"A German sniper got me at Verdun. Put a bullet right between my eyes. Was on the 17th day of October in 1917.

"They put me in the American cemetery in France. It sure was a beautiful place. In 1921, they brought me home. I'm perfectly content here at Camp Butler."

☐ A vet who died in a later war speaks:

"My name's Jerry. I was a tailgunner on a B-17 in World War II. We were flying a mission to Hamburg. Things were goin' real good. Over the target we took a lot of flak.

"Then we took a hit in our right wing tank. It was burning fiercely, then the whole plane blew up.

"I was blown clear and started falling from 27,000 feet. I hadn't had time to get my bail-out oxygen bottle, so I soon passed out. I came to somewhere around 10,000 feet.

"I was thinking it was time to pull the ripcord. Then I looked down and saw both legs were gone. All kinds of thoughts raced through my mind.

"I finally managed to yank the cord. But that didn't do any good. My chute was in shreds. My body — what was left of it — crashed to earth moments later.

"It landed in a field, near a hedgerow. A German farmer and his wife ran up. He jabbed me with a pitchfork. Guess they wanted to make sure I was done for.

"They buried me next to the hedgerow. An American Graves Registration team found me on Aug. 5, 1945, put me in a military casket and shipped me to France. I was later put on board an American ship that brought me home."

☐ Another vet tells his story:

"My name's Ralph. I was in the Korean War. Stepped on a land mine near the Chosan Reservoir.

"I was picked up by medics and taken to a forward aid station. A doctor looked at me and shook his head.

"They loaded me onto a truck. Not long after, when the truck was full, I was taken to Seoul, sealed in a G.I. casket and flown to the Zone of the Interior. For you non-military types, that's what we called the U.S.A."

☐ Ralph yields to George:
"I guess Vietnam wasn't too popular with you folks here at home, but I fought for my flag and my country. I died for them, too.
"I got it in the middle of a stinkin' jungle. A Cong frag grenade hit me. Didn't leave much.
"Please be a little more charitable, people. There's a lot of Vietnam vets left and they need your love, encouragement and understanding.
"I love it here at Camp Butler. But it does get a little lonely sometimes. So, I'm going to speak for Ned, Billy, Tommy, Jerry and Ralph.
"Please come out and visit us once in awhile. Come on Memorial Day and Veterans Day especially.
"We'll have the Avenue of Flags up and we'll be at the main gate to greet you. You won't be able to see us, of course. But we'll be there.
"You'll be able to tell. Just look for a leaf to flutter, a tree limb to bend, a ripple in Old Glory.
"We'll be all around. Come see us."

Jackson knew of Jerry's WWII experience firsthand. He, too, was a tail-gunner on a B-17. Only he was lucky; he survived.

Jackson, barely 21 years old at the time, was on 26 bombing missions over Germany with the 34th Heavy Bombardment Group, which flew out of an American air base at Mendelsham, England.

As chronicled by this columnist at the time, and reprinted in the 1977 segment of this book, Jackson returned to the village of Mendelsham, 75 miles northeast of London, for a nostalgic visit 18 years ago.

For the past several years, Jackson resided at the Illinois Veterans Home at Quincy. He died there May 31 this year. He's buried at Camp Butler.

# 1996

## ONLY IN AMERICA ~

Some people get up at the crack of dawn the day after Christmas, race to the nearest shopping mall in their ritzy automobile, stand in freezing temperatures for a half-hour until the stores open, push and shove and grab, then stand in line at a checkout counter for 30 minutes to buy a box of Christmas cards that nobody else wants for half-price.

## ANYTHING BUT ~

A quick audit of the return counters in local stores shows the most unwanted Christmas gifts were:

- Newt Gingrich mouth exercise video.
- Campbell's Soup-On-A-Rope.
- Madonna's A-Z Profanity Dictionary.
- Kinky Ken Doll.
- Michael Jackson Nose-Bob Kit.
- Bill Clinton doll. (Wind it up and it lies.)

~

- Assorted Mystery Morsels from Uncle Frank's Fish Farm.
- Barfing Barbi.
- Frisky Kitty Fruitcake.

## AD LIB ~

- Two of the big-time television talk show stars, Phil Donahue and Dick Cavett, are calling it quits.

That's a start.

## COME ON IN! ~

On a curbside marquee in front of Southside Christian Church:

"GOOD SINGING — GREAT PREACHING — FREE BMW (TWO OUT OF THREE AIN'T BAD)"

## JOGGING LANE ~

Three boys in a blue Chevy waited at Sixth and Carpenter streets for the traffic light to change Thursday afternoon. A jogger on the cross street was approaching the intersection. He was spotted by the teens. Slowly, the Chevy inched into the crosswalk. By the time the jogger arrived, his path was blocked. Still creeping, the car brushed the jogger.

BAM!

He slammed his fist on the hood of the car, leaving a big dent and causing all four corners to pop up. Panic set it, and the boys hit the door locks and froze.

The jogger kept running. Didn't even break stride.

## LIGHT(ER) SIDE ~

Then there was the Jacksonville woman who received a small package in the mail from her power company. She opened it and pulled out a night light. It was a promotional stunt, to illustrate how so much light costs so little.

She still jokes with friends that it was a total waste of energy — the power company sending it and her opening it.

She's blind.

## SALUTING THE 'SUPER' ~

A motorist pulled up behind a school bus that stopped for a red light on Stevenson Drive. Seconds later, he realized that two boys in the back of the bus were trying to attract his attention. Both were rendering that universally understood hand . . . er, uh . . . finger signal — the old single-digit salute.

They quickly gained the man's undivided attention, and much more than they bargained for. The light turned green and he changed his course. He started following the school bus, and that soon became obvious to the boys. A few minutes later, the bus stopped at Jefferson Middle School to unload. So did he.

He stood at the door and eyeballed students as they got off, searching for the finger-flippers. That turned out to be an easy task.

Word that someone was tailing the bus had spread, and everyone knew who had done what. Alighting from the bus, practically every kid pointed toward the back of the bus and spewed the names of the smart alecks. When they finally appeared, the motorist pointed them out to assistant principal Robert Bagby.

Who was that stranger following the bus?

Springfield School Superintendent Bob Hill.

## PARK SMART-ER ~

That vehicle theft alert by Park Smart, the program developed by the Anti-Car Theft Committee, Illinois Motor Vehicle Theft Prevention Council and the insurance industry, packed some good advice for motorists who don't want their cars or trucks burgled — or stolen. But besides closing windows, locking their vehicles, installing burglar alarms, etc., motorists should consider some of the more drastic measures to foil criminals. When you park your vehicle:

• Leave a pit bull in the back seat.
• If you insist on leaving valuables in your vehicle, put them in a Mueslix

cereal box. Nobody would steal that.
• Put all of your most cherished good-music cassette tapes and CDs in Barry Manilow album cases. Nobody steals those.
• Dump a gallon of chocolate pudding in the driver's seat.
• Remove and take steering wheel with you.
• Cheap anti-theft device: Tie big ball of bright-colored yarn (5-mile length recommended) to rear bumper. If vehicle is stolen, thief will leave a trail.
• Cheapest anti-theft device: The Real Club. Arm yourself with a baseball bat and stand on the hood of your car or truck.

## CATCH TO FLYING FISH ~

Flying-fish are one thing; flying fish across country, as Springfield psychologist Leslie Fyans discovered, is something else.

During a break at a seminar he participated in at Rocky Mountain National Park, Fyans and his 16-year-old son, J.P., went fishing. Between them, they caught 10 rainbow trout (or 177 inches, as they say down at the bait shop). Plenty for a fish fry at home later, Fyans decided. So he had them professionally packed in dry ice to withstand the trip.

When checking in with Delta at the Denver airport, he said he would carry the box of fish onto the plane. But the Delta rep, noting that the packing box appeared to be sturdy, insisted that the fish go with the regular baggage.

"I just knew going in that the fish wouldn't make it," says Fyans. "That's why I wanted to carry them on board."

He finally gave in to the Delta rep, who assured Fyans that not only would the box survive the cargo bay, but would not get lost because the airline's marvelous computerized baggage-tracking system is next to infallible.

It was downhill from there.

First, Fyan's flight was delayed three hours. Still, he recalled, the company that packed the fish told the two their prize catch would remain hard as a rock for 18 hours, much longer than it would take to fly to St. Louis and drive to Springfield.

After arriving in St. Louis, he took up a position alongside the designated baggage carousel. Around and around went suitcases, golf clubs, bowling balls, etc. Everything imaginable — except his rainbow trout.

"They didn't make it," Fyans says. "I just stood there, laughing. An airline employee asked me what was up."

Fyans, stressing how the Delta rep had talked him into sending his fish to the cargo hold, filled him in. He was told to report the missing box of fish to the airline. It was midnight, so Fyans decided to let Delta search for the fish, and he drove home.

The phone rang early the next morning. Delta Airlines calling. His fish had been located — in the airport at Newark, N.J. And there had been a bit of a problem. The box containing the fish had popped open. As it rumbled around the carousel, besides creating a big stink, one of the corpses bounced out. Quite a sight, not to mention the odor. Then, Fyans heard the worst part of the story:

During flight, the box of fish had been smack up against two garment bags in the baggage hold and, somewhere west of Newark, they entered the thawing stage. One bag contained three men's suits, the other a full-length fur coat. The box began leaking, the garment bags had soaked up the leakage, and the suits and fur coat reeked of fish. To be specific, the irate woman told Delta her fur coat smelled like a swamp.

Fyans was assured that the fish would be repacked and delivered to him as soon as possible. He said he no longer wanted them. Delta told him he had no choice — the airline is obligated to deliver — eventually.

After the fish were flown back to St. Louis, someone determined it would be unconscionable to make a courier drive all the way to Springfield with such stinking cargo. So it was loaded onto the next commuter flight.

Here we go again. Bad weather delayed takeoff. It didn't take long for the small plane's passengers and crew to get a good whiff of the fish. Out came the barf bags. Soon after landing at Capital Airport, the fish were delivered to Fyans in what he swears had to be record driving time from the airport to his home. He rushed the remains to the back yard for quick disposal.

~

Meanwhile, back at the Delta claims desk:

The airline shelled out $1,100 for the ruined suits and $5,500 for the fur coat. Fyans was compensated $63 for the fish.

"I've really got to give Delta credit," Fyans laughs. "They really had a good sense of humor about this."

He has thought of having an embalmer friend prepare one of the trout so he could have it mounted and sent to the airline. Something to remember him by.

"I've decided not to do that," he says. "I really don't think they'll forget me."

## PRISON CURTAIN CAPER ~

That hunger strike by death row inmates at the Pontiac state prison, protesting removal of makeshift curtains from their cell doors, ground to a humorous halt. Barely 36 hours into their snit — after passing up only a couple of meals and refusing to take showers — they gave up their cause when tempted with a heaping portion of hot dogs and baked beans.

One radio station sternly tagged that story with:

"Inmates ended their hunger strike, after eating beans and hot dogs, without incident."

Boy! If that wasn't a whiff of good news!

## MONDAY IS NOT ON THE MAP ~

Illinois, your slip is showing. People are laughing at this year's official state slogan, "Illinois: A Million Miles From Monday."

What's supposed to be attracting tourists in droves may be boring them to tears. If nothing else, it must at least be delaying their arrival as they try to figure it out on a road map.

Newsweek magazine has compared Illinois' slogan to a sleeping pill.
Too late. It's in print all over the country. We're stuck with it — for now.

But there'll be another ad campaign to attract tourists next year and the opportunity to come up with a slogan that makes sense and tells it like it is. Like:

- "Illinois: Always Under Construction"
- "Land of Lotto"
- "Land of Indictments"
- "The Shoebox State"
- "Humidor of the Midwest"
- "Here's the Graft!"
- "Nightcrawlers Bigger Than Boas"
- "Our Congressmen Serve More Time Than Your Congressmen"
- "Carp, Grey Poupon and You"
- "Illi-Noise!"

## KEY TO SUCCESS ~

"You've got to really love what you do," Springfield's Joe Hartzler, special assistant to the U.S. attorney general, said in his commencement address at North Central College in Naperville, Ill.

*Joe Hartzler*

"I don't care whether you go into microsurgery or motorcycle mechanics. If you love your work, you'll succeed."

Hartzler is lead federal prosecutor in the Oklahoma City bombing case. His wife, Lisa, is a graduate of the college.

"Nothing I do fills me with greater pride than appearing before a jury, announcing my name and stating, 'I represent the United States of America,'" he said in declaring that his passion is the process of justice.

Hartzler, diagnosed with multiple sclerosis in 1989, received an honorary doctorate degree from NCC. North Central President Harold Wilde said to Hartzler:

"In an era of great cynicism about public servants, you are the genuine article."

## CHIPS, AHOY! ~
Tip to boating buffs:

If you're shy on lifejackets, as the law requires, next best thing would be two large bags of potato chips per person. Put one under each arm. Figuring each vacuum-sealed bag contains about 50 percent air, you could stay afloat for weeks.

## OH, SINGERS! ~
Conversation between Jenny Koskey and mother-in-law Joan centered on preparations for revival services at Lord of the Harvest Christian Center. Jenny's 6-year-old son Corey and daughter Stephanie, 12, were listening. Rehearsal was scheduled for the next day, Jenny said, and all the singers had to be there.

"You mean Dad's gonna be there?" Corey chimed in.

"No," his mom replied. "I said all the singers have to be there."

"Oh," Corey sighed, "I thought you said all the sinners."

## LAUGHING GAS ~
A pair of swans have been fixtures at The Rail golf course. After they made a nest this year, the female laid two eggs. She sat on them for about a week, then both birds flew the coop. One egg was still in the nest days later. Golfer Al Burge tried to salvage it. He took the egg home, put it in a closet and then forgot all about it.

A loud boom roused him from the couch the other night. He thought something had exploded. Then he detected a gassy odor. Burge sprang into action. He called both the gas company and the fire department.

The "gas" fumes were traced to the closet. The swan egg had exploded.

## STANDING OUT IN THE CROWD ~
It had been a while since Nick Fanale Sr. of Riverton, Ill., had been to the Illinois State Fair — 1934, to be exact. But when GOP presidential nominee Bob Dole said he'd be there Saturday, that's all the prodding Fanale needed. Accompanied by Nick Jr. and granddaughter Katie, the 79-year-

old Fanale waited in line three hours to see the man.

My, how the fair has changed from 62 years ago, Fanale observed. For one thing, he couldn't believe his son had worn a T-shirt and shorts that day.

When he went to his last state fair, the elder Fanale recalled, men wore suits. Wearing a dress shirt and necktie Saturday, Fanale, to say the least, stood out in the crowd.

## MADE FOR TV ~

It was a golden moment, television-wise. So the TV cameras didn't pass it up. Lights, camera, action . . . Mayor Karen Hasara and the Department of Housing and Urban Development's Debra Torres teamed up to slam a sledgehammer into a corner of the first John Hay Homes building to bite the dust in a sweeping renewal project. Mortar flew and a few bricks fell to the ground. More entertaining than the usual groundbreakings/ribbon-cuttings for sure, any of which is right up television news' alley. But this one was a setup. Phony baloney.

The sledge and the bricks — and the two women who comprised the ceremonial wrecking crew — were real.

The phony part: Bricks had been removed from the corner of the building, then put back in place, anchored with some kind of mortar substitute, something akin to Silly Putty. Result was a Hollywood kind of prop, like the breakaway bottles and chairs used to crack someone over the head with in a staged melee.

## 'MR. FORD' ~

Glenn Sharp, who'll be eulogized at a private graveside service today, enjoyed a long reign as the dean of Springfield car salesmen. He sold Fords for 68 years, winning every award the auto manufacturer has to offer.

"Sharpie," whose trademark was a wide-brimmed felt hat and big smile, made his first sale — a Model T Ford — in the 1920s. In those days, car dealers and employees formed working parties to unload disassembled new cars from railroad boxcars, hauled them to the dealership and installed fenders, wheels, etc. Selling wasn't as complicated then, Sharp used to explain. Buyers had the choice of a coupe or a roadster, and no choice of color. All were black.

A new Model T Ford was priced at $460. When Ford produced what Sharp considered its hottest-selling car of the bygone era — 1937 — the sticker price was $1,195. And, as Sharp always boasted, that was back when financing wasn't part of the deal. Everyone paid cash.

# 1997

## LOOKING FORWARD ~

Practicing the perilous art of prognosticating, we predict for 1997:

• The Clinton administration will stay on track: a scandal a month.
• A number of manufacturers will improve anti-tampering techniques in packaging their products, thereby making it impossible for elderly people to open them.
• Some high-profile professional athletes will continue to be a rotten influence on little kids.
• Congress will act in the air bag controversy, decreeing that any car driven by a member of Congress, or cars occupied by a congressman, do not have to be equipped with factory-installed air bags — theory being that that would be redundant.

## MAKING CHANGE A LOST ART ~

A woman drove into the "surprise" lane at a fast-food restaurant at high noon and ordered a hamburger and a medium-sized Coke. She was prepared for the classic line that followed:

⌐∽

"Want fries with that?"

"No."

Moving up to the window, she tendered a $5 bill and received $1.98 change. That cost too much, she thought. Still parked at the window, she glanced into the sack. SURPRISE! French fries. No wonder the tab was so much.

She handed the sack of food and $1.98 in change back to the window jockey, requesting that the fries be removed and she be given the correct change. Out went the fries and, this time, she was handed $2.12. She was still being shorted, she pointed out. After poking several of the little squares on the cash register's "idiot" board, the frantic employee admitted she was stumped.

As the line of cars grew longer, a manager ran to her rescue. Relying on what the cash register tape was telling him, he contended the $2.12 in change was correct. Figure it out the simple way, the woman suggested.

"How much is a hamburger and medium Coke?"

"That would be $1.69," said the manager, after doing some conventional arithmetic.

"Now subtract $1.69 from $5," she coached.

"Oh, yeah," the manager muttered, counting out $3.31 in change.

By this time, the long line of drive-through patrons was a lot hotter than her hamburger.

# VALENTINE'S DAY VERSE ∼
For better or for worse:

Roses are red
Inaugural's past
Next four years
Oughta be a blast!

Roses are red
Bill's Hillary's a keeper,
Both better be good swimmers
Whitewater's gettin' deeper.

Roses are reddish
Michael Jackson's a dad
He says the kid looks like him,
Eeeee-gad!!!!

## A LITTLE LAW & ORDER ~

It's high time lawmakers get off their duffel bags and pass some common-sense legislation. Enact laws that would:

• Increase the minimum penalty for spray-painting graffiti from a slap on the wrist to spray-painting the spray-painter in a public place.
• Require any motorist who uses a cellular phone to pass a one-hand-on-the-phone/one-hand-on-the-wheel driver test.
• If — because of either faulty equipment or employee negligence — a shoplifter alarm goes off as an innocent customer exits a retail store, the customer is awarded the store.
• Require radio and TV talk show hosts to pass a competency test.
• Require self-serve businesses to pay customers the minimum hourly wage for waiting on themselves.
• Make it illegal to wear a baseball cap backward, unless the wearer's head is on backward.
• Lock up people who go nuts at the sight of a television camera.
• Determine the price of admission at a movie theater in accordance with a movie critic's review of the feature attraction. (Four stars: full price. Three stars: $1 discount. Two stars: half-price. One star: theater pays you to watch the movie.)

## EASY TIME ~

Life in federal prison at Yankton, S.D., where financial scammer Gregory Wilson is serving his six-year sentence, is described as a lot like being in college. No wonder. The minimum-security prison is the old Yankton College campus. It became a federal lockup in the late '80s, a couple of years after debts forced the college (established in 1881, it was the state's oldest) to close.

⌇

Looking in from the outside, little has changed, according to Kelly Hertz, editor of the Yankton Daily Press & Dakotan.

"If it weren't for the signs, you wouldn't know it's a prison," he says. "It looks like the quaint little college campus it was, only a lot of people think the grounds look better now than when it was a college. You see a lot of men around on the grounds, but no guards are in sight. There is a fence, but I think it's more for keeping outsiders from getting in."

A man who recently "graduated" from the Yankton facility, nestled in a residential area of the small city (population 13,000), says doing time there is "pretty sweet." It boasts about everything that a small college would have, including a running track, gymnasium, tennis courts and baseball field. About 500 inmates live in the old college dorms, which are furnished with big-screen TV sets.

"Food is excellent," says the ex-con, who prefers to remain anonymous.

There are alarms but no bars on dormitory windows, he said. Inmates perform assigned duties from 8 a.m. to 3:30 p.m. weekdays and must be in their rooms for a head-count three times a day. About two-thirds of the prisoners are serving time for drug offenses, and the rest — like Wilson — are considered white-collar criminals. In an effort to appease towns-folk, the federal government does not house hardened criminals there.

"Everything pretty much works on the honor system," says the former inmate. "There's a walk-away (an escape) once in a while, but if you run, you're sent to a tougher prison somewhere. It's (Yankton) the place to go if you've got to do time."

Inmates have a nickname for the prison at Yankton, the ex-con recalls. They refer to it as "Camp Yum-Yum."

## SPURTS AFIELD ~
Just before the Chicago Cubs broke their amazing losing streak, some local Cub fans had to endure cruel and inhumane punishment like this:

A guy parked his new car outside a south-side tavern over the noon hour. He locked it up tight and left nothing inside that might tempt a thief.

Nothing, that is, except two tickets to a Cubs game. He left them sticking out of the ashtray. He returned to find someone had smashed a side window, reached in and put two more tickets to a Cubs game in the ashtray.

(Of course it's a joke.)

## SPEAKING OF CHICAGO ~

One wag says that, every time the Shedd Aquarium pops up in the news — as it did Monday when the institution's inflatable whale was on exhibit here — he envisions a big fish tank full of cat and dog hair.

## TOUGH GUY ~

A couple put their 8-year-old son aboard an Amtrak passenger train. He was seated in a double-decker car on the Chicago-to-Dallas run. It was chilly on the train, and he wasn't dressed for it.

"I guess I should have brought a blanket," the boy commented to an elderly woman who was seated nearby and quite cozy under the blanket she'd taken along.

Motioning to the vacant seat next to her, she made him an offer she thought he couldn't refuse.

"I'll tell you what," she said. "If you come back here, I'll share my blanket with you."

"Oh," the boy replied bravely, "I like to be cold!"

## ICE (S)CREAM DREAM ~

Cool off with one of these tasty new flavors:
Pralines-n-Prunes
Preparation P (Pistachio)
Snail Swirl
Muskrat Mocha
Strawberry Smelt
Peppermint Putty
Carmel Carp
Rocky Road Salt
Beanie Baby Brickle

~

## HOLD THE PHONE! ~

When the phone rang, a 5-year-old boy answered. Conversation went something like this:

"Can I talk to your daddy?" the woman asked.

"He's in the bathtub," the boy replied.

"Can I talk to your mom?"

"She's in the bathtub, too. I'll go get her."

"No!" the caller gasped. "I'll call back later."

What the boy didn't explain was that their house has two bathrooms. His mother was in one and his dad in the other.

## JOHN WHO? ~

After a woman acquired all the attire for a Marilyn Monroe Halloween costume, she and her hubby searched Springfield for a John F. Kennedy mask for him to wear. At a costume shop in White Oaks Mall, they told a teenage sales clerk of their quest. He said they would have to tell him more about who Kennedy was so he'd know what area of the store to check.

She expressed disbelief that he didn't know Kennedy was president of the United States.

"Was he like No. 10 or something?" the kid asked.

Never mind. Her husband went to the party as Joe DiMaggio.

## HALLOWEEN SEEN ~

While it isn't unusual to see wives, girlfriends or buddies standing on the street outside the Sangamon County Jail, waving, yelling, holding signs or trying to communicate in some other awkward way with a prisoner, this scene on Halloween was different. A woman with five little kids in their trick-or-treat costumes were waving to someone — presumably their father — who was peering through an upper-story window.

Believe it or not, one kid was dressed as a prison inmate. To accent his black-and-white striped suit, he wore handcuffs and had a ball-and-chain on one leg.

## ABE'S COMIC STREAK ~

*Harry Hahn*

The recitation of the Gettysburg Address by Abraham Lincoln look-a-like Harry Hahn was apropos when a concert by the reactivated 33rd Regiment Civil War Band commemorated the 134th anniversary of the historic speech.

So was Hahn's opening line when he took the Springfield High School auditorium stage:

"Good evening, ladies and gentlemen. It's good to be back!"

In response to the laugh he got, Hahn noted that, at 188 years old, it would be good to be anywhere.

## COUNT YOUR BLESSINGS ~

There are worse things than a fly in your soup. For example:

- A mouse in your blouse.
- Pie in your eye.
- An eye in your pie.
- A cootie in your bootee.
- Rocks in your socks.
- Goo on your shoe.
- Warts in your shorts.
- Toes in your nose.

# 1998

## BUM THREAT ~

Proof positive that, when people talk on the telephone, they should speak clearly — otherwise, the party at the other end could misunderstand, suffer a panic attack and cause undo alarm. That's what happened Tuesday in Litchfield, Ill., when an employee at Wal-Mart interpreted a phone call as a bomb threat.

Not only wasn't it a bomb threat; the call was actually a wrong number, a police probe later determined.

When the employee answered the phone, the caller blurted one word. The employee thought the caller said "Bomb!" But the caller, who just happened to have misdialed, had muttered "Mom!"

## YEARN TO LEARN ~

Students in Peggy Gillespie's third-grade class at Ball Elementary proclaimed lessons they've learned. Some excerpts:

⤳

"I've learned that life is like a roll of toilet paper; you never know when it is going to run out." — Kelsey Druhot

"I've learned that if you ever want something, ask your grandparents." — Kristen Sweat

"I've learned that when you fall off a horse three times, you're an advanced horseback rider." — Rachel Chatham

## HIGHWAY PATROL ~

A motorist was hopping mad at being pulled over by a Rochester, Ill., police officer the other night on suspicion he was driving drunk. The verbal exchange between the two went like this:

"I'm never coming through this town of Riverton, Ill., again!" declared the motorist.

"You aren't in Riverton," he was informed.

"Then where am I?"

He was booked for DUI.

## PLANE TALK ~

Now that they've renamed Washington National Airport for former President Ronald Reagan, won't it be just like some congressman to push for that kind of recognition for President Clinton someday? The airport at Little Rock might appropriately be named for him. We can see the sign now! "Welcome to Bill Clinton INTERNational Airport."

## HAPPY BIRTHDAY, ABE! ~

What if Abraham Lincoln were alive today, had never gotten caught up in politics, had not been elected president and, above all, had stayed away from Ford's Theater? What if he'd never left Springfield and was still practicing law here?

Why, he'd be resting up for his birthday — his 189th! — tomorrow. What would that mean?

For one thing, he'd be the oldest barrister in the world. And, no doubt, he'd be the senior member of the longest-named law firm in the country.

Without a doubt, Abe couldn't have kept from dabbling in local politics. He probably would have served as a Sangamon County associate circuit judge for a couple of years (until his tough, no-nonsense courtroom demeanor got him booted from the bench), and, for sure, he would have (to no avail) thrown his stovepipe hat into the ring several times for a federal judgeship.

But he would not have dared take a seat on the Illinois Supreme Court, much less agreed to preside as chief justice of that august body. Abe would have been very much aware that, while filling that lofty position, someone might turn him in for racing back and forth between New Salem and Springfield in his horse and buggy, and using his clout to avoid speeding tickets.

Yep, Abe should have stuck with lawyering all this time. He could be turning an unbelievable 189 years old tomorrow.

In such a case, his co-workers would likely treat the occasion with all the dignity and respect they usually do these days.

After his early morning jog from home at Eighth and Jackson streets (despite all the sightseers, he'd still be residing there) to the "Y" for his daily swim, he'd walk to work, open the door and find his office filled with black balloons, the windows covered with black crepe paper and this sign hanging over his desk:

"ABE IS OVER THE HILL!"

## WHEN HENNY MET FRED ~

A chance and quirky meeting on a New York City street corner 35 years ago led to a close, lasting friendship between Henny Youngman, the legendary comic who died Tuesday at age 91, and Springfield publicist Fred Puglia.

"Henny Youngman! Fred Puglia! How are you?" Puglia remembers saying, reaching out to shake hands.

〜

"Yeah! Yeah! How've ya been?" a smiling Youngman replied, under the assumption he and the young Puglia had met somewhere before.

They hadn't, of course. Puglia, who grew up in the Bronx, was home on a college break, working as a vendor at Yankee Stadium at the time.

"Walk with me," Youngman said. "We'll talk."

They walked and talked, straight to lunch — at the Friar's Club. They kept in touch. Puglia says they next met a year later, again in New York City, and Youngman took him to lunch at the Stage Door Deli. Youngman was the typical showman of the day.

"He handed $10 to the headwaiter when we went in," Puglia recalls. "Every 10 minutes the entire time, they paged him: 'Mr. Youngman . . . Mr. Henny Youngman . . . telephone call for Mr. Henny Youngman.'"

Puglia booked the comic over the years, eventually bringing him to Springfield to headline "Summer Serenade" concerts sponsored by moving contractor Bob Wanless through the mid-1980s. Youngman also came to town to visit Puglia and wife Nora. He pitched a business proposition to them on one of those occasions.

Youngman, who had worked as a printer in his early comedian days and was always fascinated with the trade, wanted to open a job-printing operation in Springfield. To be called "Henny the Printer," it was to be the start of a nationwide franchise.

"Henny wanted us as partners to do marketing and public relations for the company," Puglia says. "We just couldn't work it out. He was really disappointed."

## ILLINOIS' 'SUPER' CRIMINAL ~

"Supermax," the new prison Illinois built for supermaximum security at Tamms, Ill., was designed to house the worst-of-the-worst the Department of Corrections can scrape up. So what could have been more fitting in christening the joint than making DOC's reputed No. 1 bad boy the institution's very first inmate?

Although DOC officials chose not to identify him or any of the five others who followed, he is Henry "Omar" Brisbon best known as the "I-57 Killer." As DOC puts it, the less notoriety for him, the better, largely because he likes it.

Warden George Welborn did say, without naming the 40-year-old Brisbon, that if the "First Inmate" is not the most infamous of 37,000 inmates in Illinois prisons, he ranks very close to the top.

Brisbon was considered notorious at age 17, authorities have said. He long ago earned a reputation as the state's most violent inmate.

He first went to prison in 1973 for rape and armed robbery. But while he was free on bond, awaiting trial in that case, he murdered a 25-year-old engaged couple after ramming the rear of their car south of Chicago on Interstate 57. Having tricked them into stopping, he forced them to lie on their stomachs and ordered them to "make this your last kiss" before shooting both in the back. Brisbon was accused of using the same ruse on I-57 and sadistically murdering a second young woman before he was caught.

After he was sentenced to prison for 1,000 to 3,000 years for the double murder (being 17 years old, he wasn't eligible for the death penalty), he was not charged with the later killing. He also was accused of murdering a grocery clerk by shooting him in the face with a sawed-off shotgun, but wasn't convicted of that crime either. One year after going to prison, he sharpened the end of a metal ladle stolen from the Stateville prison kitchen and murdered another inmate. For that, he was sentenced to death row.

In addition, Brisbon has been charged with 45 assaults — mostly against guards — while in prison. That includes the stabbing of three other death row inmates, infamous serial killer John Wayne Gacy among them.

Brisbon's legal challenges to the death penalty are nearing an end. If he loses, he won't have far to go; the new ultramodern execution chamber is within walking distance of his cell.

## 'AMAZING' ~

High school ensemble and solo competition was under way at Pleasant Plains Ill. High School, and Riverton, Ill., freshman Becky Piatt was singing when the quiet was shattered by the ringing of a telephone — a cellular phone that a woman in the audience had stashed in her purse.

Everyone — including Becky — heard it. But the interruption didn't phase her; she didn't miss a note, even though she was well aware that it was her mother's cell phone that was ringing.

Embarrassed to tears, Lisa Piatt, anticipating it was her 13-year-old son Clint calling, answered. It was Clint, all right, but he was calling for good reason.

"Dad phoned. They think they've found a heart for him," he told his mother.

Her husband, Ted, had been in a Peoria, Ill., hospital for more than four months awaiting a heart transplant.

As soon as Becky finished her solo, Lisa apologized to Riverton music teacher Susan Smarjesse for the distraction and told her daughter they would have to leave for Peoria immediately. A few hours later, Piatt's doctors confirmed the donor heart could be used, and they proceeded with plans for the operation that night.

Piatt, a heating/air-conditioning installer who's been off the job since suffering a heart attack 16 months ago, had become concerned that the search for a donor heart was taking so long. But he predicted several days ago that "something good was about to happen."

"It sure did," says Lisa. "We all watched the helicopter bringing his new heart land at the hospital. We were so excited. It was truly a beautiful gift."

A four-hour operation followed. Lisa says her husband is making a good recovery and could leave the hospital early next week.

Becky learned later that she placed first with her solo. She told her mother that, while singing, she followed the advice that student teacher Marie Graziano had given her.

"Think of something to inspire you," she recalls Marie telling her.

Becky thought about her father.

She sang "Amazing Grace."

## CHARGE!! ~
Talk about winning the lottery, young Michael P. Kelley has done the next best thing. He has qualified for a Bank One Platinum Visa card.

Michael, a Springfield resident, has written confirmation of the honor from Randy Christofferson, president of the big bank's credit card services company.

"You are one of a select few who appear to have demonstrated the financial credentials necessary to carry the new Bank One Platinum card," Christofferson wrote.

Suffice to say this is no small-change deal for Michael. As the bank's flier boasts, this is "the card that answers all your needs."

So, if Michael needs a 4.9 percent fixed introductory (he'd better read the fine print on that part) rate, plus $1 million worth of travel accident insurance, $3,000 worth of protection in case some airline loses his luggage and a credit line up to $100,000, he's in business.

Michael is mulling the offer. And if he decides to accept, where will he head first? Not an easy decision. Toys R Us or Isringhausen Imports?

A tough call indeed. Michael is only 4 years old.

## MIDWESTERNER'S VIEW ~
Two gents catching up on things.

One: "Is John still livin'?"

Other: "Yeah, he's down in Florida — if you call that livin'."

## MACK ONE UP ON MICHAEL ~
Qualifying for a major credit card might have put 4-year-old Michael P. Kelley in an elite group but a 9-year-old in Springfield makes an even big-

~

ger boast. He *has* a credit card. In fact, he has two cards, and they are both active.

AT&T issued a MasterCard with a $10,000 line of credit to Mack Dun Dee when the head of the household, Joe Dunbar, received his about three years ago. A couple of months later, an unsolicited Citibank Visa card addressed to Mack arrived in the mail.

Mack is a Boston terrier.

Dunbar thought it was screwy but, since the dog has the run of the house anyway, he figured Mack should have some financial responsibility, too. So he kept both credit cards and uses them when purchasing dog food and for paying for trips to the vet.

So far, Mack maintains a good credit rating. Of course, Dunbar pays the bills.

## SEASONAL TWO-STEP ~

Police were dispatched to the Jewel/Osco supermarket on South Sixth Street where a man appeared to be under the spell of a springlike Sunday morning. Officers responding couldn't help but find the guy. He was lying in a potting soil display, clutching this sign:

"WILL DANCE FOR MONEY"

## PRESIDENTIAL ADVISER ~

Joining the annual "Turn Off TV" movement last week, Rochester, Ill., teacher Peggy Cantrall had her second-graders write to President Bill Clinton to encourage him and Hillary to do likewise, and suggest three ways they could better use that time.

The list submitted by 8-year-old Matthew Butcher:

1. Read a book.
2. Plant a garden.
3. Play board games.

Mom Brenda was impressed with his ideas. But, as she read the list a second time, a significant misspelled word threw her for a loop.

When he suggested they play board games, he wrote "broad."

## CANDY 'BOMBS' AWAY! ~

There's a parallel to the "candy bombing" of blockaded Berlin, which is to be re-enacted later this month in observance of the 50th anniversary of the start of the massive airlift.

During the Korean War, Ralph Davison of Springfield, who was a navigator on a C-47 transport, often flew at low altitude over small islands off the Korean coast and could see children waving at the plane. As Christmas neared one year, he decided to treat the kids below. He collected candy bars from buddies, attached them to small parachutes fashioned from handkerchiefs and dropped them from the cargo door.

"I did it two or three times," he recalls. "You couldn't see the kids picking them up, but I'm sure they got all of them. We flew at an altitude of only 50 to 75 feet (attempting to avoid radar detection), and it was a clear area."

Davison, an Air Force retiree who now works at the Illinois Department of Transportation's division of aeronautics, at the time was unaware of the candy drops over Berlin. Although he had flown in World War II, he didn't meet the Berlin "Candy Bomber," Gail Halvorsen, until they were both serving at Wright-Patterson Air Force Base in Dayton, Ohio, in the mid-'50s. Still, Halvorsen's exploits had never been divulged publicly and Halvorsen didn't mention the subject.

"I first heard about that through friends at an Air Force reunion a year ago," Davison says. "It had just been publicized somewhere. Gail wasn't able to attend the reunion and I haven't talked to him since."

Halvorsen, 77 and living in Salt Lake City, was the subject of a story in Sunday editions of The State Journal-Register. He is currently touring Europe and will re-enact his goodwill missions by dropping candy bars and chewing gum June 26 while flying in a C-54 cargo plane over Berlin. As far as Davison knows, only he and fellow crew members knew of his Korean War-era candy drops.

## GANGWAY! ~

A mom was leading two tykes toward a department store exit Saturday afternoon.

"You know why I really want to get to the car fast?" the 3-year-old girl asked.

"No," mom replied.

"I'm gonna throw up!"

## INFERNAL KERNELS ~

Good uses for microwave popcorn that won't pop:

- Decorative stone for dollhouses.
- BBs.
- Popcorn chip cookies.
- Biodegradable ball bearings.
- Corn Kernel breakfast cereal.
- Ammunition for peashooters.
- Fat-free jawbreakers.
- Grind into coffee-free coffee.
- Crunchier croutons.
- Beanie Baby stuffing.

## GOTCHA, GRETA! ~

Psychic Greta Alexander, who died Friday, had a sense of humor second to none. She was a kidder and liked to be kidded.

She kept in touch with this column. Our phone conversations almost always started like this:

"This is Greta, darling. How are you?"

"You oughta know!"

*Greta Alexander*

## THE WAY IT WAS ~

A guy recalling his school days of a few decades ago, commenting on the new disability insurance plan Horace Mann is offering to teachers who are victims of violence in the classroom:

"When I was in school, it was the kid who hit the teacher who went on disability!"

## ONE DIP OR TWO? ~

Nominations for flavors-of-the-month at Washington, D.C., ice cream parlors:

- Monica Mocha.
- Impeach-mint.
- White Water Chocolate.
- Oval Office Orange Pineapple.
- Paula's Pistachio.
- Hillary Rodham Raspberry.
- Bubba Banana Brickle.
- Linda Tripple-Dipple.

## HORSEPLAY ~

Horses that Al Heimlich bet on at the state fair were all losers.
"I lost my shirt," Heimlich sighs. "But it doesn't matter; it was an old shirt."

## STATE FAIR DAZE ~

It was a repeat trip to the Illinois State Fair for Joe Kolb of Elkhart, Ill., and 4-year-old grandson Bradey, a preschooler at Mount Pulaski, Ill., this year. Only this time, it was more of a challenge for Grandpa to keep up — with answers, that is.

Entering the Main Gate, Bradey got an eyeful of the monstrous statue of Abe Lincoln and ducked behind Joe.

"Who's that, Grandpa?"
"Abraham Lincoln."
"What's he holding?"
"An ax."

～

"Why's he here?"
"It's a statue. It isn't real."
"Who's Abraham Lincoln?"
"He was president of the United States."
"Where does he live?"
"He died. He lives with God in Heaven."
"How'd he die?"
"He was shot."
"Why'd they shoot him?"
"Somebody was mad at him."
"A cop shoot him?"
"No, a police officer didn't shoot him."
"What's a police officer?"
"A cop."

Later in Adventure Village:

"Why are all those people screaming?"
"They're having fun?"
"Are we having fun?"
"Yes."
"Then why aren't we screaming?"

After six full hours of fairgoing, Bradey almost fell asleep on the pony ride. Joe decided it was time to head home.

Before pulling out of the parking lot, Joe used his cellular phone to call his wife. Of course, Bradey wanted to talk to her.

"Hey, Grandma, guess what!" he shouted. "Abraham Lincoln died!"

# DRUMMER BOY ～

The career of drummer Barrett Deems, who died Tuesday at age 85 in Chicago, where only a few months ago he still fronted his own big band, was no surprise to school chums here. Deems, who established himself in the music business as the world's fastest drummer, was already an act when he attended Springfield High School.

Friend Al Heimlich says Deems always had drumsticks in his pocket and drummed on anything.

"He'd go down the hallways and beat on the stairs and banisters and walls," Heimlich recalls. "When the principal saw him, he'd say, 'Quit that!' Barrett would say 'Yes, sir!' As soon as he got out of sight, he'd start again. I'd bet there are still nicks all over the place from his drumsticks."

A classmate, John LaRue, also recalls Deems' antics.

In the late 1930s, Deems paid his dues by accompanying honky-tonk piano thumpers in the roughest downtown taverns of the day. But by 1941, he had joined the nationally prominent Joe Venuti orchestra.

Deems was working with Louis Armstrong's jazz band in 1956 when it appeared in the movie "High Society," which starred Grace Kelly, Bing Crosby and Frank Sinatra. He was still with Armstrong when the band played for Kelly's wedding in Monaco a few months later.

In an interview for The State Journal-Register years ago, reporter Wayne Allen asked Deems if Kelly was really beautiful.

"If you like them skinny," Deems replied.

## CEREAL SAGA ~
Perhaps it's time for some new cereals with catchier names. Replace:

• Puffed Rice with Puffed Mice
• Shredded Wheat with Shredded Meat.
• Wheaties with Tweeties (tiny yellow bird-shaped nuggets).
• Rice Krispies with Lice Krispies.
• Captain Crunch with Corporal Crunch.
• Alpha-bits with Alpha-zits.

## A SNEAK PEAK ~
. . . at the White House dinner menu for Christmas Day:

• Turkey (Somebody say Bill?)
• Turntripp Greens
• Monicaroni & Cheese
• Impeachment Pie

## BEANIE BINGE ~

You say you'd die for a Furby but can't find one? Here's the next best thing — the latest Beanie Baby series. And just in time for Christmas. You won't be able to find these, either. Although they should, they don't exist.

• Baked Beanie
• Green Beanie
• Kidney Beanie
• Lima Beanie
• Mexican Beanie
• String Beanie
• Soup Beanie
• Chili Beanie
• Pork N. Beanie
• Jelly Beanie

## CELL PHONE 'GETS IT' ~

A Springfield man whose business depends heavily on his cellular phone took the gadget in for repair — again and again. Each time John Bavetta was told that it was in proper working order, a strong hint that *he* had some kind of hangup.

Bavetta finally figured out how he could convince the communications agent that the phone was unreliable.

He loaded his 9mm pistol and took aim.

Bam!
Bam!
Bam!

He put three shots through it. One was dead center into the battery.

Bavetta took the remains back to the phone store. Once more he asked for a replacement.

No argument this time.

~

# SHOCKING STOCKING STUFFERS ~

Still stumped on what to give the proverbial gal or guy who needs absolutely nothing this Christmas? Stump no more. "Stocking-Stuffers-Plus" (As-Not-Seen-On-TV) is here: a new line of things nobody needs. Every item for the amazingly low price of $19.95 each (plus $100 shipping & handling). Proof of citizenship required. Void where prohibited and all that jazz.

• SOUP SHOOTER: If you think the Salad Shooter's a rip, you'll be amazed at how easy you can make homemade soup with this new gadget. (Wet suit sold separately.)

• DIRTY-BIRD DROPS CLOCK: The 12 peskiest birds known to man roost on this giant clock face, each doing their thing on the designated hour. Drip pan included. (.38-caliber revolver sold separately).

• THE ZAPPER: Works on the same principle as the Clapper. Mounts on the front bumper of your car — right next to the deer whistle. Activation button attaches to dashboard. Then, whenever you're waiting for a traffic signal light to change and some guy with his thumping stereo blaring away pulls up beside you, just press the button. A laser-guided electronic signal instantaneously melts (zaps) the boom box.

• MUSTY-MUSTY: Deodorant/Shampoo/Aftershave for THE man. Guaranteed to turn any stomach. Comes in three disgusting, repulsive fragrances:

   PEE-YOO I - Smells like you had anchovies for breakfast.
   PEE-YOO II - Smells like you've just had an extremely exhausting workout at the health club and skipped the shower.
   PEE-YOO III - Smells like you've been to the sale barn and stepped in something.

• ATOMIC LOAF BREAD MAKER: Pour in flour, yeast, milk and desired additives (nuts, raisins, M&Ms, etc.), seal hatch, light fuse and run. Bread bakes in 12 seconds. Mushroom cloud dissipates within five minutes and you've got piping hot, glow-in-the-dark bread. (Note: Atomic Bread Loaf Maker is not reusable.)

• GUNN COFFEE MAKER: For real drips. Get perfect java every time. Automatically recycles coffee grounds into super-duper-absorbent gran-

~

ules for the litter box. Your cat will love the Folgers/Maxwell House aroma and you'll love the new aroma from the litter box.

• MARK McGWIRE TOOTHPICKS: Painstakingly hand-carved from the home run king's splintered ball bats. Flavors include Red Man, baseline chalk and stale stadium popcorn.

# 1999

## SNOW FUNNY ~

'Twas the day after the Big Snow and some streets in Springfield were barely passable. Among them was a side street off East Ash. A snowplow had made one sweep down the middle of the street, allowing only one lane of traffic. A woman who was trying to avoid traffic turned onto the side street. She had clear sailing for a couple of blocks, then a red pickup truck turned onto the street and headed her direction. As her car and the pickup met, the guy driving the truck yelled at her.

"Hey, lady! I don't back up for idiots!"

Shifting into reverse, she shot back.

"OK, I do!"

## NEVER TOO LATE ~

Fifty-four years ago today, John D. Roberts flew from Guam in a B-24 to bomb Japanese ground installations on Iwo Jima. It was the 22nd bombing mission that Roberts would fly with the 11th Bombardment Group, a wing of the 7th Air Force.

About five hours later, Roberts, wedged into the top gun turret of the Liberator, was over the target. A few minutes after that, he was hit. A piece of shrapnel penetrated the turret's Plexiglas bubble and hit Roberts in the mouth, knocking out several teeth and splitting his tongue.

"Now I speak with forked tongue," the Springfield native quips.

That put Roberts out of action, but only temporarily. After being dropped off on Saipan for medical treatment, he was sent to Hawaii for two months of recuperation. Roberts returned to Guam and hooked up with another bomber crew, flying 10 more missions over targets that included Nagasaki and Hiroshima.

Upon discharge at the end of World War II, he returned to his old job as a carpenter at Sangamo Electric. He retired when Sangamo was sold in the late '70s, then continued his craft at Sangamon State University (now the University of Illinois at Springfield) before moving to Rogers, Ark., six years ago. Today, the 75-year-old Roberts will be awarded the Distinguished Flying Cross in a long-overdue ceremony at Little Rock Air Force Base. Because of an administrative error, he didn't receive the medal when he should have — 54 years ago.

## IF ABE COULD SEE US NOW ~

Ahhhh . . . if only ol' Abe were with us today, his birthday, and he could stand in the well of the U.S. Senate and deliver what would someday go down in history as his "Impeachmentburg Address." It might go something like this:

"Six score and 15 years ago, I spoke of our forefathers, the birth of this new nation, conceived in liberty and dedicated to the proposition that all men — except for one scoundrel who comes to mind — are created equal.

"Naturally, none of you, with the exception of Strom Thurmond, witnessed that event.

"Well, here you are today, on my birthday — which is a darned big holiday in Illinois, I might note — at the peak of an impeachment trial. You now face the musical question — not to mention the music — what to do with President Bill Clinton?

"Do you tar and feather the rascal and send him back to Arkansas? Lemme tell you, folks, that if you do, you certainly won't be ruining the reputation of America's 'Faithful Husband of the Year.'

"Face facts, friends; you don't fool me. You could slice the stink from all this cover-my-hind-end politics in here with a butter knife. Yep, I'd bet my boots you're gonna let Slick Willie skate. You probably won't so much as make him pay Monica's dry-cleaning bill.

"But until the votes are cast and the verdict is in, I urge you to go ahead and build a fire to melt the tar. Don't take a chance on getting caught with YOUR pants down!"

Oh, well, happy birthday anyway, Abe!

## FOR THE LOVE OF . . . ~
For better or worse, this Valentine's Day, we resort to verse:

Roses are red
Clinton is shady
If he could be re-elected
Monica might be first lady

Many a congressman's face is red
Cause the impeachment trial proved silly,
It fit Democrats' plan to a T,
'Cause from Day One they chirped, "Free Willie!"

Roses are red
Hillary ain't blue
Perhaps she just
Doesn't have a clue

## 'PRINCE' PETTIT ~
He was nicknamed "Prince of Police" long ago, and the name stuck with

Springfield police officer Tony Pettit. It was inscribed on a plaque he received Monday, when Pettit retired after three decades with the Springfield Police Department.

Pettit picked up the "prince" label during the rowdy Street Machine Nationals here in the 1980s. A free-lance artist volunteered to personalize squad cars while officers were on standby for crowd control duty. Sizing up Pettit's mild, friendly manner and impressive statistics — some 280 pounds on a 6-foot-4 frame — the artist painted "Prince of Police" on one side of the squad car and "Crusher" on the other side.

Pettit's size and demeanor often proved to be a good combination when fellow officers found themselves in tight spots.

One such occasion led to a department citation — the coveted Porter Williams Award — for Pettit. When police were in a standoff with a woman wielding a sawed-off shotgun in 1985, and after she had fired two blasts, Pettit met her face-to-face and talked her into putting down the gun and surrendering.

## NO BUTTS ABOUT IT . . . ~
The R.J. Reynolds-Nabisco split boils down to this:

Nabisco was afraid its graham crackers might start tasting like Camels.

## DON'T CALL US! ~
Thrill-seekers who depend on taxpayer-supported rescuers to come running whenever they bungle their lunatic feats — as though every one of those agencies should jump at their beck and call — shouldn't. Rescuers who risk life and limb to save somebody who has no regard for their own should ignore SOS calls from:

• All mountain climbers.
• Ice fishermen in trouble in Louisiana, Georgia or Florida.
• Swimmers who flounder in the English Channel.
• Pilots of small private planes that violate Cuban air space.
• Amateur astronauts.
• Balloonists who set out to circle the globe.
• Anybody aboard a homemade submarine that sinks.
• Outboard motor boats, pontoon boats, canoes, dinghies and like pleas-

ure craft that venture more than 25 miles into either the Atlantic or Pacific ocean.

## TOOT! TOOT! ~

Three-year-old Brett Jaeger was visiting grandmother Norma Jaeger in Litchfield, Ill. Noting the mischief he was getting into, she told him he was "full of vinegar."

He stopped what he was doing, looked up at her and countered: "No, Grandma, it's just gas!"

## BEANIE BABY SOUP ~

Philosopher-at-large Smokey Joe Miller had plenty to say when he was asked if there were Beanie Babies when he was a kid.

"No," he said.

"But," he hastened to add, "if we hadda had 'em, things were so tough back then, we probably would've tore 'em open so we could cook the beans and use the cloth to patch our overalls."

*Smokey Joe Miller*

## KIDS' QUIPS ~

A pop quiz put Concordia Lutheran first-graders' imagination to the test. Preambles to common sayings were on the test sheet. The task at hand was for the kids to complete the lines. Here are some of the responses teacher Pam Billotti collected!

Don't Bite the Hand That:
. . . you write with.
Never Ever Underestimate the Power of:
. . . Jesus.
You Can Lead a Horse to Water but:
. . . don't fall in.
If You Lie Down with Dogs, You'll:
. . . get fleas.
If at First You Don't Succeed:
. . . you'll get in trouble.

A Penny Saved is:
. . . one cent.
Children Should be Seen and Not:
. . . hurt.

## A

Ackerman, J. Waldo 7, 36, 196
Ackerman, Phil 44
Adams, Barbara 234, 235
Adams, Dick 299, 300
Adams, Jordan 300
Adams, Steve 178
Aden, Mike 230, 231
Alewelt, George 67
Alexander, Greta 426
Allen, Byron 169, 170
Allen, Wayne 429
Anderson, Chuck 151
Anderson, John 143
Andrews, Richard 192
Angelo, Del 256, 257
Angelo, Dolly 327, 328
Armstrong, Duff 83
Armstrong, Louis 429
Arnett, Peter 329
Arnold, Eddie 5
Arnold, Roseanne 348
Aschoff, Lee 53, 54, 330
Auerbach, Eleanor 196, 197

## B

Bagby, Robert 401
Bagg, Bruce 221
Bailey, Debbie Powell 31, 32
Baja Marimba Band 5
Bakker, Jim 261, 262
Bakker, Tammy 261, 262
Bandor, Donna 100
Barker, Brenda 108, 109
Barry, Marion 351
Bavetta, John 430
Baxter, Ted 234
Bay City Rollers 125, 126
Becker, George 78
Beckham, Robin 281
Bergen, Justin 261
Bergen, Kathy 261
Berger, Edith 254
Berger, Myron 254, 255
Bestudik, Thomas 6
Bianco, Shirley 276
Bice, Earl 22
Biden, Joseph 274
Billotte, Pam 178, 437
Birrell, Susan 298, 299
Bitter, Janet 302
Blakely, Steve 303
Blumle, Charlotte 255
Bobbitt, Lorena 375

Bolosh, Joe 78, 79
Bond, Johnny 91
Borchers, Webber 273, 274
Borge, Victor 243
Bork, Robert 274
Bormann, Lee 195, 196
Bradley, Phil 333
Bradley, Tom 209
Brammer, Mary Ann 225
Brion, Suzanne 146
Brisbon, Henry 421
Brittin, Al 44
Broaddus, Rick 359, 360
Brooks, Lacey 41, 42, 261, 262
Brown, Jerry 351
Brown, Mike 162
Brown, Murphy 348
Browning, Bill 282
Bryant, Anita 143
Buchanan, Pat 351
Buckner, Jr. Simon Bolivar 390
Buhl, Larry 166
Bullard, Marcia 14
Bullock, Larry 247, 248
Burch, David 11
Buren, Bill 203
Burge, Al 406
Burris, Roland 365
Burris, Winona 363
Burrows, Anthony 268
Bush, George 258, 350
Bush, Ralph 39
Butchek, Mark 184, 185
Butchek, Mike 185
Butcher, Ben 346
Butcher, Brenda 424
Butcher, Helene 346
Butcher, Jonathan 346
Butcher, Matthew 346, 424
Buttafuoco, Joey 375
Buzzard, Larry 32

## C

Caliper, Frank 180, 181, 182
Campbell, Harry Lee 202
Cantrall, Peggy 424
Capone, Al 242
Carey, Luke 189
Carne, Judy 5
Carr, Howie 317
Carroll, Howard 250
Carson, Johnny 228, 229, 261, 287
Carter, Jimmy 110, 144
Cash, Johnny 125

Cauthen, Jimmy 6
Cavanagh, Joseph 40
Cavanaugh, John 59
Cavett, Dick 400
Chamberlain, William 4, 361, 362
Chamberlain, Wilt 99
Chatham, Rachel 418
Chew, Charles 225
Chic 125
Child, Julia 348
Chisam, Kelly 315, 316
Choate, Clyde 57
Christofferson, Randy 423
Clark, Debra 100
Clark, Nancy 14
Cleghorn, Emmett 243
Clinton, Bill 347, 348, 350, 351, 366, 399, 409, 411, 418, 424, 435
Clinton, Hillary 350, 351, 411, 424, 435
Close, David 386
Close, Roy 386
Cullen, Maggie 275
Coady, John 314
Cochrane, Hank 141, 142
Cody, Wayne 66
Coffey, Brenton 115
Collins, Bobby 204
Collins, Dean 43
Collins, Phil 153
Connor, Myles 316, 317, 341
Conway, William 235, 236
Coolidge, Calvin 301
Coran, Samuel 341
Cosentino, Jerry 130, 257
Costa, Eugene 162
Costello, Michael 67, 211
Coutrakon, George 58
Crifasi, Lawrence 75
Cronson, Robert 357
Crook, Jr. William 329
Crosby, Bing E. 168
Crosby, Bing 429
Cross, Christopher 157
Cullison, Stephen 182
Cunningham, Roscoe 45, 46
Cuomo, Mario 351
Curley, Moe & Larry 351
Curran, Nat 347

**D**

Dace, Florence 284, 285
Dace, Tom 284
Dahmer, Jeffrey 330
Daley, Richard 56
Dalton, Donald 307

Dangerfield, Rodney 131, 257
Daniels, Lee 250
Daughton, M. J. 2
Davidson, John 5, 250
Davison, Ralph 425
Dean, Louie 99
Deems, Barrett 357, 358, 428, 429
Delahunt, William 316, 317
DeMarco, Joe 155
Denham, Scott 153
Designe, Achille 60
Dickenson, Jack 361
Dickerson, Ray 171
Dickson, Linda 120
Dietrich, Tom 174
DiMaggio, Joe 129, 414
Dobrinic, Kathryn 314
Dodd, Charles 30
Dodson, Nancy 52
Doe, John 168
Doedtman, Carla 273
Doedtman, Jeff 273
Doedtman, Sarah 273
Dole, Bob 406
Donahue, Phil 400
Doodletown Pipers 5
Doolittle, I 96, 97
Dorman, Sam 270
Douglass, Creel 2
Downey, Maureen 223
Downs, Norman 203
Druhot, Kelsey 418
Duhs, Larry 263
Dukett, Michael 11
Dukett, Robert 11
Dunbar, Joe 424
Dunham, James 12, 13, 76, 77, 106, 107
Durbin, Dick 281, 282, 302, 303, 304
Dyer, Moses 301
Dysson, Louis 147

**E**

Easterbrook, Frank 342, 343, 345
Edgar, Brenda 280
Edgar, Jim 211, 280
Edwards, Judy 205, 206
Eickhoff, Charles 172
Eickhoff, Larry 172
Eickhoff, Nancy 172
Ellis, Larry 331
Embree, Frank 6
Emmerling, Beatrice 325, 326
Emmerling, Anson 325
Entwistle, Allen 152
Epps, Marian 295

Estill, Bob 33

**F**

Fairfield, Cecil 260
Fanale, Katie 406
Fanale, Jr. Nick 406
Fanale, Sr. Nick 406, 407
Farb, Barbara 249
Farb, Kelly 249
Fayans, J.P. 402, 403, 404
Fayans, Leslie 402, 403, 404
Feger, Harold 130, 131
Fields, W. C. 131
Finley, Ottis 134, 135, 136
Fisher, Julie 208
Fisher, Mary Ann 208
Fonda, Jane 348
Fore, Jill 326
Foreman, Helen 215, 216, 223, 301
Friedman, Simon 54
Fritz, Gerald 328
Funk, Harold 34, 35
Funt, Allen 221

**G**

Gacy, John Wayne 133, 364, 365, 366, 376, 421
Garfat, Dick 125, 126
Garletts, Diane 313, 314
Gass, Jack 392, 393
Gebel-Williams, Gunther 142
Geo-Karis, Adeline 184
Gerig, David 275, 297
Gietl, Greg 287
Gillespie, Peggy 417
Gillman, Stu 5
Gingrich, Newt 399
Gleason, Jackie 114
Gleason, Luke 233, 234
Gobble, Mary Ann 295
Gonko, Bob 81
Gore, Al 351
Gore, Tipper 351
Graziano, Marie 422
Green, Bob 285
Green, Steve 100
Griffith, Ken 279, 280
Grigsby, David 314
Guggenheim, Jay 114, 145, 146
Gutschenritter, Martin 96, 111
Gwinn, Cheryl 355

**H**

Hahn, Amanda 191
Hahn, Harry 415
Haley, Paul 141

Haley, III Paul 141
Haley, Robert 299
Hallock, John 250
Halvorsen, Gail 425
Hamburger, Joanne 173
Hanes, Murray 13
Hanson, Charles S. 73, 74, 75
Harding, Tonya 375
Harms, John 137, 138,139
Harrel, Richard 163
Harris, Vernon 116, 312
Hart, Priscilla 94
Hartman, David 223
Hartzler, Joe 405
Hartzler, Lisa 405
Hasara, Karen 407
Hawker, Linda 263, 264
Haynes, David 51, 52
Hayward, Jim 148
Hecko, Joseph 94, 95
Hefley, Bob 176
Heien, Paula 19
Heimlich, Al 427, 428, 429
Helmsley, Leona 348
Henneberry, Jim 76, 77, 79, 80
Hennessey, William 119
Hertz, Kelly 412
Hickman, Don 156
Hill, Bob 401
Hill, Mr. 218
Hinds, John 6
Hodge, Orville 18
Hoffman, Abbie 29
Hollis, H. B. 225
Holmes, J. Earl 245
Holmin, David 197
Hooper, Mr. 218, 219
Hostick, King 77, 78
Houston, Mike 146, 243, 244
Hovey, Michael 178
Hovey, Mrs. 178
Howarth, Nelson 10, 56, 333
Howell, Nic 376
Hubbard, Jr. Frank 390
Huckaby, Huck 43
Hudson, Craig 200, 201
Huff, Vicki 311
Huff, Wanda 202
Hughes, Mike 175
Humphrey, Elsie 201
Hurt, Mandy 276

Hussein, Saddam 322, 329

**I**

Icen, Dick 257

**J**

Jackson, Michael 378, 381, 399, 411
Jackson, Sean 366
Jackson, Wally 101, 102, 103, 396, 398
Jacobs, Carl 357, 358
Jaeger, Brett 437
Jaeger, Norma 437
James, Audrey 98
James, Clay 131
Janik, Jerry 243
Johnson, Lyndon 33, 34
Johnson, Tom 305
Johnson, Walter 202
Jones, Buck 43
Jones, J. David 39, 40
Jones, Reese Harold 63, 64
Jones, Selvarine 270, 271
Jost, Jim 105
Jostes, Dave 354
Judd, Meryl 272

**K**

K.C. & The Sunshine Band 125
Kane, Michael 343, 345
Kanjorski, Paul 282
Kapshandy, Steve 158
Kasten, Walter 42, 57
Katz, Allan 207
Katz, Shirley 207
Kavish, Robert 197
Kearney, Larry 242
Keating, Charles 348
Keen, Patrick 299
Kelley, Michael P. 423
Kelly, Grace 429
Kemper, David 94
Kennedy, Betty 38, 39, 40, 41
Kennedy, Frank 40
Kennedy, John F. 414
Kessler, Sara 344
Khadafy, Moammar 243
Kiesler, Kenneth 220, 366
King, Family 5
Kirby, George 5
Knight, Bobby 375
Knuppel, John 70, 71, 83, 84, 136, 137
Kolb, Hazel 287
Kolb, Joe 427, 428
Kolb, Bradey 427, 428
Komac, Dennis 242, 243, 375
Koop, C. Everett 282

Kosec, Johnathon 359
Koskey, Corey 406
Koskey, Jenny 406
Koskey, Joan 406
Koskey, Stephanie 406
Kramer-Nesbitt, Chris 378, 379
Kramer-Nesbitt, Don 378, 379
Kroll, Sherwin 388, 389

**L**

LaCombe, Laura 279
LaCombe, Abbie 279
Lacy, Alex 332
Landers, Ann 154
Langfelder, Ossie 339, 340
LaRue, John 429
Laurent, Deanna 235
Lawrence, Bill 185
Lear, Tuhran 298, 299
Lemke, Leroy 183
Letterman, David 216, 245, 287, 363
Letz, Jr. Sydney 6
Lewinsky, Monica 435
Lewis, John L. 77, 78
Liberace 5
Limbaugh, Rush 348
Lincoln, Abraham 83, 131, 170, 185, 225,
229, 245, 257, 258, 264, 265, 290, 361,
380, 415, 418, 419, 427, 428, 434, 435
Lindsay, Amy 93, 94
Linkletter, Art 227
List, Donald 272
Little, Dick 24, 25, 26
Locher, Bruce 268
Logan, Willis 136
Long, Darrell 390, 391
Lopez, Ramiro Perez 341, 342, 343, 344
Loveless, Harold 165
Lucas, Terry 229, 230
Lunt, Andy 105

**M**

Mackay, Donald 67
Madigan, Mike 250
Madonia, Frank 76, 77
Madonna 348, 399
Maggio, Anna 281
Mahr, Willard 234, 235
Makuta, Mike 253
Manilow, Barry 402
Mansberger, Floyd 229
Marcos, Imelda 261, 262
Marcussen, Walter 304
Marley, C. F. 269
Martin, Barry 327

Marvel, Tom 38
Mason, Louis 13
Mayes, Kevin 236, 237
McCarthy, Dennis 254, 255
McCarty, Don 180
McClellan, Tara 227
McCoy, Linda 131
McCoy, Richard Floyd 87, 88
McDaniel, Mike 24
McDaniel, Toby 188, 360
McDonald, Dorothy 173
McGovern, George 34
McGraw, Bob 131
McGuff, William 1, 2
McGwire, Mark 432
McKinney, George Patrick 84, 85, 86
McNabb, Bessie 351, 352
Meara, Father 23
Meiron, Angie 244
Melchiorri, Frank 266
Mellinger, Midge 155
Menendez, Erik 375
Menendez, Lyle 375
Meyer, Kevin 326, 327
Miller, Steve 98, 99
Miller, Ben 148, 153, 154
Miller, Bill 188, 189, 221, 222
Miller, Smokey Joe 275, 302, 306, 345, 437
Miller, Susan 259
Mills, Richard 316, 341, 342, 343, 345, 346, 367
Mohan, Frank 2
Monroe, Marilyn 414
Montana, Patsy 90, 91, 92, 93
Moody, Harry 209
Moore, Clayton 129
Moore, Jim 235
Morganna 230, 231
Morris, Delyte 56
Morris, Gary 164
Mullen, Kenneth 299
Mundhenke, Jonathon 354
Murakski, Slawek 362
Murphy, Eddie 33, 34

N

Neal, Lindsay 166
Nelson, Willie 126, 141, 210, 211, 250
Netznik, Mark 277
Nichols, Glen 4
Nieman, Donna 175, 176, 177
Nixon, Richard 6, 24, 34, 350

O

Oblinger, Josephine 136
O'Brien, Jack 300
Ogilvie, Richard 6, 7, 56
O'Keefe, Dan 307, 308
O'Keefe, Mary Ann 308
O'Keefe, Mike 307
O'Neill, Andy 12, 13
Osborn, Dorothy 377
Osmonds 125
Oswald, Bill 318
Overby, Joe 11
Owens, Jessie 209

P

Padget, Ned 353
Paige, Satchel 156
Palmer, Laurie 310
Parton, Dolly 348
Patton, George 297
Paul 162, 163
Paul, Rebecca 363
Peale, Norman Vincent 114
Pennington, Phil 267
Penny, Hank 91
Perot, Ross 340
Petrilli, Leno 89
Pettit, Tony 436
Philip, James 263
Piatt, Becky 421, 422, 423
Piatt, Clint 422
Piatt, Lisa 422
Piatt, Ted 422
Pickford, Ronald 181, 182
Plummer, Terry 359
Poe, Sam 302
Powell, Mary Beth 31, 32
Powell, Paul 3, 18, 34, 54, 55, 56, 57, 59, 354, 357
Presley, Elvis 100, 349, 351, 378
Presley, Lisa Marie 378
Price, Ray 141, 142
Price, Sue 275
Pryor, Richard 168
Pugh, Richard 244, 245
Puglia, Fred 419, 420
Puglia, Nora 420
Pullen, Penny 250

Q

Quayle, Dan 348, 350

R

Rand, Sally 236
Rapps, Paul 197

Reagan, Ronald 172, 173, 215, 216, 223, 234, 418
Rebel, Ned 396
Reilly, John 199
Rhodes, Jerry 45, 190
Richard, Larry 244
Richards, Kenneth 54
Richter, Norman 40, 360, 361
Ricker, Art 188
Ridder, Agnes 373
Ridder, John 373, 374
Rivera, Geraldo 242, 243
Rivers, Joan 348
Robbins, Marty 5
Roberts, Bill 211, 250
Roberts, John D. 433, 434
Roberts, L. G. 202
Robinson, Dave 139
Rock, Phil 250, 263
Rogers, Howard 146
Rogers, Smokey 91
Roncancio, German 121, 122
Roosevelt, Eleanor 246
Roosevelt, Franklin 246
Roosevelt, Teddy 374, 396
Roscetti, Erin 146
Rose, Judy 92, 93
Roundtree, Helen 275
Royko, Mike 216
Ryan, Eddie 2, 4, 39
Ryan, George 296

S

Samuels, Rich 136, 137
Santini, Michael 363, 364
Sasch, Ed 358
Schaefer, Victor 86, 87, 88
Schaub, Rob 347
Schlickman, Eugene 32
Schoenrock, Rocky 372
Schroeder, Jim 272
Schroeder, Pat 271
Schultz, Norman 61
Scott, William 18
Scroggins, Jr. Patrick 341
See, Jerry 176, 177
Serifin, Tom 140
Sgro, Sam 54, 55
Shadur, Milton 248
Sharp, Glenn 407, 408
Shaughnessy, Dick 28, 29
Shaughnessy, Pat 212
Shaver, Eric 265
Sherry, Francis 283, 284, 285
Shull, Lisa 94, 95

Simmons, Richard 166, 167
Simon, Paul 56
Simpson, Anna 183
Sims, Erskin 378
Sims, Lydel 28
Sinatra, Frank 429
Skaggs, Dan 375
Skelton, Red 246
Slaven, Jay 22, 23
Smarjesse, Susan 422
Smith, A. Ray 156
Smith, Bill 107
Smith, Kent 310
Smith, Larry 143
Smith, Lewis 395
Smith, Marguerite 395
Snow, Hank 350
Sothern, Georgia 236
Spice, Robert 153, 154
Spinney, Karen 317
Spinney, Jack 316, 317
Squires, Belle 38
Squires, Bob 57, 58
Stadtman, Vickie 120
Stadtman, Steve 120
Stanhoven, Steve 168
Stevenson, Adlai 68, 221, 234, 251
Stinebaugh, Rick 298, 299
Stockus, Joanne 150
Stockus, Tony 149, 150
Stoker, Bob 6
Stokes, Marion 331, 332
Stone, Nick 113
Stover, David 216, 217
Stuckey, Tim 187
Suarez, Silver 2, 13
Suer, Howard 254, 255
Sullivan, John 164
Sutter, Gus 301
Sutton, Bud 59
Sutton, Pat 13
Sweat, Kristen 418
Swink, Floyd 148

T

Talkington, Penny 51, 52
Tapscott, George 186, 187
Taylor, Harry 373, 374, 375
Taylor, Joe 388
Telford, William 14, 76, 77, 79, 80, 81, 106, 107
Templeman, Andrew 42
Tendick, Ron 301
Terrell, Raymond 268
Thomas, Randy Lee 298, 299

Thompson, Duke 63, 64
Thompson, Jayne 305
Thompson, Jim 106, 124, 125, 132, 139, 144, 154, 155, 185, 210, 211, 223, 225, 227, 250, 251, 261, 305, 351
Thompson, Murray 259
Thompson, Samantha 227, 305
Thurmond, Strom 434
Tiny Tim 306
Tomlin, Fred 195, 196
Torres, Debra 407
Tretter, Mike 340
Trudeau, Ed 306, 307
Truman, Harry 68, 77, 78
Tucker, Angie 347
Tulley, Florence 130
Turner, William 94, 95
Turnock, Bernard 251
Twain, Mark 328
Tyhurst, Gene 18
Tyler, Joyce 295, 296
Tyler, Ken 295, 296

**V**

Vadalabene, Sam 225
VanPickerill, Ryan 90
VanTine, Kent 371
VanTine, Richard 371
Varney, Jim 305
Vazzi, Jim 314
Venuti, Joe 429
Verticchio, Paul 13
Vu, Hung Manh 76

**W**

Wacaser, Lyle 44
Walch, Billy 255
Walden, Holly 359
Walker, Dan 41, 74
Walker, Jim 163
Wall, David E. 38
Wall, John 23
Wall, Mrs. Lloyd 38
Wanless, Bob 420
Ward, Pat 77, 107
Ward, Terry 200, 201
Webster, Susan 317
Wedeking, Jerry 11, 58, 361, 362
Weiss, John 204
Welborn, George 421
Welch, Robert 163
Welk, Douglas 165, 166
Wells, Kitty 92
Werries, Larry 172
Weston, John 165

White, Bruce 206
White, Howard Lee 55
Whitehurst, Henry 202
Wilburn Brothers 92
Wilde, Harold 405
Wilkins, Chuck 293
Wilkins, Miranda 293
Willhite, Darlene 240
Williams, Eleanor 378
Williams, Hank 92
Williams, Jr. Hank 211
Williams, Porter 436
Williams, Ron 313
Williams, Wanda 144
Williamson, Bob 45
Wills, Bob 91
Wilson, Clarence Eugene 167
Wilson, Gregory 411
Winfrey, Oprah 349
Wohler, Mark 290, 291, 292, 296, 297
Wood, Jr. Harlington 67, 343, 345
Woodward, Cindy 143
Woodward, Jim 262
Wright, Jolene 234, 235
Wynette, Tammy 164

**Y**

Yates, Richard 374
Young, Faron 5
Young, James 57
Youngman, Henny 419, 420

**Z**

Zappa, Leo 268
Ziegler, Jr. Roy 41